To George:

For his early and consistent support for the Conference that yielded this book.

With great Appreciation

Service as Mandate

NE✕US

NEW HISTORIES OF SCIENCE, TECHNOLOGY, THE ENVIRONMENT, AGRICULTURE & MEDICINE

NEXUS is a book series devoted to the publication of high-quality scholarship in the history of the sciences and allied fields. Its broad reach encompasses science, technology, the environment, agriculture, and medicine, but also includes intersections with other types of knowledge, such as music, urban planning, or educational policy. Its essential concern is with the interface of nature and culture, broadly conceived, and it embraces an emerging intellectual constellation of new syntheses, methods, and approaches in the study of people and nature through time.

SERVICE AS MANDATE

How American Land-Grant Universities Shaped the Modern World

1920–2015

ALAN I MARCUS

THE UNIVERSITY OF ALABAMA PRESS   TUSCALOOSA

The University of Alabama Press
Tuscaloosa, Alabama 35487–0380
uapress.ua.edu

Inquiries about reproducing material from this work should be
addressed to the University of Alabama Press.

Typeface: Scala Pro

Manufactured in the United States of America
Cover photograph: Lab technician reviewing chemical sam-
ples; courtesy of the Special Collections Department, Iowa
State University Library
Cover design: Michele Myatt Quinn

∞
The paper on which this book is printed meets the minimum
requirements of American National Standard for Information
Sciences—Permanence of Paper for Printed Library Materials,
ANSI Z39.48–1984.

Cataloging-in-Publication data is available from the Library
of Congress.
ISBN: 978-0-8173-1888-8
E-ISBN: 978-0-8173-8897-3

To land-grant universities, their stakeholders, and their critics

Contents

Acknowledgments

This volume resulted from a national conference, "Thinking Land-Grants: A 'Cerebration' of the 150th Anniversary of the Morrill Land-Grant Act." Held October 3–6, 2012, at Mississippi State University, the conference brought some forty scholars together from across America. The essays included here are revisions and expansions of some of the papers presented at that event.

Pulling off such a significant meeting required considerable support. Mark E. Keenum, Mississippi State University president; Jerome A. Gilbert, provost and executive vice president; Gregory A. Bohach, vice president for Agriculture, Forestry and Veterinary Medicine; David Shaw, vice president for Research and Economic Development; Don Zant, vice president for Budget and Planning; George Hopper, dean of Agriculture and Life Sciences and director of the Mississippi Agricultural and Forestry Experiment Station; and Gary L. Myers, dean of Arts & Sciences all jumped at the opportunity to back the effort. They gladly provided the funding necessary to bring in speakers and to conduct conference affairs as well as the moral support to see it through. Of special note was the magnificent trip to the Mississippi Delta where we visited cotton fields, watched a working cotton gin, ate at a commissary, and hung out at a blues joint. I thank Reuben Moore and Joe Street for helping to arrange that epic event. The graduate students of the Department of History helped with local arrangements—driving shuttles, making airport runs, guiding visitors. In turn, they got to meet scholars in a way that few neophyte historians do. Karrie Barfield spearheaded the transportation effort and in the process learned vital life lessons. Pam Wasson, the Department of History's administrative assistant, was her usual indispensible self and coordinated everything. Patsy Humphrey ran the department office while Pam was otherwise engaged.

Jean Marcus graciously hosted a catfish fry at our house for nearly one hundred people and our son, Gregory, provided logistical support, collecting garbage, emptying and restocking containers, and dragging coolers of soft drinks and ice wherever they were needed. Haley Jade entertained as necessary and removed food that had fallen on the floor. Without their help, the entire conference would have lacked je ne sais quoi.

Following the event a handful of graduate students participated in a colloquium on historical editing. There they took the various conference essays and grappled with thorny issues of organization and editing, creating themes and introductions, and writing head and section notes. In a sense, the colloquium enabled them to see a historical product constructed in a fashion quite different than a single-authored piece would be. It was my hope that by starting with completed pieces and then establishing a framework in which to house them, this would permit the students to recognize the steps they would naturally encounter when they undertook their own studies. Time will tell how successful I was.

Two of my Mississippi State colleagues, Jim Giesen and Mark Hersey, read a version of the introduction for this volume and provided wise counsel.

I would be remiss if I did not thank the University of Alabama Press for its support. Curtis L. Clark, director, Daniel Waterman, editor in chief, and Elizabeth Motherwell, environmental editor, as well as the entire Alabama Press staff, were helpful every step of the way. Two anonymous readers kindly shared their insights and made this a better book.

Finally, it gives me great pleasure to thank the contributors to the volume for their hard work, perception, and historical vision. It is very much their production.

Service as Mandate

Introduction

ALAN I MARCUS

Few federal initiatives have been as successful as the Morrill Land-Grant College Act. The 1862 act fostered a series of institutions that opened educational opportunities to a significant segment of the American public. They produced the country's scientific, technical, and agricultural leaders, spawned innovations that changed the face of the nation, and helped create the modern world. Tens of millions of students have passed through their doors. These men and women became entrepreneurs or scholars or got well-paying jobs, raised families, and sent their sons and daughters to college. Industries and businesses rose because of research done at these places, which helped fuel the postwar boom that made America the leader of the free world.

Champions of these institutions tout a "land-grant ethos," a fundamental sense and purpose that have always characterized such schools. In 1890 and again in 1994 their successes appeared so abundant that Congress reopened the Morrill Act to incorporate those who had been ineligible to reap the initial measure's myriad benefits. The manifest achievements of the land-grants ought not be construed to suggest that they have not been without their significant foibles and far greater flaws. Nor have these colleges remained unchanged as their foremost proponents loudly assert. In their century and a half of existence, land-grants have been redefined and reconceptualized any number of times. They bear only a cursory resemblance to their original incarnations.

The 150th anniversary of the Morrill Act in 2012 gave its modern-day partisans the opportunity to do some stocktaking. So proud were they of the institutions' virtues that they held an epic celebration. The Smithsonian Institution hosted a two-week-long exhibit at the National Mall recounting the many splendors that the act had produced over the course of the previous century and a half. Virtually all the nation's land-grant institutions participated in what was a display of past, present, and future science and technology. Nor was that all. The American Chemical Society, the world's largest scientific organization, held at its annual meeting no less than three sessions that considered the implications of the Morrill Act on chemistry. One was a special presidential session, which was followed by an hour-and-a-half-long news conference. Penn State, Illinois, Florida, and Mississippi State each held a large national or international conference to discuss the act's past and in some cases its future.

This process of inquiry and the outpouring of scholarship gratified the Association of Public and Land-Grant Universities (APLU). The single entity joining all state and land-grant universities, the APLU partnered with Mississippi State to create the Virtual Archives of Land-Grant History. Still in its nascent stage, the archives will become the portal through which to enter and search the archives of the various land-grant universities and the central clearinghouse for the history of the land-grant experience.

The recent flurry of scholarly activity on land-grants has helped elucidate just how they became educational juggernauts. It has also reminded us that that was not always so. The initial act was a compromise among a variety of positions and it passed only because the southern states were in rebellion. Few in that region wanted to use public lands for educational purposes.

This volume is the second of a two-volume effort that traces the changes among America's land-grants over the past century and a half. It stems from the papers presented at the Mississippi State conference, which in tone was different than the others. Its organizers titled it "Thinking Land-Grants" and called it a "cerebration," not a celebration. The event was explicitly about the history of those institutions, warts and all. Apparent dead ends were to be followed and unexplored areas uncovered. It was to be a historical investigation, not a self-congratulation.

The first volume covered aspects of the period from before the act's passage to about 1930. It sought to explain how and why the land-grant institutions developed as they did and how they came to put considerable faith in and effort into science and technology. That book did not try to be all-encompassing. It is not nor was it meant to be a de facto history of the land-grant movement. It was a series of scenes, vignettes, and episodes in the history of land-grants, which, when weaved together, demonstrate the fundamental thrusts and tenets of how Morrill land-grant universities came to assume the forms and purposes that they have exhibited.

This volume follows the same organic approach. But rather than focus on how land-grants developed, this collection examines how land-grant universities participated in and reflected the making and shaping of the modern world. It primarily covers the period after about 1920 and carries the analysis to the present day.

The difference in theme and focus is intentional. Land-grants in this more modern period have played a far more extensive role in American life than they had earlier. Since at least the turn of the twentieth century, land-grant universities have become quintessentially American institutions. With the possible exception of government, land-grants have more completely incorporated the fundamental American arrogance that virtually everything can be made better or at least less objectionable. Action in the present shapes the future, and targeted action in the present enhances the future. Fatalism, nihilism, and the paralysis associated with the existential dilemma have never made significant inroads among twentieth- and twenty-first-century Americans. Americans have always treated the future as if plastic, putty to be manipulated.

Not only have land-grants championed that ethic, but it has come to define them. These schools embrace the American passion for defining anything not favored a "problem" as well as its corollary, an unwavering confidence that virtually all present "problems" can be mitigated through planned, concerted, or individual action. The repeated attempts to erect "solutions" to perceived public problems remain the most conspicuous land-grant university activity since about 1900.

That sense of engagement has led land-grants to work in an extraordinary number of critically important areas. The schools' late nineteenth-century decision to pursue science, coupled with their subsequent linkage of science to service to cement their fortune, has positioned these institutions most favorably. Science and technology, including the social and behavioral sciences, emerged in the twentieth century as the primary mechanism through which to make social and other adjustments. Science, applied rigorously and relentlessly—almost religiously—to the body politic and its myriad constituent endeavors, has promised to right whatever is wrong.

These interventions often have gone less smoothly than their advocates anticipated. Kerfuffles, even bitter disputes, have sometimes ensued with land-grant universities in the center of the action. Rarely have the land-grants shied away from controversy. The contentiousness regularly enveloping these institutions has proven unavoidable; to a large degree, it is inherent in the characteristically American notion animating the entire framework.

This future-dependent formulation—action in the present shapes the future, and targeted action in the present enhances the future—hinges on an approximation of consensus, a society-wide set of similar desires, ambitions, and goals. But American society and its members' ambitions are not now nor have they ever been monolithic. Manifestly more visible since the 1950s, Americans have increasingly consciously group identified and achieved collective voice. That pluralistic reality has undercut many land-grant activities. Resolutions to the "problems" of one group frequently produced or revealed other problems or became problems to others. Those so aggrieved acted like their predecessors and demanded amelioration of these newly uncovered "problems." Put simply, a snowball effect has often occurred. Responses to criticisms and pressures have produced many times efforts to refashion society, the social order, and its practices. And on numerous occasions, those modified and altered activities have yielded situations and conditions that others demanded be revised or adjusted.

Anger and frustration usually mark these disputes. Indeed, the notion responsible for them—the nearly rabid conviction that action now will have significant impact on the future—intensifies feelings precisely because the subsequent situation seems so readily mitigated. With resolution not just possible but so tantalizingly close, each refusal or failure to act in the method desired by the disillusioned generates renewed or sharpened hostility. A sense of desperation sometimes leads to individual action. It becomes the last resort, the last hope for spurring group and then official action.

Ironically, the perception that action in the present can temper the future provides little true solace. Since possibilities are essentially plastic, they can be mediated, interceded, or interposed almost ad infinitum. There can be no contentment, only endless process. Satisfaction is in abeyance, at best a temporary phenomenon; there is no permanent peace in the relentless, never-ending search for something better or less bad.

Land-grants are prominent players in this perpetual drama. They engage in what is in essence a Sisyphean labor. The schools embody change and posit science as mechanism. But since change often impacts people and groups differentially, land-grant universities find themselves embroiled in frequent controversy. It is inherent in and endemic to the intellectual milieu in which they function.

Stepping back a bit, the key feature of twentieth-century land-grants has not been what is often celebrated: opening up higher education to the

American masses. Democracy's colleges did that, of course, but they have become what they are because of their exquisite political sensitivity. The act creating them mandated that they pursue their tasks in the "manner that the respective state legislatures prescribe." Each land-grant has operated according to the demands and dictates of that state's legislature, and those legislatures have responded to various constituencies within that state. In conjunction with the nineteenth-century union of science to service, the schools have been repeatedly mandated by legislatures to come directly to bear on issue after issue in the interests of the state. The preeminence of the federal government has added yet another legislature and other sets of interests to the mix. Congressional action has imposed any number of duties and obligations on land-grants.

State and federal interests, of course, exist within the political sphere. Popularly elected legislatures circumscribed land-grant university activities just as surely as they ascribed duties. Land-grants, their agendas, and their functioning have been debated in almost every public forum: trade and professional societies, newspapers and other media, legislatures and electoral contests, even houses of worship. They have been lauded and chastened, hailed and condemned. Land-grant activities appear so controversial, and are often heavily politicized, because their initiatives seem so critical to the citizens of the states in which the schools reside. It is the lot of land-grant universities—and their genius.

✳✳✳

As it had since well before the Morrill Land-Grant Act's 1862 passage, rural America dominated state legislatures. They, in turn, favored agriculture; service-oriented agricultural sciences at land-grant schools dwarfed in numbers and power other scientific endeavors. Mechanics arts—engineering—gained a foothold a subject at a time by demonstrating practical utility. Engineers first seized on agriculture-related equipment—steam engines—to ensconce themselves within the new colleges. As each new technology associated with transportation, electric power, and construction emerged, engineers branched out to cover those areas. It remained until about 1920 for land-grants to develop a full complement of engineering specialties.

The creation of engineering divisions corresponded to a national demographic shift. The 1920 US Census reported that for the first time 50 percent of the nation's population lived in communities of 2,500 or more residents, places identified as urban. Rural-dominated legislatures recognized the needs of the emergent urban and industrial sector, which reduced agriculture's sway over the schools within state bureaucracies. But it would be wrong to contend that agricultural scientists lost clout at land-grants. The rise of the federal government and its interest in agriculture gave agricultural scientists an additional foothold. Before 1890, the US Department of Agriculture (USDA) had become a cabinet department and the Hatch Act of 1887 had provided reliable, persisting funding for land-grant agricultural science. Both loosened state grasp and diminished state legislative influence, as did the land-grants' decision in 1887 to form themselves into a national organization, the Association of American Agricultural Colleges and Experiment Stations. This group began to coordinate nationwide some land-grant policies and activities. An engineering complement, the Land-Grant College Engineering Association, mimicked its functions in 1912 as engineers sought to achieve parity with their agricultural counterparts.

Rural control of state legislatures persisted beyond World War II, but national action fueled earlier land-grant growth. Federal legislation even spurred land-grants into new areas. By expanding experiment station mandates, congressional acts established beachheads from which land-grant scientists could legitimate new concerns and institutionalize new disciplines. The 1906 Adams Act, for example, privileged basic science research. Practical concerns remained paramount, but the act recognized that nondirected original research into the principles of life was perhaps more effective for solving problems in the long run. Understanding the basic sciences and exploring their parameters seemed fundamental to building a successful knowledge system and provided a potent justification for stand-alone chemistry, biology, physics, and mathematics departments. Passage of the Smith-Lever Act in 1914, which established in each county an agent to carry USDA and land-grant science to residents, provided the de facto completion of the national agricultural knowledge system; it placed each land-grant in intimate connection with its state's citizenry.

Land-grants helped the nationalist agenda by combining their agricultural and engineering associations right after World War I to form the American Association of Land-Grant Colleges. Additional federal legislation and funding further expanded land-grant possibilities. In 1925 the Purnell Act authorized experiment station expenditures to support sociological and economics research, which led directly to the creation of agricultural economics and rural sociology departments. The Bankhead-Jones Act of

1935 provided additional funding to solidify land-grant standing and work during the Great Depression as well as broadened station mandates to justify original research into the production of agricultural by-products, land and water conservation, and virtually anything that could be tenuously tied to any aspect of agricultural activity. Finally, the Agricultural Adjustment Act of 1946 demanded that a quarter of its funds be spent on regional problems, a stipulation that forced land-grants to work collectively on issues they had in common.

World War II proved to be a landmark for the land-grants and further redefined their agendas. For the first time, agriculture played second fiddle to the provision of technical competence and officer training. Dragooned into the war effort, land-grants trained men to engage in the myriad activities that supported millions of soldiers waging war across oceans. College campuses were drafted to house student soldiers and to offer them short courses in technical areas to build bridges, fix tanks and airplanes, and pursue a slew of other tasks. Land-grant faculty often were relocated to engage in top-secret projects, including radar and the atomic bomb, two technologies thought to be instrumental in ending the war.

The tumult surrounding mobilization and deployment radically changed the face of land-grants. The effects of the GI Bill pushed the schools in yet another direction. The war had forced men and women to delay going to college, creating an artificial bubble at the war's conclusion. The GI Bill democratized higher education by providing funds for veterans to gain college degrees, which caused land-grant college enrollment to skyrocket. Persons in unprecedented number sought degrees that would lead to careers in an exploding number of fields. Land-grant curricula became broader. The schools' physical plants strained under the onslaught. Quonset huts and other temporary shelters housed students until permanent facilities could be built. Sewage and water supplies proved inadequate. Heat and electricity sources demanded expansion.

Veterans helped transform schools other than land-grants, but the lessons of the war as interpreted by the federal government bore especially heavily on the 1862 schools. Science and technology had proven essential to winning the war; they now seemed critical to winning the peace. The Marshall Plan redeveloped Europe as a bulwark against Soviet expansionism, and Japan was rebuilt as a hedge against the Chinese communists. Each activity depended on technical prowess and acumen. Americans also demanded the spoils of war; education was one factor and single-family dwellings another.

Engineering graduates flocked to jobs—high-paying jobs. Science graduates found careers as lucrative. If that were not reason enough for land-grants to flourish, there was also the Cold War. America competed with the Soviet Union for world domination. A scientifically and technologically dependent military might serve to protect the nation, but sending American technological and agricultural knowhow around the globe provided unaligned countries a demonstration of American power and attendant prosperity.

These massive changes in postwar American society struck those at home as unprecedented. Critics complained that the fabric of American life had been torn and its essential threads lost. A whole stream of children entered the scene—a later consequence of the postwar bubble—and the parents of these baby boomers worried about the ability of their children to adjust to the changing—and troubling—times. Psychologists, particularly child psychologists, met the challenge and land-grants led the charge in creating an elite to help Americans cope with the postwar world. Emphasis on citizenship in their parlance but coping, fitting in, and conforming in ours brought an investigation into and an appreciation for the various groups that comprised America and their stories. Questions of what it meant to be an American or even human soon became fodder for the land-grants as they devoted attention to the humanities and saw that each graduate was firmly grounded in the Western democratic tradition. Great books courses soon became land-grant staples.

The growth of the humanities, psychology, child psychology, and the behavioral and social sciences beyond agriculture stretched land-grants and extended their influence markedly. As important was the predominance of science and technology in American affairs. It increased land-grant cachet and the schools acted to shed the remnants of their cow college past. Graduate education provided the vehicle through which land-grants got state legislatures and regents to remove the agricultural or A&M college designation and to relabel them universities. This relabeling was at least as important symbolically as substantively. Land-grants would be vital elements in fostering America's scientific and technical future.

Agricultural science stood as a crucial part of this nexus. The food for peace program established agricultural science and technology as a most important foreign policy weapon, and efforts to provide indigenous peoples with the latest agricultural science and technology to increase production seemed a robust barrier to the communist menace. The USDA organized these programs and land-grant universities carried them to fruition. A new

USDA Agricultural Research Service coordinated the department's research and oversaw that of the state experiment stations to increase effectiveness while reducing cost.

The land-grants capitalized on the newly recognized importance of science and technology. As specialists in these areas, they were no longer willing to be considered third-rate institutions. Their tradition of excellence in these areas raised their stock nationally, and they made preparations to join an association with the haughty state universities. Negotiations proved complicated, but Congress's passage in 1958 of the National Defense Education Act (NDEA), which provided loans to students at low, deferred interest with easily achievable stipulations for forgiveness, enabled land-grants and others to raise tuition markedly. Using the new money to fund a state-of-the-art scientific infrastructure begot additional research and more graduate students. The drive to build up science facilities enhanced land-grants, and the long-discussed organizational merger with state universities was consummated in 1963.

The ascension of the land-grants and their emergence as a decisive factor in higher education occurred just before the latter was struck by the continuing World War II–created demographic onslaught: baby boomers entering college. Coupled with the federal government's willingness to sponsor a Great Society that would come to bear on America's social problems and to enact a Higher Education Act to help fund that quest, land-grants gained further visibility as they consciously attempted to prepare to answer the queries of an inquisitive generation. Chanting mantras such as "the system does not work anymore" and "never trust anyone over thirty," the baby boomers demanded relevance from land-grant universities, a trait those institutions always claimed. Boomers wanted to know and they wanted the skills and initiatives to change the social milieu. These were heady times for students and even headier times for land-grants. Their student bodies demanded an education and increasingly that seemed disconnected to the ability to earn a livelihood.

The baby boomer crusade coincided with Clark Kerr's recognition of something he called the multiversity. Higher education could no longer be knowledge for knowledge's sake or directed to an immediate practical end. It needed instead to incorporate a multitude of approaches and purposes. It needed to be all things to all people, to serve all the diverse interests of the public, including the abject criticism of state practices. It would be a community of communities, outrageous and unruly, yet vibrant and forward moving. It was almost an evolving life form and America's great hope and salvation. The multiversity would guide the nation's endeavors, not just its scientific and technical ones.

Whether because of Kerr or the pressure exerted by the baby boomers, land-grant universities created many new stand-alone departments, especially in the humanities and social sciences. Political science, philosophy, and history now became independent entities with seats at the land-grant table. Courses focusing on African Americans and women came soon after. These disciplines and approaches seemed to hold some answers to questions that seemed then central to the experience of America's youth.

These hotbeds of inquiry often bubbled over into active demonstrations and weakened the long land-grant connection to the military. Students questioned not only the role of military research on campus but also ROTC. At some land-grants, students had been referred to as cadets from the beginning and subjected to something like military discipline while at college. A few universities now severed military bonds, while others made participation in ROTC optional. The student unrest and change of the later 1960s and early 1970s were disorienting and caused state legislatures to gasp. Rarely did they blame the chaos on expansion of the university curriculum. They almost always found other culprits; administrators and out-of-state students were especially favored. But while legislatures did not make the land-grants revert to their previous monofocal existence, the great stagflation and oil embargo of the mid-1970s led to a reemergence of practical matters. Universities, particularly land-grant universities, now seemed essential to ending the nation's economic ills. Science undertaken at these institutions and funded by federal dollars would overcome a distressing decline in productivity and reliance on foreign energy and fuel an American economic renaissance. What remained was to create a mechanism through which to unleash university science to private enterprise.

While the economic downturn of the 1970s and after was a national phenomenon, almost every state legislature demanded that land-grant universities lead that state to prosperity now and in the future. Stanford Research Park, the Research Triangle in North Carolina, and the Route 128 corridor around the Massachusetts Institute of Technology were posited as models of desirability and possibility. Each area had experienced a concentration of new high-tech industries, complete with high-paying jobs. Each industrial cluster rose in that location as neighboring universities nurtured nascent attempts of entrepreneurs to translate into marketable products the science and technology generated at nearby schools. Legislatures wanted universities to copy that blueprint—including their agricultural research units—and expected a quick return on their investment.

State universities without land-grant designation and agricultural sectors received a similar legislative dictum. Their origins and much of their history had not prepared them to provide the assistance states now demanded except in a few circumscribed areas. Because of legislative directives, state universities attempted to fortify those places where emergent technologies might blossom. In effect, legislatures demanded that state universities function very much like land-grants always had. The economic chaos of the later 1970s and 1980s led states to adopt for all state institutions a land-grant-like model in hope of staving off economic catastrophe.

Congress joined the land-grant university-dependent economic revitalization movement by passing in 1980 two major technology transfer acts. The Bayh-Dole Act dealt with science and technology funded by federal money, the primary financier of land-grant research. It permitted universities, small businesses, and nonprofits to own and patent devices derived from federally funded investigations. The Stevenson-Wydler Technology Innovation Act required federal laboratories, many of which were located near or on land-grant university campuses, to actively engage in transferring their science to universities and entrepreneurs. The act mandated that each laboratory must use a certain percentage of its budget to encourage nonfederal entities to consider establishing industries and products based on federal laboratory research.

Land-grants tried to capitalize on their respective research strengths to comply with this new state-sponsored industrial mandate. Anxiousness and more than a hint of desperation had accompanied the state's prescriptions. Land-grants and other state universities were given the task of transforming the state's economy. Their continued state support seemed to hinge on their success. The magnitude of the situation drove the universities in a particular direction; it privileged those fields likely to produce spinoffs at the expense of the other facets of the "multiversity."

The new university obligation of ensuring a prosperous state economy lay outside land-grant capabilities. Land-grants could and did work to that end, but guaranteeing a state's economic well-being was a daunting task. State economic success involved factors from a far larger matrix than those inside state borders. Dissatisfaction was all but inevitable. Legislatures would almost surely remain unsatisfied.

Land-grant investment in areas likely to produce an economic miracle had ironic consequences. Building up scientific and technological infrastructure and establishing industrial incubators and other mechanisms to foster new business required dramatically increased funding. Land-grants responded in four distinct ways. In some cases, they cut back on functions other than those that might produce immediate economic benefits. They closed down or deemphasized areas with little student demand or with little chance for quick economic success. In others, they established branch campuses in major cities, places with great student demand and venture capital. They also worked to increase external support significantly, although not from legislatures, which expected universities to accomplish this transformation without massive state assistance. Private enterprise, especially contracts, federal grants, and project-specific direct congressional appropriation, known as earmarks or political pork, became the primary means to develop the financial resources to pursue state economic ends.

Prospects for gaining further revenue from the federal government appeared dim with Ronald Reagan's election. He had promised to get government off the backs of citizens. Universities and others feared the Reagan program would result in a sharp decrease in federal science spending. To prepare themselves for what seemed the inevitable severe decline in federal research support, universities raised tuition to create additional revenue for the new state purposes; they passed some of the costs of the new effort on to students and their families.

This move was not unprecedented. A similar tuition spike had occurred in the later 1960s and 1970s at the height of the initial baby boomer entrance into college. But there it gobbled up the NDEA money, low-interest, easily forgivable loans. The Higher Education Act of 1965, the 1972 Title IX Higher Education Amendments, and the Middle Income Student Assistance Act of 1978 perpetuated the policy of loaning students cheap money that universities could capture through higher tuition and fees to fund an activity deemed in the national interest. Indeed, at least since the end of World War II, American statesmen and women recognized a compelling national need to expand the number of college graduates, to broaden curricula, and to enhance university infrastructures, especially in science and technology. The various programs enacted by Congress were predicated upon those three objectives. The rhetoric and campaign of Reagan was of a very different order. Rather than consider college graduation and university research essential to the public weal, Reaganites treated each as a special interest, as a burden perpetuated by government rather than a blessing on the nation. Each was just another middle-class entitlement, an inappropriate "tax" on everyone not attending college or engaging in research. And Reaganites promised to unburden Americans from this oligarchical impediment.

To these men and women, education had only individual—personal— benefits, not national ones. Individuals who attended college married better, got better jobs, received higher wages, and stayed happier and healthier. Those were individual benefits. Science and technology that directly served national foreign policy ends remained of national importance and deserved continued federal support, but university programs to restore economic prosperity or complete the American dream served only individual ends. They needed to compete in the marketplace.

The Reagan administration never actually accomplished what it had pledged it would do. In fact, federal funding nearly tripled during his two administrations. Higher education and scientific research received a healthy share of the expanded largesse. Nonetheless, a new tone had been set and a new thrust undertaken. Higher education was a personal concern. And as such, universities and their programs were subjected to individual scrutiny. Each consumer needed to weigh the options available and then pick the institution that best fitted his/her goals. A plethora of personal factors went into choosing a university; academics was only one. Over the course of the past few decades, colleges have actively competed for students by highlighting the amenities that young people and their parents wanted: jobs, new apartment-like dorms with private bedrooms and baths, a physically attractive campus, winning sports teams, scholarships, helpful administrators, multiple dining options, a student-oriented recreation center, coffee shops, friendly guides and students, an active student affairs office.

The case that higher education constituted a personal, not national, benefit gained further traction with the fall of the Soviet Union and the end of the Cold War. Gone was a serious goad and potent demonstration of high national purpose, a major impetus for land-grant university funding for the previous half century. With no other national mandate recognized as replacing it, the personalization of higher education quickened and calls for privatization of state and land-grant universities materialized. Many university functions have now been contracted out, and states have drastically reduced their percentage of public university budgets. University boards of trustees have been reticent to raise tuition for fear of hurting school marketability or fomenting brouhaha among state legislators. The situation has been exacerbated with the rise of distance education. Schools lacking laboratories, classrooms, and even instructors sell courses directly to students, reducing their overhead to near zero and with appreciably lower tuition. Universities, especially land-grant universities, counter these virtual schools by accentuating benefits from place-based education, such as service learning, student engagement, learning communities, and quality enhancement programs.

The Great Recession of 2008 and its aftermath have further reconfigured the land-grant scene. Collapse of state tax revenues caused legislatures to curtail support for universities by 20 percent or more. Parts of the American Recovery and Reinvestment Act of 2009–commonly known as the federal stimulus package–temporarily lessened the pain. Universities also acted in other ways. Shortly before and during the early days of the recession many of the professors hired to teach the baby boom generation reached retirement age. Although a portion deferred retirement because of the economic collapse, a goodly number left academia. Universities replaced only a small percentage with tenure-track faculty and then primarily in areas of traditional strength. Temporary, time-limited faculty, often without benefits and always poorly paid, took up the slack in other areas.

As the recession neared its conclusion, administrators at state-supported universities did not act to restore their schools to what they had been. Instead of restocking all the various disciplines, land-grant and other universities used the recession to reshape efforts. Places of traditional strength and places of economic promise absorbed a major portion of the renewed funds. In general, land-grants retrenched somewhat from the efforts that had broadened them in the 1960s and 1970s. They concentrated on reestablishing and reequipping those areas likely to generate external funding and to spur economic development. Their thrust was to move strongly back to science and technology and to areas of high student demand.

It is that latter thrust that has proved most revealing. Management has become the new land-grant panacea. Used in this context, management is not a subject but a mechanism—a metaphor, really—to improve on the present without additional resources. It takes the status quo and "improves" upon it through intervention; management is simply employing "scientific" principles to take things as they are now and redistribute them or proportion them in a different way to create new practices thought to be more effective, efficacious, or sustainable.

Agricultural colleges within land-grants have been especially avid in embracing this approach. Enrollments are burgeoning as students now flock to major in an impressive number of au courant managerial specialties, each of which promises to fashion a better tomorrow. Choices include integrated pest management, environmental economics and management, floral management, turf management, enterprise management, gin management and technology, natural resource and environmental management, management policy and law, and poultry management. There are many more.

That managerial approach to the future has become so compelling within American society that its tangible product is millions of jobs in a wide variety of service and other industries and businesses. Managing and regulating life and living are among America's leading endeavors. Dieticians and nutritionists manage the eating habits of groups as diverse as diabetics, the obese, cancer patients, and children. Every sports complex and golf course has a resident turf manager. Human resource management departments ride herd over virtually every enterprise. The departments of the interior and natural resources are awash with environmental managers. Financial management gurus manage portfolios for the rich and not so rich. Pain and chronic illness management specialists bridge the divide between social and medical science. Extension agents and journalists avail themselves of the opportunities of information science to manage their messages. Case managers manage the entire web of programs and services that constitutes the social safety net. Environmental law manages the "rights" of natural phenomena and landscapes and is exceedingly big business. Life coaches harmonize the myriad factors of human existence to ensure success, happiness, and longevity.

Management's comfortable home at land-grants stems from their similar premises. That notion—action in the present to create a better or less objectionable future—has powered these schools for at least a century. These quintessentially American institutions have repeatedly proven their mettle by serving as engines for a presumed better future in a slew of diverse arenas. In the meanwhile, their efforts toward improvement have often produced controversy; initiatives to resolve one series of issues frequently reveal or create new problems or problems for other groups. In today's parlance, land-grant universities manage. Their critics find only mismanagement.

Part One

Whose University?

Land-grant universities' many constituencies often take proprietary interest in the institutions. That is natural, of course. It reflects a profound faith in the universities' ability to affect the status quo. That faith is also an obligation; stakeholders regularly demand that their schools take action whenever some such perturbance is identified.

Sometimes land-grant-orchestrated change occurs sub rosa. It fails to generate critical comment or even much notice. Real disturbances occur when a university action draws prolonged public scrutiny. That frequently happens when schools seek to modify services or redefine missions. It may even happen when established activities no longer match current assumptions or expectations. In all of these cases, groups may object and often mobilize to force the land-grant to right that perceived wrong.

In each of these instances, the very important question of whose university it is takes center stage. Numerous constituencies claim a voice in discussions and demand a seat at the table during deliberations. Control and authority are at its heart. Determining the present and future direction of the institution—at least in the matter under consideration—is the goal. What transpires and how it occurs leave an important legacy both inside and outside the university and help frame future discussion.

Men in the Food Lab, Women in the Engine Shop

Gendered Stereotype Breaking in Land-Grant Technical Programs

AMY SUE BIX

Democracy's colleges promised higher education opportunities to the sons and daughters of America's working classes. Many land-grants had incorporated that promise in their degree programs by establishing majors aimed specifically at one sex. At their inception, home economics and engineering were among the disciplines considered discrete by gender. This bias remained well into the 1970s, about a hundred years later, before that supposed assumption came under strenuous attack.

Bix's essay provides a necessary corrective. She shows that a not negligible portion of both curricula contained members of the opposite sex almost from their beginnings. Students chose to major in what they wished rather than in some curriculum designated appropriate for them.

These gender-benders did not escape notice. Sometimes they endured ridicule and questioning. But their successes in receiving the degrees of their choice proved the persistent flexibility of land-grants as well as their openness to change. By permitting students to take courses of study initially designed for members of the opposite sex, land-grants ultimately helped weaken barriers traditionally raised to keep men and women in separate spheres.

✳✳✳

At first glance, the early land-grant college system seems to embody the ultimate "separate spheres" division of the sexes, in which male students studied "agriculture and the mechanic arts,"[1] while female students took liberal arts, became teachers, and were concentrated in home economics. Crucial elements of that simple structure are at least partly true. Land-grant schools both reflected and reinforced conventional associations of engineering with masculinity and of domestic science with femininity. But in many ways, the more interesting part is where the paths grew more tangled and flexible, where the gendered history of land-grant education proves more complex. Seemingly straightforward boundaries assigning men and women to different academic fields turned out to be more permeable than they might initially appear. Both as individuals and in small groups, female students entered engineering from the late 1800s onward, while occasionally, some men pursued domestic-science classwork. Elements of gendered crossing-over occurred relatively early; indeed, the openness and novelty of land-grant colleges made them the *only* institutions in American higher education where young women and men of the late 1800s and early 1900s could experiment with choices of study most strictly associated with the other sex.

ESTABLISHMENT OF LAND-GRANT COEDUCATION AND CONVENTIONAL GENDERING OF ACADEMIC SUBJECTS

College coeducation in the United States originated at Oberlin, which began admitting female and African American students alongside white men soon after its founding in 1833, reflecting its reform-minded commitment to learning as a vehicle for cultural uplift. The notion of coeducation spread gradually before and after the Civil War, gaining particular momentum in midwestern and western states, while trailing in the conservative South. Some all-male schools adopted coeducation with reluctance as an economic strategy to boost enrollment, and especially in such cases, female students were often shunted aside with second-rate facilities, barred from receiving certain honors, and excluded from male-led extracurriculars or reduced to subordinate status.[2]

The Morrill Land-Grant Act, as passed in 1862, specified nothing with regard to coeducation; it did not stipulate and did not forbid teaching women and men in the same institution. Land-grant schools did not all open as mixed sex; especially in New England and the South, precedents of separate education often lingered. But historians such as Julie Roy Jeffrey and Andrea Radke-Moss have argued that an experimental frontier mentality made coeducation appealing in "western" locales that proved eager to differentiate themselves from stodgy East Coast tradition. As husbands of educated women, progressive college presidents such as Iowa State's Adonijah Welch and Kansas State's John Anderson favored elements of women's rights. Supporters also believed that by having male and female students share a campus, states could save money and use women's "civilizing" presence to tame the roughhousing and violence of an all-male atmosphere.[3]

To many nineteenth-century parents, social observers, and even college faculty and administrators themselves, the whole notion of female higher education remained controversial. Critics had worried for years that advanced intellectual work for women risked transforming them into unnatural creatures, masculinized and diverted from proper feminine interest in home and family. Adding to such fears, respected Boston doctor Edward Clarke warned in 1873 that overly demanding college work endangered women during the most "susceptible" years of biological development and would foster a national epidemic of "female physical degeneracy." A teenage girl who tried to study as hard as boys did was "deranging the tides of her organization," Clarke worried, "divert[ing] blood from the reproductive apparatus to the head" so that "the ovaries . . . cease to grow [until] . . . the brain and the whole nervous system, disturbed . . . became neuralgic and hysterical." Clarke cited case studies of women whose long hours of study led to menstrual disorders and infertility, including one female student at "a Western college" who graduated at the top of her class but soon "began to show signs of failure." While "she had mastered . . . the secrets of chemistry, . . . she steadily ignored her woman's *make* . . . [trying] to compass man's intellectual attainment in a man's way, and died in the effort" from apparent "degeneration" of the brain. Clarke's book, *Sex in Education*, particularly condemned the new popularity of coeducation in "Western colleges" such as Iowa and Michigan, warning that their first female graduates might already have incurred serious "physical defects."[4]

Despite such criticism, coeducation represented an integral part of many of the earliest land-grant schools; by offering affordable, locally accessible education to both young men and women, founders hoped to enhance state development, economic growth, and social well-being. At mixed-sex schools, leaders had to consider how one of the Morrill Act's main missions—providing practical training centered on agriculture and mechanic arts—could apply to female pupils. Trustees at Iowa State College, which admitted women from its start in 1869, declared, "If young men are to be educated to fit them for successful, intelligent and practical farmers and mechanics, is it not as essential that young women should be educated in a manner that will qualify them to properly understand and discharge their duties as wives of farmers and mechanics? We must teach the girls through our Agricultural College to acquire by practice a thorough knowledge of the art of conducting a well-regulated household." Iowa State adopted a "ladies' course of study," and its first official class in domestic economy appeared in 1871, under the title "Chemistry as Applied to Domestic Economy."[5] Kansas State University created its domestic economy program in 1873–74, which started primarily as sewing, with additional lectures on hygiene, food chemistry, and dairying. President Anderson declared, "A girl has a right to an education as precisely adapted to a woman's work as is a boy's preparatory to a man's work." By 1877, Kansas State began offering women cooking and baking classes in its new "kitchen laboratory."[6]

Land-grants did not begin in the 1860s by shunting all female students into home economics; indeed, that discipline did not exist as a coherent intellectual field when the Morrill Act passed. At some of the earliest land-grants, subjects for male and female students often overlapped, especially for first-year work in literature, philosophy, mathematics, and other basics. Even after Iowa State identified a distinct "ladies' course" in the 1870s, domestic economy remained a minor part of the curriculum; other requirements dominated, including liberal arts (history, political economy, Shakespeare, "study of words") and sciences (multiple courses in chemistry, botany, physics, psychology, anatomy, mineralogy, and meteorology).[7] Early land-grants did not immediately offer women the option of earning degrees in domestic economy; the University of Wisconsin-Madison only established home economics as a department in 1903 and the University of Nebraska in 1908, while the University of California did not create its first domestic science classes until 1912. Female students instead claimed undergraduate degrees in general studies or science, especially favoring chemistry and botany; by the early 1900s, a small but tangible number chose other areas, including library science, commerce and business, pharmacology, and, as we shall see, even engineering.[8]

Nevertheless, home economics increasingly served as a convenient default for female land-grant students, a gender-appropriate and hence respectable academic base to prepare them for marriage and "scientific home-making" and/or employment as teachers, extension workers, "women's page" reporters, or other gender-appropriate jobs. According to Radke-Moss, sixty-four out of sixty-six female students at Oregon Agricultural

College in 1892–93 majored in household economy, while twenty-six of the forty women who graduated from Utah State Agricultural College from 1894 to 1909 took domestic science degrees.[9] Land-grant programs served as a vehicle to propagate the field, as early female graduates secured posts to inaugurate home-ec teaching in other colleges and in secondary schools. The field gained academic credibility with the formation of the American Home Economics Association in 1909, building on a decade of annual conferences held in Lake Placid, New York, where influential women and men defined the goals of their new discipline and outlined possible directions for teaching, research, and social impact.[10]

During the late 1800s and early 1900s, land-grant colleges also institutionalized their teaching of engineering, expanding to encompass civil engineering, mechanical, mining, electrical, and a variety of other subdisciplines. As an occupation, engineering had been masculinized from its start in early modern Europe, growing out of traditions where rulers called on ingenious innovators to devise formidable new weapons, defense systems, and manufacturing machinery. Engineering training retained that military connection in the United States, centered on early nineteenth-century classes at West Point. But entry to the field did not depend on formal education; the majority of technical workers for many decades learned through hands-on experience in factories and in the field, helping build the Erie Canal and national railroad networks. These informal and academic contexts of engineering training had one thing in common: few women found a welcome on bridge construction sites or in heavy industry. As Ruth Oldenziel and other historians have noted, nineteenth- and early twentieth-century culture reinforced the single-sex identity of engineering through literary and professional rhetoric that added a epic tone to technical work, depicting engineers as macho heroes who built roads to conquer the wilderness.[11] When land-grant schools added engineering departments, they naturally echoed those assumptions of engineering's masculinity.

By the early twentieth century, in both philosophy and practice, higher-education authorities had established engineering as primarily an appropriate field for male students and home economics as primarily suitable for women; indeed, those gender identities formed key parts of each field's self-image. But even as land-grant colleges steered men into engineering and women into home economics, they also created a potential for gender crossover that could not have been duplicated anywhere else in American higher education at that time. During the 1800s, colleges in the United

States multiplied dramatically, fragmenting to serve young people of different classes, genders, races, ethnicities, and locales. The culture at all-male schools varied widely; small New England colleges such as Amherst and Williams prepared men of modest background for teaching and the ministry, while institutions such as the University of Virginia focused on instilling gentlemanly character. Old-fashioned presidents still placed classical knowledge at the center of study, while innovators elsewhere experimented with broadening classwork to include more sciences and social sciences, architecture, and engineering. But across the board, from Harvard, Yale, and Princeton to newer and smaller schools, men's curriculum expansion stopped short of home economics. Fundamentally there was no logical reason for all-male colleges to embrace the study of domestic science.[12]

Nineteenth-century Americans also created a range of new schools to offer women opportunities for extended academic study, though as with men's colleges, female seminaries differed radically in their visions of the purpose of education and hence its content. Many finishing-school-type academies stressed music and similar arts as the means to instill proper feminine virtues in upper-class young ladies; others prepared women to meet an expanding nation's need for schoolteachers at relatively low wages. Some, such as Mount Holyoke and Bryn Mawr, aimed to match elite men's colleges in academic rigor and graduated pioneering generations of female scientists and other ambitious alumnae.[13] Precisely for that reason, home economics never formed a major component of instruction at the "Seven Sisters"; many proud women faculty and administrators scorned it as beneath their intellectual dignity, too vocationally oriented.[14]

As much as the women's colleges of the 1800s and early 1900s differed from each other in some aspects, none offered female students a specialized training in engineering; technical studies simply had no place either in the ideal of cultivated feminine skills or in copies of the Harvard model. The engineering programs of West Point and all-male schools such as the Georgia Institute of Technology, Rensselaer Polytechnic Institute (RPI), and the California Institute of Technology excluded female students by definition. In short, all-male schools had no rationale or framework for offering men studies in home economics, and all-female schools gave women no opportunity to study engineering or, often, home economics. Instead, it was the Morrill Act schools that most commonly welcomed both genders and developed programs in both areas, under the banner of "useful arts." That history set the stage for a few individuals and small groups in the late 1800s and early 1900s to explore studies that defied gender stereotypes. Land-grant colleges were by no means gender neutral or automatically fair to women, but inadvertently, by their very broadness, they created conditions under which a small but growing number of women would infiltrate men's fields and vice versa.

The very breadth of land-grant training allowed gender crossovers in other academic areas; over the past 150 years, the male-female composition of both agriculture and veterinary medicine has also shifted. Vet-med in particular transitioned from emphasizing large-animal farm practice to small-pet care, a change accompanied and facilitated by the entry of more female students. While such stories are crucial to the history of gender in land-grant colleges, this chapter focuses on the fields of engineering and home economics. Specialists in the history of engineering have just begun to trace the experiences of the earliest women in that discipline, while historians of home economics have largely reiterated and reinforced perceptions of the field as by definition female; there is little scholarship on the history of male home-ec students. Yet it is clear that both female engineering students and male home economics students existed, starting early in land-grant college history.

HOME ECONOMICS AS EARLY TWENTIETH-CENTURY TECHNICAL EDUCATION FOR WOMEN

By the early 1900s, domestic science professors conspicuously modeled their philosophy and teaching after (and in cooperation with) their institution's science and engineering programs. Land-grant schools carefully branded home-ec workspaces as "laboratories," terminology meant to differentiate their teaching from the unscientific bread-baking and dressmaking duties of mothers and grandmothers. In 1914–15, the Home Economics Department at the University of Wisconsin boasted of having "two food laboratories, two applied chemistry laboratories, one dietetic laboratory with practice kitchen . . . , one weaving laboratory, a textile laboratory, a dressmaking laboratory, a house architecture and house decoration laboratory, an art and design laboratory, [and] one applied arts laboratory . . . all . . . fully equipped with apparatus." Iowa State students referred to their course in textile chemistry and laundering techniques with the nickname "scrub lab."[15]

Domestic-science teaching and research grew increasingly technical, incorporating elements of not just chemistry, physics, and biology but also engineering. At Iowa State in 1924, household administration graduate student Eloise Davison test-taught a class focused on making women into modern "household engineers," skilled in evaluating, purchasing, using, and maintaining the new types of kitchen equipment appearing on the market. Davison observed, "The whole modern period in which we live is an age of machinery," so the "average homemaker" simply must "overcome" her lack of experience with technology.[16] Significantly, the new class was a cooperative venture of Iowa State's home-ec division and its agricultural engineering department. By 1929, Iowa State promoted equipment studies to the status of a department; its initial roster included not only female home-ec faculty but also mechanical engineering professor Herbert Sayre, signifying the perceived connection between engineering and equipment studies. Elements of engineering authority and masculine representation gave the new discipline legitimacy, but from the outset, women defined the field.[17]

Other home-ec schools, including University of Minnesota, Purdue, Ohio State, and Washington State University, followed Iowa State in creating household-equipment courses. Equipment curricula embedded technical lessons squarely inside culturally acceptable boundaries of women's knowledge; they incorporated engineering and science principles while safely segregating female students into alternate programs centered around their presumed sphere of interest: domestic life. Dozens of female students each year took multiple classes in equipment mechanics, gas and electric appliances, and refrigeration and home lighting, as well as an equipment seminar and "electrical laboratory."

Professors insisted that students learn scientific and technical principles to understand how and why appliances worked (or didn't). Hands-on experience reinforced theory; in "electrical lab," students deliberately overloaded circuits, reading voltmeters and ammeters at each stage. Exercises assigned women to dismantle refrigerators and ranges, to assess construction quality and analyze how various features applied fundamental physics principles of temperature control. Seniors in home-refrigeration classes inspected installation of furnaces and air conditioners on local construction sites. Their final project involved planning a full household heating and cooling system, including technical specifications and cost estimates. Female students visited metallurgical and chemical testing labs of the Hoover Vacuum Cleaner Company, as well as General Electric's Kitchen Institute.[18]

Equipment courses undoubtedly thrived in part because women's knowledge of domestic science did not challenge men's leadership of pure science and engineering. Far from feeling threatened, Iowa State engineering faculty cooperated in equipment teaching and research. But quite powerfully, equipment training served to subvert the notion of women's technical ignorance. Faculty and students conducted technical research and published results in experiment station newsletters and leading home-ec journals.

Men in Cooking and Home Economics Classes
before World War II

It was not automatically predetermined that all subjects later identified with domestic science must inevitably have been identified as in the women's sphere. Ellen Swallow Richards linked her research and teaching in water purity at MIT to the male-dominated world of chemistry. Her protégé, Marion Talbot, tried to establish a sanitary science program within the Sociology Department at the University of Chicago in the 1890s, envisioning a field in which male and female experts together would reform city planning and address urban problems by applying insights from the physical, biological, and social sciences.[19] The American Home Economics Association was headed by female presidents, but especially before World War I, influential men filled a number of its other leadership posts and helped edit its journal, including nutrition specialists C. F. Langworthy and Howard Knight, plus household-economics and accounting experts William Morse Cole and Benjamin Andrews, the latter a longtime professor in household arts at Columbia University's Teachers College.[20]

Even as gendered philosophies of land-grant schools linked home economics to female enrollment, authorities within the discipline continued to assert its universal applicability. In 1913, US Department of Agriculture nutritionist Langworthy noted that men often encountered topics such as food adulteration, dietetics, and environmental hygiene in science and medicine classes. He cited West Point and Annapolis cadet room inspections and clothing regulations as inculcating a sense of "ship housekeeping . . . [that] involves cleanliness and order and much that can be called home economics, though this grouping is without doubt far from the minds" of military authorities. "Men sometimes take courses in household arts at Teachers' College, Columbia University," Langworthy noted, and such instances, combined with trade-school and military vocational cooking lessons, Boy Scout experience, and informal home lessons from mothers, meant that men's home-ec study, "though scattered and often incidental, is nevertheless fairly considerable in amount."[21]

Teachers of home economics clearly positioned daily preparation of home meals as women's work, but food preparation elsewhere could shift into male territory. Between 1931 and 1940, Iowa State's home-ec department offered a course called "Fundamentals of Food Selection and Preparation," specifically for men, with "principles of cookery, meal planning and preparation adapted to forestry, engineering, scout camps, and organized houses."[22] Some men who registered were fraternity stewards who wanted to gain confidence in planning "well-balanced" meals; others liked the idea of being able to survive, even just on "simple dishes," "if ever put on their own." The course combined lecture and regular weekly "laboratory" sessions, where men prepared beef stock, boned rib roasts, and created "man-made" cookies and cakes. Instructor Louise L'Engle commented that the men's "skill would put to shame some of the home-ec girls who flunk the 'practical.'"[23]

Reports of Iowa State men whipping up a full dinner that included sweet-potato soufflé and jellied vegetable lime salad elicited banter from fellow students, both men and women. One female home-ec student quipped that college women should consider making a "leap year proposal" to a veteran of the class, since "perhaps he'll agree to cook her bridge luncheons for her, and he'll do it well." The male students themselves joked that they "suppose all the girls will be after them now." But such comments underlined the fact that the course only meant to teach men cooking for temporary circumstances ("when the wife is away on a visit") or in masculine contexts such as camping, a message that often appeared in other early twentieth-century discussions of "manly cooking."[24] There was no intention or desire for men to take over or routinely share women's obligation of producing breakfast, lunch, and dinner for a full family every day. The magazine produced by Iowa State's home-ec department commented, "Certainly the man who has taken Foods will appreciate the time and effort his wife spends in preparing meals and will recognize good food when he gets it."[25]

Cooking courses aimed at a male student constituency began to be offered at a number of other land-grant schools in this era, including state colleges and universities in Maine, Colorado, Minnesota, Idaho, and Washington.[26] For several years prior to World War I, Professor Abby Marlatt, "chairman" of the Home Economics Department at the University of Wisconsin, taught "camp cookery," listed as part of a roster of classes taught by women and, the rest of which were almost exclusively intended for female students. According to the 1913–14 catalog, the course was "intended especially for the Forest Rangers . . . [and] considers the food values, fundamentals of cookery practice, balanced ration, and practice in using camp cookery utensils."[27]

In fact, even with the overwhelming female associations of home economics, social concerns about food, family, and home fostered the creation of some courses targeted to men that extended well beyond camp cooking. In 1925, at the request of male students, Dean Nora Talbot at Stillwater's Oklahoma A&M College created a three-month lecture and laboratory course where her home-ec faculty taught nutrition, "table practice," "standards of social conduct," family economic life and relationships, and "selection and appreciation of dress in relationship to appropriateness and right values." Though a few men dropped after discovering that home economics was not a "snap course," popular demand from male students filled two sections in the following quarter. "For some time, home economics enthusiasts have dreamed, studied, and talked about the importance of educating the men as well as the women to an appreciation of the standards of home life," instructor Florence Schertz declared. "The time when the school of home economics caters to women only is passing."[28]

Following similar impulses, North Dakota Agricultural College offered a class titled "Home Economics for Men," which attracted an average of fifty-six students per year from 1926 to 1929. The course aimed to inform young men that they should not expect a "modern girl" to follow their mothers' "old fashioned" lives, since "women have changed and progressed and . . . [in] the rapidly changing world, the home too is changing." In order to promote marriage stability amid such flux, the course addressed "relationships between college men and women, courtship, engagements, family finance, incompatibility, other causes of divorce, preparation for parenthood, child training, health and recreation of the family, and . . . good standards of family life."[29] During the 1920s and 1930s, some home economists campaigned to expand their discipline to incorporate new studies of child development that could draw male as well as female students. But as historian Julia Grant has detailed, these "grandiose hopes that the participation of fathers in parent education classes would contribute to the construction of a more egalitarian family" did not sway male professors in psychology, sociology, and medicine, who feared that connections to feminized home economics would undermine their scientific stature.[30]

Cornell offers the most dramatic example of gendered redefinition in the teaching of cooking and food science, plus decoration, textiles, design, and more. After World War I, the US hospitality industry enjoyed strong economic growth, and leaders felt pressure to modernize. Well-heeled clientele had high expectations for service, and hotels had expanded into complex operations that needed well-organized meal service, laundry, housekeeping, and maintenance.[31] To handle such demands, the newly formed American Hotel Association (AHA) sought to transform hotel management into an expert profession. While earlier generations of hoteliers learned on the job, advocates envisioned creating a new class of university graduates who combined knowledge of accounting, institutional efficiency, and business psychology with training in customer care, hospitality law, building engineering, and more. Given New York State's importance to the tourism and business-travel industry, Buffalo hotel owner John McFarland Howie approached Cornell as a natural site to develop the first bachelor's degrees in hospitality management. Though Cornell's president, classicist Jacob Gould Schurman, initially scorned the proposal as trade-school rubbish, Howie found key allies in home-ec faculty Martha Van Rensselaer and Flora Rose, who in 1911 had overcome resistance from fellow faculty to become the first women promoted to full-professor rank at the college. The School of Home Economics was housed within Cornell's Agriculture College, whose dean, Albert Mann, endorsed plans to create a hotel-training curriculum "centered around home economics."[32]

Cornell's hospitality-management program opened in 1922, as part of the School of Home Economics, and was headed by Howard Meek, a mathematician who had earned his college tuition through summer work in resort hotels. The first class of twenty-two was entirely male, including some "sons of hotelmen," and up to World War II, men comprised the vast majority of degree candidates. Iowa State, Wisconsin, and other land-grants routinely trained female majors in institutional management, and numerous alumnae took jobs running restaurants and cafeterias, dormitories, clubs, and similar businesses. But the older men who dominated the AHA envisioned hotel management as an entirely male profession, and in being unfriendly to women, Cornell's hospitality program reflected that. One of the relatively few women who enrolled, 1926 graduate Dorothy Daly Johnson, recalled that Meek "had not wanted *any* women in the course and he gave all five of us a particularly hard time."[33]

The roughly one hundred men (plus a handful of women) pursuing hotel-management degrees in the early 1920s followed a curriculum that crossed disciplinary lines and thus defied associated gender stereotypes. The class called "Hotel Engineering" taught building planning and construction, kitchen design, and specifications for elevators and plumbing, heating, cooling, refrigeration, electrical, and other large-scale technological systems. Photographs show male students, shirtsleeves rolled up, working on steam engines and boilers in Cornell shops. In other photos, the men donned white aprons to work in a food-preparation laboratory, a context virtually identical to that of female home-ec majors in the same era. Male hospitality students took a battery of classes in cookery, foods, and nutrition, and, like female home-ec majors, their chemistry courses explained theory through applied lessons in mixing salad dressing. They studied mechanical drawing, economics, and accounting but also took required classes in textiles, decoration, and furnishing. As the program grew, female home-ec specialists, including designer Annette Warner and textile expert Beulah Blackmore, spent increasing amounts of time working with male hospitality students, while food-science instructors Jessie Boys, Irene Dahlber, and Anna Driscoll played key roles in shaping the program.[34]

The fact that the hospitality degree required male students to spend more time in kitchens and decorating studios than in machine shop, taking lessons from the same female faculty who taught female home-ec majors, did not erase all traditional gender expectations at Cornell. Indeed, the hotel school was built on—and throughout its early years reflected—assumptions that family cooking and household management were feminine chores, while a parallel knowledge of linens and cooking became masculinized when applied for pay in hotel employment.

But officially, male hotel-management students were enrolled in the home economics school, and other Cornellians teased them with the line, "Boy, you're going to make some girl a good wife." To add to the apparent gender oddity, the hospitality major proved popular among pre–World War II Cornell athletes. Robert Beck, former hotel-school dean, recalled that hotel majors comprised fourteen out of twenty starters on Cornell's 1939 football team, unbeaten and ranked first in the country. Beck remembered, "When Cornell defeated Ohio State, the Big Ten Champion that year, one news report read, 'Never in the annals of football has a Big Ten Champion been defeated by a team, two-thirds of whom were enrolled in the College of Home Economics.'"[35]

At other land-grant schools, individual men filtered into home economics. The University of Wisconsin had a scattering of male students who took textile chemistry and institutional management; Phillip Dakin's experience in "advanced draperies" class and his role in producing the school's 1933 student fashion show drew admiration from professionals, who subsequently engaged him as a theatrical designer.[36] In other instances, men potentially interested in home economics may have been discouraged or deterred by hostile faculty, counselors, and administrators. The University of Illinois restricted men from entering its Woman's Building, the site of its Department of Household Science, as well as the swimming pool and gymnasium for female students.[37] Upon entering Kansas State in the late 1930s, Harry Martin intended to major in chemical engineering but, inspired by his part-time job in college food service, shifted to dietetics, nutrition, and food management. "There was no men's bathroom in the building," Martin recalled. "Many male students took courses in the department, but I was the only one who attempted to complete the program. I called in one day and the administration said, 'You're not going to be able to get a degree.' . . . They didn't want to give a home economics degree to a man." The school's president had simply vetoed awarding Martin a home-ec diploma, as confirmed later by College of Home Economics dean Ruth Hoeflin, who arranged for Martin and nineteen other men to receive belated home-ec degrees in 1980.[38]

Women in Engineering Classes before World War II

Meanwhile, on the mechanic arts side of the land-grant equation, it was some of the land-grant schools that provided America's first female engineering graduates at a time when Caltech, Georgia Tech, RPI, and other technical schools remained all-male institutions. Just six years after the University of California-Berkeley opened, Elizabeth Bragg Cumming was the first woman to earn a civil engineering degree there, in 1876, writing a thesis on a technical issue in surveying. In the 1890s, Iowa State granted civil engineering bachelor's degrees to sisters Elmina and Alda Wilson. After Elmina proceeded to earn her engineering master's degree from Iowa State, the school hired her to head its drafting room, then promoted her. As assistant professor of civil engineering, she helped plan a new campus water system. Bertha Lamme completed a mechanical engineering degree at Ohio State in 1893, then designed motors at Westinghouse.[39]

In the early twentieth century, simply being a woman studying engineering was unusual enough to get your picture on the front page of campus papers at Iowa State and elsewhere. Under the cute headline "Beauty Meets Resistance," the *Penn State Engineer* noted in 1934 that Olga Smith had become the first female enrolled in electrical engineering. Isolation made the experience hard for many of these individuals; one woman in engineering at Cornell said: "A girl has to want . . . pretty badly to go through with the course in spite of the unconscious brutality of . . . [male] classmates. . . . She must be ready to be misunderstood, as . . . many . . . will conclude that she took engineering . . . to catch a husband. She must do alone lab reports and other work men do in groups—because men who are willing to face the scorn of their peers and . . . work with her are more interested in flirting than in computations. She must be prepared for a lonely academic career; she cannot approach her classmates to exchange notes without appearing bold." But slowly, the number of female engineering students at land-grant schools such as Illinois, Ohio State, Penn State, and Purdue began to add up, one or two at a time.[40]

At Cornell alone by 1938, more than twenty women had received engineering degrees; classmates attached the nicknames "Sibley Sue" and "Slide Rule Sadie" to these female engineering majors. Nora Stanton Blatch earned a civil engineering honors degree in 1905, then worked for construction companies and the water-supply board in New York City. Olive Dennis established a thirty-year career as an engineer and designer at the B&O Railroad. Female engineering students such as Blatch and Dennis remained a curiosity. Remarking on the intriguing rarity, a 1920s paper ran the headline "Three Coeds Invade Engineering Courses and Compete with Men at Cornell University: Stand Well in Their Studies." Alongside a photo of mechanical engineering junior Jeannette Knowles working on a compression-testing machine, the article noted that the three represented "the greatest number of women students ever enrolled [in engineering] at one time" at Cornell, attending class alongside over eight hundred men.[41]

Administrators did not encourage women to enroll in engineering; in fact, they did just the opposite. Gladys Tapman had to remind Cornell of its promise of instruction in any subject *regardless of sex*, before the dean agreed to accept her into civil engineering, where she completed her degree in 1934.[42] Observers assumed that women literally did not belong in engineering; when Esther Knudsen and Ursulla Quinn arrived at the University of Minnesota as civil engineering majors in 1921, male classmates heard "the click-click of women's heels upon the tiles of man's last retreat at the University" and helpfully rushed to redirect the presumably lost female students to their proper building. Knudsen and Quinn both received engineering degrees in 1925, as the University of Minnesota student newspaper explained in an article reading, "Co-ed Engineers: Man's Domains Are Again Invaded. . . . and Man's sacred domains will be sacred no longer."[43]

An attempt at concerted change came at Purdue in the 1930s, where progressive president Edward Elliott supported bold thinking about opportunities for women. Elliott hired respected engineer Lillian Gilbreth to teach industrial management and mentor female students. Elliott also recruited famed aviator Amelia Earhart as another career consultant. Purdue had recently opened its first residence for women; with Earhart's high-profile appointment, female enrollment jumped 50 percent, and the new dorm overflowed. Both Gilbreth and Earhart encouraged female students to combine marriage with careers in engineering or science. In summer 1940, Ellen Zeigler and Kathleen Lux joined seventy Purdue men at the school's civil engineering camp, where the female "camper-ettes" joined men in playing baseball, swimming, and learning to use surveying equipment.[44] Still, gender crossing in land-grant culture remained limited; as at other schools, few Purdue women chose to enroll in engineering, and among that handful, attrition proved high.[45]

Women in Engineering Studies during World War II

It is, of course, impossible to estimate how many land-grant female students before World War II were interested in engineering, only to be sidetracked by self-doubts or steered into more traditionally feminine fields. World War II proved a crucial transition. As employers ran short of manpower, they began placing "Rosie the Riveter" on the shop floor; companies also sought to hire female engineers. Wartime pressures justified stretching gender boundaries, at least temporarily. The federal government, schools, and industry urged female students to serve their country by taking more engineering and science courses. At Penn State, at least sixty-five women signed up for special war classes in airplane and ship drafting.[46]

Companies desperate for wartime help began recruiting women who had math and science skills, then gave those women customized crash courses to make them engineering aides. In one of the most elaborate programs, in 1942, the Curtiss-Wright airplane company began training what they called "Curtiss-Wright Cadettes," giving over six hundred women a ten-month immersion in engineering math and mechanics, theory of flight, airplane materials, drafting, job terminology, and aircraft production. It was no coincidence that five out of the seven colleges handling Cadette training were land-grants: Cornell, Iowa State, Minnesota, Penn State, and Purdue (the other two were RPI and the University of Texas).[47]

The announcement of the Cadette program elicited joking about the notion of female engineers. Faculty had to adjust; Minnesota Cadettes remembered a "reputedly tough professor who strode into his first class and suddenly burst into uncontrollable laughter, eventually recovering to admit that he had never before faced 25 females wielding slide rules." But Cadettes could claim to be doing their part for the war effort, and on that patriotic ground they were welcomed. Moreover, some skeptics ended up pleasantly surprised by women's ability. Cadettes' presence forced men to face questions about gender and technical work. Purdue's 1943 yearbook noted, "Tradition . . . seems destined to vanish as demand for manpower opens careers for women in . . . fields heretofore . . . practically uninvaded by the fair sex." An Iowa State publication editorialized, "Girls in the wind tunnel, the shop . . . caused engineers to wonder, then acknowledge, and finally resign themselves to the fact that there would be similar incursions as long as the war continues, and perhaps even after."[48]

Recognizing that many female students were still daunted by the prospect of entering the traditionally male world of engineering, inventive staff at Purdue sought special pathways to make women more comfortable with technical studies. In 1943, Purdue's engineering school teamed up with the home-ec school to start a new program named "Housing." Fifteen female students promptly enrolled, combining home-ec studies with physics, math, chemistry, and six general engineering classes, plus specialized work in civil, mechanical, and electrical engineering. Professors gave women technical knowledge of construction and remodeling, suggesting that graduates could find employment as consultants to home buyers or as lab technicians conducting research for building manufacturers. Based on the assumption that female students were natural authorities on the home, the program seemed to offer a safe middle ground for technical exploration. It reportedly appealed to women who were "glad of the opportunity to get something a little more revolutionary than the traditionally feminine field of home economics and yet not have to go to the extreme of entering the engineering schools that [men] insist upon preserving for themselves."[49]

The next year Purdue created another crossover course, meant to offer female home-ec majors intensive shop training. Nine women signed up to study plumbing, electrical appliances, and metal finishes. Instructors reported having to force women out of the machine shop after hours, as they practiced using precision measuring instruments, cutting and shaping wood, and filing, soldering, and riveting metal. Applying new skills, the women designed and made bookends, wastebaskets, dishes, jewelry, ashtrays, and model railroad cars. Professor O. D. Lascoe argued that even housewives needed to understand modern engineering terminology and techniques. Again, the course underlined wartime erasure of strict gender lines. One observer commented that in machine shop, home-ec women "don their slacks, pin back their hair and really assume the role of a woman engineer," stepping into "a field which, heretofore, was practically unheard of in women's circles."[50]

At Iowa State, household-equipment majors found their mechanical knowledge in sudden demand, a valuable wartime commodity. Representatives of the Naval Research Lab traveled to Ames to interview equipment majors for engineering posts. At the suggestion of these recruiters, the home-ec program added extra work in algebra, trigonometry, and calculus to accelerate the women's preparation for emergency employment. Home-ec majors could also sign up for special wartime electrical engineering classes; they earned the nickname WIRES (Women Interested in Real Electrical Subjects). Iowa State engineering professors reported that they had originally planned to give "these girls . . . elementary background [as] a gentle transition from biscuit baking." As things turned out, one instructor said, anyone "who expect[ed] to see the girls changing a fuse or repairing a toaster cord [was] sadly disappointed. Baby stuff! They learned those things in their own equipment lab when they were freshmen." WIRES were ready to pursue "more rugged topics" such as magnetic circuits, vector diagrams, transformers, and synchronous motors. Though Iowa State's class yielded only a handful of graduates, WIRES immediately entered wartime testing and design work for General Electric (GE), Western Electric, and General Motors.[51] Other Iowa State home-equipment students entered wartime engineering through on-the-job learning. Nine signed up for special training with GE to become engineering aides. During the day, they made calculations and graphs, calibrated instruments, and tested radio transmitters, receivers, and airplane motors. In the evenings, they studied engineering theory and practiced using slide rules.[52]

Such connections between corporate engineering employment and Iowa State home-ec training continued into the postwar years. After finishing her home-equipment degree in 1951, Pat Traylor became a GE engineering aide, testing a new navy automatic pilot system and working on the manufacture of gas turbines. Traylor wrote that once she moved into the grease pits, "I made those test engineers swallow their guffaws about Home Ec majors!

I was certainly glad I had physics and household equipment mechanics courses and could use testing instruments."[53]

Women's classes in housing, household equipment, and shop and men's occasional classes in camp and military cooking did not in themselves aim to revolutionize the standard gender divisions of land-grant education. Such courses situated cross-gender study within very limited contexts and specific circumstances. Indeed, their definition reinforced men's customary links to public life and masculine space and women's emotional and practical ties to the home. At the same time, such nontraditional courses represented more than just idiosyncrasies. Their existence illustrated the potential gender flexibility of land-grant disciplines, foreshadowing a significant long-term trend, the broadening and redefinition of the original scope of home economics to make room for men, and especially the movement of women into mainstream engineering.

Along with the wartime crash courses designed to train women as temporary engineering aides in defense industries, World War II brought a burst of propaganda encouraging undergraduate women to pursue full engineering degrees. A Penn State magazine editorialized: "Here's to the Victory girl. . . . The girl who wields a slide rule as deftly as a Lord and Taylor creation. . . . She jumbles up all the old theories about this being a man's world. She can tell an engineer . . . to go to hell. She can even talk to . . . them about dynamos and two-way sockets without feeling like a damn fool. . . . Neat."[54] Schools were besieged by wartime employers searching for women who held engineering degrees. The University of Illinois flatly told companies not to bother coming to interview the lone eligible female graduating in February 1943 since she already "had countless offers for positions."[55]

Before the war, the one or two women enrolled at any one time at schools such as Cornell or Penn State were an anomaly. Wartime support brought extraordinary jumps in their numbers at many schools. By 1945, Purdue alone had eighty-eight women majoring in engineering, where a critical mass made life easier; aeronautics major Helen Hoskinson remarked, "Now that lady engineers are not a novelty on this campus, people no longer stare at the sight of a girl clutching a slide rule."[56] Among other land-grant schools, there were fifty female engineering students at Ohio State, forty-eight at the University of Minnesota, thirty-seven at Cornell, thirty-two at Illinois, twenty-seven at Wisconsin, and twenty-six at Iowa State. Overall, in November 1945, colleges and universities reported a total of 48,977 men enrolled in engineering courses and 1,801 women (at a time when Caltech,

Georgia Tech, and some other engineering schools still refused to admit women at all).[57]

World War II brought a number of "firsts" for female students in engineering, as their enrollment climbed. In 1944, Iowa State civil engineering major Ruth Best joined thirty-three men selected for the Guard of Saint Patrick, one of the school's main honor societies. The engineering magazine reported, "A woman invaded the Guard of Saint Patrick for the first time in the history of Iowa State College," an initiation traditionally celebrated with an "informal smoker." The next year the Guard welcomed two more women, including Maxine Goodson, Iowa State's first woman graduate in chemical engineering. Eloise Heckert became the first female member of Iowa State's chapter of Pi Tau Sigma, the honorary mechanical engineering fraternity; she had earned the highest grade point average in the entire first-year engineering class.[58] In 1945, as the first woman elected to edit Iowa State's engineering magazine, architectural engineering junior Mary Krumboltz wrote an editorial declaring, "Slide-rule-pushing girls are no longer a rarity. . . . We see them on our own campus and they are not the problem they were once expected to be. In fact, they are a problem only inasmuch as their fellow students and instructors choose to make them one."[59]

Even as wartime educators begged female students to enter engineering, many women still encountered resistance. Purdue's Helen Hoskinson reported that one engineering professor turned and left the classroom when he saw her sitting there the first day. "He was sure someone had made a mistake and didn't think it was he." Other Purdue women complained that professors still spiked lectures with hoary sexist jokes. Patronizing male classmates annoyed women; one insisted that while she was serious about her studies, "there are too many boys who think you [women] take engineering to get dates."[60] Everyday experiences continually reinforced women's sense of historically being outsiders; the frustration of trying to find ladies' rooms reminded them that engineering schools were literally built for the opposite sex. One anonymous author commented:

> All young women, who have come to Penn State
> Listen to me, and let me relate
> The story of one who has learned the hard way
> That technical schools are no place to stay.
> When you've stood all morning and you've "got to go,"
> First, you'll suspect—and then you'll know

That the [engineering] buildings were made for men at Penn State;

I assure you, my dears, they're not for his mate. . . .

So take my advice, and switch to Home Ec

If you don't want to become a physical wreck.[61]

MEN IN HOME ECONOMICS DURING AND AFTER WORLD WAR II

What about the other side of the equation, men studying home-ec subjects traditionally gendered female? During World War II, Iowa State's naval training program ran special courses for electricians, diesel mechanics, and firemen. Alongside that, Iowa State ran multiple sessions of a Cooks and Bakers School that prepared navy men to handle food preparation onboard submarines, aircraft carriers, troop-transport ships, PT boats, and at onshore stations. The program, headed by Iowa State home-ec professor Fern Gleiser, former head of the school's institutional management department, trained 280 men between 1942 and 1944. The navy had standard cooking procedures and expectations but no precedent for formal instruction in quantity cooking, so Gleiser and other Iowa State civilian faculty had to develop their own curriculum.[62]

The naval training four-month course included 132 hours of lecture and 432 hours of "laboratory" practice, conducted in regular college kitchens and meat-handling facilities. Iowa State taught navy students to use and maintain ranges, steamers, slicing and grinding and mixing machines, and a wide range of other kitchen equipment, to follow sanitation rules, to issue supplies, and to understand different types of storage. Like land-grant female home-ec majors, these military men learned to plan meals with an understanding of vitamins, minerals, and nutrition. They studied the dietary function, characteristics, and comparative advantages and disadvantages of fresh, frozen, canned, and dehydrated vegetables, as well as how to cook and serve each and combine them for optimum color, shape, flavor, and harmony with the main dish. Iowa State's female experts taught the men to master a long list of baking terminology, the characteristics of different varieties and grades of flour, and the chemistry of fermentation and yeast action. Students learned the reasons why pie crusts came out tough, soggy, doughy, burned, shrunken, or too thick or too thin, plus techniques for preventing such pastry problems. Iowa State course material described the perfect cake as "a work of art flawless in every way," teaching students to make angel-food, devil's food, sponge, marble, gingerbread, jelly-roll, and at least eight other types of cakes in loaf, layer, and sheet form, plus multiple types of cookies, fruit cobblers, doughnuts, cream puffs, pies, puddings, coffeecakes, and other sweets. Under supervision by Iowa State institutional management instructor Mabel Anderson, navy men practiced making at least sixteen types of dressings, gravies, and sauces, a curriculum that in many ways replicated the civilian peacetime instruction given to young women studying home economics.[63]

Meanwhile, as civilian men vanished from Cornell during the war, male enrollment in its hospitality program plunged. While only twenty women had completed hotel-management degrees in the decade from 1933 to 1943, the program attracted forty-one women in 1944, comprising exactly one-third of the class of 122 students.[64]

Wartime provided an immediate rationale for military men to study food preparation, food chemistry, and nutrition under the guidance of female home-ec teachers. However, after World War II ended, powerful peacetime "norms" reasserted contrasting gender roles. Rhetoric from government, advertisers, and social commentators encouraged middle-class white men and women in particular to strive for an idealized convention of a bread-winning husband and homemaking wife, and to make room to rehire men, many employers discharged those "Rosie the Riveter" women who did not voluntarily quit. While wartime propaganda had pressured female college students to consider majors or at least taking some coursework in engineering, science, and math, postwar messages and trends in academic options reverted to a divide along the most traditional gender expectations. Of the 1,598 male students entering Iowa State in 1955, 890 (55.7 percent) chose to enroll in the division of engineering, 410 (25.6 percent) chose agriculture, 295 (18.5 percent) chose science, and just 3 men (0.2 percent) chose home economics. Of the 508 female students, 446 (87.8 percent) chose to enroll in home economics, a college that encompassed a range of areas, such as physical education. Fifty-one Iowa State women (10.0 percent) enrolled in science, while just 5 women (1 percent) chose agriculture, and 6 (1.2 percent) engineering.[65] The Iowa State figures seem to have been typical of those of most postwar land-grant colleges. Margaret Rossiter has reported that nationwide, "only 97 men majored in home economics at the bachelor's degree level in 1947–48."[66]

But beneath this broad male-female gulf, subtle distinctions revealed a more complicated gendering of subject matter. Iowa State College split the study of foods into several subdivisions that conveyed distinctly different implications for men and women. In 1947, Iowa State's home economics division had a "curriculum in foods and nutrition," while its Agriculture College contained a Department of Dairy and Food Industry, and the Science Division offered a curriculum in food technology, each with a unique gender profile. The home-ec "foods and nutrition" program supported majors in dietetics, nutrition, experimental cookery, and related sciences (such as chemistry). In 1947, all students in this program were female; the dietetics major enrolled no men and 130 women, experimental cookery had 32 women, foods and nutrition had 15 women, and 9 women majored in "related sciences." In sharp contrast, the Agriculture College's Department of Dairy and Food Industry was oriented toward the dairy business, stressing milk testing and inspection, cheese manufacture, dairy chemistry, and bacteriology. In 1947, it enrolled 95 men and just 1 woman. But the Science Division's "food technology" program had more room for gender crossover, under its focus on the "technological application of the sciences and engineering arts to the manufacture, transportation, storage, distribution, and utilization of food." Students undertook heavy requirements in chemistry, physics, and math, plus a three-month internship in a "branch of the food industry." Between 1946 and 1956, Iowa State graduated at least two women and five men in the food-technology major. The related program in "chemical technology" enrolled five women, amid seventy-four men, in 1947.[67]

As Margaret Rossiter has detailed, from the 1940s through the 1970s, many land-grant home-ec programs were racked by tensions with male central administrators, who scorned female instructors as an outdated embarrassment and rushed to replace them with younger male faculty. Rossiter depicts the outcome as a devastating story in which universities marginalized or excluded female staff from what had historically been one of the few areas where professional women had been able to secure advancement, exercise leadership, and serve as role models for new generations of students. "The changes could be brutal and humiliating, involving such deliberate ruptures with the past as . . . appointment of male deans lacking qualifications in the field," Rossiter writes.[68]

In the short term, female home economists at Cornell, Penn State, Wisconsin, and a number of other colleges lost ground in a zero-sum game with the odds stacked against women. But the longer evolution of home economics reveals a more tangled story about how evolving social mores and ideals of higher education played out in reshaping the self-defined scope of an entire discipline and its traditional associations of gender. Women professors and administrators ultimately succeeded in reasserting their place in a rapidly changing field, establishing strong teaching programs and international research in areas ranging from marketing and consumer behavior and environmental science to high-tech textile research and development of nutritional space food for NASA.[69]

Stereotypes of both men and women continued to permeate discussions of home economics and color expectations. In 1960, the University of Nebraska's Arnold Baragar, associate professor of housing and equipment, hailed "the invasion of men into the teaching and research areas" as "an interesting and encouraging endorsement of the home economics profession."[70] While Baragar praised male faculty ready "to compete with women in home economics" as a positive indicator of male interest in the "improvement of family living," he added that "men students in home economics are another story. I cannot conceive of men taking an entire home economics curriculum at the undergraduate level."[71] Loyal Horton, an Illinois college food-service director, quickly riposted that "not only can I conceive this but I did it and I am no quirk of nature," having "invaded" the institution-administration major at Michigan State around 1946 with more than a dozen other men.[72]

As it happened, the American Home Economics Association (AHEA) soon proved the error in Baragar's assumption that it was unimaginable for college men to choose a concentration in home economics. In a 1965 survey, 65 out of 306 home-ec departments in coeducational schools reported that their list of 1964–65 majors included at least one male student; Oklahoma State University had 185 male undergraduate majors, and Penn State had 107. Those sixty-five programs together enrolled 701 men, almost 1.5 percent of the 48,000 students pursuing bachelor's degrees in home economics across the country that year. Out of those 701 men, 297 chose to specialize in food-service management, 178 in applied art (often covering areas such as housing and interior design), and 117 in institution administration.[73]

Absorbing men into a program designed around female students presented campus authorities with specific challenges. The University of Wisconsin, like other land-grant schools, required home-ec majors to practice applying their lessons under official supervision by spending several weeks living in a home-management practice house. As men's enrollment grew during the 1960s, program leaders felt they could not allow the male and female classmates to live together. Engineering programs faced a parallel difficulty in figuring out how to integrate women; MIT leaders agonized over how to provide proper accommodations for female majors at the outdoor camps used for training civil engineering students.[74]

At the level of students' individual experiences during the postwar period, men studying home economics and women studying engineering faced parallel tensions, encountering suspicion and hostility from classmates and even faculty of the opposite gender. One man who earned a home-ec education bachelor's degree in the late 1970s reported that of professors at his state university, "There were those that were encouraging and supporting and those that were discouraging and wanted me out of there . . . I had to do some fighting. . . . I . . . understood where . . . having a guy with a beard and cowboy boots . . . sitting . . . with girls . . . with very nice outfits . . . and scarves, probably looked pretty much out of place." He recalled some "very harsh" grading and professors who "didn't want to talk to me." Gendered assumptions were embedded in official bureaucracy; just as women in postwar engineering programs received university correspondence addressed to "Mister," this man remembered getting letters calling him "Ms." and filling out forms that asked him to indicate a "husband's occupation." And just as male engineering majors accused female classmates of adopting feminine wiles to elicit special treatment from susceptible teachers, one man who completed a 2002 state-university degree in family and consumer sciences education remembered female classmates with Bs and Cs saying, "You're getting the A because you're the guy. . . . They're being easy on you because they don't want to discourage you. They want you to stay in."[75]

During the late 1960s and afterward, those who were proponents (male and female) of bringing more men into home economics, as faculty and as students at all levels, cited feminist-influenced ideas about the changing nature of the family and a vision in which "Free to Be You and Me"-era boys and girls grew up to share domestic responsibilities. "Nowadays homemaking is man's work too . . . a joint husband-wife adventure," Luther Baker Jr., chairman of Central Washington State College's Home Economics Department and associate professor of family life, wrote in 1969. Denouncing the trap of gender stereotypes, Baker added, "There is no good reason why a dietician, nutritionist, textiles expert, housing specialist, or any other practitioner in the various areas of home economics should not be male. . . . With challenging exposure during the public school years, increasing numbers of qualified men could be lured into the exciting and fruitful adventure of home economics."[76] Bemoaning the absence of men as junior high and high school home-ec teachers, male and female home-ec faculty at Ohio

State University and the University of Idaho in 1990 called for instituting new "recruitment and retention strategies . . . [and] career awareness opportunities directed specifically toward males, recruitment literature for men, and scholarships for male home economics majors." They advocated having established male professionals serve as role models and mentors, to tell their stories at schools and meetings and hence "personalize [and] affirm" a nontraditionally gendered choice of work. That plan for actively courting and supporting male home-ec majors strikingly paralleled the measures that the Society of Women Engineers and other activists had already instituted to promote the recruitment and success of female engineering majors in American colleges.[77]

As it turned out, during these same decades, students, faculty, administrators, and others at land-grants and other colleges engaged in an impassioned intellectual and emotional debate over the very essence of the discipline of home economics. In 1969, Cornell adopted the new name "Department of Human Ecology" to represent desired modernization and broadening of the field, and by the mid-1980s, more than 70 of the 387 colleges offering undergraduate home-ec degrees had also rebranded themselves. Names play a crucial role in how a discipline is perceived, by both insiders and outsiders; while some observers bemoaned a painful destruction of tradition, others welcomed the promise to invest teaching and research with renewed vigor and relevance. Not coincidentally, as schools redefined home-ec programs as "family and consumer sciences," "human development," or "human sciences" and merged their traditional scope with elements of economics, education, and business training, the number of male students rose. In 1969, men had comprised just 1.7 percent of home-ec undergraduate students nationwide; by 1983, that figure had more than tripled, to 5.8 percent. University of Missouri football player Robert Curry told reporters that his home-ec major and ambition to run and own day-care centers had earned him "some ribbing from the guys at first. . . . But they're catching on."[78]

Historians, sociologists, and psychologists have emphasized the disincentives for men to enter fields previously associated with women, such as nursing, social work, and elementary education and child care, which typically carry lower pay, benefits, and prestige. While those occupations might appeal to men for reasons having to do with personal satisfaction or economic necessity, only all but the most self-confident men who opted for "women's work" could ignore emotionally fraught conflicts of gender identity, heightened external scrutiny, or peer stigmatization. Just as women who entered engineering programs faced both internal and externally imposed pressure to assess what statement that nontraditional direction made about their femininity, so men who enjoyed home economics found that preference often raised culturally laden questions about masculinity.[79]

Under the influence of feminist thinking, some reform-minded school districts of the 1970s started requiring or encouraging all boys and girls to take both home economics and shop, though students and parents sometimes reacted negatively. By the 1990s, the reinterpretation of home economics as "work and family studies" or "life-management education" reinvigorated that trend, encouraging secondary schools to replace lessons in cooking and sewing with units on relationships and parenting skills, communication, nutrition, and "teen living." In 1968, boys accounted for only 4.2 percent of the 2.2 million pupils taking home-ec classes in seventh-through twelfth-grade home-ec classes, but by 1993, enrollment had reached 5.3 million, with 41.5 percent boys.[80]

By 2004–5, men made up 27 percent of the students in the University of Georgia's College of Family and Consumer Sciences.[81] In 2005, Iowa State University combined its College of Family and Consumer Sciences with its College of Education to form a new College of Human Sciences, offering degrees in early childhood, elementary, and secondary education, entrepreneurial studies, kinesiology and health, diet and exercise, dietetics, hospitality and event management, nutritional, culinary, and food science, family finance, apparel merchandising and design, family services, and more. Under that widened umbrella, men comprised about 20 percent of Iowa State's College of Human Sciences in 2010.[82] Eighteen men majored in the apparel program in 2009, for example, compared to just three in 1995. Some observers attributed male interest to popular-culture trends such as the television reality show *Project Runway* that gave high-visibility appeal to the glamor of modern clothing design, a movement echoed in culinary science by new media attention to "foodie" culture and the transformation of chefs into celebrities.[83] At Oklahoma State University, which still had a separate education college, men earned 62 out of 430 undergraduate degrees in human sciences in 2008–9 (14.4 percent), 58 out of 461 in 2009–10 (12.6 percent), and 52 out of 370 in 2010–11 (14 percent).[84] Over the long term, the gender shift in home economics and the repositioning of the discipline again showed the flexibility embedded within the land-grant model, enabling its teaching and research to stay relevant over the decades, to a wider audience.

Women in Engineering after World War II

World War II did not magically remove all institutional barriers to women wishing to study engineering. Toward war's end, Cornell started to worry about women taking up too much room on campus. To make room for male veterans, administrators imposed an artificial cap, ordering all departments except home economics to block admission of any new female undergraduates for spring 1945. The engineering dean had already approved admission of nineteen first-year women to join eighteen already enrolled; Cornell's vice president scolded the engineering school for exceeding its quota of twenty-five women and forbade it from accepting even one more woman that semester.[85]

Postwar numbers of female engineering students plunged steeply, but they never entirely vanished; after reaching new lows in the early 1950s, female ranks again climbed, finally approaching World War II levels by 1957. In 1949, there were 763 female students enrolled in engineering at schools across the United States; by 1957, that total had more than doubled to 1,783. Since men's engineering enrollment also rose over that period, female students still constituted well below 1 percent of the total engineering-student population. During the 1950s, roughly 10 to 15 percent of all male college graduates earned degrees in engineering; by contrast, women completing engineering degrees amounted to 0.2 percent or less of all female college graduates.[86]

Even though female undergraduates remained a tiny minority, some land-grant engineering schools acknowledged their presence and occasionally even sought to recruit more. In 1952, the University of Illinois's engineering school bulletin courting potential students carried two images of female students working alongside men in machine shop and encouraged female high school students with good grades in math and science to "seriously consider the possibilities of engineering careers."[87]

But many male and female parents, counselors, high school and college teachers, and even university administrators still refused to believe that women could or should seek technical degrees on equal terms with male classmates. In 1955 Eric Walker, dean of engineering at Penn State, wrote an article titled "Women Are NOT for Engineering" in which he asserted that investing time and effort to teach female students didn't make sense, since most simply did not have the "basic capabilities" needed to handle technical work.[88] At most land-grants during the 1950s, female engineering majors faced a campus climate that remained chilly, or even toxic, discouraging some to the point of dropping out.

To combat both overt discrimination and more subtle discouragement, a core of activist female engineering faculty and professionals mobilized, incorporating as the Society of Women Engineers (SWE) in 1952. Purdue's engineering women formed a student section two years later, followed soon by other land-grants such as Iowa State. College SWE chapters undertook a wide range of activities to provide mentoring, networking, and other forms of support; they paired first-year women with "big sisters," hosted talks by industry representatives, organized panel discussions, distributed women's résumés, and more. To encourage more girls to view engineering as a real and exciting career option, college women gave presentations at elementary and secondary schools, ran Girl Scout programs and summer camps, and helped with SWE's national outreach efforts.[89]

SWE's support for women in engineering came at a time when the climate of the field had started to change at a number of institutions. The early 1960s extended the distinct upward trend of female enrollment; for example, the Engineering College at the University of Illinois had twelve women enrolled in early 1960 but twenty-four in 1963, twenty-six in 1964, thirty-four in fall 1965, and thirty-seven in spring 1966.[90]

SWE chapters multiplied and extended their efforts, calling attention to such issues as sexual harassment and highlighting ways in which women engineers' concerns were connected to broader issues of the second-wave feminist movement. Meanwhile, a crucial core of allies, some faculty (male and female) and administrators at land-grants, organized institutional efforts to encourage more young women to consider studying engineering and to help them succeed. Today, it is virtually impossible to find a land-grant campus that does not have programs supporting women in science and engineering. In the 1950s, women were less than 1 percent of all engineering students in the United States; in 2010, women comprised 18.1 percent. Out of the twenty-five schools that granted the highest numbers of engineering degrees to women in 2011, seventeen of them were land-grants.[91]

Conclusion

This history of how small groups of students made nontraditional choices at land-grant schools offers revealing lessons about the powerful ways in which different fields of study became associated with a particular gender and about the circumstances that permitted stretching those "normal" boundaries. Gendered connotations of home economics and engineering did not disappear, as revealed in ongoing jests about men learning to cook and women learning to use machinery. Few, if anyone, anticipated (or perhaps even desired) a time when both those fields would draw equal numbers of female and male majors.

Instead, it was the multidimensional definitions of science and technology within the land-grant context that allowed room for small-scale crossovers to occur more gradually. In shaping a new hospitality degree that required male students to master both the female-led area of food science and the masculine study of hotel-building technology, Cornell literally brought hundreds of men into the home-ec kitchens. In redefining household studies to include an expertise in refrigerators and other equipment, Iowa State and other land-grant schools gave female students an accepted gateway to technical studies at a time when they were discouraged from pursuing traditional engineering degrees. Special programs set up for particular purposes encouraged opportunities for further crossovers. By institutionalizing a specific course in its catalog, Iowa State's home-ec program endorsed the value of teaching men to cook, albeit for appropriately gendered use in fraternities, on camping trips, and in outdoor labor. The Iowa State WIRES program, Purdue's housing and shop classes for women, validated the idea of giving women access to technical knowledge and hands-on tool experience.

The histories of men learning traditionally female subjects and women learning traditionally male subjects were not precisely parallel. Starting in the late 1800s, Elizabeth Bragg Cumming, the Wilson sisters, Bertha Lamme, and a few other women earned engineering degrees, one by one. Land-grant schools did not set up any special curriculum just for them; those women earned civil and mechanical engineering degrees identical to those of men. Their individual interests in engineering studies drew them to follow that unusual path, often defying administrators and faculty who regarded that choice as inappropriate. By contrast, men entered home economics in sizable numbers at Cornell only after the growing hotel business encouraged the school to create a uniquely masculinized degree that would facilitate men's employment in the new profession of hospitality management. For its part, the engineering profession displayed no active interest in welcoming women until World War II, when the national manpower emergency fostered temporary efforts such as the special wartime technical classes program and Curtiss-Wright training to draw female students into engineering.

After World War II, gender patterns in the fields of both home economics and engineering changed. Margaret Rossiter has argued that it was the quest for academic prestige that led several universities to maneuver more male faculty and administrators into home economics after the war, at great personal cost to the female pioneers who had built and sustained that field. By contrast, no schools of that era made concerted efforts to court female engineering faculty or deans, and doing so would not have increased respect for a department.

During the postwar period, a number of the nation's women engineers sought to make that field more appealing and accessible to new generations of young women. The Society of Women Engineers organized outreach efforts, mentorship programs, and other forms of encouragement for women with talent and interest in technical work. Such campaigns gained strength during the 1960s and beyond, finding support from the second-wave feminist movement, civil rights law, and broader social shifts in education and gender. Today it is virtually impossible to find a land-grant school (or other university) that does not boast about having a SWE chapter and a wide variety of other support mechanisms for women interested in engineering. By contrast, while some advocates from the 1960s onward favored bringing more men into home economics at all levels (secondary, undergraduate, graduate, faculty) to reflect both a desirable broadening of the field and a modernization of family realities, there were few organized efforts or national support mechanisms to attract more men. The increase in male students during this era reflected something different: the redefinition of the discipline and its increasing overlap with fields such as education, often as a result of financial pressure in university administration or other institutional trends.[92]

Today the historically gendered fields of engineering and home economics (however relabeled in today's parlance) remain far from achieving gender parity. Indeed, both disciplines still stand out as among the most gender imbalanced in the modern university. In the United States in 2009–10, women earned 87.7 percent of all bachelor's degrees in "family and consumer sciences/human sciences" (FCS/HS); the highest percentage female among twenty different fields listed by the US Department of Education, and little changed from the 87.5 percent figure of 1999–2000. The field had grown during that decade; in 1999–2000, US colleges issued a total of 16,321 bachelor's degrees in FCS/HS, 14,288 to women; in 2009–10, the nation produced 21,818 FCS/HS graduates, 19,132 of whom were women. In dramatic contrast, just 16.8 percent of all bachelor's degrees in engineering and engineering technologies in 2009–10 went to women, the lowest percentage female of all listed areas. That figure represented a significant drop from the 1999–2000 level of 18.6 percent, though the total number of engineering degrees earned by women rose, from 13,655 out of 73,323 in 1999–2000 to 14,896 out of 88,729 in 2009–10.[93]

Many activists for women in engineering bemoan the fact that the dramatic increase over the 1980s and 1990s in women's share of degrees has leveled out, apparently stalling or even declining substantively in certain specialties. Gendered stereotypes continue to exert a powerful influence over perceptions; despite the best efforts of the feminist movement and reform-minded educators, many Americans still reflexively associate technology and engineering with men and link food and household-related interests primarily with women.

In the big picture, however, land-grant colleges helped alter an essential reality of gender and academic discipline. While a woman choosing to study engineering in the late 1800s or the early 1900s was likely to face criticism or discouragement in many quarters, while a man in Cornell's home-ec hospitality program in the 1920s became the target of jokes, students making similar choices today encounter far less (if any) opposition and ridicule. It was the land-grant schools that first created the chance for such crossovers, a gender-bending opportunity that would have historically been impossible at either traditionally all-male or all-female colleges.

Men studying foods, textiles, home decor, and clothing design and women studying engineering were certainly not what the authors of the Morrill Act had envisioned. But such gender crossovers came to represent a key part of land-grants' 150-year history. They reflected broader cultural patterns, including the influence of World War II, second-wave feminism, civil rights law, and social trends such as new emphasis on nutrition and consumer sciences. Land-grant history thus represents a strong case study of a bigger historical question of how American society has gendered different forms of knowledge and how popular assumptions about what's proper for men and proper for women have been reshaped, at least partially, over decades.

NOTES

1. "An Act Donating Public Lands to the Several States and Territories Which May Provide Colleges for the Benefit of Agriculture and the Mechanic Arts," July 2, 1862, http://memory.loc.gov/cgi-bin/ampage?collId=llsl&fileName=012/llsl012.db&recNum=534 (accessed December 20, 2012).

2. Rosalind Rosenberg, "The Limits of Access: The History of Coeducation in America," in *Women and Higher Education in American History*, ed. John Mack Faragher and Florence Howe (New York: W. W. Norton, 1988), pp. 107–29.

3. Julie Roy Jeffrey, *Frontier Women: "Civilizing" the West? 1840–1880* (New York: Hill and Wang, 1998); Andrea G. Radke-Moss, *Bright Epoch: Women and Coeducation in the American West* (Lincoln: University of Nebraska Press, 2008). For background, see Mary Ann Dzuback, "Gender and the Politics of Knowledge," *History of Education Quarterly* 43 (Summer 2003): 171–95.

4. Edward H. Clarke, *Sex in Education, or, A Fair Chance for Girls* (Boston: James R. Osgood and Co., 1873), pp. 28, 47, 84, 103–4, 126, 144.

5. Ercel S. Eppright and Elizabeth Storm Ferguson, *A Century of Home Economics at Iowa State University: A Proud Past, a Lively Present, a Future Promise* (Ames: Iowa State University Press, 1971).

6. "Department of Household Economy," *College Symposium of the Kansas State Agricultural College* (Topeka: Hall and O'Donald Litho. Co., 1891), http://skyways.lib.ks.us/genweb/archives/statewide/schools/ksu/1891/56.html (accessed December 9, 2012). See also V. R. Gunn, "Industrialists, Not Butterflies: Women's Higher Education at Kansas State Agricultural College, 1873–1882," *Kansas History* 18 (1995): 2–17.

7. Eppright and Ferguson, *A Century of Home Economics at Iowa State University*, 3.

8. Radke-Moss, *Bright Epoch*; Lynn D. Gordon, *Gender and Higher Education in the Progressive Era* (New Haven: Yale University Press, 1990).

9. Radke-Moss, *Bright Epoch*, pp. 166–67.

10. Sarah Stage, "Introduction: Home Economics: What's in a Name?" and "Ellen Richards and the Social Significance of the Home Economics Movement," in *Rethinking Home Economics: Women and the History of a Profession*, ed. Sarah Stage and Virginia B. Vincenti (Ithaca: Cornell University Press, 1997). See also Megan J. Elias, *Stir It Up: Home Economics in American Culture* (Philadelphia: University of Pennsylvania Press, 2008).

11. Ruth Oldenziel, *Making Technology Masculine: Men, Women, and Modern Machines in America, 1870–1945* (Amsterdam: Amsterdam University Press, 1999).

12. John R. Thelin, *A History of American Higher Education* (Baltimore: Johns Hopkins University Press, 2011).

13. Ibid.; Helen L. Horowitz, *Alma Mater: Design and Experience in the Women's Colleges from Their Nineteenth-Century Beginnings to the 1930s* (New York: Knopf, 1984); Margaret Rossiter, *Women Scientists in America: Struggles and Strategies to 1940* (Baltimore: Johns Hopkins University Press, 1982).

14. Vassar incorporated some elements of home economics under the label "euthenics" from the 1920s through the 1950s, but such classes failed to attract many women and were not widely imitated among the other colleges that made up the Seven Sisters. Barbara Sicherman, "College and Careers: Historical Perspectives on the Lives and Work Patterns of Women College Graduates," in *Women and Higher Education in American History,* ed. Faragher and Howe, pp. 130–64.

15. "College of Agriculture: Courses in Home Economics, 1914–1915," *Bulletin of the University of Wisconsin,* serial no. 660, General Series, no. 472 (Madison, 1914): 5.

16. Eloise Davison, "A Course in Home Economics: A Report of a Successful Course Offered to Sophomore Women at Iowa State College" (Master's thesis, Iowa State College, 1924), 6–9, 21. See also Eloise Davison, "Electricity and the Farm Home," *Journal of Home Economics* 18 (1926): 215–16.

17. Amy Sue Bix, "Equipped for Life: Gendered Technical Training and Consumerism in Home-Economics, 1920–1980," *Technology and Culture* 43, no. 4 (October 2002): 728–54.

18. Elizabeth Beveridge, *Choosing and Using Home Equipment* (Ames: Iowa State University Press, 1968), 50; "Brief Outlines of Courses in Household Equipment Taken by Majors," n.d., box 3, folder 14, Louise Jenison Peet Papers, Iowa State University Archives; Faith Madden, *Household Equipment Experiments* (Ames: Iowa State College Press, 1952), 67; Virginia Berry, "Equipment Students Travel," *The Iowa Homemaker* (May 1937): 11.

19. Rosalind Rosenberg, *Beyond Separate Spheres: Intellectual Roots of Modern Feminism* (New Haven: Yale University Press, 1982).

20. Royston J. Lawson, "Men and Home Economics in the U.S.: 1900–1975," *Journal of Home Economics* (Spring 1993): 47–52.

21. C. F. Langworthy, "Home Economics Work in the United States for Men and Boys," *Journal of Home Economics* 5, no. 3 (1913): 239–48.

22. Iowa State College catalog, 1939–1940, p. 288.

23. Kathryn Soth, "It's Leap Year, Girls . . . And These Men Can Cook!" *The Iowa Homemaker* 12, no. 2 (May 1932): 1, 13.

24. Jessamyn Neuhaus, *Manly Meals and Mom's Home Cooking: Cookbooks and Gender in Modern America* (Baltimore: Johns Hopkins University Press, 2003).

25. Soth, "It's Leap Year, Girls," 1, 13.

26. Lawson, "Men and Home Economics in the U.S."; Langworthy, "Home Economics Work in the United States for Men and Boys."

27. "College of Agriculture: Courses in Home Economics, 1913–1914," *Bulletin of the University of Wisconsin,* no. 575, General Series, no. 399 (Madison, 1913): 28, 30.

28. Florence D. Schertz, "Home Economics for College Men," *Journal of Home Economics* 18, no. 7 (1926): 398–400.

29. Alba Bales, "A Course in Home Economics for College Men," *Journal of Home Economics* 21, no. 6 (1929): 427–29.

30. Julia Grant, "Modernizing Mothers: Home Economics and the Parent Education

Movement, 1920–1945," in *Rethinking Home Economics,* ed. Stage and Vincenti, 69. For more on the history of child-development ideas and practices, see Hamilton Cravens, *Beyond Head Start: The Iowa Station and America's Children* (Chapel Hill: University of North Carolina Press, 1993).

31. Molly Berger, *Hotel Dreams: Luxury, Technology, and Urban Ambition in America, 1829–1929* (Baltimore: Johns Hopkins University Press, 2011).

32. Brad Edmondson, *Hospitality Leadership: The Cornell Hotel School* (Ithaca, NY: Cornell Society of Hotelmen, 1996), 12.

33. Ibid., 50.

34. Ibid.

35. Ibid., 52; Robert Beck, introduction to *Hospitality Leadership,* xi.

36. Rima D. Apple and Joyce Coleman, "Domestic Science to Human Ecology," *The Challenge of Constantly Changing Times: From Home Economics to Human Ecology at the University of Wisconsin-Madison, 1903–2003* (Madison: Parallel Press, University of Wisconsin-Madison Libraries, 2003), 77.

37. Paula A. Treichler, "Isabel Bevier and Home Economics," in *No Boundaries: University of Illinois Vignettes,* ed. Lillian Hoddeson (Urbana: University of Illinois Press, 2004), 31–54.

38. "People in the News," *Pittsburgh Press,* May 17, 1980, A3, http://news.google. com/newspapers?nid=1144&dat=19800516&id=HWFhAAAAIBAJ&sjid=kFwEAAAA-IBAJ&pg=6560,263790 (accessed December 15, 2012); "Degree Given 40 Years Later," *Lakeland Ledger,* May 17, 1980, 2, http://news.google.com/newspapers?nid=1346&-dat=19800517&id=cI4sAAAAIBAJ&sjid=IfsDAAAAIBAJ&pg=4413,321741 (accessed December 15, 2012). See also "State Reports—Kansas," *AHEA Action* 7, no. 1 (August 1980): 5.

39. For Cumming, see *Women in Transportation: Changing America's History* (Washington, DC: US Department of Transportation, 1998), 11. On the Wilson sisters, see Richard Weingardt, "Elmina and Alda Wilson," *Leadership and Management in Engineering* 10, no. 4 (2010): 192–96; Elmina Wilson, *Modern Conveniences for the Farm Home,* USDA Farmers' Bulletin no. 270 (Washington, DC: GPO, 1906); "Elmina Wilson, Alda Wilson," *The Arrow of Pi Beta Phi* 21 (1904): 93; and Iowa State University websites: http://www.lib.iastate.edu/arch/rgrp/21–7–24.html and http://www-archive. ccee.iastate.edu/who-we-are/department-history/marston-water-tower.html (accessed January 3, 2012). For Lamme, see Margaret Ingels, "Petticoats and Slide Rules" (1952), in *Women in Engineering: Pioneers and Trailblazers,* ed. Margaret Layne (Reston, VA: ASCE, 2009): 85–97; Jeff Meade, "Ahead of Their Time" (1993), in *Women in Engineering,* ed. Layne, 137–40; Martha Moore Trescott, "Women in the Intellectual Development of Engineering," in *Women of Science: Righting the Record,* ed. Gabriele Kass-Simon and Patricia Farnes (Bloomington: Indiana University Press, 1990); and Martha Moore Trescott, *New Images, New Paths: A History of Women in Engineering in the United States, 1850–1980* (Dallas: T&L Enterprises, 1996).

40. "Beauty Meets Resistance," *Penn State Engineer,* October 1934; and Raymond

Howes, "Concerning Sibley Sues," *Cornell Alumni News*, October 13, 1938, 30.

41. Marilyn Ogilvie and Joy Harvey, eds., "Barney, Nora Stanton (Blatch) De Forest," *The Biographical Dictionary of Women in Science* (New York: Routledge, 2000), 82–83; "Woman a Civil Engineer: First of Her Sex to Enter the Heretofore Masculine Profession," *Spokane [WA] Spokesman Review*, August 26, 1923; Alumni folder, "Dennis, Olive Wetzel," Cornell University archives; Alice Goff, "Women Can Be Engineers" (1946), in *Women in Engineering*, ed. Layne, 155–77; "Three Coeds Invade Engineering Courses and Compete with Men at Cornell University: Stand Well in Their Studies," *Cornell Daily Sun*, 1923; Cornell University archives, #16/3/860.

42. "Light Shed on Engineering Job by an Expert Feminine Touch," *New York Times*, March 31, 1940.

43. Harold Peterson, "Co-ed Engineers: Man's Domains Are Again Invaded," *The Minnesota Techno-log*, May 1925, 11.

44. Ellen Zeigler, "Ross Camp," *Purdue Engineer*, October 1940, 10, 14; Kathleen Lux, "Following the Civils," *Purdue Engineer*, November 1941, 42.

45. Jane Lancaster, *Making Time: Lillian Moller Gilbreth—A Life beyond "Cheaper by the Dozen"* (Boston: Northeastern University Press, 2006); Robert Topping, *A Century and Beyond: The History of Purdue University* (Lafayette, IN: Purdue University Press, 1988); Susan Butler, *East to the Dawn: The Life of Amelia Earhart* (Cambridge, MA: DaCapo Press, 2009); Ray Boomhower, "The Aviatrix and the University: Amelia Earhart at Purdue University," *Traces of Indiana and Midwestern History* 6, no. 3 (1994): 36–41; John Norberg, *Wings of Their Dreams: Purdue in Flight* (Lafayette, IN: Purdue University Press, 2003); Zeigler, "Ross Camp," 10, 14; Lux, "Following the Civils," 42.

46. "We the Women," *The Daily Collegian [Penn State]*, October 10, 1942, 3. For more, see Amy Sue Bix, "Engineering National Defense: Technical Education at Land-Grant Institutions during World War II," in *Engineering in a Land-Grant Context: The Past, Present, and Future of an Idea*, ed. Alan Marcus (West Lafayette, IN: Purdue University Press, 2005), 105–33.

47. Amy Sue Bix, "From 'Engineeresses' to 'Girl Engineers' to 'Good Engineers': A History of Women's American Engineering Education," *National Women's Studies Association Journal* 16, no. 1 (Spring 2004): 27–49.

48. Marjorie Allen, "Cadette Column," *Iowa State Daily Student*, March 5, 1943: 2; "Fifty Years of Aeronautical Engineering: University of Minnesota, 1929 to 1979" (Department of Aerospace Engineering and Mechanics, University of Minnesota, Minneapolis, 1979); Purdue University yearbook, *The Purdue Debris*, 1943, 20.

49. Martha Lee Riggs, "Coeds Prove Themselves Good Engineering Students," *Purdue Exponent*, December 11, 1943, 3.

50. Martha McCulloch, "Lascoe Organizes New GE 41 Course for Campus Coeds," *Purdue Exponent*, August 26, 1944, 1; Elinor Hilton, "Shop Course Alleviates Christmas Present Problems of Coed Students," *Purdue Exponent*, December 5, 1944, 1, 4.

51. "Interview Women for Naval Jobs," *Iowa State Daily Student*, October 9, 1942, 3; "Require Equipment Majors to Add 5-Hour Course," *Iowa State Daily Student*, October

15, 1942, 4; Ben Willis, "The Wires Take Over," *Iowa Engineer*, October 1943, 41; "Dr. Peet Visits Iowa State Women Doing Engineering Work," *Iowa State Daily*, November 7, 1942, 4; "EE Course for Women," *Iowa Engineer*, January 1943, 107.

52. Bette Simpson, "Engineering Enlists Women," *The Iowa Homemaker*, November 1942, 7. See also Frances Madigan, "Women Choose Engineering Careers," *The Iowa Homemaker*, April 1943, 15; and "Girls, Girls, Girls: G-E Campus News," *Cornell Engineer*, November 1942, back cover.

53. Beverly Gould, "Meet Miss Engineer," *The Iowa Homemaker*, February 1953, 7.

54. "They'll Help Play 'Taps' for Japs," *Daily Texan*, January 6, 1942, 1; "Wimmin,'" *Froth*, August 1942, 6.

55. G. A. McConnell to Kenneth Meade, December 19, 1942 and March 29, 1943, box 70, folder "dean of women," 2/9/1, Willard Papers, University of Illinois Archives.

56. Peggy Stefen, "Coed Engineer Comes Through Over Comments of ME Faculty," *Purdue Exponent*, July 22, 1943, 1; "University's 30 Girl Engineers Have Gripe; Male Engineers Scorn Their Big Ambitions," *Purdue Exponent*, August 9, 1944.

57. "Enrollment of Undergraduate Civilian Engineering Students, as of November 5, 1945," *Journal of Engineering Education* 36 (1946): 388–94.

58. "Guard Pledges Woman," *Iowa Engineer*, January 1944, 100; "Pi Tau Sigma Elects," *Iowa Engineer*, April 1944, 155; "Woman Leads Engineers," *Iowa State Daily*, May 22, 1943, 5; "Graduates in Chem. E.," *Iowa Engineer*, July 1945, 22.

59. Mary Krumbholtz, "Women in Engineering," *Iowa Engineer*, May 1945, 176; "Engineer Staff Announced," *Iowa Engineer*, July 1945, 20.

60. "University's 30 Girl Engineers Have Gripe"; Peggy Stefen, "Coed Engineer Comes Through Over Comments of ME Faculty."

61. "Lend a Helping Hand," *The Daily Collegian*, September 22, 1942, 2.

62. Iowa State College report, "War Training Programs—World War II: Naval Training Schools," v. A VIII, April 1, 1945, Special Collections Department, Parks Library, Iowa State University. See also Helen Hudson, "New Navy Kitchen Serves," *The Iowa Homemaker*, April 1943, 7, and Virginia Bates, "Navy Learns to Cook," *The Iowa Homemaker*, November 1942, 9.

63. "Bakery" and "Pastry" booklets, Naval Training School, Iowa State College, Cooks and Bakers, n.d., ca. fall 1942, box 5, folder 5, "Naval Training School, ISC: Cooks and Bakers," RS 12/9/3, Special Collections Department, Parks Library, Iowa State University.

64. Cornell made the Hotel School a separate college in 1954, no longer officially part of the College of Home Economics. Edmondson, *Hospitality Leadership*.

65. Economic Research Service, US Department of Agriculture, *Progress of Rural and Urban Students Entering Iowa State University, Fall, 1955*, Agricultural Economic Report No. 12, 1962, pp. 8, 21.

66. Margaret W. Rossiter, "The Men Move In: Home Economics, 1950–1970," in *Rethinking Home Economics*, ed. Stage and Vincenti, 99.

67. Iowa State College catalog, 1952–53, pp. 144, 232; "Enrollment Figures," RS

7/2/3, file 1/2, Special Collections Department, Parks Library, Iowa State University; Becky Jordan, Iowa State University archivist, personal correspondence with the author, September 14, 2012. In 1990, the Agriculture College's former Dairy and Food Industry Department merged with the former Home Economics College's Foods and Nutrition Program, forming a new Department of Food Science and Human Nutrition, jointly administered by the two colleges.

68. Rossiter, "The Men Move In," 109. For more, see Margaret W. Rossiter, *Women Scientists in America: Before Affirmative Action, 1940–1972* (Baltimore: Johns Hopkins University Press, 1995).

69. Rima D. Apple, "Liberal Arts of Vocational Training? Home Economics Education for Girls," in *Rethinking Home Economics*, ed. Stage and Vincenti.

70. Arnold Baragar, "Opportunities for Men in Home Economics," *Journal of Home Economics* 52, no. 10 (1960): 833.

71. Ibid.

72. Loyal E. Horton, "Our Readers Say: Men in Home Economics," *Journal of Home Economics* 53, no. 3 (1961): 159.

73. "Male Students Choose Home Economics Major," *Journal of Home Economics* 57, no. 3 (1965): 166, 242.

74. Apple and Coleman, "Domestic Science to Human Ecology."

75. Carol Werhan, "Why Men Enter the Gendered Profession of Family and Consumer Sciences Education: An Exploratory Case Study" (PhD diss., University of Akron, 2008), 46–47, 49–50, 64.

76. Luther G. Baker Jr., "The Enigma of Men in Home Economics," *Journal of Home Economics* 61, no. 5 (May 1969): 371–73.

77. Ruth E. Dohner, C. Michael Loyd, and Laurie Stenberg, "Men: The Other Professionals in Home Economics Education," *Journal of Home Economics* 82, no 4 (Winter 1990): 32–36.

78. "From Consumer Affairs to Arms Control Policy," *New York Times*, June 27, 1985.

79. Ben Lupton, "Explaining Men's Entry into Female-Concentrated Occupations: Issues of Masculinity and Social Class," *Gender, Work, and Organization* 13, no. 2 (2006): 103–28; Paul Sargent, "Between a Rock and a Hard Place: Men Caught in the Gender Bind of Early Childhood Education," *Journal of Men's Studies* 12, no. 3 (2004): 173–92; Paul Sargent, "The Gendering of Men in Early Childhood Education," *Sex Roles* 52 (2005): 251–59; Simon Cross and Barbara Bagihole, "Girls' Jobs for the Boys? Men, Masculinity and Non-Traditional Occupations," *Gender, Work, and Organization* 9, no. 2 (2002): 204–26; Christine L. Williams, ed., *Doing "Women's Work": Men in Nontraditional Occupations* (Newbury Park, CA: Sage, 1993).

80. Lisa M. Miller, "Where the Boys Are: Home Ec," *New York Times*, December 16, 1993.

81. "Strategic Plan," University of Georgia, Family and Consumer Sciences, n.d., ca. 2005, http://www.aplu.org/NetCommunity/Document.Doc?id=2285 (accessed December 28, 2012).

82. Diane Heldt, "Women Students Are 'Big Man' on Many College Campuses," *Cedar Rapids Gazette*, July 14, 2010.

83. "Weaving a Fashion Network," *Visions* (Ames: Iowa State University, 2010), http://visions.isualum.org/summer10/coverstory2.asp (accessed December 28, 2012).

84. Oklahoma State University, "OSU Student Profile," Fall 2011, 58, http://vpaf.okstate.edu/irim/StudentProfile/2011/PDF/2011StudentProfile.pdf (accessed December 28, 2012).

85. George Sabine to S. C. Hollister, November 22, 1944 and July 4, 1945, Hollister to Sabine, July 2, 1945, 16/2/2077, box 44, 71, Cornell University Archives.

86. Lee Fuhrman, "Tech Girls Carve Academic Niche: Doing Fine Job, Officials Find," *Atlanta Constitution*, November 26, 1953.

87. University of Illinois "Careers in Engineering" bulletin, June 1952, vol. 49, no. 71, and University of Illinois "Careers in Engineering" bulletin, April 1954, vol. 51, no. 57, both in 11/1/870, University of Illinois Archives.

88. Eric Walker, "Women Are NOT for Engineering," *Penn State Engineer*, May 1955, 9, 20.

89. Bix, "From 'Engineeresses' to 'Girl Engineers' to 'Good Engineers.'"

90. *Engineering Outlook at the University of Illinois* 1, no. 4 (July 1960): 4; "Newsletter—Dept. of General Engineering, University of Illinois," vol. 8, no. 1, October 1965, 11/7/809, University of Illinois archives; *Engineering Outlook at the University of Illinois* 7, no. 3 (March 1966): 4.

91. Brian L. Yoder, "Engineering by the Numbers," American Society for Engineering Education, 2012, 13, http://www.asee.org/papers-and-publications/publications/college-profiles/2011-profile-engineering-statistics.pdf (accessed October 14, 2012).

92. Virginia B. Vincenti, "Home Economics Moves into the Twenty-First Century," in *Rethinking Home Economics*, ed. Stage and Vincenti.

93. US Department of Education, National Center for Education Statistics, *The Condition of Education 2012* (Washington, DC: US Department of Education, 2012), 259. See also Stephanie Woodham Burge, "Academic Programs: Undergraduate, Graduate, and Professional," in *Gender and Higher Education*, ed. Barbara J. Bank (Baltimore: Johns Hopkins University Press, 2011).

2

What's in a Name?

Students and Alumni and the Meaning of Home Economics

Who is the university? Who "owns" the land-grant university? These questions are often contested. Land-grant universities encompass and serve many different missions. Groups within the land-grant constellation of interests often jostle for influence and power. They select specific issues that galvanize them, that enable them to act as if they were a single group, and use that authority to exert control over the university's direction.

Faculties, administrations, farmers, and industry have garnered the most attention from land-grant scholars, but other groups also claim ownership of facets of the university. This chapter examines two of these groups: alumni and students. Aside from their participation in antiwar demonstrations, both have gotten short shrift from historians. Kay chooses a relatively small event: attempts in the last half of the twentieth century to rename and rebrand home economics. Initially proposed by faculty and administrators who wanted to raise the status of home economics within the university—competing for external research funding was crucial—the name-change campaign ran afoul of both students and alumni. Each group had important reasons to become involved. Changing home economics' name was no insignificant matter. Identity—what the name had signified and was signifying and what the home economics division had become—was a critical point of contention.

***

"Home economics, now human ecology . . . has sustained me from 1939 to NOW. I have found that a woman with a degree in home economics is so resourceful that she can always find a job. It prepared a woman for life— jobs, home, self, community."[1] In her 1990 letter to Kansas State University president Jon Wefald, MarBeth Busch Carmony articulated why she valued her education at Kansas State, the land-grant university of Kansas. Mrs. Carmony saw her degree as a woman's degree. She understood that her tasks were different than those undertaken by her husband or other men and was proud of it. Her daily tasks as a woman required expertise and her college education had provided it.

Mrs. Carmony's epistle reaffirmed what college had provided her: a good women's education. Her sentiments also illustrated the larger point that universities do more than research. They teach students to become productive community members. Because each student is a transient presence on a college campus, involvement with university bureaucracies is often ephemeral. They seem to leave few lasting marks on their institutions. University committees that reserve a seat for a student representative frequently see such seats go unfilled.

But it would be a serious mistake for historians to dismiss all students and their interactions within the university setting as inconsequential. They sometimes make quite a splash. In the 1960s and 1970s, free speech movements, Vietnam protests, and crusades for gender and racial equality all were student driven and helped change the character of America. But putting this obvious example aside, students may be students for a short while, but they are alumni for the rest of their lives. The relationships and friendships nurtured as students often become lifelong touchstones. As significant, alumni gain in political, economic, intellectual, and other significance once they graduate. Their student tenure is one of the least powerful times of their lives. Yet it is that period in which attachments are formed. Alumni, then, are able to wield clout that their student selves rarely dreamed of. They possess real power to influence the course of their treasured university.

Alumni in this version may appear to be nothing more than former students. They retain connections to their alma mater and expect it to remain faithful to the ideals and sentiments they encountered while they were in residence. But times change and so do land-grant universities. Present-day students at an institution are quite different from its graduates. When alumni examine what their institutions have become, they often are aghast. Fundamental principles sometimes seem to have been discarded and a new agenda put in place. Alumni, then, are not former students per se but students locked in a time and place that might be vastly different from the present-day climate.

Questions of identity rest at the heart of the matter. Alumni expect their institutions to favor the programs that helped define them and their careers; they expect institutions to be familiar, even comforting. Sometimes something as simple as changing the name of a treasured department or college can cause great consternation. With appropriate homage to Shakespeare, a rose by another name does not necessarily smell as sweet. That is because a name is not simply a name. It is much more. It is a new direction, a new emphasis, a new program. In the course of these changes, things are left behind as others become integrated into the college corpus. The result is often a reshaping that sometimes leaves alumni alienated.

The 1960s were a time of fundamental reshuffling on college campuses. Land-grant universities aspired to become comprehensive institutions, serving a far broader swath of American society than they had earlier. These chaotic times were also marked by student activism, and while much of that activism concentrated on American international and social policies, it also extended to university functions. Students saw a correlation between what went on in virtually every university sphere and what was happening in the world. Chanting mantras such as "never trust anyone over thirty," students felt empowered to construct a world more to their liking, one that seemed to them to be saner, more rational, and more democratic.

This fervent reassessment of established practice also had a gendered component. For nearly a century, home economics had been considered a woman's domain within land-grant universities. The activism of the 1960s, however, took direct aim at the doctrine of separate spheres. Departments and colleges of home economics, integral parts of land-grant institutions,[2] served as a major focus of the more general debate over the place of women in American society.

This concern and hand-wringing were new. Up to this point, students rarely became intertwined in the development of programmatic missions, curricula, or research agendas. Alumni also had rarely been visibly involved in such decisions. To be sure, as college benefactors alumni had clout, but usually they worked behind the scenes. Then again, only the most generous were able to sway land-grants in a particular direction.

The battles in the 1960s and after over home economics energized a substantial portion of the alumni and student populations. But almost universally during the early period of these conflicts faculty and administrators settled disputes. When name changes were the issue, students and alumni rarely found themselves on the same side. As a rule, students wanted a name change from home economics to something else, while alumni chose the status quo. Even in the few instances where students and alumni favored a similar course of action, that commonality of interests usually failed to create a joint agenda. Vocal alumni almost always cast themselves as the sole beacons of tradition and heritage; they almost always disregarded students' opinions. Alumni also positioned themselves in direct opposition to university faculty, almost all of whom wanted the college to be seen as more contemporary and relevant than the name "home economics" might suggest.

Traditionalist alumni certainly had history on their side. Home economics (initially called "domestic science") had long been an integral part of land-grant universities. The first course in the discipline was offered at Iowa State (1871), with the oldest continually operating program at Kansas State (1873).[3] Ellen Swallow Richards, who was an instructor at MIT, is regarded as the founder of home economics.[4] With help from Melvil Dewey, the New York State librarian, Richards and similarly interested colleagues gathered at Lake Placid, beginning in 1899, to discuss this nascent field.[5] Over a decade's worth of conferences, standard secondary school and college curricula were established, a name agreed upon, and a professional organization created. By 1908, when the conference ended and the Home Economics Association was launched, conference members and attendees represented most of country's land-grant institutions.

Few people challenged the presence of women at land-grant institutions, tucked away in the school of home economics. On some campuses, only women were admitted to the home economics programs.[6] Graduates had many career choices, including teaching, dietetics, institutional management, interior design, journalism, or running a private household.[7] Federal, state, and local governments also hired home economics graduates. Many Children's Labor Bureau staff had training in child development.[8] During World War I, Herbert Hoover relied on the Office of Home Economics to create menus for "meatless Monday" and "wheat-less Wednesday." During the Great Depression, extension service specialists taught budgeting, clever cookery, and basic cooking and sewing skills long forgotten in the era of convenience. During World War II, home economists helped American with rationing, limited food and clothing options, budgeting, and child care and to do more with less.[9]

The postwar science and technology boom changed the face of American higher education. Institutions increasingly emphasized research and outside funding for that research.[10] The postwar influx of students courtesy of the GI Bill had repercussions including a lack of housing, particularly for married students, and fewer seats for women and minorities. Women often dropped out of college upon marriage. But not all women dropped out, not all women married, and many of these women attended college with a single purpose in mind: to get a degree that would get them a job.[11] For these women, home economics offered a practical education, one that could be used both inside and outside the home, for private and public consumption.

Home economics units in colleges and universities, like agriculture, had long been the beneficiary of federal legislation. This legislation simultaneously provided revenue and shaped public perceptions. Some large grants went to create home economics extension (Smith-Lever Act) and had to be matched by state funds. Another significant revenue stream was for vocational education (Smith-Hughes Act).[12] The former provided for extension service agents, the latter for occupation-directed education, including teacher training. In secondary schools, many home economics teachers taught basic cooking and sewing skills as part of the holistic view of home economics and "right living."

Home economics at the college level suffered from a stereotype problem. Just as metal or wood shop was offered as vocational education for junior and senior high school boys, so home economics—cooking or sewing—was created as vocational education for junior and senior high school girls. This gave rise to, or reinforced, the popular perception that home economics was "just stitchin' and stirrin'."[13] Home economics seemed merely technique, not scientific. While home economics students in college may have had some classes on sewing or cooking basics, they also took classes on textile history, properties of fabric, kitchen chemistry, and other topics. The home economics core curriculum typically included mathematics, physics, biology, chemistry and organic chemistry, genetics, microbiology, economics, sociology, psychology, and art history.

That was the state of the home economics art at the onset of the 1960s. A name change would enable the discipline to seem more relevant to contemporary society and its problems. It would emphasize research—scholarly inquiry—and capture the interest of serious-minded college students. Home economics programs would thus be positioned for the present and the future.[14] Often a new academic leader or monumental programmatic anniversary provided the opportunity for change. A select committee would examine the department or college on all levels. Admissions, recruiting, job success, curriculum, research, resident instruction, and extension services all would undergo scrutiny. The issue of a name change was usually broached. Had home economics as a traditional construct and label outlived its utility? Would a name other than "home economics" be more compelling for students, prospective employers, and the general public? Would more research dollars, or male students and faculty, be attracted to a differently named field?[15] The select committee might survey students and examine names of similar programs at peer institutions. If the name was deemed inappropriate, faculty voted, selected a new name, and brought the matter to the board of regents.[16]

The key to all this was the desire of the faculty and ultimately the administration to shuck the worn-out name and concept of home economics and to replace it with something both more modern and indicative of what actually occurred at home economics colleges. To these institutions and their employees, members of the home economics disciplines were scientists, building new knowledge and creating a fundamentally better way of living. They were not simply teaching young women how to be good wives and mothers. They were setting out the scientific parameters for modern life and living. They were leading and creating as much as dispensing wisdom, and they demanded recognition of these new endeavors. A change from the old-fashioned home economics seemed essential.

Two early and very different examples of responses to a reexamination of home economics make this faculty- and administrator-driven pattern undeniably clear. Pennsylvania State University became the first school to engage in this intensely introspective process. In 1959 Grace Henderson, dean of the College of Home Economics, seized on Penn State's centennial and a presidential request for some long-range planning. The president explicitly asked Henderson to ponder how, and where, to best "place" the School of Home Economics for the next quarter and a half centuries. Henderson saw the need to make her school more research driven and more appealing to potential students, and, as she mentioned to a colleague in a letter, changing the name might also send the right signal to potential students and employers.[17]

Henderson's group proceeded, albeit slowly. By 1966, the Penn State program changed its core materials and the requirements for majors, and it underwent a complete assessment of its curriculum. It also changed the program's name from Home Economics to Human Development. During the entire rebranding process, only the faculty and administration participated.[18]

Neither alumni nor students were invited, or involved, although they were informed occasionally.

Students did not seem in any way disturbed by Penn State's action. The contrast could not have been more stark when compared to the student anti-Vietnam protests of spring 1970, which included looting, protests, a sit-in, calls for dialogue with university administration, and a bomb threat.[19] Faculty committees studied the matter. One recommended a public affairs series on current events, organized by the president, with "suitable faculty and student participation"; a one-week, non-credit period for full discussion on these topics; college-level lectures and discussion facilitated by deans; and a comprehensive list of all special topics courses, compiled by the provost's office.[20] The students' actions, and the administration's response, cost President Eric Walker his position.[21]

Cornell handled the matter of the name change very differently than had Penn State. The retirement of Cornell's dean of the College of Home Economics precipitated the college's self-examination.[22] What started as a dean's contemplation of the future of her college in 1961 shifted when Cornell's president requested a self-study of the college as a whole in 1964.[23] The categories under discussion were the focus of the college; the role of public service; the problem of organization; and the name itself.[24] The challenge from president James Perkins was to envision the role of home economics in Ithaca, in New York State, and in a global setting, in the present and the future. In 1965, the President's Committee to Study the College of Home Economics presented its findings to the college.

International experts in the new components of home economics served as outside evaluators in the process. The team included Francena Nolan Miller, chair of the committee, home economics, University of Connecticut; P. J. Flory, chemist, Stanford University; Alfred Harper, biochemistry and nutrition, University of Wisconsin-Madison; Helen Lamale, Bureau of Labor Statistics; and Francis Palmer, child studies, New York University.[25] This blue-ribbon committee focused on the future and its findings reflected that intentional bias. It urged the college to be bold and take advantage of the unique resources—faculty expertise, money, grant opportunities—that the college had to offer:[26] "Cornell has an exciting opportunity to make an important departure from the departmental lines of traditional American education. The Administration, faculty and students are receptive to significant change which would align the college with the problems of today's society and the standards of the University proper . . . because of Cornell's reputation, change will be watched by the academic community throughout the nation and prove an opportunity for impact beyond your campus."[27] In effect, committee members simply called on Cornell to institutionalize their specialties within the school.

The committee issued its final report in December 1966. Subcommittee reports on focus and name, admissions and recruiting, counseling and advising, residential teaching policy, public service, and field stations were all incorporated into the document. That was not the end of the involvement of these outside experts. In July 1967, subcommittees began to address each concern. The subcommittee working on the name generated at least as much attention as those covering other topics, including whether the college should move from a departmental structure to one based around social issues, such as poverty or hunger. Each subcommittee submitted updates to, and provided reports at, faculty meetings.[28] Finally in late 1967, the faculty voted to change the name of the college from home economics to human development and the environment.[29] The Cornell administration rejected that new name as unwieldy. In 1968, the faculty again voted a name change, this time choosing human ecology. Cornell's president and the state's board of trustees agreed and in 1969 Cornell's Home Economics became Human Ecology.[30]

Neither students nor alumni participated in any public way in the Cornell matter. This was especially interesting since it came on the heels of major disruptions on many college campuses. The model for student activism was already in place, but Cornell's students failed to use it in an effort to influence the reshaping of their home economics college.

Perhaps the apparent inaction stemmed from an agreement with the principles and process. Perhaps students did not recognize their abiding interest in the matter. Or perhaps students were more concerned with ending the Vietnam War. Students were not marginalized but were certainly ignored in this entire process; they were never asked to serve on a committee or to participate in any meaningful discussion. No matter what the case, students willfully remained absent from the discussion.

In the following decade or so, academic home economics changed little outwardly. The status of women showed no such constancy, however. The women's movement and Title IX legislation increased educational access and job opportunities for women. Formerly single-sex schools were now coeducational, and gender-segregated programs, such as home economics and engineering, drew increasingly from the opposite sex.[31] Home economics administrators welcomed the challenge to make their school relevant and appealing to women.

Saddled with popular stereotypes, administrators struggled to find ways to deconstruct "home economics" to appeal to the brightest students—those bound for medical or graduate school or for classrooms of their own. When name changes were proposed in the 1980s and beyond at several land-grant home economics colleges or departments, letters of support for the change from students, faculty members, and alumni often mentioned the stigma of studying something that could be considered solely women's work.[32] Students noted that their peers denigrated their classes, faculty worried their grant applications and professional publications were hindered, and alumni complained that working men and women did not appreciate the holistic view that home economics graduates brought to their occupational and personal lives. The public or popular perception did not reflect the true state of the field.

Home economics self-examinations were aimed at generating more credibility for these departments within the university itself. Faculty did research, developed community relationships, and prepared their students for a range of professional endeavors, but this was not widely recognized on some campuses.[33] Having "home economics" in a department's name was a disservice to students; it hampered graduates seeking jobs as well as the recruitment of new students.[34]

The mid-1980s were also a period of economic crisis, with an extended recession and major cutbacks in social services. In state legislatures eager to trim budgets, higher education was an easy target. The Iowa Board of Regents in 1986–87 decided that Iowa State must change the name of its College of Home Economics. Discussion was straightforward. One board member claimed that "a name change was a way of changing perception."[35] Seizing the moment, at the February 1987 meeting, another board member stated "that the board frequently gets approval for a name change, and she wanted to know when they were going to change the name of the College of Home Economics because she believe[d] the name is a disadvantage. She stated she has raised the question each of her six years on the board, but there has been no effort to do anything about it."[36] Perhaps sensing the writing on the wall, the College of Home Economics changed its name to Family and Consumer Science with very little fanfare or discussion.[37] The board of regents, the instigator, approved the name change in 1987. "The university went through a consensus process for identifying a new name for the college," the regents' minutes noted. "The result of the suggestions from faculty, and a preference poll concluded with the new name 'College of Family and Consumer Sciences.' It was hoped that this new name would enhance opportunities for greater fulfillment of the college's mission."[38]

The name change in the Iowa system was unprecedented. It occurred within a relatively short amount of time and moved forward smoothly. To be sure, when the board of regents "suggests" a change, it is in the best interests of everyone to comply; the name was likely to change with or without the will of the unit involved. Without regent impetus, change was usually slow in coming. Students and alumni often put a brake on the process. When things got really bogged down, it was often because alumni were involved; when things moved along, it was often despite student involvement.

The process at Florida State proved more typical. After working on program development and curricular change, clarifying the mission, and articulating long-range goals, in the fall of 1987 the Ad Hoc Name Change Committee asked whether the name of the school—the College of Home Economics—was appropriate, given the mission statement. Committee members included faculty, undergraduate and graduate students, and alumni, so past and current student opinion was deemed important. The committee's surveying was also inclusive. Questionnaires, different for each group, were sent to employers—including local utilities, school districts, dept stores—administrators, alumni, home economics teachers, extension home economists, students, and faculty. Alumni were asked whether a name change would be beneficial to the future growth of the school, and whether it would affect their involvement in the college. However, the survey noted that "only College faculty have both the right and the responsibility to make the decisions as to the new name." The students were largely asked about the impact of the name on their current status and future employment.[39]

Faculty voted in September 1988 to accept the report and its conclusion that the name was inappropriate. Another faculty committee was appointed to identify two alternative names and submit those names, with rationales, at a faculty meeting in February 1989.[40] The faculty chose the College of Human Science as the new name. The name went up the appropriate channels and was officially in place later that same year. Student sentiment was quite positive. "I'm so pleased with the name change for our college to Human Service," wrote a student to the dean. "I'm hoping it will be possible to have that printed on our diplomas this spring. I graduate April 29th with a BS in Child Development and Family Relationships—is it feasible to get the new college name on my diploma?"[41]

The situation at the University of Georgia started similarly, but things soon took a dramatic turn. First suggested by dean Emily Quinn Pou in 1985, the name change did not go into effect until 1990.[42] It was the culmination of Pou's fifteen-year effort to make the college central, relevant, and important. Over that period, Pou led a curricular expansion and strengthening campaign. Five new majors had been created and three doctoral programs added.[43] Very much thinking about process, the dean first broached the name change with faculty and then launched extensive surveys the following semester (spring 1986) among constituent groups: alumni, employers, extension agents and specialists, faculty, home economics teachers, staff, and students.[44] A rough tally suggests that thirty-three alumni respondents supported a change of name, sixteen were opposed, and ten were neutral. In a perceptive comment, one alumna wrote, "I personally have never objected to being identified with home economics but I understand the position of those who desire the change. Obviously, a lot of work may be needed to be done to gain support of older alumni."[45] Among current students, many saw advantages to a new college name and forty-nine could think of no disadvantages. Unconsciously echoing the alumna just mentioned, one student commented that "The name sounds out of date, old timey. We need a new modern, professional name for today's new look. 'Home Economics' sounds like an old lady."[46]

Plans proceeded apace, with alumni apprised of discussion both by the survey and via articles appearing in their UGA newsletter, *Highlights*. Despite those publicity efforts, few alumni responded to the surveys and articles. Many expressed surprise that serious change might be afoot in the fall of 1987.[47] Just as Dean Pou was submitting the request to change the name of the college to the new president, several formerly silent alumni sprang into action. This group, the "ad hoc alumni committee of six," asked to meet with the president, drafted a position paper, and sent out an emergency letter to all alumni informing them of the possible name change and asking one question: should the name be changed?[48] When the meeting with the dean and president and alumni yielded no decision, the committee of six informed its members of this latest development and offered instructions for writing local regents to dissuade them from voting to change the name of the college. The weight and volume of letters from the alumni, sent directly to regents and the chancellor of the Georgia system, were enough to convince the chancellor to defer the decision in January 1988 and ask for more careful consideration at the University of Georgia.[49]

Another round of discussion commenced. An advisory committee, the

College of Home Economics Name Change Consideration Committee, was created. It replicated the previous committee's work. It surveyed all relevant parties, examined names in use at other institutions of similar rank, especially in the South, held open meetings, and held faculty votes. As this long process was winding down in the fall of 1989, only two things differed from 1986. First, the new name of the College of Home Economics, the College of Family and Consumer Science, emerged as a more comfortable, more desired and/or less objectionable name than "College of Human Ecology."[50] Second, anticipating a repeated deluge of letters from alumni to the president, Dean Pou wrote to all students in the college and encouraged their own letter-writing campaign.[51] All sides—alumni, employers, faculty, students, and parents—wrote letters both in favor of and in opposition to a new name.

One well-informed parent wrote to President Charles Knapp, "For the third time, I strongly urge you to recommend the name change for the College of Home Economics. It is quite clear that politics have played a major role in delaying this decision. . . . What will it take for you to stop stalling and make a decision? I find it appalling that alumni have the power to dictate and interfere with the normal operations of the college."[52] In response to Pou's encouragement and the circulation of information, the students were remarkably well informed. "I think it is terrible that alumni have enough power to influence this decision," wrote one student. "Actions should be taken to do what is best for the students—*not* what is best for a retired group of old women."[53]

Students wrote about the fact that the name "home economics" did not elicit respect from their peers and future employers, and they mentioned being dogged by stereotypes that belied their hard work and the hours of science and social science courses that were invisible behind the name "home economics." Other students who could not suggest alternatives still wanted a new name. Students just declaring a major within the college or transferring from elsewhere also wanted a different name; the reputation of the college was attractive, but the name was not.

Alumni letters poured in again, this time with more complexity. The emergency appeal sent out to alumni included a form letter, and many of the letters to President Knapp were this letter verbatim.[54] Several women promised to revoke gifts, current and future, if the name change went through.[55] "How would you like your name changed after all these years," asked one writer. "What is a name? It's what people identify you by and what you go by. The most important title you hold."[56] As several writers also (correctly) pointed out, the American Home Economics Association (AHEA) had not changed *its* name, so why be different?[57] Discussion regarding a name change had begun within the AHEA on the floor of annual meetings in the early 1970s, but a decision to move forward did not crystallize until the mid-1980s, culminating in a multi-organizational meeting in Scottsdale in 1993. The majority decision, although a painfully achieved consensus for some, was to change the words "home economics" in the name to "family and consumer science."[58] By this point, all of the leading academic programs had long since changed their names to something other than "home economics."

Having gone through the process, twice, both Dean Pou and President Knapp were undeterred. In spite of the outpouring of letters, or perhaps bolstered by them—many alumni and most students supported the change—the request for a new name went to the regents and was approved. "Home economics" disappeared from the lexicon in University of Georgia System universities.[59]

During the nearly ten years it took Georgia to change the name of its home economics college, several other programs made the leap. Each system looking at change began the process by comparing itself to its peers. The University of Alabama, Florida State University, Texas Tech, and the University of Tennessee all changed the name of their home economics colleges in this period. Then, in the fall of 1990, one of the oldest home economics programs in the country, one that had changed its name with much fanfare but little flap, was suddenly under siege.

In 1985, Dean Barbara Stowe laid out a rationale, and plan, for changing the name of Kansas State's school of home economics.[60] Within six months,[61] the new name—College of Human Ecology—was in place, approved by all necessary parties. The college continued to examine its mission and celebrated its 125th anniversary in 1988. Beginning in fall 1989, the college, along with others on campus, engaged in strategic planning for "Vision 2020," a university-wide initiative. Final reports were delivered in June and July 1990, at the end of the 1989–90 academic year.[62] Early in the fall 1990 semester, plans were clearly afoot for reorganization across the university, driven in large part by economic considerations.[63] Plans were vague, but faculty voted on them.[64] Students were aware of these plans and occasionally their exclusion from them.[65]

Things changed dramatically in October 1990 President Jon Wefald announced that in an effort to save money and avoid needless duplication or competition with the University of Kansas or Fort Hays State University, the Colleges of Architecture and Human Ecology would merge with other colleges within the university. To say that this came out of nowhere would, perhaps, be an understatement. Everyone was blindsided by this announcement. As one alumna and heavy donor wrote to the president, "Needless to say, your initial action in eliminating the College of Human Ecology was a real surprise."[66] Students and alumni, with some help from faculty and staff, quickly entered the fray.[67]

The president of the alumni association, Carolyn Robey, printed out and mailed off—aided by students—a letter to all alumni, informing them of this turn of events, soliciting their help. Letters quickly came back, mailed to President Wefald (with copies often sent to Robey). MarBeth Carmony wrote the president that "I had read the letter of October 27, 1990 from the College of Human Ecology and if I had not had a serious fall on the ice I would have written you a letter that would have sizzled your fingers. Since I couldn't write, I'm grateful you had a productive learning experience and wrote to the alumni of the College."[68] Students and alumni across the state wrote letters to editors even as the story appeared elsewhere in the newspaper.[69] Students, faculty, and alumni even marched together to protest this unexpected turn of events. In terms of crisis management, all went smoothly for the college as it mobilized all available parties. Students worked late into the night stuffing envelopes and making banners and placards. The march and rally were dramatic, aided, no doubt, by the architecture students lying as if in graves with T-squares at their heads. But it was the human ecology students and alumni who were visible, loud, and prepared with talking points. The immediate public backlash, the avalanche of letters from alumni and concerned supporters, and the (negative) publicity engendered by the rally *may* have been factors in President Wefald's decision to cancel the changes to the colleges.

"You do make a difference!" Wefald and Dean Stowe wrote in a joint letter to alumni. "Your letters, calls, and visits to our offices expressing your views on the KSU Reorganization Plan which proposed significant reduction in the College of Human Ecology were many and clearly stated. As you know, the draft prepared for the reorganization at KSU was taken off the table." Wefald had come to realize that the faculty and the students were committed. The college "has an incredible support base throughout the state," he added.[70] The program at Kansas State was secure, reinforced by the value placed on it by students past (the alumni), current, and future. Unlike the student involvement at the University of Georgia in the name-changing process for its college of home economics, the student action at Kansas State was unplanned and unsolicited, although very much welcome. That everyone seemed to rally together made a difference. Students placed an advertisement in the campus newspaper, the *Kansas State Collegian*, noting their happiness. The faculty expressed its gratitude to the students in the newspapers, too.[71]

The almost-change in Kansas was defeated by a mixture of organized (alumni) and spontaneous (student) action. Together these entities, along with faculty and staff across the university, helped alter the decision. These lessons—about how and when to initiate change—were well heeded. The AHEA, in its final push to change its name, adhered to the tenet of "process" (and inclusion). When Iowa State decided to change its college's name again in 2004, it was deliberative, transparent, and all-inclusive. Meetings were held specifically for students, others specifically for alumni. Multiple meetings and opportunities were provided to ensure a wide net was cast. Consensus emerged, as the facilitators hoped it would, and the new name was adopted largely without controversy or complaint.[72]

What are the lessons to be learned? As soon as students graduate from institutions, their memories, attitudes, and attachments may change and become far more solidified than imagined. That so many alumni, at multiple institutions, so clearly worked to preserve *their* programs, at *their* institutions, speaks to the power of memory. Change in the here and now often runs afoul of what had been or had seemed to be.

Notes

1. MarBeth Busch Carmony to President Wefald, November 27, 1990, RG 02/01, President's office, box 6, folder 31, Richard L. D. and Marjorie J. Morse Department of Special Collections, Kansas State University Libraries.

2. From "domestic science" to "home economics," the name changes for such university departments that began in the 1960s yielded a plethora of names, including human ecology, human development, family and consumer sciences, human resources, and more. In 1993, the American Home Economics Association changed its name to the American Association of Family and Consumer Sciences (AAFCS). For simplicity's sake, I will use the term "home economics" for pre-1965 and "human ecology" for post-1965.

The schools under discussion are a legacy of the 1862 Morrill Land Grant Act.

Similar activism may have occurred on 1890 land-grant campuses, but a lack of archival sources has led to a focus on the 1862 rather than the 1890 campuses. On the latter, see Mary Wyatt, "A Comparison of Preservice Home Economics Education Programs in Predominantly Black and White Southern Institutions of Higher Education" (PhD diss., Florida State University, 1980); and Penny Ralston, "Black Participation in Home Economics," *Journal of Home Economics* (hereafter *JHE*) 70, no. 5 (1978): 34–37.

3. See Ercel S. Eppright and Elizabeth Storm Ferguson, *A Century of Home Economics at Iowa State: A Proud Past, a Lively Present, a Future Promise* (Ames: Iowa State Home Economics Alumni Association, 1971); Ruth Hoeflin, *History of a College: From Woman's Course to Home Economics to Human Ecology* (Manhattan, KS: Ag Press, 1988); and "History of the College," http://www.he.k-state.edu/about/what-is-human-ecology/history.php (accessed June 10, 2013). For the history of home economics, see Sarah Leavitt, *From Catherine Beecher to Martha Stewart: A Cultural History of Domestic Advice* (Chapel Hill: University of North Carolina Press, 2002), 44–51; Nancy Tomes, *The Gospel of Germs: Men, Women, and the Microbe in American Life* (Cambridge, MA: Harvard University Press, 1998), chapter 6; and Glenna Matthews, *Just a Housewife: The Rise and Fall of Domesticity in America* (New York: Oxford University Press, 1987), chapter 6.

4. Caroline Hunt, *The Life of Ellen H. Richards* (Boston: Whitcomb & Barrows, 1912); Robert Clarke, *Ellen Richards: The Woman Who Founded Ecology* (Chicago: Follett Publishing, 1973); Margaret Rossiter, *Women Scientists in America: Struggles and Strategies to 1940* (Baltimore: Johns Hopkins University Press, 1982), 30–31, 68–70; Sarah Stage, "Ellen Richards and the Social Significance of the Home Economics Movement," in *Rethinking Home Economics: Women and the History of Profession*, ed. Sarah Stage and Virginia Vincenti (Ithaca, NY: Cornell University Press, 1997), 17–33.

5. See Emma Weigley, "It Might Have Been Euthenics: The Lake Placid Conferences and the Home Economics Movement," *American Quarterly* 26, no. 1 (January 1974): 79–96; Judy Annette Jax, "A Comparative Analysis of the Meaning of Home Economics: The 1899–1908 Lake Placid Conferences and 'Home Economics: A Definition'" (PhD diss., University of Minnesota, 1981); Megan J. Elias, *Stir It Up: Home Economics in American Culture* (Philadelphia: University of Pennsylvania Press, 2008); and Carolyn Goldstein, *Creating Consumers: Home Economics in Twentieth-Century America* (Chapel Hill: University of North Carolina Press, 2012).

6. Linda Fritschner, "The Rise and Fall of Home Economics: A Study with Implications for Women, Education, and Change" (PhD diss., University of California-Davis, 1973).

7. Particularly in the Midwest, this education was incorporated into notions of modernity. Marilyn Irvin Holt, *Linoleum, Better Babies, and the Modern Farm Woman, 1890–1930* (Albuquerque: University of New Mexico Press, 1995); Lynn Curry, *Modern Mothers in the Heartland: Gender, Health and Progressives in Illinois, 1900–1930* (Columbus: Ohio State University Press, 1999).

8. Molly Ladd-Taylor, *Raising a Baby the Government Way: Mothers' Letters to the*

Children's Bureau, 1915–1932 (New Brunswick, NJ: Rutgers University Press, 1986); Kriste Lindenmeyer, *A Right to Childhood: The U.S. Children's Bureau and Child Welfare, 1912–1946* (Urbana: University of Illinois Press, 1997).

9. See Goldstein, *Creating Consumers*; and Paul Betters, *The Bureau of Home Economics: Its History, Activities and Organization* (Washington, DC: Brookings Institution, 1930).

10. Clark Kerr, *The Great Transformation in Higher Education, 1960–1980* (Albany: State University of New York Press, 1991); Hugh Davis Graham and Nancy Diamond, *The Rise of American Research Universities: Elites and Challenges in the Postwar Era* (Baltimore: Johns Hopkins University Press, 1997).

11. Susan Hartmann, *The Home Front and Beyond: American Women in the 1940s* (Boston: Twayne, 1983); Eugenia Kaledin, *Mothers and More: Women in the 1950s* (Boston: Twayne, 1985); Ruth Rosen, *The World Split Open: How the Modern Women's Movement Changed America* (New York: Penguin, 2000), chapter 1; author interview with Barbara Goldstein, Cornell '57, June 9, 2011.

12. Federal funding from these two pieces of legislation continues to provide revenue. Great Society legislation also provided further research dollars. The emphasis on research funding streams in the postwar era shifted the conversation from community service and relationships to bench science, something not previously a part of everyone's consciousness.

13. See Elias, *Stir It Up*, especially chapter 3; Margaret Rossiter, *Women Scientists in America: Before Affirmative Action, 1940–1972* (Baltimore: Johns Hopkins University Press, 1995), especially chapter 8; Hazel Taylor Spitze, "Yes, our nation is at risk but . . . " *JHE* 74, no. 2 (1984): 50–52; author interview with Julia Faultinson Anderson and Frances Smith, former associate dean and faculty members, Iowa State College of Home Economics, respectively, August 2008.

14. Jessie Harris, "Panorama of Home Economics and a Re-affirmation of Our Philosophy and Objectives in the Land Grant Colleges" (paper presented to Home Economics Division at the Association of Land Grant Colleges and Universities annual meeting, November 8, 1959, box 16, College of Home Economics Records, Pennsylvania State University [hereafter cited as PSU CHE]). See also M. Virginia Richards, "The Postmodern Perspective on Home Economics History," *Journal of Family and Consumer Science* 92, no. 1 (2000): 81–84.

15. Rhonda Trainor, "Home Economics: Where (Some of) the Boys Are," *Florida Vocational Journal* (April 1980): 22–25; Lawrence Royston, "Men and Home Economics, in the United States, 1900–1975," *JHE* 85, no. 1 (1993): 22–25; Gwen Kay, "Men in Home Economics? Taking a Discipline More Seriously" (paper presented at Agricultural History Society annual meeting, June 16, 2011).

16. Patricia Durey Murphy, "What's in a Name?" *JHE* 59, no. 5 (1967): 702–7; Barbara Stowe, Kansas State University, "Name Change to Human Ecology: A Logical Process at KSU" and Nancy Belck and Julia Miller, "Panel Discussion: Name Changes in Home Economics Units" (both papers presented at a joint meeting of the Association of Administrators of Home Economics and the National Council of Administrators of

Home Economics, February 1986, box 2, College of Home Economics Records, Oregon State University [hereafter OSU]); Helen McHugh, Margaret Hazeleus, and Rex Culp, "The Review Process for a College Name: A Case Study of Colorado State University," n.d., box 2, OSU.

17. Grace Henderson to Ralph Tyler, December 2, 1959, box 51, PSU CHE.

18. The Penn State Board of Trustees redesignated the School of Home Economics the School of Human Development in 1966. The name change was in place in 1967. In another common trope, the first dean of the newly named school was a man.

19. "Chronology of Events on University Park Campus," box 13, College of Human Development, Pennsylvania State University (hereafter PSU CHD).

20. There was a joint Inter-College Council Board–Council of Academic Deans Committee on Campus Disruptions, aka the "Tension Committee"; their first meeting was May 1, 1970, near the end of the semester as the students were about to depart for home. "Report of the Senate Committee on Resident Instruction, Recommendations for Facilitation of Student Consideration of Public Issues," box 13, PSU CHD.

21. Tom Bates, *RADS: The 1970 Bombing of the Army Math Research Center at the University of Wisconsin and Its Aftermath* (New York: Harper Collins, 1992).

22. Flora Rose and Esther Stocks, *A Growing College: Home Economics at Cornell University* (Ithaca, NY: Cornell University Press, 1969); Lynn Benson, "Gender and the Marginalization of Women at Cornell University: A History of Home Economics/ Human Ecology" (Master's thesis, Cornell University, 1999); Gwen Kay, "A Growing College, Redux: When Home Economics Became Human Ecology," 2008 CHE Fellow Talk in the History of Home Economics, March 2008 in possession of the author.

23. The president asked the College of Agriculture to conduct a similar study. Cornell, a private university, housed four statutory colleges of the State of New York: Agriculture, Home Economics, Industrial Labor Relations, and Veterinary Medicine.

24. "Selective Transcript from Meeting, December 15, 1965," box 78, New York State College of Home Economics, Cornell University (hereafter NYSCHE).

25. Letters to evaluation team, 1966, box 78, NYSCHE.

26. Urie Bronfenbrenner, for example, a distinguished member of Cornell's Department of Child Development and Family Relationships, is widely hailed as the "father of Head Start." His expertise, reputation, access to people, and monies were but one example of the unparalleled opportunities that Cornell could create if it chose to tackle social problems beyond the confines of a small town in upstate New York.

27. Francis Palmer, "Interim Report to the President's Committee to Study the College of Home Economics," box 78, NYSCHE.

28. The committee on admissions and recruiting reported out at the March 17 faculty meeting; college focus and name reported on March 28; counseling and advising on March 31; field stations on April 11; residential teaching policy and public service on May 3, 1967. Box 78, NYSCHE.

29. Ad hoc committee on focus and name to Faculty re: summary of ballots, runoff ballot, May 4, 1967, box 78, NYSCHE.

30. David Knapp to Lois Stilwell, January 29, 1969, box 79, NYSCHE; Benson,

"Gender and the Marginalization of Women at Cornell University," 98–105. Follow-ing the adoption of the new name, a reorganization plan went into effect, reflecting standing committees, department councils, administrative organization, and depart-ment-level organization.

31. Previously, at many land-grant campuses, men could not enroll in the home economics unit. Men had to be enrolled in another school on campus to be able to take home economics classes. For more on education and the women's movement, see Ann Mari May, ed., *The "Woman Question" and Higher Education* (Northampton, MA: Edward Elgar Publishing, 2009); Gail Collins, *When Everything Changed: The Amazing Journey of American Women from 1960 to the Present* (New York: Little, Brown, 2009); and Rosen, *The World Split Open*, 265–67.

32. To date, I have examined institutions in Florida (Florida State), Georgia (Uni-versity of Georgia, Fort Valley State), Iowa (Iowa State, Northern Iowa State, University of Iowa), Kansas (Kansas State), New York (Cornell), Oregon (Oregon State), Pennsyl-vania (Penn State), and Texas (Texas Tech, Texas Women's University). The papers of the AAFCS offer some reflection but mostly from an administrator/organization perspective.

33. Students with degrees in human ecology, depending on their major, might get jobs in dietetics or nutrition, as teachers, as journalists, as consumer affairs personnel, as interior designers, as merchandisers, as child care specialists, as family therapists, as clothing designers, as institutional managers, and more.

34. As Margaret Sitton, dean of the College of Home Economics, commented in notes for a presentation to all college deans at Florida State, one graduate student was working in child development but his degree would be in home economics, and a recent graduate working at the Pentagon as head of family services for the army also had a doctorate in home economics. Similarly ranked institutions—Purdue, Auburn, the University of Alabama, the University of Tennessee—competing for graduate stu-dents did better, in part because they had changed their names already. Notes, April 13, 1989, box 12, folder 7, Home Economics Name Study (1989), College of Human Science Records, Special Collections, Florida State University Libraries, Tallahassee (hereafter FSU).

35. Iowa State University Academic Planning, September 17 and October 15, 1986, RS 01 State Board of Regents Minutes, Iowa State Board of Regents, 1986/87, Univer-sity Archives, Iowa State University (hereafter IA BoR).

36. Minutes, February 18–19, 1987, IA BoR.

37. This change was reflected as well in merger discussions between the depart-ments of Home Economics Education and Home Economics Studies. The downsizing was necessitated by reallocations of funds, but the merger did not happen. However, the names of the departments needed to change as the name of the school was chang-ing. Minutes, 1986–87 (September 15, October 13, March 2, April 13, May 4), RS 12/7/3, Dep't of Family and Consumer Science Education, box 2: 1982–90, folder 4: 1985–1986, University Archives, Iowa State University.

38. Minutes, April 22–23, 1987, IA BoR.

39. The questionnaires and the data can be found in box 12, folder 7, FSU.

40. Sixty-two percent thought a name change would be beneficial, while 17 percent disagreed. On the other hand, only 13 percent thought a new name would impact their involvement. This last was an important point, as alumni at other institutions frequently employed the threat of withheld contributions as a measure of their displeasure. "Alumni questionnaires" (blank and with data), box 12, folder 7, FSU.

41. Margaret Sitton, "FSU College of Home Economics Factors to Consider in the Identification of a New Name," October 1988, box 12, folder 7, FSU. Students also responded to the statement "I believe that the name of the College of Home Economics should be changed." Among undergraduates, 15 percent were unsure, 77 percent agreed with the proposition, and 6 percent disagreed. Among graduate students, 10 percent were unsure, 77 percent agreed, and 13 percent disagreed. Margaret [Sitton, dean,] to Gus Turnbull, [provost], February 15, 1989, box 12, folder 7, FSU; Jean Fortianos to Dean Sitton, February 20, 1989, box 12, folder 7, FSU.

42. For placement of Georgia's shifts within the larger changes surrounding home economics, see Martha Virginia Richards, "The Evolution of a Profession: From Home Economics to Family and Consumer Science" (D.Ed. diss., University of South Carolina, 1998), especially chapter 5, "Name Change: A Case Study at the University of Georgia."

43. The breadth and depth of Pou's enhancements to the College of Home Economics were contained in an executive summary accompanying the proposal to the chancellor and board of regents to rename the college, May 22, 1990, RG 2–17, Family & Consumer Sciences, UGA 06174:17, College of Family and Consumer Science Papers (1916–2006), box 17, folder 10, Hargrett Rare Book & University Archives, University of Georgia (hereafter UGA FCS).

44. The original survey plus results can be found in box 17, folders 2–9, UGA FCS.

45. Box 17, folder 2, UGA FCS. This respondent was anonymous, as were all others. Nowhere on the form did it ask for alumni to mention their class, by year or decade, so it is difficult to determine if there were generational differences.

46. Five others wrote similar sentiments, more diplomatic than the anonymous student who wrote that "home economics is a weeny word," which encapsulated twenty-three other comments. Box 17, folder 9, UGA FCS.

47. "Name Consideration Report," *Highlights* 9, no. 1 (Fall 1987): 4; box 17, folder 13, UGA FCS.

48. This is detailed in the information packet sent to each regent. Box 17, folder 1, UGA FCS; the meeting is recounted in Charles Knapp to Chancellor H. Dean Propst, October 19, 1987, box 17, folder 10, UGA FCS. The members of the committee were Doe Harden, a retired home economist, past president of the UGA College of Home Economics Alumni Association (CHEAA); Nancy Hyte, a home economist in private business, past district director of the CHEAA; Marian McCullers, vice president of Atlanta Gas & Light, distinguished alumna of the CHEAA; Kathy Palmer, attorney,

past district director of the CHEAA; Norma Spivey, Georgia Department of Education, past president of the Georgia Home Economics Association; and Lynda Talmadge, home economist, past president of the CHEAA.

49. H. Dean Propst, Chancellor, to President Charles Knapp, January 5, 1988, box 17, folder 10, UGA FCS.

50. The loss of "home" in the name was central to many respondents of older generations. Using "family" instead of "human" seemed to assuage this fear of loss of identity and sense of self.

51. Emily Quinn Pou to 910 currently enrolled students in the College of Home Economics, April 4, 1990, box 17, folder 10, UGA FCS. Also, Coordinating Committee Opposed to a Name Change to UGA Home Economics Alumni, December 1989, box 17, folder 11, UGA FCS.

52. Debbie Phillips to President Knapp, April 19, 1990, box 17, folder 10, UGA FCS.

53. Peggy Grace to President Knapp, n.d. (ca. April 1990), box 17, folder 10, UGA FCS.

54. Coordinating Committee on the Name Change to UGA Home Economics Alumni re: pending name change of the College of Home Economics, n.d. (ca. December 1989), box 17, folder 11, UGA FCS.

55. Mary Louise Price Elkin expressed a disinterest in adding additional monies to scholarships she endowed. Martha Nell Allman similarly noted that she would change her will, ensuring that monies formerly earmarked for the College of Home Economics instead went to the College of Education. Mary Louise Elkin to President Knapp, n.d. (ca. April 1990), and Martha Nell Allman to President Knapp, April 19, 1990, both in box 17, folder 21, UGA FCS.

56. Mrs. Jean D. Robinson to Dr. Knapp, May 1, 1990, box 17, folder 11, UGA FCS.

57. Those who noted this included Helen B. Sasser, Dale Marie Narasou, Judy McCleskey (all alumni, in letters to Dr. Knapp), and Marilyn Horn (faculty, University of Nevada, Reno, to Regent Thomas H. Frier Sr.), box 17, folder 11, UGA FCS.

58. On the name change, see Gwen Kay, "Scottsdale: The Beginning of the End, or the End of the Beginning? Changing Names, Keeping Identity," at Home Economics: Classroom, Corporate and Cultural Interpretations Revisited, University of Georgia, February 27, 2012, and Goldstein, *Creating Consumers*, chapter 8.

59. Georgia College, in Milledgeville, had previously changed the name of its home economics college. The non-impact of this—no higher enrollments, no quick increase in research monies—was cited by Georgia alumni.

60. Barbara Stowe, "Household Economy to Human Ecology: A Case for Name Change" (an address to faculty), March 8, 1985, Human Ecology, box 14, folder 10, Richard L. D. and Marjorie J. Morse Department of Special Collections, Kansas State University Libraries (hereafter HE KSU).

61. "Why the College of Home Economics Changed Its Name" (media statement), October 21, 1985, box 14, folder 10, HE KSU.

62. Kansas State University College of Human Ecology updated strategic plans, May

1990; Jim Koelliker to Faculty Senate Committee on University Planning (FSCOUP), June 25, 1990, box 14, folder 14, HE KSU.

63. "Reorganization Set for 1990–91" and "Anxiety Created," letter to the editor, *Kansas State Collegian*, September 7, 1990, file 1, Vertical File, Kansas State University Reorganization, 1990–91, Richard L. D. and Marjorie J. Morse Department of Special Collections, Kansas State University Libraries (hereafter VF KSU).

64. "Teachers to Vote on Reorganization Plan," *Kansas State Collegian*, September 11, 1990, file 1, VF KSU.

65. "Reorganization Should Include Student Voice," *Kansas State Collegian*, August 27, 1990, file 1, VF KSU.

66. The letter ended, "It is that time of the year when Bryan and I make our contributions as President's Club members [minimum lifetime giving of $25,000]. Hopefully the past shifting of the Human Ecology program is behind us and we can continue to make contributions to the colleges from which we received our degrees, Agriculture and Home Economics." Marjorie Hamon Warta to President Wefald, December 28, 1990, box 6, file 31, HE KSU.

67. Photographs from personal papers of Virginia Moxley, dean, College of Human Ecology, and a scrapbook compiled by Carolyn Robey, past president of the alumni association. I am grateful to Dean Moxley for sharing these documents and photographs.

68. MarBeth Busch Carmony to President Wefald, November 27, 1990, box 6, folder 31, HE KSU.

69. Letters and articles appeared in the *Manhattan Mercury* ("More than Ever, a Need to Talk," November 1, 1990), the *Topeka Capital-Journal* ("Plan Targets College of Human Ecology," October 30, 1990), and elsewhere, file 1, VF, KSU

70. Jon Wefald and Barbara Stowe to Dear Alumnus, November 9, 1990, box 1, folder 3, HE KSU.

71. *Kansas State Collegian*, file 1, VF KSU.

72. The entire process is documented in binders prepared by the dean's office staff. RS 8/6/177, Iowa State University; University Councils and Committees; Planning Committee for the Combination of the Colleges of Education and Family and Consumer Sciences, box 1 in entirety, University Archives, Iowa State University.

3

The 1890 Land-Grant Colleges

From the New Deal to the Black Farmers' Class-Action Lawsuit, 1930s–2010s

Valerie Grim

The 1890 land-grant colleges initially embarked upon a mission not dissimilar to that of the 1862 colleges. They sought to prepare the sons and daughters of America's Black men and women in the "several pursuits and professions of life." These colleges hoped to provide students with the skills necessary to support themselves, their families, and their communities. That soon proved impossible. Within a few short decades of Booker T. Washington's "Cast Your buckets where you stand" speech, these new colleges and universities, led by a series of engaged presidents, realized that racial discrimination blocked their ability to accomplish what they had set out to do. As a consequence of that fatal impediment to Black economic success, these administrators and their schools gradually altered their mission. They focused much of their attention on securing the rights to which Blacks as Americans were entitled. To assist them in this quest, they formed themselves into an organization of presidents: these men worked collectively with little regard for state strictures and sought to involve the federal government in their equal rights battle. That collective took as articles of faith that the work of the Black land-grants had to be the fight for civil rights, self-determination, and self-agency for Black Americans. Black land-grant activities affirmed daily that supporting the struggles of disenfranchised people was work of the highest moral imperative. Only through that endeavor could the Black land-grants ultimately deliver on their original promise.

✳✳✳

The 1862 Morrill Land-Grant College Act, undertaken while the southern states were in rebellion, excluded those states until they were readmitted to the Union. When these states established their Morrill colleges, their segregationist policies practically excluded Blacks and left African American farm families without the support needed to develop an agricultural and mechanical arts education for young Blacks. Acknowledging a tremendous outcry from Blacks and their supporters, Congress, in 1890, passed a second Morrill Act. This act prohibited racial discrimination by compelling states either to permit Blacks to enter extant Morrill Act schools or to establish new, separate institutions of higher learning for African Americans. New schools formed by this act became known as the Black or 1890 land-grant colleges. Seventeen states, predominantly in the South, created separate land-grant institutions. Although each school's history was different, all of the 1890 land-grants experienced chronic underfunding, difficulties establishing a collegiate curriculum based in the agricultural and the mechanical arts, and discrimination in accessing federal funds for agricultural education. From the beginning and well into the twentieth century, money remained a major issue, but it did not prevent these institutions from establishing successful programs and activities that helped rural African American farm communities. Nor did lack of access to governmental agricultural programs inhibit the presidents of Black land-grants and their constituencies from working together to improve African American rural and farm life.[1]

The chapter focuses on a broad range of issues and topics to examine how the 1890 land-grant institutions addressed issues that Black families faced living in rural and agricultural America. Discussions will focus on presidential leadership and the president's operating philosophies concerning the mission of Black land-grants, their reactions to and assessment of certain components of the New Deal and related subsequential federal farm programs, educational outreach that addressed farm, family, and community needs, partnerships with government agencies and organizations, and Black land-grants' responses to the Black farmers' lawsuit against the USDA. Looking across the experiences of Black land-grants reveals how the educational mission of the Black land-grants changed over time. Their initial goal, which involved training adults and students to act as their own agent of change, eventually gave way to focusing on social and political situations that were constraining Blacks. Black land-grants challenged the premise that higher education should be exclusively for whites, although leaders of Black land-grants during the pre-Civil Rights era accepted the ideology of separate but equal, as long as such an approach led to the democratization of the American society and opportunities for educated Blacks. This collective understood that the work of Black land-grants entailed the fight for civil rights, self-determination, and self-agency. Black land-grant activities affirmed daily that supporting the struggles of Black Americans was work of the highest moral imperative.

Leaders of Black land-grants were committed to supporting the educational, social, economic, and cultural needs of Black rural and agricultural communities. Although Black land-grants deeply affected Black life, they were significantly hindered by having to rely upon resources from the federal government, state farm agents, and state offices that were opposed to equality and Black progress. The struggle for inclusion and full democratic participation began with the vision and work of the presidents of the Black land-grants. Their efforts were sustained by various communities, groups, and organizations, as well as social, political, and economic forces that helped keep the 1890 land-grant institutions relevant.

LEADERSHIP: PRESIDENTS OF THE BLACK LAND-GRANT COLLEGES AND UNIVERSITIES, 1930S–1950S

At the 1923 Southern Conference on Education in Negro Land-Grant Colleges, held at Tuskegee Institute, the Association of Negro Land-Grant Colleges was formed. Its purpose was to discover and address problems commonly faced by the constituencies the Black land-grants were to serve. Each of the seventeen schools would freely exchange ideas and stand willing to contribute pertinent knowledge and information. The founders recognized that the functions of the association were broad and needed to involve other historically Black colleges and universities, such as Hampton and Tuskegee institutes. They also realized they needed to collaborate with Black families, institutions, and organizations outside of academia. As a consequence, the presidents in March 1924 changed the name of their collective to the Conference of Presidents of Negro Land-Grant Colleges—a name that identified this group until its termination in 1956.[2]

During the early years of the conference, the presidents worked to gain respect and recognition for their colleges as institutions of higher learning.

They faced the major issues of funding, staffing, and curriculum. Funding was severely limited; the seventeen institutions were not eligible for some of the resources available to their white land-grant counterparts. The 1890 institutions had difficulty carrying out their missions. The federal government's lack of enforcement of federal nondiscriminatory laws meant that the 1890 institutions received less than one-twentieth the funds given to the 1862 white land-grants. The presidents at the seventeen Black colleges addressed the policy neglect and discrimination in 1935 at the group's annual meeting. They complained to Henry A. Wallace, then secretary of agriculture, that the Black colleges had received less than had been promised and that in 1933, "not one of the states that supported a separate land-grant college for Blacks had established an agricultural experiment sub-station in connection with the institutions responsible for serving Blacks in this capacity. Records of the federal government show that in the seventeen states providing land-grant outreach, Blacks comprised twenty-three percent of the population, but received only six percent of funds appropriated to the relevant states to support the work of black land-grant institutions."[3]

The 1890 institutions' initial mission was to train teachers to educate Black children in public and private schools; the Black land-grants functioned as normal schools, not as land-grant ones. In the states with Black land-grant institutions in 1928, Blacks were predominantly enrolled in private colleges—9,395 (73 percent) versus only 3,527 (27 percent) in Black land-grants. The land-grants understood that remedial work was necessary for a large portion of their student population so they concentrated on preparing students to seek a college degree. They emphasized the liberal arts: the classics, humanities, and basic sciences. Agriculture and mechanical arts training was minimal, offered either in separate institutes or through an occasional course. Black land-grants could not even attract trained teachers in these technical fields. States offered these specialists salaries that were slightly more than half of what white professors with similar training, ability, and experience received. It was not until 1931 that Black land-grants enrolled more students directly seeking a college degree than those requiring extensive college preparatory courses.[4] Early Black colleges had to spend most of their funding on subcollegiate-level institution. Despite these struggles, by the 1930s most of the 1890 land-grant colleges developed a bona fide four-year, standard degree program and received accreditation for their curriculum.

The 1930s were critical years for the Conference of Presidents. The desperation of the Great Depression exacerbated the rural Black condition. The Black land-grants tried to ameliorate the situation. They worked to secure credit for Black farmers and establish ways to better utilize farm credits. The presidents of Black land-grants believed that solid economic footing for Black farmers was a major institutional objective in the 1930s, and they recognized that their conference had to be a public voice. They defined making credit available to Black farmers as a sign of inclusion and democratic participation, a kind of democracy that would result in significant improvement in farmers' standard of living. Therefore, they agitated for changes in credit policies and credit mechanisms, which would improve the condition and status of Black farmers.

Black land-grant institutions' presidents in the 1930s championed diversity of learning and living. At their 1934 conference, building knowledge dominated conversation. The group argued that to ensure farm profitability, students should receive a strong, general agricultural course, including classes on animal husbandry, field crops, vegetable growing, dairying, farm management, economics, rural sociology, diseases, plant families, and poultry husbandry. The presidents recognized that teachers also required professional training to provide the instruction that diversified rural and farm culture demanded.[5] Educational training Educational training for teachers at the vocational high schools as well as at the mechanical and agricultural colleges was a major topic, since these individuals were responsible for implementing workshops and programs in communities to improve knowledge associated with farming and home economics, so that the youth and adults would gain a better understanding regarding how to improve their standard of living and income as skilled rural laborers. The 1935 conference gave overwhelming attention to the type of curricula (secondary and collegiate) needed at the agricultural and mechanical schools to prepare students for extension work. The presidents wanted to chart best practices as a way of establishing past and present trends for extension agent training.[6] The 1937 conference focused on soil conservation. It called on their agricultural specialists and field staff to address soil-conservation needs typically experienced by Black farmers. That agenda included participation in land-grant conservation programs, which entailed training farmers in new methods of production and encouraging the planting of crops such as pulpwood trees to preserve forests.[7] The 1937 conference also emphasized new and evolving opportunities for land-grant colleges. The keynote address discussed how the land-grants could move beyond agriculture to include training related to industry, business, home economics, and health.[8] The 1938 conference continued a discussion of the aforementioned issues addressed at the 1937 conference as essential needs that had to be addressed if the Black community was to survive the Great Depression. Suggestions for Black farm families' improvement in such areas as agriculture and business would require Black land-grants establishing better relationships with the USDA and its Federal Tenant Purchase Program. It also called on the land-grant schools to participate in rural development efforts, engage in rural rehabilitation, create and maintain cooperatives, and organize local agricultural conferences.[9]

That complicated, critical agenda fueled conference discussions throughout the 1930s. It also provided the foundation for the meetings in the 1940s and 1950s. The presidents continued to expand curriculum areas to better prepare their students for a wider variety of opportunities. They also sought equal opportunities for graduates who had been denied positions because of their race, and they help land-grants as a group adjust to social change. The latter included helping Black farmers keep abreast of changing New Deal policies and their evolving consequences.

Black Land-Grants' Reaction and Assessment of New Deal Policies

The presidents of Black land-grants also examined the implications of federal policies, including the sometimes negative effects and behaviors that federal offices spawned. In 1933, for example, the presidents of these institutions looked at the role of small southern farms in relation to the Future Land Utilization Program.[10] They found too little effort went into helping the smallest farmers: African American growers and producers. The presidents called for a federal redress of the imbalance. Later at the 1937 conference, they sought to restore Black farm tenants' confidence and morale. The presidents stipulated that Black land-grants study the local conditions of tenancy and make recommendations to alleviate unfavorable situations.[11] In 1938, the presidents worked together to develop a good relationship with the Farm Security Administration.[12] These leaders also addressed the impact of the Farm Credit Administration, demanding that it work through their institutions to provide services essential to equipping rural people with requisite farm management and finances knowledge.[13] Addresses given at a conference of Black agricultural leaders and farmers at Prairie View, Texas, in August 1936 discussed the importance of Black farmers to the Agricultural Adjustment Act

(AAA) and the Soil Conservation and Domestic Allotment Act.[14] In short, the presidents believed it was the responsibility of their institutions to establish logical approaches to address the needs of Black rural farmers and find ways to develop greater effectiveness in extension programs.[15]

Academics, intellectuals, and journalists, the majority of whom were Black, regularly criticized federal agencies and offices and New Deal farm programs because of the limited resources provided to Black land-grants and the communities they were supposed to serve. In 1936, Ralph J. Bunche declared that New Deal programs were primarily a means to enhance middle-class capitalism while simultaneously worsening the condition of the poor.[16] J. Phil Campbell showed the meager benefits the Federal Emergency Relief Administration provided Black farm families in terms of income improvement, rural rehabilitation, training for industrial employment, development of rural work centers, and rural education.[17] In 1936, *Crisis* magazine published an article titled "A Black Inventory of the New Deal." In it, John R. Davis decried the Agricultural Adjustment Administration and Public Works projects for their failure to help Black citizens.[18] He expanded the critique later that year in the *Journal of Negro Education*. He argued that New Deal policies did little to help Black farm families; they gave minimal attention to their poor standard of living, the need for crop and acreage reduction, mass unemployment, evictions, terrorism against tenant farmers and sharecroppers, and robbery.[19] Public critiques of New Deal farm programs, along with a sustained assessment of the ways in which Black farmers and rural communities and their land-grant institutions were being treated, enabled the presidents of the 1890 colleges to establish additional and different kinds of collaborations and partnerships. Through these new mechanisms, the voices of the Black land-grants could be heard and their constituencies might be included in public farm policy. But it would be some decades later following the 1960s uprisings when constituencies of Black land-grants and of Black farmers began to be heard.

Collaborations and Partnerships with Government Agencies and Organizations

Black land-grant colleges and federal offices sometimes collaborated to resolve issues among the Black rural and farm populations, often with mixed results. For example, in Louisiana, Black farmers and sharecroppers viewed the federal government's agricultural programs as a cross between confusion and tolerance. They objected to the activities of state officials, local bankers, and merchants. But in 1937, life for Black farmers and rural communities seemed to be improving: a study of farming and industrial employment conducted in the Southeast by the Federal Emergency Relief Administration showed comparable social and economic data for part-time farmers and for nonfarming industrial workers. By 1939, studies indicated that federal policies had gained traction among Black people. The Farm Security Administration Rehabilitation Program studied 50,000 Black families as part of a survey of 116,000 typical southern families and found only small differences between black and white families.[20]

The fruitful collaboration between federal offices and Black land-grants encouraged these schools to seek additional collaboration. At the nineteenth annual conference meeting in Chicago in 1941, the Conference of Presidents' theme was "Cooperation with Federal Agencies with Particular Reference to Agricultural Extension Services and the National Defense Program." Thomas N. Roberts, a special assistant to the director of personnel at the US Department of Agriculture (USDA), gave a paper that showed nearly nonexistent Black involvement in agency activities except in the extension service and the Farm Security Administration. Discussion ensued but no commentator attributed the imbalance to racism. No one argued that the USDA needed to reach out to Black land-grants. In 1942, at a meeting of the presidents of Black land-grants at Hampton Institute, the group broached again partnering with the federal government to help Blacks on farms and in rural communities. This time, they included the voice of a major Black intellectual, W. E. B. DuBois, in the mix. DuBois submitted a proposal to the Black land-grants presidents assessing the impact of the nation's entry into World War II and the economic and social changes the war would bring to Americans, especially Black people. Working under the conference theme "National Planning for the Prosecution and Winning of the War, Long-Time Issues of Postwar Collapse and Reconstruction, and Their Effects upon the Negro Land-Grant Colleges," the presidents wrestled with questions of how to involve their institutions and students in three major areas: the armed forces, war industries, and agriculture. Maintaining that a job applicant's skill and ability should be the only factors considered by an employer, not race, religion, or any other condition, they spoke with a stronger political voice. They registered special concern that the USDA was employing Blacks primarily in custodial positions, that the navy not only was refusing to recognize Negro colleges as participating in the V-1 program but had not worked out a plan for the employment of Negro officers, and that Black colleges continued to be drastically underfunded because states were not sharing equitably the funds designated for land-grant colleges.[21]

These ongoing struggles for inclusion and sustained efforts to empower rural Blacks and Black farmers through education and employment prompted the presidents of the Black land-grants to send representatives to Washington, DC to speak with President Harry S. Truman. They met with him on October 22, 1946. Because Blacks had fought in uniform and participated in wartime productions programs, presidents of the Black land-grants and their representatives wanted President Truman to know that Black colleges were willing and ready to help educate Americans, especially with the support of the G.I. Bill created to educate veterans. In a prepared statement presented by Drs. Sherman D. Scruggs of Lincoln University, Rufus B. Atwood of Kentucky State College, and John W. Davis of West Virginia State College, they declared:

> We represent officially the publicly supported land-grant colleges of seventeen southern states in which approximately seventy-five percent of Negroes of America live. . . . The progress of these colleges is important to the advancement of the South and the Nation. They are located in states which are rich in the number of children and poor in wealth; where a separate school system is maintained for Negroes; where schools for Negro youth are conducted in churches, lodges, old stores, tenant houses, or whatever building is available; where oftentimes in entire counties, high schools for Negroes do not exist and where publicly supported professional training for Negroes is nonexistent. The Director of Selective Service has pointed out that of 347,038 registrants of the first two registrations prior to Pearl Harbor, 220,052 were Negroes. . . . Equalizing educational opportunity for all American youth is important to our National well-being. Federal Aid to education in areas of need is a necessity.[22]

They concluded their statement by asking President Truman to consider four areas of concern: (1) expanding personnel and support for the cooperative agricultural and home economics extension service work for needed programs in adult education; (2) providing for organized research in the institutions and appropriate access to experimental station facilities within the respective states, so that current information essential for sound agricultural and rural life be made readily available; (3) activating additional ROTC units in the interest of military preparedness and peace; and (4) making equipment, surplus property, buildings, and land more easily available to meet the demands being made on the Black land-grant institutions for training veterans.[23] Within this presentation, the presidents reminded President Truman that "Racism is probably the weakest link in our democracy, and it is time in our own interest as a nation to do something about it."[24]

Black college presidents remained diligent in their efforts to attack racism and discrimination. A most critical moment happened in the 1950s when the presidents complained that much discrimination existed in federal projects and outreach programs. A letter concerning the Tennessee Valley Authority (TVA) to Dr. Lewis Webster Jones, president of the University of Arkansas and head of the Executive Committee of the Land-Grant College Association, from R. B. Atwood, president of Kentucky State College and secretary of the Negro Conference, put the case simply: "As you know, the TVA will not enter into research or other projects with the Negro Land-Grant Colleges because it has already contracted with the white land-grant colleges in each Valley State. Our requests to the TVA have met with little success. Several institutions have requested that their college farms be made TVA test Demonstration Farms; we also have a Cooperative Social Studies Project (sociological) for which we need financial support, and which, some of us feel, falls within the area of research aidable from TVA funds. It is suggested that your Committee can aid the Negro Land-Grant Colleges and establish and maintain a closer, more active working relationship with the TVA, at least in the seven states located in the TVA region."[25] On February 1, 1951, after one year and three months of discussion, the TVA entered into a research agreement with the land-grant colleges in the Tennessee Valley and the Conference of Presidents of Negro Land-Grant Colleges. The title of the agreement was "Study of Social and Economic Change as It Affects the Negro Population of the Tennessee Valley Region."[26] The presidents of North Carolina A&T, Alcorn A&M, Fort Valley State College, Kentucky State College, Virginia State College, and Tennessee A&I State College participated; their universities were located in the Tennessee Valley region. They conducted the study in three phases. In phase one, each school analyzed census data that related to population, farm mechanization, farm electrification, selected crops, farm tenure, occupations, and other trends from 1920 to 1950 in each county of the seven-state region. In phase two, the schools studied census data to determine whether there had been an increase or decrease in Black farm ownership. In phase three, the universities provided recommendations for training and service programs based on the research findings.[27]

Black land-grant institutions' collaborations and partnerships with government agencies and community organizations increased in particular from the 1940s through the 1970s. Research studies and community projects were established with such offices as the US Farmers Administration, the US Bureau of Agricultural Economics, the US Extension Service, the US Office of Education, the state experiment stations, the US Bureau of Labor Statistics, the US Census Bureau, and the US Commission on Civil Rights. Many of these efforts involved collecting data about the work that Black land-grants were doing regarding farm life and standards of living, collegiate agricultural education, farm-ownership programs, rural employment, equal opportunity and equal treatment of the 1890 institutions and the constituents they served, participation in federal farm programs, and youth programs for rural and farm children.[28] Working with and through these offices, the presidents of the Black land-grants labored to enhance the physical, material, cultural, economic, and social life of their students and the communities these land-grants were established to serve.

The Work of Black Land-Grant Colleges: Conferences, Extension, and Cooperatives

The real-life work of Black land-grants evolved through their outreach. The presidents of Black land-grants believed the 1890 act had created the opportunity to expand, define programs for, and better determine Blacks' educational needs.[29] They believed defining and implementing an educational mission that included these objectives were critical to empowering Black farmers and rural communities to become more progressive and independent.

Conferences were one of the ways Black land-grants chose to exercise leadership and engage in community building to empower people. Sessions at these conferences educated Black youth, farmers, and women. Discussions at conferences organized by Black land-grants focused on issues related to improving standards of living as well as questions that attempted to define ways Black rural and agricultural communities could move forward through partnerships with the 1980 institutions. In doing so, conference leaders encouraged Blacks to develop not only community philosophies about progress, but strategies that would allow them to continue participating in life conferences, the kinds that would help Black rural families understand how to modernize and adjust to rural and agricultural changes. Everyone who was engaged in helping farm families improve their lives and communities needed to be trained to give assistance.

Black land-grants' presidents utilized provocative thematic approaches at their conferences to address issues that their institutions were facing. At the thirteenth annual conference, held in Washington, DC, in 1935, the theme was "The Need of the Negro Land-Grant Colleges." This meeting featured eight guest speakers, including Henry A. Wallace, secretary of agriculture. From the US Department of Commerce, Eugene Knicles Jones, in a talk titled "Studying Vocational Opportunities for Negroes," emphasized that for Black Americans to be able to take advantage of increasing opportunities, Black land-grant colleges must have the resources and personnel to prepare students. He said it was crucial for each Black land-grant college to have a field agent, whose chief duties would be compiling the types of occupations that would be available to graduates as well as placing graduates in positions that offered apprenticeship privileges, and instituting a follow-up system to check on the vocational progress of graduates. He advised Black land-grants to hold annual conferences emphasizing consumer and growers' cooperatives, credit unions, agricultural economics, small farm ownership, and crop diversification. Erwin H. Shinn of the extension service gave a speech titled "Professional Training of Negro Extension Work." He emphasized curricula that those who held federal positions related to agriculture wanted to see developed in Black land-grants. These included training (1) teachers of agriculture, home economics, and the related sciences for both college and secondary positions; (2) extension workers in agriculture and home economics and to some extent subject-matter specialists in these fields; and (3) practical farming and farm homemaking and their scientific underpinnings.[30]

At the regional conference of Black land-grant presidents meeting In Petersburg, Virginia in 1937, district agents, persons working in groups that had been divided by the 1890 presidents into districts based upon geographical location, emphasized similar types of training and thinking. Their meeting focused on the need for farm ownership, advancement in tenant farming, problems associated with cotton production, more effective utilization of extension services, advanced farm and home demonstrations, and participation in government programs. In 1939, the Black land-grant institution of the University of Arkansas-Pine Bluff convened a conference for state supervisors and Black teachers involved with providing agricultural education. Through reports, speeches, and roundtable discussions involving fifty-one participants from fourteen states and the District of Columbia, the meeting focused primarily on methods of instruction in agriculture and mechanics. It also emphasized farmer and teacher training in vocational and agricultural fields and in technical education. Its final thrust was means to increase community participation in government programs run by Black land-grants.[31]

One of the leading institutions involved in organizing Black land-grant conferences was Tuskegee University. In 1950, with the support of the seventeen Black land-grants, Tuskegee held a conference to address the problems of small Black farmers in the South. Discussions focused on problems, changes, and trends in southern agriculture, major areas in which targeted research could solve problems, and the types of programs that would enable Black farmers to become economically secure.[32] Each of the aforementioned Black land-grant conferences stressed the specific needs of Black farmers within the context of farm, family, and community.

Between 1930 and 1960, the presidents of the Black land-grants defended their colleges in the face of what they considered unfair criticism. They objected to statements and points of view put forth that they believed were out of step with reality. For example, in a 1935 letter to Henry A. Wallace, they wrote: "The magnitude of the educational program for white citizens may attract so much attention that attention is distracted from how little is being done for the Negro citizens. . . . All of this may happen unwittingly, but the fact remains that as the program for white citizens proceeds and expands, the program for Negro citizens lags behind, and at a low level. The minds of many citizens, both white and colored, become confused and then, sometimes complacent; we assume that all is well with our citizens; what is generally considered to be everybody's business turns out to be no nobody's business—and the Negro suffers."[33]

In addition to meetings set up to further the professional development of administrative leaders at the 1890 land-grants, the Conference of Presidents of Negro Land-Grant Colleges partnered with the presidents of some Black private and public colleges to provide an array of services. The expanded programming was designed to prepare students and adults in rural communities for a variety of occupations. Within this context, the presidents of Atlanta University, Central State College in Ohio, Hampton Institute, Howard University, Savannah State College, Texas Southern University, and

Tuskegee were given associate membership in the conference. To be more inclusive of the voices of Black researchers and scholars and of Black institutions of higher education that were concerned about the needs of poor Black people, the aforementioned associated colleges and institutes, which did not carry the land-grant designation, agreed to utilized their faculty, primarily in the social sciences, to conduct research concerning problems Black Americans in rural communities faced. For example, Professor E. Franklin Frazier, a sociologist at Howard University, served as coordinator of a research program called "The Land-Grant Program in Cooperative Social Studies." With a group of other scholars, he conducted research on Black communities and their experiences with demographic changes, land tenure, availability of health care, changing economic problems, occupational opportunities, and the quality and variations within family relations. Other leading scholars involved in the project included W. E. B. DuBois of Atlanta University, Ambrose Coliver (assistant to the commissioner of the US Department of Education), and Charles S. Johnson of Fisk University, all of whom worked together to address specific problems facing the Black community. With the addition of the associate institutions, Black land-grants were able to shift their attention primarily from a single focus on rural development and agricultural education to preparing members of the Black community and students so as to raise the standard of living for Black families, to overcome inequality, poverty, and poor health, to deal with rapid mechanization and industrialization, and to call for the integration of higher education.[34]

Especially in the 1950s, Black farmers found a rhythm for developing alliances and organizations to address the needs created by segregation, discrimination, and oppression. In 1956, for example, Black farmers in Clarendon County, North Carolina, organized the Clarendon County Improvement Association to circumvent discrimination. It provided small loans, farm supplies, and services to Blacks. When area gins would not accept cotton from Black farmers, the cooperative transported it to distant facilities. When Black growers could not sell their goods because of discrimination, Black farmers and producers formed vegetable cooperatives. In the 1960s, the Federation of Southern Cooperatives was created by representatives from twenty-two cooperatives throughout the South. Many of the initiators of cooperative development were religious leaders and churches active in improving life in Black communities. In the early 1970s, some Black churches and cooperatives bought land for self-sufficient farm settlement and market production. Through the mid to late 1970s and into the 1980s and 1990s, Black farmers cooperatives gained some financial stability and, as a collective, developed several operations, including vegetable-packing facilities to serve large supermarkets. They also established high earning pecan businesses, while some of the pepper growers created their own brand of hot sauce. Further, in the 1990s, the development of Southern Alternatives, a pecan-marketing cooperative in Georgia, exemplified a new emphasis on commercialization, with Black growers removing the middlemen from the profit-making process. Hoping to keep Black farming alive and pass it on to future generations, Black cooperatives are currently taking steps to teach younger generations about farming,[35] sometimes with the help of Black land-grant institutions.[36] Four modern, up-to-date, cooperative cotton gins were owned and profitably operated by Black farmers in the Delta section of eastern Arkansas. Agricultural cooperatives had been started by poor Black farmers in Harris County, Georgia, and Halifax County, Virginia.[37] Many *New York Times* articles have discussed the actions of Black cooperatives and their attitudes about surviving as independent participants in agricultural production.[38]

Revitalizing Black Farm Life, Family Living, and Community Struggles (1950s–1990s)

As the African American community exerted greater pressure for inclusion and equality and the right to engage in society as full citizens, the presidents of the Black land-grants stepped up their outreach. Between the 1950s and the 1970s, these institutions focused more intensely on quality-of-life issues. Family, farm, and community formed the core of Black land-grants' work. Diversification in farming emerged as a major development that would help Black farm families earn a profitable living and depend less on the production of cotton. Black land-grant presidents supported dairying and poultry and livestock production as farming enterprises. North Carolina A&T University focused, for instance, on dairying and emphasized a course of study that would be useful for anyone wishing to transition to dairying. Supervisors provided farmers with results of surveys that showed progress, as a small percentage of Blacks experienced profit-making with dairying, and they cited cases where at least two Black families had experienced great success.[39]

Land acquisition remained a critical need for Black farmers during the Civil Rights Movement. This idea was not new, but the ways in which the presidents addressed it were different. By now, sufficient evidence showed that the Farmers Home Administration and the Agricultural Stabilization and Conservation Service had been ineffective in helping Blacks transition into landowners. In the 1960s, Black farmers began to ask how the Black land-grants could help with racialized issues when the presidents had dissolved their own independent organization (the Conference of Presidents of Negro Land-Grant Colleges) and had joined the dominant white association (now called the Association of Land-Grant Colleges and Universities). During the first twenty years after the end of World War II, racism in American agriculture became more entrenched. The influence of racial factors and the impact of economic demands, such as profit-making on land tenure in the South had devastating consequences for Black farmers. Comparisons between Blacks and whites revealed great disparities in the differences of land, in the opportunities to purchase available land, and in mortgage titles.[40]

Black land-grants began to focus their energy and training on the homes and health of rural Blacks. Nutritional needs were a serious health-related issue. Through surveys of southern communities, Black land-grants discovered alarming nutritional deficiencies among rural Blacks, as evidenced by the large number of cases of indigestion, constipation, low vitality, and general physical disability. The extension service encouraged Black farm families to grow gardens and to cure and can pork products by providing demonstrations on food planting and food preparation.[41]

While organizing leadership conferences to discern how best to inform and educate Black rural and farm communities, the presidents of the Black land-grants engaged in safe politics as far as voicing opposition to discrimination involving Black farmers. Farm conferences paid tribute to the country's Black farmers and to Black agricultural leaders for their patriotic contributions during World War II. The presidents critiqued both federal offices and their leaders' failure to implement policies or to recognize the success of Black farmers. These conservative approaches prevented their constituencies from becoming dismayed by politics or fearful of retaliation because of positions the presidents had taken on farm programs.

Health was perhaps the most important family-life issue that Black land-grant presidents tackled. Segregation made it difficult for Blacks, especially southern ones, to get access to competent medical care. Black researchers decried incidences of illness, the lack of available health care, and the cost of medical services, as well as the effects that income, location, and occupational status had in terms of Blacks' access to such services.[42] Black land-grants held health fairs and conferences on health, and they sent extension workers into communities to help provide basic medical care, to recommend clinics and doctors, and to work with elderly and young adults regarding prevention of common colds and childhood measles and chicken pox.

The socioeconomic situation of Black farmers and rural communities remained a critical issue. Therefore, revitalizing such communities had to involve protest. Although the presidents of the 1890 institutions did not actively or directly engage in the Civil Rights or Black Power movements, their researchers did through the print media. In this way, Black land-grants helped articulate the struggles and needs of Black rural and farm communities. Although federal agencies increased funding and programming for these populations, support remained limited and sometimes was not provided in a timely manner. The Black land-grant presidents, students, and community supporters reached out to media outlets for help in voicing the needs of these historically Black institutions. Among the hundreds of leading media outlets that gave their voices to this struggle, *Opportunity*, *Atlantic Monthly*, the *New York Times*, the *New Republic*, the *Nation*, *Civil Rights Digest*, and *Ebony* publicized the struggles of Black farm communities. For example, *Opportunity* published articles that discussed white violence against Black farmers because some Black workers and landowners were perceived to be too political, as they associated with socialist and communist groups whom the white elite believed were encouraging Blacks to retaliate against whites with violence at Camp Hill, Alabama.[43] The *Atlantic Monthly* reported that Black sharecroppers in the Arkansas and Mississippi deltas showed aggression toward what they perceived as oppression. Newspaper articles described the attitudes and responses of both the white landowners and Black sharecroppers and the dishonest methods of exploitation typically used by both groups.[44] *Social Forces* detailed attempts by community leaders to suppress efforts by communists to organize Black tenant farmers in east-central Alabama into a sharecroppers' union. Articles in the New York Times provided details about battles over wages. Writers often focused on the state of Mississippi. In 1965, they reported that forty-eight Black tenant farmers, including women and children, in southeast Greenville, Mississippi, were determined to keep their strike going through the winter to emphasize their demands for better wages and working conditions. They had adequate provisions for the winter and were running a cooperative workshop to generate income. Cash contributions for the cause were being sought from many different sources, including northern philanthropists.

The strikers were urging other Black tenant farmers throughout the South to walk off their jobs at planting time in the spring.[45] According to *The Nation*, thousands of sharecroppers in the Mississippi Delta faced eviction and loss of income as a result of the one-dollar increase in the minimum wage. Delta planters announced that workers would be replaced by a more intensive use of weed-killing chemicals and mechanical cotton-pickers. The writer repeated popular suggestions offered by presidents of the 1890s, leaders of the Black communities, and by white farmers who were rapidly modernizing their farms through technology.[46]

The public outcry from Blacks about discrimination and segregation led the presidents of Black land-grants to ask the federal government and the USDA for more funds and additional extension agents to help the 1890s achieve their work agricultural, mechanical, and technical work with Black communities. Newspaper reports and editorials helped shed light on the federal government's neglect in implementing and enforcing federal farm programs and civil rights protections to ensure democratic participation. Emmett Peter Jr. discussed in *The New Republic* how Secretary of Agriculture Orville Freeman had instructed Agriculture Extension and other USDA agencies in the South to end discrimination and to encourage Black farmers to participate in the federal programs to which they were entitled. He appointed a fifteen-member advisory committee to review the department's plans and monitor progress.[47] In 1968, *Civil Rights Digest* documented racial discrimination against Blacks in the Cooperative Extensive Service, especially in salaries, promotions, and services, outlined new USDA regulations for eliminating these practices, and established procedures for filing complaints.[48] Through a photojournalistic piece by James Peppler, *Civil Rights Digest* also illustrated poverty, discrimination, and the economic dependency of rural Black citizens, particularly in sixteen Alabama counties.[49]

One of the ways in which the Black land-grants could address the struggles of Black farmers and rural communities was through extension services, home economics, and research. The formal extension work of the 1890 land-grants took place via the Cooperative Extension Service after 1914. Extension remained segregated through the 1970s in some places, but it nonetheless delivered significant training, courses, programs, health care, and other services. Extension in the Black land-grants remained woefully underfunded until 1972, when the presidents of the Black land-grants and their allies complained bitterly about the USDA. Only then did Congress establish extension programs to redress the imbalance: the Agricultural

Environmental and Consumer Protection Appropriation Act provided opportunities for predominantly Black land-grant institutions to plan extension education programs on their own. This act became the foundation of the 1980 extension redraft. It gave colleges and universities autonomy to parcel out funds set aside by Congress according to local priorities.[50]

Of the various extension efforts, home economics had the greatest immediate impact on the social and material conditions of rural Blacks and Black farmers. According to Walter Washing, president of Alcorn State University in Mississippi, "Some economics programs not only integrate knowledge and services from various disciplines to enable individuals and families to improve their quality of well-being, but home economics uniquely touches the hearts and spirits of people and bestow[s] on them human value, character, and dignity—the very preservation and progression of humanity."[51] The presidents of the Black land-grants believed that home economics held answers to many problems. It came to bear on health, health care, nutrition, sanitation, and domestic activities such as sewing, dressmaking, needlework, costume design, and hat making. By creating domestic science programs and bringing this kind of training into the community, the Black land-grant presidents established home economics units at their colleges to help individuals and families become self-sustaining and contributing members of society. Home economics programs were tremendous successes, both for students and for the communities the Black institutions served. These programs bolstered respectability for Black people as progressive home managers and provided skills necessary for community leadership and support. While the teaching of home economics at each of these 1890 land-grants has changed dramatically over the years, the fundamental purpose has not deviated from the original mission. In the twenty-first century, the presidents remain vested in building humanity among Black people by training students who can help develop strategies for managing life situations.[52]

The success of the extension and home economics programs encouraged the presidents of the Black land-grants to pursue research as the final frontier for addressing the needs and concerns of Blacks living on farms and in rural America. For seventy-seven years (1890–1967), these institutions lacked state and federal financial support for research. The 1890 act specified that the new schools were not eligible for Hatch Act funds or those subsequent to them. During this period, funding for experimentation and research was bringing increased status and recognition to white land-grant universities. State research support for the Black land-grants lagged far behind, but formal federal research support began in 1967 with development of the Cooperative State Research Service (CSRS). The CSRS was a response to pressure from Black faculties and their supporters. With increased funding for research at the Black land-grants came many changes in rural and farm life. CSRS has promoted better understanding of health, nutrition, home economics, and life needs, household and farm management, crop and produce diversification, the development of markets, improvement in livestock production, and more profitable farming techniques. According to Leedell W. Neyland, each of the Black land-grants, along with Tuskegee and Hampton universities, has made great strides in agricultural research since 1967, when the CSRS first organized federal support.[53] Nevertheless, the Black land-grants have had to conduct their research within a climate of discrimination and segregation while a disproportionate amount of funds have been allocated to the white land-grants. Researchers and presidents at the Black land-grants continue to request more funding. The advocacy of the presidents on behalf of their constituencies is one of the main reasons why many Blacks continue to see the land-grant system as ideal for accessing higher education.[54]

BLACK FARMERS' COLLABORATION WITH BLACK ORGANIZATIONS AND OTHER BLACK INSTITUTIONS

Beginning in the 1950s, researchers in the marketing and production wing of the USDA published studies to illuminate issues related to the participation of rural Blacks and Black farmers in American agriculture. The result of these efforts, *Success Stories: Negro Farmers*, primarily provided information about individual Black farmers in USDA programs.[55] Articles about Black self-help successes began to appear in the popular press. These included stories about a wealthy young Black farmer in Beaufort, North Carolina,[56] a communal farm near Wayside, Mississippi,[57] a multipurpose center in Bricks, North Carolina,[58] a 376-acre Black Muslim farm in Ashville, Alabama,[59] a former sharecropper who became a wealthy farmer in Jackson, Georgia,[60] and the National Baptist Convention's purchase of 5,000 acres of land in Liberia for the purpose of setting up a Black version of the Peace Corps.[61] In 1963, Tuskegee Institute announced plans for an experimental training program to prepare impoverished Black tenant farmers for city life. In keeping with their emphasis on collaborating with Black farmers, Black organizations, and Black community institutions, such as churches, Black land-grants executed plans that included rural and urban Blacks working together to address city poverty. For example, farmers who worked with extension agents from Tuskegee studied city life, giving special attention to the ways in which they could help Blacks—many of whom were rural migrants, former tenants, and sharecroppers from the South—grow food in yards and other limited city spaces to help with the chronic issues of health and nutrition poor Blacks faced daily within their inner-city environments.[62]

Despite the success some Black farmers experienced, the vast majority had unpleasant encounters with the USDA and the local offices created to assist them. Discrimination and intimidation were so prevalent that the USDA issued an order to treat all clients equally. Responding to the passage of the Civil Rights Act of 1964, many groups demanded that racial segregation and discrimination be abolished. The presidents of Black land-grants, members of their faculties and their supporters, and members of the associated institutions urged the USDA to provide equal opportunities and additional support for the 1890 colleges. Movement toward research appropriations began in 1965, when Congress authorized the USDA to fund research at colleges and institutions that were ineligible under previous legislation. Congress's Public Law 89-106 made it possible for Black land-grants to get funding from the National Academy of Sciences while shoring up funding for agricultural and food research and greater assistance for agricultural experimental stations in the states where the Black land-grants existed. Conversations concerning the increasing need for more funding for 1890 institutions grew less polite in the 1960s following the passage of the Civil Rights Acts of 1964 and the Voting Rights of 1965. These pieces of legislations made it possible for the presidents of Black land-grants to focus on the need for increased research allocations to their institutions. Support for Black land-grants' struggle to obtain more funding came from the National Association of State Universities and Land-Grant Colleges (NASULGC) and the Rural Sociological Society (RSS). Because of this collaborative approach and pressure from allies, Black land-grants received $8,880,000 in 1972.[63] From the 1970s onward, funds for research at Black land-grants continued to increase.

In the 1970s and the 1980s, the funding needs of Black farmers did not receive the same attention as did funding requests from the presidents of the Black land-grants. Lack of access to these dollars remained a great concern, but the USDA responded slowly to discrimination complaints. It issued statements reminding its agents, as well as state and local offices, that discrimination would not be tolerated. Despite these efforts, discrimination was tolerated, and Black farmers persisted with their complaints well into the 1980s. Struggles around this issue peaked in the 1990s, when Black farmers brought a class-action suit against the USDA.

THE BLACK FARMERS' LAWSUIT AGAINST THE USDA

Complaints about discrimination made it difficult for the USDA to claim a strong civil rights record in agriculture and farming in the 1980s. Based on past practices, Black farmers charged that the USDA had consistently tolerated racial discrimination in distributing program benefits, which mostly went to white farmers and excluded minority and limited-resource farmers and ranchers. Many Black farmers and those working for the USDA now view the 1980s as the critical period, when racist practices and retaliation against protesters peaked. The resurgence of conservatism during this time was accompanied by a rapid decline in access to certain public agricultural programs. In the 1990s, the USDA attempted to ameliorate that criticism but seemed unable to establish the right kind of policies that Black and small farmers needed. By the 1990s, Black farmers and their advocates complained that the way in which the USDA allowed local county committees to function disrupted their ability to farm successfully and profitably. At least 94 percent of county committees had no female or minority representation, even though women and minorities comprised a considerable portion of the southern farm population. Minority producers were 4.7 percent of eligible voters but held only 2.9 percent of county committee seats. Women constituted 28.8 percent of eligible voters but held only 1.5 percent of county committee seats. The General Accounting Office found that in 1995, only 36 of the 101 counties with the largest concentration of minority farmers had at least one minority county committee member.[64]

Despite legislation created to help minorities remain in agriculture, the number of African-American farmers had decreased by 98 percent by 1997, while the number of white Americans who farmed declined by 66 percent. Documentation of Black land loss began in 1971, when the Black Economic Research Center (BERC) sponsored a two-day conference at Clark College in Atlanta. It argued that between 1950 and 1969, the number of acres of farmland fully or partly owned by Blacks had dropped from 12 million to 5.5 million. The reduction continued because Black farmers could not acquire capital and, as some Black farmers believed, the USDA allowed white land-owners to manipulate local USDA offices to maintain their domination of agricultural life and production. Due to Blacks' struggle to hold onto land, an Emergency Land Fund (ELF) was created to help Black farmers acquire land as well as maintain ownership. This work led to collaboration between ELF and BERC to implement a strategy of tracking Black land loss. A report by R. S. Browne from the 1971 conference that was published in 1973 described the outcome of a dozen projects dealing with this particular issue.[65]

During the 1990s, Black farmers became increasingly vocal in blaming the USDA of racial discrimination. They charged that the USDA had long tolerated the unequal distribution of program benefits and the misuse of power to influence landownership and farm profitability. They blamed the USDA for enforcing regulations that, intentionally or not, prevented minority and limited-resource farmers and ranchers from accessing the benefits of the same programs that had enabled larger nonminority producers to weather changes in agriculture since the 1930s. They accused the USDA of exhibiting insensitivity toward the differing needs of minority and limited-resource farmers and maintained that it had neglected its responsibility to reach out and serve all.

The 1990s were ripe for protest. Some Black farmers demanded action that would produce results. On December 12, 1996, Black farmers from every region of the country demonstrated outside the White House, calling upon President Bill Clinton to demand fair treatment in implementing federal agricultural lending programs. Thereafter, Daniel R. Glickman, secretary of agriculture, established the Civil Rights Action Team (CRAT) within the USDA to investigate the Black farmers' charges. He authorized listening sessions throughout America to field complaints and ordered the USDA to produce a summary in a timely manner.

The USDA sponsored twelve listening sessions in eleven different locations in January 1997 to learn about Black and minority farming experiences. Nine listening sessions were held with farmers and producers, typically called customers, and three with USDA staff employees. Each session was designed to address gender and race as they related to interactions between USDA local offices and African Americans, Native Americans, Hispanics, and Asians. Farmers and staff employees who did not speak at the listening sessions were allowed to submit recorded or written statements to CRAT. In addition, the USDA established an e-mail address, a fax number, and a hotline for comments. Details varied from family to family, but the general themes focused on loan processing, delays in approval of loans, and lack of information and help necessary to participate in USDA programs. Farmers, too, orally documented their concern about declining number of minority farmers and farms; many indicated they believed that the USDA was involved in a conspiracy to take land from minority farmers so that wealthy landowners could gain access to it.

At these sessions, farmers described a pattern of discriminatory behavior. The most serious accusation concerned how Black farmers were treated personally and how their farm business was not treated as a serious agricultural enterprise. Some claimed that their paperwork was dismissed and that they had been disrespected. Others emphasized loans that had arrived long after planting season, arbitrary reductions in loan amounts, and a much higher rejection rate than that experienced by white applicants. An overwhelming majority of Black farmers accused the USDA of ignoring research that would help small-scale and limited-resource farmers, and of failing to include minority populations in outreach efforts to raise awareness of federal programs. Finally, minority farmers indicated that official complaints of discrimination had been processed slowly, if at all, and that the USDA often continued with foreclosure proceedings even when a relevant discrimination complaint had been filed. Members of CRAT heard more than thirty separate complaints at the USDA-authorized listening sessions.[66]

Meanwhile, some Black farmers and their advocates developed grassroots strategies to enable them to be heard. Their activism included protest marches in Detroit, Chicago, Atlanta, Washington, DC, and other major cities. They organized letter-writing campaigns, sent messages to churches, e-mailed local and national politicians, conducted major fund-raisers to help farmers, and established national and regional farm organizations to address media questions concerning the struggle. Among the many issues they raised, none seemed more pressing than the fight against Black farm foreclosure and the snail's pace at which the USDA handled complaints. Black farmers clearly linked these two issues to the ready loss of land and farms.

The Black farmer protest led to *Pigford v. Glickman*, a 1999 class-action lawsuit against the USDA. Black land-grant institutions were largely absent from this battle. Tuskegee and other institutions held conferences concerning the lawsuit and continuous Black land loss.

Developments within the state of Kentucky were critical to events surrounding the lawsuit. Major protests occurred there, especially in the Henderson area. Harry Young, an African American farmer, received considerable publicity for opposing USDA agents. The House of Representatives in the Kentucky General Assembly passed a provision urging the Kentucky Department of Agriculture, Kentucky State University (a Black land-grant), the University of Kentucky's College of Agriculture, and the Governor's Office of Agricultural Policy to assess the economic conditions and needs of Black farmers in Kentucky, to cooperate with other stakeholders (including the USDA), and to identify the Black farmers in Kentucky who were affected by the Pigford case. The economic and demographic data were to include an analysis of the impact of Black farmers on Kentucky's economy. Kentucky State University took the lead in contacting other Black land-grants to identify programs that were being offered to help Black farmers. All information was to be reported to the Kentucky Joint Committee on Agriculture by July 1, 2012. To date, however, there has been no effort on the part of the state or the Black land-grants that shows a significant involvement with the current struggles of Black farmers and the implications of the class-action lawsuit in this way. Only Tuskegee, an associated partner, has been involved in organizing meetings and holding forums. This lack of participation may be the result of institutions that have had, and still have to have, a working relationship with the USDA and that still need its resources. Many claimants in the lawsuit continue to experience difficulties securing compensation for the discrimination they have experienced, even though other groups, such as Latinos, women, and Native Americans, have successfully utilized the Black farmers' class-action legislation to sue for justice for themselves.[67]

BLACK LAND-GRANTS AND THE FUTURE

Although it appears that an overwhelming majority of Black land-grants were not involved in directly supporting the Black farmers in the Pigford case, it is clear that they collectively believe that their next level of involvement with Black rural communities and farmers should focus on entrepreneurship and outreach. They have to remain engaged with federal offices and they have to continue recruiting African American students with an interest in agriculture and rural life. Much of their work centers on empowering communities through entrepreneurship, helping small-scale and limited farmers with food and crop production, increasingly utilizing technology and digitalization to improve constituent services, and developing relationships with federal agencies to shore up funding. Toward this end, rural development cooperative agreements with the 1890 institutions have been created to strengthen the capacity of rural communities to undertake innovative, comprehensive, citizen-led, long-term strategies for community and economic development. In other contexts, many Black land-grants are expanding their research capacity by developing expertise in areas such as homeland security and national defense, cyberinfrastructure, environmental observatories, food security, energy expenditures, genomics, and material science. These new initiatives do not diminish other Black land-grants' efforts. As long as students are interested in higher education from agricultural and rural perspectives, Black land-grants will be vital to the social, political, and economic life of all people, especially African Americans.

Black land-grant leaders must remain engaged and continue to voice their concerns about discrimination, the racialization of their schools and constituencies, and the ways in which they have been excluded from federal and state opportunities. This spirit must guide the Black land-grants in considering the plight of Black farmers and rural Blacks, just as the presidents who created the Conference of Presidents of Negro Land-Grant Colleges did as they implemented the 1890 land-grant vision. There can be no implementation without full representation and understanding that all the work is, indeed, political. The work that the Black land-grants have performed on behalf of Black people has been not only useful and effective but lifesaving, educationally relevant, and socially engaged; it has empowered Blacks to think differently about democracy and participation. Although not perfect, the Black land-grants have worked hard to improve the educational, social, and economic order that makes life livable for the people they were created to serve.

Notes

1. For a discussion of the early history of Black land-grant colleges and universities, see Leedell W. Neyland, *Historically Black Land-Grant Institutions and the Development of Agriculture and Economics* (Tallahassee: Florida A&M University Foundation, 1990); Barbara Cotton, ed., *The 1890 Land-Grant Colleges: A Centennial Review* (Washington, DC: Agricultural History Society, 1992); Wayne F. Urban, *Black Scholar: Horace Mann Bond, 1904–1972* (Athens: University of Georgia Press, 1992); and Ralph D. Christy and Lionel Williamson, eds., *A Century of Service: Land-Grant Colleges and Universities, 1890–1990* (New Brunswick, NJ: Transaction Publishers, 1992).

2. See Neyland, *Historically Black Land-Grant Institutions*, 77–93.

3. Ibid.

4. John W. Davis, *Land-Grant Colleges for Negroes* (Institute: West Virginia State College Bulletin, Series 21, Number 5, April 1934), 12.

5. Rufus B. Atwood, "Agriculture in the Negro Land Grant College," *Conference of Presidents of Negro Land Grant Colleges, Proceedings* 13 (November 1935): 41–46. See also Davis, *Land-Grant Colleges for Negroes.*

6. Erwin Henry Shinn, "Professional Training for Negro Extension Work," *Conference of Presidents of Negro Land Grant Colleges, Proceedings* 13 (November 1935): 27–37.

7. F. D. Bluford, "What Part Should the Negro Land Grant Colleges Play in Soil Conservation?" *Conference of Presidents of Land Grant Colleges, Proceedings* 15 (November 1937): 64–67.

8. Arthur Howe, "New Fields of Opportunity and How the Land Grant Colleges Can Meet Them," *Southern Workman* 67, no. 2 (February 1938): 37–44.

9. John W. Davis, "Negro Land Grant Colleges," *School and Society* 47, no. 1213 (March 26, 1938): 44–413.

10. Benjamin F. Huebert, "The Role of the Small Southern Farm in the Future Land Utilization Program," *Opportunity* 11, no. 9 (September 1933): 264–68.

11. J. B. Watson, "Ways and Means of Relief for Farm Tenancy," *Conference of Presidents of Negro Land Grant Colleges, Proceedings* 15 (November 1937): 53–56.

12. Issac Fisher, "Conferences of Presidents of Negro Land-Grants Colleges," *Proceedings of the Annual Conferences of the Presidents of Negro Land-Grant Colleges, 1932–1933 and 1935–1938* (November 1938): 52–56.

13. George F. Hudson, "Educational Implications of the Farm Credit Administration," *Conference of Presidents of Negro Land-Grant Colleges, Proceedings* 16 (November 1938): 48–52.

14. Cully A. Cobb, "The Negro Farmer and the AAA," Addresses 1, Agricultural Adjustment Administration, Agricultural Conservation Program, Southern Region, Washington, DC, 1936.

15. Erwin Henry Shinn, "The Need for an Enlarged Program of Agricultural Extension Service in Negro Land-Grant Colleges," *Conference of Presidents of Negro Land-Grant Colleges, Proceedings* 16 (November 1938): 32–41.

16. "Aid to Negroes under FSA Rehabilitation Program," in handbook of labor statistics, 1941, *U.S. Bureau of Labor Statistics Bulletin* 694, no. 1 (1942): 599.

17. Ibid.

18. Ibid.

19. John R. Davis, "A Survey of Problems of the Negro under the New Deal," *Journal of Negro Education* 5, no. 1 (January 1936): 3–13.

20. "Aid to Negroes under FSA Rehabilitation Program," 599.

21. Neyland, *Historically Black Land-Grant Institutions,* 83.

22. "Statement of Presidents of Land-Grant Colleges for Negroes as presented to the Honorable Harry S. Truman, President of the United States, White House, Washington, DC, October 22, 1946." In *Historically Black Land-Grant Institutions and the*

Development of Agriculture and Economics, 1890–1990, Leedell W. Neyland (Tallahassee, FL: Florida A&M University Foundation, Inc., 1990): 83–84.

23. Neyland, *Historically Black Land-Grant Institutions*, 85.

24. *Proceedings of the Conference of the Presidents of Negro Land-Grant Colleges*, special session, Atlantic City, February 21–26, 1948: 103.

25. President R. B. Atwood, Kentucky State College and Secretary of the Conference, to President Lewis Webster Jones, President of the University of Arkansas, Fayetteville, November 8, 1949.

26. *Proceedings of the Conference of Presidents of Negro Land-Grant Colleges*, October 17–19, 1950, Frankfurt, Kentucky State College, 34. See also Neyland, *Historically Black Land-Grant Institutions*, 87.

27. Neyland, *Historically Black Land-Grant Institutions*, 87. According to the agreement between the TVA and the presidents of the selected Black land-grants, the TVA was responsible for taking care of the expenses associated with maintaining the office of the director, including the salary, travel, material, and supplies. The participating 1890 institutions had to contribute research personnel services, office space, supplies, and facilities. The effective date of this agreement's initiation was February 20, 1951, and it was scheduled to expire on February 20, 1953.

28. See US Census Bureau, *The Negro Farmer in US, Census of Agriculture, 1930* (Washington, DC: GPO, 1933); US Office of Education, *Negro Conference*, US Office of Education, Vocational Division, Miscellaneous Publication 2377 (Beltsville, MD: National Agricultural Library, 1940); United States Bureau of Agricultural Economics, *Farm Tenancy in Arkansas* (Washington, DC: GPO, 1941); United States Department of Agriculture, Office of Personnel, *The Negro, the USDA, and the Negro Land-Grant College* (Washington, DC: USDA, October 25, 1945); United States Extension Service, War Food Administration, *1940 Rural Farm Negro and Rural Negro Youth, Ages 10–19 and 4-H Club Negro Enrollment, Ages 10–20 for the Years, 1941–1944* (Washington, DC: Extension Service, 1945); United States Department of Agriculture, Office of Personnel, *Negro Employment in the USDA*, September 30, 1945–January 31, 1946 (Washington, DC: USDA, 1946); United States Farmers Home Administration, *How Supervised Credit Programs Help Negro Farm Families Better Live—As Shown by Reports of Articles from the Nation's Press* (Washington, DC: Farmers Home Administration, 1951); Arnold C. Anderson and Mary Jean Bowman, "Tenure Changes and the Agricultural Ladder in Southern Agriculture," *Kentucky Agricultural Experiment Station*, Bulletin 634, 1955; Nelson L. Leray and Wayne C. Rahrer, "Employment of Black Manpower in Calvert County, Maryland," *Maryland Experiment Station* Bulletin 467, March 1960; Nelson L. Leray, George Wilber, and Grady B. Crowe, "Plantation Organization and the Resident Labor Force, Delta Area, Mississippi," *Mississippi Agricultural Experiment Station*, Bulletin 606, October 1960; Leslie J. Silverman, *Follow-up of Project Uplift, the MDTA E & D Project Conducted by Florida A&M University, BSSR 369* (Washington, DC: Bureau of Social Science Research, July 1964, 1967); R. Steptoe and B. Clark, "The Plight of Rural Southern Blacks and Some Policy Implications," *Southern University*

A&M College Bulletin 55, July 1969: 21–35; US Commission on Civil Rights, *Equal Opportunity in Farm Programs: An Appraisal of Services Rendered by Agencies of the USDA* (Washington, DC: GPO, February 1965); US Commission on Civil Rights, Alabama State Advisory Committee, *The Agricultural Stabilization and Conservation Service in Alabama Black Belt* (Washington, DC: GPO, 1968).

29. John W. Davis, "The Negro Land-Grant College," *Journal of Negro Education* 2, no. 3 (July 1933): 312–28.

30. Neyland, *Historically Black Land-Grant Institutions*, 79.

31. "Conference of Presidents of Negro Land-Grants," *Proceedings*, 1939, University of Arkansas-Pine Bluff. See also Clyde L. Orr, "An Analytical Study of the Conference of Presidents of Negro Land-Grant Colleges" (unpublished dissertation, Lexington, KY: University of Kentucky, 1959) and Joel Schor, *Agriculture in the Black Land-Grant System to 1930* (Tallahassee: Florida A7M University, 1982).

32. Lewis Wade Jones, "Changing Status of the Negro in Southern Agriculture," *Tuskegee Institute Rural Life Information Series Bulletin*, June 3, 1950. See also William N. Elam, "Report of Conference of State Supervisors and Negro Teacher Trainers in Agricultural Education," US Office of Education, Vocational Division, Miscellaneous Publication 2377 (National Agricultural Library, Beltsville, Maryland, 1940).

33. "Conference of Presidents of Negro Land-Grants to the Honorable Henry A. Wallace, Secretary of Agriculture, Washington, DC," November 1935. Letter was presented while the presidents were holding their annual conference in Washington, DC. A copy of the letter exists in the archive of Kentucky State University Library, Frankfurt, Kentucky. See also Clyde L. Orr, "An Analytical Study of the Conference of Presidents of Negro Land-Grant Colleges" (unpublished dissertation, Lexington, KY: University of Kentucky, 1959). At the President of Negro Land-Grants Conference in Washington, DC, in 1935, where the letter that was to be delivered to Henry A. Wallace was read, conference participants discussed a number of critical needs. These included the need for more monetary and human resources as well as the desire of young people to have an organization that they could utilize as their own to learn more about vocational training. Research on new farm techniques, improved ways to conserve the soil, and farm diversification remained important discussions because Black farmers and the agents working with them wanted up-to-date information. Conference participants also discussed activities for New Farmers of America (NFA), which was organized in Tuskegee, Alabama in 1935 and became a national organization for African American young men. The NFA was a youth organization established with the support of the presidents of the Black land-grants to educate Black youth about vocational agriculture and the mechanical arts.

34. Neyland, *Historically Black Land-Grant Institutions*, 87–93.

35. "Closing Ranks on Poverty: Cooperatives Give New Hope to Poor People of the South," *Ebony* 26, no. 10 (August 1971): 86–90, 94–96.

36. United States Department of Agriculture, *Black Farmers in America, 1865–2000: The Pursuit of Independent Farming and the Role of Cooperatives* (Washington,

DC: USDA, Rural Cooperatives Service, RBS Research Report 194, 2003), 1–19.

37. Isabella C. Wilson, "Sickness and Medical Care among the Negro Population in a Delta Area of Arkansas," *Arkansas Agricultural Experiment Station*, Bulletin 372, March 1939.

38. Ibid.

39. W. L. Kennedy, "Opportunities in Dairying for Negro Farmers of North Carolina," *Journal of Dairy Science* 38 (November 1955): 1301–4.

40. Monroe N. Work, "Racial Factors and Economic Forces in Land Tenure in the South," *Social Forces* 15, no. 2 (December 1936): 205–15.

41. E. B. Evans, "What Do Negro Farmers Eat?" *Extension Service Review* 14, no. 3 (March 1943): 44.

42. Wilson, "Sickness and Medical Care among the Negro Population in a Delta Area of Arkansas."

43. "Communism and the Negro Tenant Farmer," *Opportunity* 9, no. 8 (August 1931): 234–35. Newspaper reporters indicated that some members of the white establishment characterized the action as social, while others called it political. Reports as well as newspaper and magazine articles discussed editorials that explained the cause of the outbreak of violence at places like Camp Hill, Alabama, as an attempt by Black sharecroppers to organize with the assistance of communists. This particular editorial argues that Blacks knew nothing about communist philosophy but assumed they did know about miserable wages, grinding work, debt, poor schools, forced labor, and peonage.

44. David Lewis Cohn, "Sharecropping in the Delta," *Atlantic Monthly* 159, no. 5 (May 1937): 579–88.

45. Gene Roberts, "Striking Negro Farmers Brace for Cold Weather," *New York Times*, November 17, 1965, p. 25, col. 1.

46. "Off the Land," *Nation* 204, no. 9 (February 27, 1967): 262.

47. Emmett Peter Jr., "On the Outside Looking Out," *New Republic* 152, no. 26 (June 26, 1965): 18.

48. William Payne, "Job Opportunity for Farm Agents," *Civil Rights Digest* 1, no. 3 (Fall 1968): 13–15.

49. James Peppler, "Commission on Hearing on Rural Poor Black Belt, Alabama," *Civil Rights Digest* 1, no. 2 (Summer 1968): 20–28.

50. Neyland, *Historically Black Land-Grant Institutions*, 147–89.

51. Quoted in ibid., 190.

52. For a discussion of the development of home economics at the seventeen Black land-grants, see C. Vincent, *Southern University and A&M College: Its Agricultural Development* (Baton Rouge: Southern University and A&M College, 1990); E. Fields, *Historical Profile of Home Economics Programs at 1890 Colleges/Universities* (Baton Rouge: Southern University and A&M College, Home Economics Unit, 1990); M. Furness, *Historical Profile of Home Economics Programs at 1890 Colleges/Universities* (Normal: Alabama A&M University, Division of Home Economics, 1990); R. D. Pace, *Historical*

Profile of Home Economics Programs at 1890s Colleges/Universities (Tuskegee, AL: Tuskegee University, Department of Home Economics, 1990); E. Noel, *Historical Profile of Home Economics Programs at 1890 Colleges and Universities* (Prairie View, TX: Prairie View A&M University, Department of Home Economics, 1990); H. Walston, *Historical Sketch: Kentucky State University* (Frankfort: Kentucky State University, Department of Home Economics, 1990); D. Conteh, *Historical Profile of Home Economics at 1890 Colleges/Universities* (Fort Valley, GA: Department of Home Economics, 1990); E. G. Neal, *Historical Profile of Home Economics at 1890 Colleges/Universities* (Pine Bluff: University of Arkansas, Department of Home Economics, 1990); M. W. McCray, *Historical Profile of Home Economics Programs at 1890 Colleges/Universities* (Petersburg: Virginia State University, Department of Human Ecology, 1990); R. Kellam, *Historical Profile of Home Economics at 1890 Colleges and Universities* (Langston, OK: Langston University, Department of Home Economics, 1990); E. W. Adams, *Historical Profile of Home Economics Programs at 1890 Colleges/Universities* (Dover: Delaware State College, Department of Home Economics, 1990); V. Caples, *A People and a Spirit Serving the Nations of the World* (Normal: Alabama A&M University, 1990); J. Smith Huam and E. Glover, *Historical Profile of Home Economics Programs at 1890 Colleges/Universities* (Lorman, MS: Alcorn State University Department of Home Economics, 1990); *Historical Profile of Home Economics Programs at 1890 Colleges/Universities* (Nashville: Tennessee State University, Department of Home Economics, 1990); W. Funchess, *Historical Profile of Home Economics at 1890 Colleges/Universities* (Orangeburg: South Carolina State College, Department of Home Economics, 1990); M. Kumelachew, *Historical Profile of Home Economics Programs at 1890 Colleges/Universities* (Princess Anne: University of Maryland Eastern Shore, Department of Human Ecology, 1990); and *Historical Profile of Home Economics Programs at 1890 Colleges/Universities* (Greensboro: North Carolina A&T, 1990).

53. Neyland, *Historically Black Land-Grant Institutions*, 110–19.

54. Ibid., 110–46.

55. James P. Davis, ed., *Success Stories: Negro Farmers*, 16 vols. (Little Rock, AR: US Production and Marketing Administration, Field Services Branch, 1948–1954).

56. "New Booker T. Washington: Cast His Buckets," *Ebony* 20, no. 3 (January 1965): 66–68, 70–71.

57. Roy Reed, "Negroes Start Communal Farm to Escape Mississippi Poverty," *New York Times*, July 25, 1966, p. 17, col. 1.

58. Warren Marr, "Self-Help in the Black Belt," *Crisis* 75, no. 8 (October 1968): 283–87.

59. James T. Wooten, "Black Muslims Would Sell Farm to Klan," *New York Times*, March 17, 1970, p. 32, col. 2.

60. "1000 Acre Tycoon: Former Georgia Sharecropper Finds Fortune in Cotton Ranching," *Ebony* 27, no. 9 (July 1972): 90–94, 96.

61. John Wicklein, "Group of Baptists Spurs Farm Plan," *New York Times*, March 15, 1967, p. 39, col. 2.

62. John D. Pomfret, "Farmers in South Study City Life," *New York Times*, September 22, 1963, p. 86, col. 1.

63. Neyland, *Historically Black Land-Grant Institutions*, 110–13.

64. See US Department of Agriculture, Civil Rights Action Team (CRAT), *Civil Rights at the U.S. Department of Agriculture* (Washington, DC: Government Printing Office, 1997). See also Valerie Grim, "Between Forty Acres and a Class Action Lawsuit: Black Farmers, Civil Rights, and Protest against the US Department of Agriculture, 1997–2010," in *Beyond Forty Acres and a Mule: African American Landowning Families since Reconstruction*, ed. Debra A. Reid and Evan P. Bennett (Gainesville: University Press of Florida, 2012), 271–96.

65. R. S. Browne, "Only Six Million Acres: The Decline of Black Owned Land in the Rural South" (New York: Black Economic Research Center, 1973).

66. Although the listening sessions created a forum for dialogue, none of them produced any real solutions to problems or answers to questions that affected Black farmers' ability to survive. But the USDA ordered CRAT to gather data, and plenty of it was found. Only a fraction of the findings from the oral testimonies from the twelve listening sessions was included in the February 1997 report the CRAT team prepared. But the report made possible a Black farmers' lawsuit because the CRAT team indicated discrimination had taken place and the USDA was liable. Overall, the report found little accountability within the USDA, especially in its local offices, and county officials who had allegedly discriminated against minority farmers went unpunished. See Pete Daniel, *Dispossession: Discrimination against African American Farmers in the Age of Civil Rights* (Chapel Hill: University of North Carolina Press, 2013).

67. See also Grim, "Between Forty Acres and a Class Action Lawsuit."

Part Two

From National to Local

Addressing land-grant colleges and universities as part of a "land-grant system" has become commonplace. There are numerous explanations for why this is so. The most common stems from the fact that since Washington is the source of most funding and legislation, a federally guided system must naturally result. The formation of all sorts of cooperative land-grant associations to embark upon concerted action nationwide is another indication of systemic action. Still another explanation targets the various programs and activities that engage land-grants. One of the premier methods to establish a new program or procedure is to adopt what is commonly called "best practices." Best practices is little more than land-grant universities copying one another; a program or procedure that worked well at one institution is thought to work well at all institutions. Land-grant universities are deemed so similar that such a transfer among them seems almost instinctive.

The truth is quite the opposite. The proliferation of cooperative and best practice groups as well as the creation of national commissions and the explosion of consultants truly undercut the reality of a comprehensive land-grant system. Indeed, these various homogenizing structures demonstrate just how tenuous the system has become; a flourishing system would not require mechanisms to foment common, consistent policies, practices, and activities. They would arise organically and no mechanisms would be needed to spur their introduction and dissemination.

In reality, the land-grant system has long since collapsed. Inaugurated by passage of the Hatch Act and the creation of the Association of American Agricultural Colleges and Experiment Stations in 1887 and the elevation of the USDA to cabinet status two years later, the system flourished until at least the 1950s. It has been under assault since that time. Localities and state clients have moved decisively to reexert control over their precious institutions. The federal government has been increasingly reticent to provide money for a wide range of new national tasks. In many cases, Washington has labored hard to cut back funding for established programs, even as powerful lobbying groups plea for the status quo. A rise in pork barrel spending has been a consequence. Congress has proven willing to designate special funding to individual land-grants to accomplish a mission of predominantly local interest. This allows Washington to reward certain interests and places while decreasing appropriations overall. The result has been striking. Land-grants now have significantly less in common substantively with each other than they had a hundred years ago.

4

The Evolution of a Public Research System

The Economic Research Service and the Land-Grant Universities

ANNE B. EFFLAND

The federal government originally expanded its control over agricultural research through an almost painless means. It enacted legislation that gave experiment stations and land-grant colleges new privileges and duties and provided funding to implement those new activities. Almost always the money came directly from the United States Department of Agriculture (USDA); the USDA served as the federal agency that coordinated the new tasks. Its assumption of new responsibilities indirectly caused the centralization of established tasks. The department naturally accrued under its umbrella activities previously held by individual land-grants and stations.

The establishment of the Bureau of Agricultural Economics in 1922 was a milestone in the federal agricultural research effort. The agency used economics to predict and plan the agricultural future. Its scientists rotated between the land-grants and the USDA; the same people served both, although not at the same time. The reorganization of USDA agencies in 1953 interrupted federal leadership of agricultural economics research, while at the same time further centralizing federal control of research in the agricultural sciences. The establishment of the Agricultural Research Service consolidated all agricultural science research into one large agency of the USDA. The agency was to provide central oversight and guide virtually all public agricultural science research undertaken in America, while public agricultural economics research became progressively more decentralized.

Effland's essay documents, from the perspective of Washington, why and how that model of grand synthesis crumbled and ultimately collapsed for agricultural economics research.[1]

✱✱✱

On April 8, 1983, almost twenty-two years to the day since its founding, the Economic Research Service of the USDA ended its longstanding field office system. That system had linked the agency to the land-grant college and university system through a network of researchers working in positions located in state agricultural experiment stations, agricultural economics departments, and other colocated field research institutions. The field office system dated back to the 1920s, when it was organized under the first agricultural economics research agency in USDA, the Bureau of Agricultural Economics. The closing of the field offices represented a break in a long-established research relationship and an evolution in the structure of the public agricultural economics research system. Many factors played into this evolution—the maturing of the agricultural economics discipline, the growth of the land-grant universities, and increasing federal budget pressures—but central to the transformation was a changing vision of the appropriate roles of the federal and state institutions that make up the public agricultural economics research system.

The USDA and the land-grant university system are linked through a network of formal and informal relationships. Although the land-grant universities are independent state-based institutions, they have been formally linked to the national USDA research system for most of their history. As early as 1885, before the department had achieved cabinet status, Commissioner of Agriculture Norman J. Colman spearheaded a joint effort with the state land-grant colleges and experiment stations to promote cooperation between the USDA and the colleges and to secure federal funding for the state experiment stations. In the view of Colman and many state leaders, collaboration among the growing scientific research programs of the colleges, experiment stations, and the USDA promised a rapid expansion in the nation's agricultural research. The passage of the Hatch Act in 1887 secured financial support for the experiment stations, and the creation of the Office of Experiment Stations in the USDA in 1888 established the department as the national hub for sharing research plans and results among the participants in the new federal-state research system.[2]

In 1906, the Adams Act doubled the funding to the state experiment stations while increasing the USDA's supervision of funded projects, and in 1925, the Purnell Act again increased funding and authorized support for economic, sociological, and home economics research at the state experiment stations. The Purnell Act expanded the federal-state research relationship into new areas that were already becoming established within the land-grant and federal research communities. Agricultural economics research at the state experiment stations expanded from 234 projects in 36 states at a cost of $353,839 in 1924–25, prior to the Purnell Act, to 332 projects in 46 states with expenditures of $608,000 in the first year of the act. Within another year spending had increased to $768,781 and over 90 percent of agricultural economics research at the state experiment stations was funded by the Purnell Act.[3]

The Research and Marketing Act of 1946 expanded federal research support yet again, this time establishing a formula that divided available funding according to each state's share of the total US rural and farm population. It also directed funding into research in the areas of marketing and distribution and added a system of regional research committees to fund projects with an explicit regional focus. Following the reorganization of the USDA's research bureaus into the Agricultural Research Service in 1953, amendments to the Hatch Act in 1955 consolidated the research expansions under the Purnell Act and the Research and Marketing Act under a single law governing federal support for state land-grant and experiment station research.[4]

Parallel to this growing funding relationship between the USDA and the land-grants has been the development of a system of field offices within the research agencies of the USDA. The scientific bureaus and research services built a widespread network of field research stations frequently colocated with the land-grant colleges and universities and linked directly to university programs through graduate student funding and cooperative research with faculty. Among the earliest of these were the regional research laboratories established under the 1935 Bankhead-Jones Act. Nine laboratories were established—most colocated with already existing state experiment stations—in South Carolina, Pennsylvania, Illinois, Iowa, Idaho, Alabama, Michigan, California, and New York. In the area of agricultural economics, however, the field office system was established earlier. Even before the Purnell Act had expanded USDA funding for the state experiment stations to include economics and other social sciences, field offices for agricultural economics research came into being as part of the new Bureau of Agricultural Economics in 1922. The BAE's field office system continued the local-national partnership that characterized the early development of farm management and rural organization in the USDA.[5]

The Department of Agriculture began some early research in the area of farm management, marketing, and rural organizations in the first decades of the twentieth century. Paralleling the approach of leaders in the early development of the physical agricultural sciences, early leaders in developing the fields of agricultural economics and rural sociology worked in both the land-grant system and the USDA. Land-grant and government scientists moved relatively freely between the university and federal research settings in developing their new disciplines and fields of research. In the area of farm management, a precursor to agricultural economics, W. J. Spillman, a USDA agronomist investigating grass and forage plants, began studying farm production and financial practices on successful farms in 1901, which led to the establishment of the USDA Office of Farm Management in 1905. Headed by Spillman, the Office of Farm Management continued to study and demonstrate efficient farm management practices on both private farms and USDA-operated demonstration farms. They began an extension program in 1911 that worked through the state land-grant colleges to educate farmers about newly developed and tested farm production and management practices.[6]

At the same time, Professor Henry C. Taylor at the University of Wisconsin was developing the field of agricultural economics, for which he wrote the first textbook in 1905,[7] and sending students to the USDA's Office of Farm Management. He moved into leadership positions in the department, heading the Office of Farm Management and Farm Economics in 1919 and the newly formed Bureau of Markets and Crop Estimates in 1921. In 1922, he became the chief of the new Bureau of Agricultural Economics, which he had been instrumental in organizing. He remained for only a few years, until 1925, when he was replaced by another land-grant professor, Thomas Cooper, dean of the College of Agriculture and director of the Agricultural Experiment Station at the University of Kentucky.[8]

The BAE, in a sense, was a product of the land-grant university system. Key land-grant university leaders in the emerging field of agricultural economics—particularly Taylor, George F. Warren of Cornell University, John D. Black of the University of Minnesota (and later Harvard University), and Theodore W. Schultz of Iowa State College (and later University of Chicago)—played an essential role in the organization and then in the leadership of a bureau dedicated to economics work in the Department of Agriculture. These and other leaders of the BAE trained in the land-grant universities and alternately held positions in the BAE and on land-grant faculties. Their developmental work on price estimation, market outlook, farm management, and land economics, among other topics, was the cooperative result of work at the land-grant universities and in the BAE, and interactions between the BAE and the land-grants led to mutual development of agricultural economics work in the universities and in the Department of Agriculture. Individuals moved relatively frequently between faculty positions and service at the USDA, and there appears to have been close professional relationships among university and BAE field staff working at experiment stations and university departments.[9]

During the years in which the BAE was active, most farms were relatively small and disadvantaged economically. The BAE's purpose included both pursuing research that could help reduce the disadvantages of the agricultural sector through better policies and helping the operators of these many small farms adjust to the economic changes around them by developing effective means for getting information about agricultural markets and farm management to individual farmers. The BAE worked closely with the land-grant universities in both of these areas. It was established with 148 field offices employing 936 staff, comparable to the 990 staff in the Washington headquarters office. Most of the early field offices were responsible for inspection and regulatory activities, but many were also actively engaged in joint research with university economics departments and experiment station staff, especially after passage of the Purnell Act in 1925.[10]

Other types of field work were added to the BAE's responsibilities throughout the 1930s, beginning with the transfer of the Farm Security Administration's land utilization work to the BAE in 1937. To facilitate this work, the BAE established a regional office system. The field staff expanded markedly in 1939 when the Program Planning Division of the Agricultural Adjustment Administration was transferred to the BAE as the Division of State and Local Planning. These state- and county-level offices conducted land-utilization studies and established community-level agricultural and land-use planning programs. Renamed the Agricultural Planning Field Service in February 1942, this program was discontinued by July of that year as Congress moved to end the BAE's involvement in local planning activities. By June 1946, the regional offices were closed.[11]

BAE economists helped strengthen university research and analytical capabilities, and universities trained new generations of agricultural economists with expertise in farm management and economic adjustment. Through the field offices, BAE economists also gathered information on conditions at the local and regional levels that supported the analysis of national-level problems. After a reorganization in 1947 that moved the technical assistance work in marketing and transportation to the Production and Marketing Administration, each of the four divisions of the new agency incorporated at least some field offices. The assistant chief for Production Economics managed field staff in two divisions—Land Economics and Farm Management and Costs. The assistant chief for Prices and Marketing managed a field staff in the Marketing and Transportation division. The assistant chief for Farm Population managed a field staff for both its divisions—Special Surveys and Farm Population and Rural Welfare. The assistant chief for Agricultural Estimates managed field staff in forty-one state offices, the Chicago Dairy Office, and research laboratories in Ames, Iowa, and Raleigh, North Carolina. These offices contributed to all six divisions of the agricultural estimates work—Statistics, Field Crops, Fruit and Vegetables, Livestock and Poultry, Dairy, Agricultural Prices, and Special Farm Statistics. This combination of local and national fed the development of a strong network of analytical capacity on the agricultural economic questions that could meet a range of informational needs of producers and policymakers.[12]

The BAE story is much better known to historians than is that of the Economic Research Service (ERS), so there is no need to dwell too long on it. But it is important to the story of the ERS and the land-grant universities to establish that the BAE's history was one of leadership and close relationships with the land-grant system in developing the new field of agricultural economics. Through a shared cast of characters coming and going from Washington and a formal institutional structure that colocated BAE staff with university departments and research stations in the field, the BAE maintained a strong central role in coordinating agricultural economics research. That role reached its peak during the agency's years as formal policy coordinator for the USDA, when the regional office structure played a critical part in facilitating the land-use planning fieldwork from 1937 to 1946.[13]

When the BAE was disbanded in 1953 as part of a wider USDA reorganization of the research bureau system, the centralized leadership of economics research in the USDA ended. BAE staff working on farm management, land economics, and agricultural finance were assigned to the new Agricultural Research Service (ARS). Those working on marketing and transportation and on rural population and communities were assigned to the new Agricultural Marketing Service (AMS). The educational, field office, and cooperative research systems continued as before, with the ARS and AMS managing their portions of the field office system according to different models—the ARS used a decentralized, topically oriented management system, while the AMS managed all field offices out of its area administrative offices. Without the central core of leadership the BAE had provided, university links with the field offices became stronger and research work was less coordinated nationally. Within the wider reorganization, the ARS was assigned to the Federal-States Relations group, along with the Forest Service, Soil Conservation Service, Federal Extension Service, Agricultural Conservation Program Service, and Farmer Cooperative Service, all of which operated extensive field systems, though not all in conjunction with the land-grant university system. The AMS moved into the Marketing and Foreign Agriculture group with the Foreign Agricultural Service and Commodity Exchange Authority, neither of which operated field offices, at least in the United States.[14]

For the February 1954 issue of its professional journal, the *Journal of Farm Economics*, the American Farm Economic Association commissioned a group of agricultural economists to comment on the recent reorganization of the USDA that included the breakup of the BAE. O. V. Wells, the last chief of the BAE and the new director of the AMS, provided a rationale for the changes that focused on the intention of the Secretary of Agriculture to focus the work of the USDA along the lines of problem areas, rather than disciplines. Wells suggested that the new organization offered more opportunities for agricultural economists to apply themselves directly to broader problems and to work with teams of scientists and program staff to solve agricultural problems. He went on to suggest that "the reorganization does place some greater responsibility upon the Departments of Agricultural Economics in the land-grant colleges and universities and upon the American Farm Economic Association for defining and maintaining the integral character of agricultural economics than has been the case over most of the time since the Bureau of Agricultural Economics was organized."[15]

Other contributors to the roundtable, including former USDA and BAE leaders Paul Appleby, H. C. Taylor, Howard Tolley, and university economists Raymond Penn and Theodore Schultz, disputed the value of dividing the USDA's agricultural economists along program lines. Among their concerns, the likelihood that action program demands would force short-term analysis to overshadow long-term, fundamental research priorities weighed most heavily. But concerns about the ability of the land-grant system to replace the disciplinary leadership and policy research provided by the BAE also ranked high, as did concerns about the potential deterioration in the quality of economists willing to work in the USDA without the kind of prestige that had accompanied the BAE's reputation within the discipline. In effect, the reorganization removed the central, independent source of economics information and policy analysis that previous secretaries had relied on for background and context for policy decisions.[16]

According to both historians and economists who worked in Washington and in the field, however, the separation from the central planning and policy work of the department created by the reorganization actually allowed the USDA's economics staff to refocus on more fundamental farm economics research and applications. And while leaders in agricultural economics expressed worries about the loss of a well-regarded centralized economics research institution in Washington, the links between the new economics divisions within the ARS and AMS and the land-grant departments continued essentially unchanged. The USDA supported the field offices, opportunities for graduate education, and cooperative research projects that had begun under the BAE. The regional research councils established under the Research and Marketing Act continued to operate as part of the responsibility of the ARS director, although they also funded projects in the areas of work relocated to the AMS. And the land-grant universities did experience a period of growth and expanding research capacity in the 1950s and 1960s that allowed them to take on a stronger role in leading the discipline.[17]

The election of John F. Kennedy in 1960 ushered in a period of renewed belief in an activist federal government. Kennedy's campaign farm policy advisor, Willard Cochrane, an agricultural economist from the University of Minnesota, believed this approach required a strong analytical capability within the federal bureaucracy that could provide the kind of intelligence needed for effective policymaking. For the USDA, that meant, in Cochrane's vision, reestablishing a single agricultural economics research agency in the USDA, along the lines of the BAE. Kennedy's secretary of agriculture, Orville Freeman, tapped Cochrane to bring this new agency into being and established the Economic Research Service in 1961 by drawing back together most of the divisions of the former BAE that had been moved to the ARS and AMS, with the addition of the international economic analysis work from the Foreign Agricultural Service (FAS). Instead of becoming part of the ERS, the statistical work of the former BAE formed the core of the Statistical Reporting Service (SRS). In a key bureaucratic change from the BAE, the reorganization placed some distance between the ERS and the secretary, to protect the research function from too-close identification with the administration's policy choices. The use of the BAE to implement the agricultural planning policies of Franklin Roosevelt's New Deal contributed to the political hostility that led to its demise. To guard against that possibility, the ERS and SRS became twin services under the director of Agricultural Economics, similar to the organization of other areas of work in the USDA. The Staff Economists Group rounded out the organizational unit, providing policy-oriented economic advice directly to the secretary and in effect serving as a buffer between the economic analysis carried out by the ERS and the policy decisions made by the secretary.[18]

With the security of being removed from direct policy deliberations, the ERS could move forward with a broad mission of research to support the expanding policy responsibilities of the USDA. The ERS's work included the traditional production economics and marketing research that had been the core focus of economics research in the department since even before the BAE, as well as expanded research on rural development and natural resources and research in new areas like food and international development. The ERS's early leaders, particularly Cochrane and the first ERS administrator, Nathan Koffsky, envisioned an agency focused on national and international policy issues of immediate concern. They recognized the necessity of supporting long-term basic research that undergirded the short-term analysis, but their emphasis, especially Cochrane's, was on the ERS's capacity to provide economic intelligence as needed to its constituents—the secretary of agriculture, Congress, and the wider public—to be "a staff agency to the Nation," in Cochrane's words.[19]

Cochrane and Koffsky believed that the quality of economic research would improve with the intellectual interaction resulting from reconsolidating the various branches of economic research that were formerly part of the BAE. As noted earlier, economists who opposed the breakup of the BAE had expressed concerns about the effects on staff and the department's ability to retain high-quality researchers and recruit newly trained agricultural economists. In Cochrane's view, "The *esprit de corps* of the dispersed economic workers in USDA, as of January 1, 1961, was at a low ebb and we knew that morale would be raised by bringing them together into one agency that understood and appreciated their efforts."[20]

At the same time, they believed that a reconsolidated economics research agency would need to work hard to persuade Congress and the public that it was worth what it cost. As O. V. Wells had noted in 1953, securing funds for economics research on its own could be difficult, and his experience of the near doubling of his budget for marketing research after it became part of the AMS seems to support that view. ERS budgets were relatively flat through the 1960s, providing sufficient additions to meet salary increases but rarely offering additional funds for new areas of research or additional staff. Cochrane and Koffsky understood that much of the work of the agency would need to be clearly useful for solving immediate problems. In their view, the more the agency focused on applied research with direct applications to current policy questions, the longer it was likely to survive under congressional scrutiny. It had no natural constituency to support it politically and thus would always be a potential target for budget cutting.[21]

This emphasis among the ERS's leaders on a clear, nationally focused mission and an orientation to provide short-term economic intelligence to policymakers placed the field office system, and thus the agency's relationship with the land-grant universities, under pressure almost from the beginning. As early as 1963, the Economics Research Advisory Committee (in operation since the 1953 reorganization of the USDA) recommended "a division of labor in economics research" among the ERS, the land-grant colleges and universities, and the private sector. Made up of fourteen members—five from the land-grants, five from the private sector, an agricultural journalist, and three USDA economics and research managers (Cochrane, Koffsky, and James F. Lankford, ARS research coordinator)—the committee suggested that the ERS should function "as a national intelligence center for agriculture."[22]

Soon after, however, an internal group tasked with examining the ERS's work with other agencies concluded that the ERS had a responsibility to work with the land-grant colleges and other state agencies to develop economic intelligence and was "in a unique position to lead in guiding and coordinating economic research." In their examination, they also considered the role of field offices and concluded that they had the potential to improve research coordination, responsiveness to local and regional needs, and opportunities to recruit and retain personnel. The group noted that the university setting often provided "a better research environment" than could be found in Washington. They recommended that a task force be formed to more carefully examine the field office structure with an eye to improving their effectiveness in these areas and their management. A group of field staff also had an opportunity to submit recommendations, the main thrust of which was the need to improve communication and exchange between field and headquarters staff, including a greater role for field staff in planning research, but without eliminating field staff's ability to independently pursue relevant research at their field sites.[23]

Acknowledging the strength of the field office system but noting the internal management problems inherent in focusing the work of so many different field locations on evolving national and regional priorities, Koffsky returned again in 1965 to the question of how best to organize and administer the ERS's field offices and to balance the work of the ERS and its university cooperators. Koffsky tasked his management team with examining a wide range of program issues at the ERS, including the field office structure and relations with other agencies and the land-grant colleges and universities. Koffsky's Program Evaluation Committee, after gathering specific details of the field structure and the work done by field staff, concluded that the ERS field office system "presents many difficult problems" and that it was "in need of an overhaul."[24]

While the committee's recommendations did not detail their assessment of these problems, their recommended solutions made clear that the problems revolved around effective headquarters management of field offices. The committee's subtask force on field offices suggested a number of possible steps that could be taken individually or severally, all of which tended toward more centralized supervision of the field system and a reduction of the number of field offices by concentrating and refocusing them as "centers of excellence" dedicated to major priority research efforts. They further revealed their critiques of the field office structure as it was then organized by describing their assessment of the strengths of concentration. Most important, they believed that concentrating resources on "an organized, balanced, regional, and national attack on specific problems" would avoid "diffusing these resources throughout the universe of problems." They also cited the ability of such a system to support prioritization of research problems, reduce duplication, allow for an efficient distribution of expertise, and facilitate the planning and evaluation of research programs.[25]

The subtask force acknowledged the need to consider relations with the land-grant colleges and universities carefully in this potential reorganization.

Another subcommittee had been tasked with evaluating ERS relationships with cooperators, including the state experiment stations and university agricultural economics departments. They had concluded that relationships with university cooperators were very good but "could be quickly upset if our present field staff arrangements are changed drastically." They recommended that these relationships be carefully considered in any decisions regarding the reorganization of the field offices.[26]

Koffsky responded with an agency-wide memorandum accepting the recommendations of both subcommittees. He made clear his intention to attempt to refocus the field office system on concentrated "operational centers" by requesting each division director to identify which current locations might be best suited for development into such centers. At the same time, however, he requested that directors indicate which offices primarily served university-based training and recruitment of new staff; which currently operated as effective "research and service" locations, presumably with long-term regional projects best addressed in cooperation with their university or other partners; and which were located with cooperators who might be willing to take over the work of the ERS field staff. Koffsky's memorandum made clear that he recognized the need to maintain good relations with cooperating agencies and universities and acknowledged that there could be cases in which more than one field office continued to operate as satellite "points" associated with the new concentrated centers. But he also revealed his long-term view of the evolution of the ERS's research organization, asserting that "The time is approaching when the staff of the Service must further concentrate its people and facilities to improve the quality of its research product, to reduce further the fragmentation of research efforts both in Washington and in the field, and to more effectively mobilize our people, in concert with our cooperating agencies, for more effective research."[27]

At the core of these efforts were two separate visions of how the work of the ERS and university economists should be oriented. From the early days of the BAE, before university agricultural economics departments and the agricultural economics research profession had consolidated a secure role, BAE research economists and rural sociologists led the way in developing the data, research questions, and mathematically based methods that built the reputation of these disciplines and pioneered the application of economics and other social sciences to public policy. Their integration with the land-grants and other universities, through rotating appointments in government and in teaching and research in the emerging academic departments in agricultural economics and rural sociology, built an integrated profession, without a highly developed distinction in the type of work pursued in the two locations.

But as the profession, and the civil service, developed during the mid-twentieth century and government budgets at the federal level in particular began to constrict, questions about the appropriate "division of labor between USDA and university economists," to quote Willard Cochrane, came to the fore.[28]

Cochrane's vision, expressed in a 1965 article in the *Journal of Farm Economics* after his return to his academic position, divided the work between Washington and the universities on the basis of "economic intelligence" and "creative analysis." In a view shared by other leaders in the reorganization of agricultural economics work in the USDA in the 1950s and 1960s, including Don Paarlberg and John Schnittker, the comparative advantage of USDA economists was in analyzing the "constant inflow of basic economic intelligence regarding crops, prices, incomes, production, stocks" and collecting the "necessary data to formulate the many alternative program mechanics and crank through the quantitative results." The comparative advantage of university economists was in "creative analysis and methodological studies that take time, involve new relationships and methods and lead to needed new and improved estimates," as well as in "constructive criticism" of USDA analyses from their more politically separated vantage point and outreach to farmers and the public to explain policy problems and "the economic and social consequences of different general approaches to these problems."[29]

The opposing vision, held by USDA economists, saw a more integrated research profession. Described in a pair of responses to Cochrane's article, proponents of a more integrated approach remembered the significant research contributions of USDA economists in the BAE and in the years before the ERS. They suggested that Cochrane, Paarlberg, and Schnittker, all of whom had held high-level management and advisory positions as economists in the USDA, proposed an unworkable, unrealistic division, failing to note the political pitfalls of associating ERS research with political objectives and the absolute necessity that USDA economists engage in creative thinking in their work. One of these proponents, Fred Waugh, a well-respected research economist in the ERS, summed up his opposition to Cochrane's views in the following question: "Should universities have a monopoly on brains?"[30] Waugh, whose methodological and program-related research as a USDA economist had achieved acclaim throughout the profession, suggested there was "an obvious alternative" division of labor: national-level researchers should attend to national- and international-level problems and state-level researchers should attend to state and local problems. In fact, however, he indicated that his own view was that no division of labor was required.[31]

An ERS examination of publicly supported economic research in agricultural marketing suggested, however, that the idea of university economists, especially land-grant university economists, actually focusing their work exclusively on state, rather than regional or even national, economic problems was unrealistic. According to the unidentified author of this report, the agricultural economy had become so interdependent that almost no research could be limited to a single state, recommending instead a natural division along the lines of subsectors of that economy—presumably commodity groups and regional production and marketing areas. The author did suggest, however, a different natural division of labor between economists in Washington and the states related to the political constraints on research. In some cases, USDA economists might not be legally allowed to produce research that might contradict the official position of the US government (e.g., in the case of legal proceedings on regulatory actions); in these situations, university economists could provide the needed research. Similarly, in cases where research at the state level might run into local political opposition, USDA economists at the national level, or even university economists from other states, would be better placed to pursue that work.[32]

Meanwhile, as these program evaluations and disciplinary debates considered the larger questions, university relations continued in much the same fashion for those in the field and within the cooperative regional research structure as they had during the years in which the department's economic research was carried out under the ARS and AMS. Secretary Freeman had acknowledged prominently in his announcement of the reorganization of agricultural economics work in the department that the USDA worked cooperatively with the state departments of agriculture and land-grant colleges and universities in carrying out this work. According to that announcement, field staff made up nearly half of the new agency's workforce when the ERS was established in 1961, 800 of the total staff of 1,800. A 1965 inventory identified about 200 professional field staff associated with the three main ERS research divisions—Marketing Economics, Farm Production Economics, and Resource Development Economics. They were located in thirty-nine states, most colocated with land-grant universities, with additional staff in the Economics and Statistical Analysis Division located in several of the same locations.[33]

In keeping with the ERS vision that field staff should work on regional or at least multistate issues, most of the work carried out in these field stations focused on regional- or national-level research. The Marketing Economics Division fielded thirty-seven economists in twenty-three locations during 1965—four at the ARS Regional Utilization Laboratories in Pennsylvania, Illinois, Louisiana, and California and the remainder at land-grant universities, some as regional research leaders, some as part-time graduate students, and the others conducting joint research with land-grant university faculty. Their research focused on marketing problems of such key regional commodities as cotton, livestock, dairy, vegetables, and eggs. The majority of field research in the Farm Production Economics Division was part of the regional and national adjustment studies coordinated through the regional research committees and nationally by the ERS. Field station economists at the University of New Hampshire and University of Minnesota, for example, coordinated the regional dairy adjustment studies in the Northeast and Great Lake states, while those at Purdue University, Texas A&M University, Montana State University, and Oregon State University coordinated regional livestock studies.[34]

The Resource Development Economics Division operated its field offices through its branch structure, with field staff working on area economic development projects in Appalachia through regional research centers at state experiment stations at West Virginia University, Pennsylvania State University, Cornell University, and the Virginia Polytechnic Institute. Similar projects operated in the Ozarks, the Great Lake states, and the Southeast, headquartered at the state experiment stations in those regions. The Land and Water Branch operated similarly through regional research centers and state universities already specializing in land and water utilization, tenure and legal issues, income distribution, and urban expansion. Field work under the River Basin and Watershed Branch operated slightly differently, since it involved cooperation not only with the land-grant universities but also with other state and federal government agencies, including the Soil Conservation Service and the ARS. Five field sections (headquartered at Logan, Utah; Stillwater, Oklahoma; East Lansing, Michigan; Little Rock, Arkansas; and Upper Darby, Pennsylvania) carried out economic research and planning activities for river basin and watershed development and conservation programs.[35]

Many of these field offices retained staff who had been in place prior to the establishment of the ERS, as well as research programs that had been in existence prior to 1961. In 1965, a little over one-fourth of field office staff had been working at their field locations since before 1961. Most had been in place in the mid-1950s, but some had worked in field locations since the offices had been part of the BAE; one USDA economist had been at the field office at the University of California-Berkeley since before the establishment of the BAE. Although ERS staff at field offices had specific subject-area assignments and were officially managed by headquarters staff, in most cases they were fully integrated into the university research system. They frequently participated in joint research with university faculty and experiment station staff, publishing a great deal of their work jointly with their university colleagues through the experiment stations and sometimes the state departments of agriculture, rather than through the ERS. ERS field staff appreciated the academic working environment and opportunities for teaching and cross-disciplinary research with physical scientists that were possible in the university setting. Moreover, as one ERS manager noted, "We have found that working jointly with a land-grant college group who are well acquainted, interested, and enthusiastic about research of mutual interest that much more can be accomplished than working as a separate body."[36]

Many at headquarters also valued the field office system and its role in maintaining close relationships between the ERS and the land-grant system. ERS field offices provided funding to help support graduate students, employment opportunities for students after completing their degrees; close collaborative research relationships between the ERS and university faculty and experiment station research staffs; skilled economic analysis of local, state, and regional agricultural issues; and a rich source of local, state, and regional economic information to contribute to the national work going on in Washington. In fact, funding for field offices and regionally based research increased during the 1960s and 1970s, in part because of rising interest in rural economic development and natural resources, though much of this funding came through the transfer of funds from other USDA agencies for specific projects. Transfer funding varied from year to year (supporting, for example, 56 full-time equivalents in 1965, 123 in 1968, and 80 in 1972), which created challenges for ERS planning and research programs, but both initiatives also expanded ERS research into new areas of policy interest that enhanced the ERS's reputation beyond traditional agriculture issues.[37]

To accommodate the new work, the former Resource Development Economics Division split into two new divisions—the Economic Development Division (EDD) and the Natural Resource Economics Division (NRED)—reflecting the new emphases. Both new divisions worked closely with the land-grant universities through the longstanding field structure, as well as through cooperative research locations shared with state-level USDA offices and the state departments of agriculture. Even in cases where ERS economists were not working specifically in the new areas, their presence at the land-grant universities provided a direct channel of communication between the ERS and the states about data and state-level activities in the new areas.[38]

Some of the pressure on the field offices also eased in the 1970s when an improved budget situation allowed the new administrator, Quentin West, to secure increased appropriations for the ERS. However, West also instituted a thorough review of the agency with an eye toward reorganization, in part with the intention of better integrating the field work through a newly popular management approach: "management by objective." A key change included eliminating the distinctions between field offices and Washington headquarters, with field staff organized together with other staff into "program areas." West centralized work planning and priorities and planned to reallocate staff as projects arose and were completed. The realignment assigned some program area leaders to locations outside Washington where field office facilities offered better support. In some respects, this reorganization built on the earlier "centers of excellence" idea, although in a much broader way that incorporated Washington headquarters as simply one of a number of potential center locations. West also explicitly adopted Waugh's vision of the natural research split between the ERS and the universities. An ERS mission statement drafted during West's 1972 review referred to "University Support" as one of eight ERS missions, and described its purpose as being "to foster continued development of university-based professionals and their institutions," with particular emphasis on "developing capability to analyze local and regional issues counterpart to national issues examined by ERS."[39]

West's program review offers a glimpse of the changing field structure, following nearly ten years after the initial reviews under Koffsky in 1963 and 1965. The total number of professional staff located in the field had risen to over three hundred, but most of that increase had been in NRED on work funded through the Soil Conservation Service river basin, watershed evaluation, and Resource Conservation & Development studies. Nearly two-thirds of the division's staff and two-thirds of its funding came from these cooperative programs. The NRED field offices were primarily colocated with other federal agencies cooperating in these studies, rather than in land-grant university economics departments, and SCS and other cooperating agencies jointly planned the use of these funds with the ERS. Land-grant institutions housed some of the data-processing facilities supporting water resources planning studies, however, and some staff working on ERS program research in the area of natural resources and environmental economics studies continued to share space and work cooperatively with the land-grant university faculty.[40]

Only twenty-two economists assigned to the EDD operated in the field in 1972, all as project managers on cooperative projects between the EDD and university staff. Plans called for an increase to thirty field staff by 1974, operating cooperatively on five major projects across the division and in direct cooperation with Washington economists on joint projects. The Marketing Economics Division maintained a field staff of thirty-six professionals, virtually the same number as in 1965 but distributed somewhat differently. The number assisting the ARS Regional Utilization Laboratories doubled from four to eight, as efforts to assist in the commercialization of new technologies and program planning received additional emphasis. Another five ERS field staff were assigned to ARS cotton laboratories facilities in South Carolina and Mississippi and a wheat laboratory in Kansas to conduct research on quality evaluation. Two other staff assisted with the Agricultural Stabilization and Conservation Service merchandising program in Kansas City, Missouri, and the remainder were located at land-grant universities pursuing relevant cooperative research with university faculty and in some cases pursuing graduate degrees funded by the ERS.[41]

Formerly the largest field staff, the sixty-nine field economists in the Farm Production Economics Division worked at thirty different locations, almost all land-grant university economics departments. Over the preceding decade, however, the research projects had moved from cooperatively funded joint work between ERS and university economists to a more parallel arrangement, with ERS economists paying a share of support staff and data-processing costs and working on related but separate research programs. ERS economists frequently continued to hold teaching positions and faculty privileges, however, and worked with graduate students on ERS-funded projects. An additional two field staff from the Economics and

Statistical Analysis Division worked in Denver as part of a seventeen-state cooperative livestock outlook and market information project.[42]

Only five years later, in 1977, budget pressures had returned and a new administration brought a critical eye to spending across the federal system. A new management system called "zero-base" budgeting upended years of foundational budgets that allowed traditional program areas to continue without much scrutiny—all spending was reviewed and all program areas and research projects examined for relevance and value. ERS field offices and relationships with university researchers fell under this new comprehensive review of spending. The new administration, in the person of Howard Hjort, economic advisor to Secretary of Agriculture Bob Bergland, supported the maintenance of good relations between the ERS and the land-grant universities, but he made it clear that the ERS had to be able to explain and justify how ERS staff in the field contributed to the agency's research and relevance. Hjort suggested, as West had done only a few years previously, that ERS staff needed to concentrate on national and international research questions, leaving state-level research to their university colleagues. He reestablished the Cochrane vision as well, reminding ERS managers that university research tended toward long-term problems, while ERS research required a shorter-term focus. Hjort viewed the offer of a link between these two approaches as one of the benefits of the ERS-university partnership, with each institution supporting the relevance of the other as long-term research informed short-term analysis and short-term analysis helped guide the identification of long-term issues.[43]

As part of this review of the ERS and its programs under the new administration, John Lee, director of the National Economic Analysis Division, prepared a study of the ERS's role and value to other public and private research organizations and federal program agencies. Addressing the relationship between the ERS and the land-grant university system, Lee recounted some of the history of the ERS and preceding BAE, ARS, and AMS field office systems, pointing out the change in the farm economy that reduced the need for the federal agricultural economics agency to focus on local- and farm-level management problems. He noted that university faculties and economics extension staff had increased in the 1950s, taking on a greater role in addressing local and regional farm problems. In response, and despite universities' continued requests for additional ERS field staff to assist in researching these regional and local problems, ERS field staff had been reallocated over the previous two decades to locations where its research on national policy issues could benefit from complementary strengths at land-grant universities.[44]

Lee's report referred to the idea of the ERS as "the economic intelligence arm"[45] of the federal government, echoing Willard Cochrane and other early supporters of the ERS's national orientation. He also emphasized the ability of the ERS to assemble large teams to tackle major research problems of national scope and at the same time to respond quickly to requests for economic analysis at the national policy level. Lee noted, however, the complementarity of university and ERS research and their shared responsibility for the further development of the agricultural economics discipline. As a result, he recommended that the ERS find an effective new way to combine the complementary expertise and resources of the ERS and the university system that recognized the changing budget and disciplinary context in which they both worked.[46]

Lee's analysis of the changed research context, which he completed before becoming administrator, reached the same conclusion advocated by previous ERS administrators and USDA directors of economics: the ERS's responsibilities lay in attending to research and policy issues at the national and international levels, with some attention to regional topics when those drove national policy. As in the past, this assessment directly threatened the allocation of staff to field offices, most of them at land-grant universities. By 1982, when Secretary of Agriculture John Block appointed John Lee the new ERS administrator, the tension between the field offices and headquarters had reached a critical point. The continued escalation of budget pressures as Lee began his tenure further strengthened his conviction that he would finally have to bring about the consolidation of the ERS as a Washington-based agency.[47]

Budget pressures had been building since the late 1970s but reached a critical point under the new Reagan administration. Until 1980, Congress had tightened budgets only by making smaller annual increases, allowing the ERS an essentially stable budget foundation after inflation. But real budget reductions followed the new administration's commitment to tackling federal spending. The ERS's inflation-adjusted budget fell by 20 percent between FY1979 and FY1983 and further reductions were expected. The ERS also lost $1.5 million in reimbursement income for programs in natural resources planning and rural economic development, and while the loss of $1.6 million in mandated pay increases helped meet budget reduction targets with fewer losses to non-salary expenses, it contributed to falling morale.[48]

Lee's reconceptualization of field work in the agency hinged on defining the field and Washington staff as a single entity. Under this conception, all staff worked for the agency and location assignments depended on the current research program. As the research program changed, ERS staff could expect to be relocated as needed—into or out of Washington—and to remain in their assigned locations temporarily as projects required. For university-based field locations, this new conception ended the idea of long-term regional research locations that remained in place and addressed regional research issues as they changed over time. It also entailed a stronger emphasis on cooperative arrangements with the university base—complementarities with university staff associated with specific research issues, clear research benefits for both parties, and identifiable synergies among ERS staff assigned to the same field location. No longer would ERS field staff be seen as a separate staff "type" with pro forma association with headquarters and expectations of continuing research relationships with university faculty over a career and across multiple project areas.[49]

At the same time John Lee was reevaluating ERS research priorities and its staffing structure, the US General Accounting Office (GAO) carried out a review of the ERS research program, examining both its fulfillment of its research mission and its role as a national leader in public agricultural economics research. At the core of this review was identifying the appropriate roles of the full range of participants in that public economics research system, including the land-grant universities. GAO investigators interviewed both current and former USDA officials as well as leading agricultural economists in the land-grant university system. The investigators began their analysis from the position that the ERS and the land-grant university departments of agricultural economics together composed a "US agricultural economics research and analysis system." Following its investigation, the GAO concluded that the ERS was failing in its responsibility to lead the planning and coordination of public research in agricultural economics for the nation.[50]

The GAO investigators interviewed a number of former managers of the ERS and the USDA economics research system, as well as leaders from the land-grant university system and the agricultural economics profession.[51] The GAO investigators also drew on the records of an ad hoc committee on ERS-University linkages that had been organized in August 1979. According to the GAO's report, both ERS and land-grant representatives on the committee had agreed that improved planning would be beneficial for identifying priority research areas. They had also agreed that the ERS should take a leadership role in this process but that specific projects should be planned, implemented, and funded jointly by both the ERS and the land-grant universities and include other agencies as appropriate.[52]

Four years later, however, the planning process had stalled. The former ERS administrator interviewed by the GAO investigators indicated that ERS efforts to formalize planning had been greeted with little interest by the land-grant universities. He believed that was the result of conflicting demands on their time and concerns about allowing the federal government to influence their research direction. He concluded that jointly identifying priority research areas as the ad hoc committee had begun to do might be possible, but actual planning to the level of identifying who would do which part of the work might be less likely. The land-grant university officials interviewed by the GAO recognized the importance of coordinated research planning to a more comprehensive coverage of agricultural economics research priorities and agreed that the ERS's national position made it the natural choice for leadership of such an effort. But they repeated the same concerns about allowing the USDA to "dictate" state university research. By the 1980s, land-grant universities' budgets matched or exceeded (in total) the budget of the ERS, making them "at least equal to that of ERS." The current ERS administrator interviewed by the GAO reinforced the reality of this perception, pointing out that the ERS was not a cooperative research agency like the Cooperative State Research Service and thus had no formal authority over land-grant university research activities. At best, the ERS could exert informal leadership by the use of persuasion in planning and coordination.[53]

A key finding in the GAO investigation was that the views of both the members of the ad hoc committee and other leaders in public agricultural economics research reflected an assumption that these two major research partners should be pursuing different types of work. Opinions varied, however, as to whether the differentiation should be between macroeconomic and microeconomic problems, national/international and local/regional problems, applied research and basic research, or service to national policymakers and service to state policymakers. In fact, both the ERS and the land-grant university departments pursued some of all of these types of research. Some members of the ad hoc committee suggested that rather than separating the areas of work between these two partners, clarifying their missions and roles would allow them "to more easily identify areas of mutual interest and facilitate productive cooperative activities."[54]

A number of experts consulted by the GAO expressed concern that the ERS's capacity for producing high-quality, long-term research had been sacrificed as pressures to respond to short-term staff work increased while staff numbers fell. Agricultural economists from the land-grant universities lamented this change, suggesting that the ERS should consider splitting the staff into two groups, one to focus on long-term, fundamental economics research and the other to focus on staff work. One economist even suggested dispersing the research program more broadly among other USDA agencies, although without removing that function from the ERS altogether. ERS field staff echoed these concerns and suggested as well that the emphasis between the two mission focuses varied with different administrations, making staffing choices difficult. Under different sets of priorities the ERS would want to hire more PhD economists to pursue fundamental research, but under others, they would want more economists with master's degrees to do staff analysis. Similarly, some priorities would require placing more staff in the field to pursue long-term research in cooperation with land-grant university faculty and experiment station staff, while other priorities would mean bringing more staff into headquarters to support increased levels of work there.[55]

The GAO study examined the ERS's field office structure as part of its investigation of the agency's relations with the land-grant universities. As with responses to questions about the mission of the ERS, views of federal administrators, land-grant university departments, and field and headquarters staff varied widely. Some believed the field offices enhanced cooperative work between the land-grants and the ERS; others thought the dispersion of staff away from headquarters weakened the agency's flexibility in responding to new research and policy priorities. The GAO noted that the role of field offices in the ERS had been an open question for most of the agency's existence and had been examined most recently in a series of regional conferences held with agency staff in 1979. The call for a clarification of research priorities and the role of field staff in meeting them had not yet been addressed by the time of the GAO study, four years later. No written policy regarding the role of field staff in the agency's future had been developed, but the gradual decline in the number of field offices and their dispersion were generally regarded as the result of an unwritten policy to phase out the field offices.[56]

In 1983, that unwritten policy became official policy. As part of a broader assessment of the ERS's mission and research program, John Lee outlined a new staff location and mobility policy that formalized his vision of a single Washington-based staff with the program and location flexibility to meet changing research priorities and staff development needs. The official policy fleshed out the details and finally brought certainty to what had been an open question for twenty years. After a two-year transition period, all ERS staff would be assigned to Washington, DC. Lee's policy allowed for temporary field assignments for specific time-limited projects approved by the administrator, which could never exceed three years, with the additional proviso that no staff could be approved for consecutive assignments that kept them from Washington for more than three years. Additionally, the long tradition of assigning staff to university locations to earn advanced degrees pursuing research of interest to ERS came to an end, although one-year relocations for specific, approved training opportunities remained an option. Lee explained in his memo to staff that the new policy had become necessary in the face of increasingly limited budgets. With a declining staff and reduced funding for data collection, travel, and other research support, ERS management could no longer afford to have staff resources more or less permanently allocated to field office locations and unavailable for assignment to urgent policy research demands. The ERS would focus instead on enhancing its working relationships with other agencies and with other parts of the public research system.[57]

A group of senior field staff expressed concern that ending the field office system would disrupt cooperative relationships with the land-grant universities and possibly lead to their unwillingness to work with the ERS in the future. Field staff who had worked outside Washington most or all of their careers, often at the same field location, valued their working relationships with university faculty and experiment station staff and believed their research had contributed to the development of national intelligence on the agricultural economy, natural resource use, and rural community problems. They feared a wholly Washington focus would distract the agency from continuing to invest in maintaining a close knowledge of conditions across the country. In their view, the development of national policy solutions to agricultural and rural problems depended on in-depth knowledge of those problems and of the implications of solutions in specific places. For example, analysis of range and irrigation policy issues benefited from regional studies in the West, just as analysis of cotton policy issues benefited from regional studies in the South and analysis of rural development benefited from direct research in rural communities. Field staff also expressed concern that the pressures of short-term policy analysis on staff in Washington would overshadow long-term economic research. And they believed the loss of ERS support for field research at the land-grant universities would reduce the agency's ability to recruit new staff who were drawn to the agency through work on ERS-funded projects at their universities.[58]

Not all ERS field staff viewed the location policy negatively, however. A number who had served in both field offices and Washington headquarters supported the new location policy, particularly those who moved into management positions or moved in and out of Washington on assignments in the course of their careers. ERS staff who had worked in both field offices and headquarters management remembered the change in their own views once they moved into headquarters from the field. Some came to see the work of ERS staff as duplicating that being pursued by university professors. Others acknowledged the quality and contributions of field staff research but found that project planning at the state and regional levels was ineffective for meshing these individual projects into a nationally usable whole. Moreover, Washington managers found it could be difficult to influence the research focus and time allocations of staff in the field, whose identification with their university colleagues and involvement in joint research could interfere with their responsiveness to changing ERS priorities, especially when many had been in place since before the ERS was established.[59]

In some cases, of course, synergies with university faculty and facilities led to useful collaborations. One manager acknowledged "these regional involvements gave us an opportunity to encourage research in the States along the lines we were following, and gave us the opportunity to draw some very able University people into our research work," but believed that it was "often at high cost."[60] As managers found their own headquarters staffs pressured by budget reductions, however, not being able to make full use of field personnel for agency research priorities became an increasingly serious concern. In addition, the separation of ERS field staff from the short-term policy analysis demands in Washington forced a greater reliance on headquarters staff for this growing area of work. Finally, field staff were often recruited while in graduate school and earned degrees on research projects funded by the ERS, only to decline to move to Washington at the end of their degree program. For managers, this inability to bring highly educated researchers into the headquarters mix could be frustrating, limiting the ERS's access to the recently trained PhDs in whom they had invested.[61]

By the time the new location policy was put in place, however, only 127 staff remained in the field, and two-thirds of those were in the NRED, nearly half of whom were attached to the river basins project funded by SCS. Estimates by those involved all suggest that only about 25 of those staff elected to remain with the ERS and make the move to Washington. In many cases, moving families proved too difficult; for others, living conditions and costs in Washington were unappealing. Those who remained in the field chose from a range of options. Many older staff were able to retire, some staff moved to other federal or state government agencies or to private employment, and others retooled and moved into new areas of work.[62]

The change in the ERS's field staffing policy occurred in the context of a more comprehensive reassessment of the ERS's mission and the development of a long-term plan that refocused the agency's research around new policy priorities, especially international demand and trade, natural resources, and rural development. Centralizing the staff in Washington occurred as part of a broader "regrouping" to clarify the agency's purpose and direction at a time of intense questioning of the status quo in the federal bureaucracy. As the only national-level public agricultural economic and social science research institution, the agency had to focus on the "broad public policy issues." This new vision of the ERS, however, placed the agency within a broader public economics and social science research network. The ERS clearly shared research and policy interests with economic and statistical agencies throughout the federal system and with the land-grant university and state experiment station system. Though it no longer supported long-term field relationships with the state universities, the ERS expected to continue cooperative analyses and coordinate with university research that contributed to aggregate studies of national and international issues and that helped build the data and knowledge underlying effective applied policy research. And along the lines anticipated by the 1979 ad hoc committee on ERS-university linkages and recommended by the 1983 GAO study, the ERS's long-term plan called for the agency to participate in coordinated, cooperative planning of social science research priorities for agriculture and rural areas.[63]

The ERS's renewed mission would include participation in the full range of public food and agriculture research planning, including federal and regional research councils, the regional experiment station associations, and the USDA/land-grant regional research committee structure. ERS management also reiterated its commitment to cooperative research projects with individual university researchers and research consortia, to promoting short-term staff and faculty exchanges when appropriate, and to supporting staff involvement in professional associations. Lee and other ERS leaders recognized the value to both ERS staff and university colleagues of opportunities for specific field-based assignments to contribute research goals, provide enhanced experiences and training, and strengthen ERS relationships with land-grant universities and other research institutions. While continuing budget pressures made temporary field assignments for ERS staff rare in the end, land-grant and other university faculty did embrace the continued opportunity to spend sabbaticals in residence at the ERS, as had been the practice since the days of the BAE.[64]

The end of the ERS field office system changed the relationship between the ERS and its land-grant partners in real ways. The most immediate loss, according to those who witnessed or experienced the relocation process, was the highly qualified staff who elected not to accept reassignment to Washington. Perhaps of equal concern, the ERS lost some direct working links to experts in the universities. While collaboration and cooperation continued both informally and through formal agreements, the continuity of daily, long-term contact could not be fully replaced. Other observers noted the loss of proximity to issues of concern in the agricultural sector and to the multidisciplinary problem-solving context of the land-grant universities. Finally, moving ERS staff out of field locations removed a small but real link to state-level political support in Congress.[65]

While some within the land-grant university system favored differentiating the ERS mission from their own, university departments and experiment stations valued having ERS staff at their locations. Their links to the national policy arena contributed a direct knowledge of relevant national policy issues to joint research projects and their expertise expanded the breadth and depth of the departments' and stations' research capacity. ERS staff often held faculty status and shared in teaching and advising, especially graduate students, and in some cases had been graduate students themselves at the universities where they worked. Moreover, while most of these departments had expanded in the 1950s and 1960s, by the 1980s state resources were growing thinner, amplifying the loss of ERS funding to support field offices and joint research projects.[66]

Just a few years after the last field office closed, the ERS celebrated its thirtieth anniversary. As part of that celebration, the agency sponsored a conference to review its historical development and encourage discussion of the agency's changing mission and program over time. One of the sessions of that conference, "ERS and the Land-Grant Universities," offered an opportunity to assess the effects of the decision to end the ERS field office system on the public agricultural economics research system. Two speakers addressed the topic: R. J. Hildreth, managing director of the Farm Foundation, former assistant director of the Texas A&M experiment station, and former president of the American Agricultural Economics Association, and Burt Sundquist, professor and former chair, Department of Agricultural Economics, University of Minnesota, and former ERS field staff member in that department, as well as former ERS branch chief, division director, and deputy administrator. In the audience were a mix of current and former ERS and land-grant university economists.[67]

Hildreth, who had worked with field staff while at the Texas A&M experiment station in the 1950s, laid the groundwork for his recommendations for the future of ERS and land-grant university cooperation by noting the damage he thought had been done by moving ERS field staff to Washington. While he acknowledged the necessity for this "clearly rational decision,"[68] he believed the change had affected the ERS and land-grant university relationship negatively. The loss of institutional memory among staff who had worked many years in the field affected the ERS's store of knowledge of local- and state-level agricultural conditions. And although the expectation had been that the land-grant universities and the ERS might develop a working system to draw together such local and state details into national research programs, Hildreth observed that communications along those lines had actually fallen off in the years since the relocation. He observed, however, that the continued linkages facilitated by the formal regional research system might be a useful model for exploring more formal working relationships that might reverse the negative effects of losing the field office connection.[69]

Hildreth emphasized the commonality of interest between the ERS and the land-grant universities and suggested that a more formal division of labor, at least on some issues, would support the full range of analytical needs policymakers and the public fairly expected from the public agricultural economics research system. His vision echoed that of many previous observers—that the ERS was in a position to respond to the needs of Congress and national policymakers, while the land-grant universities could do the same for individual firms and state policymakers. He didn't recommend a strict division of research effort, however, but greater cooperation to help each other serve their different publics. He further suggested that both the ERS and the land-grant university agricultural economics departments could benefit from a coordinated effort to educate the public on the value of continued funding of all parts of the public economics research system.[70]

Like Hildreth, Sundquist did not suggest a return to an ERS field presence but rather a cooperative approach based on the comparative advantage of the two primary partners in the national agricultural economics research system. While prefacing his comments with the caveat that he did not believe the creativity of individual economists in either the universities or the ERS should be limited by their institutions' comparative research advantages, he did suggest that for the public research system as a whole, some specialization could have value. Not unlike Hildreth, and many others before them, Sundquist noted the ERS's capacity for short-term policy analysis and national and international situation and outlook reporting. Both of these specializations he attributed to the ERS's location in Washington, close to national policymakers and policy support agencies, as well as to data collection agencies and national commodity and agricultural industry organizations. According to Sundquist, what was most important for the ERS's relationship with land-grant economists, however, was the agency's role in developing and analyzing national economic data. Because of declining budgets at the state level, land-grant universities could no longer support nationally reliable economic data collection. In Sundquist's view, the entire public research system had a stake in the ERS's continued collection and development of high-quality data, and especially in its further development of electronic systems for making that data and supporting research widely available. For their part, the land-grant universities could provide the professional education of agricultural economists and rural social scientists, who were necessary for sustaining and improving the public research system in the long term. The land-grants were also best equipped to bring a multidisciplinary approach to social and economic research questions and to pursue analysis of state and local policy questions. The ERS had lost the role it once had in these three areas with the closing of the field offices.[71]

The audience's response to Hildreth and Sundquist reflected many of the same issues that had been raised in earlier discussions of how the ERS and the land-grant universities could best share agricultural economics work. Much as Fred Waugh had in 1965, ERS researchers objected to the idea of limiting them to short-term analysis and data development. Others wondered (as had land-grant leaders who had been interviewed by the GAO in

1983) how a national planning process could direct universities and individual faculty and graduate students to adjust their research orientations to a coordinated cooperative plan. As had happened in these earlier discussions on creating a national plan for public agricultural research, most saw great merit in the idea, but few agreed on the implementation or at least on the likelihood that it could be accomplished.[72]

Hildreth singled out the regional research activities of the ERS and the state experiment stations as a particularly successful collaboration over the years. Participation in the regional research system dated back to the period of the BAE and remained a core focus of the field offices throughout their history. Hildreth suggested, and others have agreed, that building on these formal frameworks tied to the wider public agricultural research system held a strong possibility for continued coordination of economics research planning between the ERS and the land-grant universities. Within this system operated through the Cooperative State Research Service (now the National Institute for Food and Agriculture), the ERS and the land-grant universities cooperated as peer institutions, each committing resources and staff to jointly planned and mutually beneficial research efforts and avoiding the problem of hierarchy in implementing shared research. While the level of participation in regional research activities could vary, with more or less cooperation from the ERS and/or land-grant departments, during some periods and in some regions collaboration secured strong funding and high-quality researchers for priority projects over a relatively long term.[73]

In more recent decades, as the relocation of field office staff has receded further into the past, the issue of the ERS's relationship with the land-grant universities has lost some of its immediacy. To some extent, increased familiarity with the new relationship has eased concerns. Modern communications and electronic data sharing capacity have to a large extent mitigated the loss of daily direct personal contact between the ERS and land-grant university colleagues in field offices. Formal cooperation and more informal direct peer collaborations have also continued to secure links among the institutions. Following the recommendations of a number of observers in the mid-1980s, the ERS has also continued to have a leadership role in the wider profession of agricultural economics and to support regular exchanges of ideas between its staff and land-grant faculty by sponsoring workshops, conferences, and seminars, as well as funding cooperative research agreements between ERS staff and university faculty and supporting participation in multi-institutional projects like the International Agricultural Trade Research Consortium and the Global Trade Analysis Project.

Individual staff members also maintain informal working collaborations with university colleagues developed in graduate school and through participation in professional associations.[74]

Over the course of nearly one hundred years, the public agricultural economics research system has undergone a series of changes culminating in the current institutional structure of an essentially nonhierarchical peer relationship between the national-level economics research agency and the land-grant universities and experiment stations. This chapter focuses on the national side of this story, examining how the field office systems of the BAE, ARS/AMS, and eventually ERS developed, changed, and ultimately ended, but at the same time, the story builds a context for the land-grant university experience as part of a larger, integrated public research framework. Examining this framework from both sides sheds light on how public agricultural research works in the United States and how and why the institutional structures have evolved in the face of changing research capacities, priorities, and funding at the national and state levels.

In the case of public agricultural economics research, early development succeeded through a back-and-forth channeling of new state university agricultural economics departments and a growing federal Department of Agriculture. Following a period of ascendancy at the federal level during the peak years of the BAE, growing capacity at the land-grant universities and weakening influence at the national level led to the emergence of a new model of specialization between the new federal agricultural economics research institution, the ERS, and its land-grant university partners. While that model never really took hold in the sense of dividing public economics research into two distinctly different realms, it did help build a vision of peer partnership, rather than hierarchy, between the institutions. Questions may remain as to whether this vision strengthens or weakens the public research system—whether it leads to greater innovation and creativity by allowing individuals greater freedom in what research to pursue, for example, or whether it leads to duplication of research efforts and a declining critical mass of support for continued public investment. But it seems certain that this evolution cultivated and protected a strong informal research infrastructure—those professional research relationships forged in graduate school and through collaborative research projects and professional interactions that persist no matter what the formal institutional structure is. It may well be that in the end this informal infrastructure provides the strongest basis for an integrated public research system, continuing the fluid interchange of personnel and ideas that built the system in the first place.

Notes

1. The views expressed in this chapter are those of the author and should not be interpreted as representing the views of the Economic Research Service or the US Department of Agriculture.

2. Gladys L. Baker, Wayne D. Rasmussen, Vivian Wiser, and Jane M. Porter, *Century of Service: The First 100 Years of the United States Department of Agriculture* (Washington, DC: US Department of Agriculture, February 1963), 24–25.

3. Joel P. Kunze, "The Purnell Act and Agricultural Economics," *Agricultural History* 62, no. 2 (1988): 143; Norwood Allen Kerr, *The Legacy: A Centennial History of the State Agricultural Experiment Stations, 1887–1987* (Columbia: Missouri Agricultural Experiment Station, University of Missouri, 1987), 65–71.

4. Baker et al., *Century of Service*, 55, 128, 341–42; Kerr, *The Legacy*, 97–99; "Science and Education Activities of the USDA: 1961–1968" (unpublished manuscript produced by staff of the Agricultural History Branch, Economic Research Service, USDA, n.d., in possession of the author), 1–2.

5. Baker et al., *Century of Service*, 227.

6. Ibid., 43–45. There are several good sources on the early years of the rural social sciences disciplines in the universities and the USDA. See especially Gladys L. Baker and Wayne D. Rasmussen, "Economic Research in the Department of Agriculture: A Historical Perspective," *Agricultural Economics Research* 27, no. 3–4 (July–October 1975): 53–72; Richard Lowitt, ed., *Journal of a Tamed Bureaucrat: Nils A. Olsen and the BAE, 1925–1935* (Ames: Iowa State University Press, 1980); Harry McDean, "Professionalism in the Rural Social Sciences, 1896–1919," *Agricultural History* 58, no. 3 (1984): 373–92; Harry McDean, "Professionalism, Policy, and Farm Economists in the Early Bureau of Agricultural Economics," *Agricultural History* 57, no. 1 (1983): 64–82; Kunze, "The Purnell Act and Agricultural Economics," 131–49; Joel P. Kunze, "Public Service vs. Professional Responsibility," in *Economics and Public Service: Proceedings of the 30th Anniversary ERS Conference* (Washington, DC: US Department of Agriculture, Economic Research Service, AGES 9138, July 1991), 76–83; Jess Gilbert and Ellen Baker, "Wisconsin Economists and New Deal Agricultural Policy: The Legacy of Progressive Professors," *Wisconsin Magazine of History* 80, no. 4 (Summer 1997): 287–97; and Olaf F. Larsen and Julie N. Zimmerman, *Sociology in Government: The Galpin-Taylor Years in the U.S. Department of Agriculture, 1919–1953* (University Park: Pennsylvania State University Press, 2003).

7. Henry C. Taylor and Anne Dewees Taylor, *The Story of Agricultural Economics in the United States, 1840–1932* (Ames: Iowa State College Press, 1952).

8. Baker and Rasmussen, "Economic Research," 53–55.

9. There are a number of sources that discuss the story of the BAE's origins and development. I have drawn particularly on Taylor and Taylor, *The Story of Agricultural Economics in the United States*; Joel Kunze, "The Profession and the Public: Agricultural Economics and Public Service, 1920s and 1930s," in *Economics and Public Service,*

76–83; Gilbert and Baker, "Wisconsin Economists and New Deal Agricultural Policy," 287–97; and John F. Geweke, James T. Bonnen, Andrew A. White, and Jeffrey J. Koshel, eds., *Sowing Seeds of Change: Informing Public Policy in the Economic Research Service of USDA* (Washington, DC: National Academy Press, 1999).

10. "ERS and Its Research Program," pp. 8–9, FF Economic Research Service (2), box 1.4/23, USDA History Collection, Special Collections, National Agricultural Library, Beltsville, Maryland (hereafter USDA History Collection); "Organization of Marketing Research, 5/18/82," prepared by Vivian Wiser, Agricultural History Branch, FF I.5XIH13, Economic Research Service, January–June 1982, box 1.5/24, USDA History Collection.

11. "ERS and Its Research Program," 8–9; "Organization of Marketing Research."

12. "ERS and Its Research Program," 8–9; "Organization of Marketing Research."

13. Baker and Rasmussen, "Economic Research," 53–72; Baker et al., *Century of Service*, 499–500.

14. "Organization of Marketing Research"; Baker et al., *Century of Service*, 376–77; author interviews with Velmar Davis, May 14, 2011, and Melvin Cotner, September 20, 2012, former ARS and ERS economists, Washington, DC, in possession of the author, The ERS 50th Anniversary Collection, Special Collections, National Agricultural Library.

15. O.V. Wells, "Agricultural Economics under the USDA Reorganization of November 2, 1953," *Journal of Farm Economics*, 35, no. 1 (1954): 5.

16. See Paul H. Appleby, H. C. Taylor, Howard M. Tolley, Raymond J. Penn, and Theodore W. Schultz, "The Fragmentation of the BAE," *Journal of Farm Economics* 36 (February 1954): 5–21.

17. Baker and Rasmussen, "Economic Research," 53–72; author interviews with Davis, Cotner; "ERS and the Land-Grant Universities," in *Economics and Public Service*, 50; R. J. Hildreth presentation, Audio O86A/B, Meetings at the ERS Conference, April 4, 1991, box 8.2, USDA History Collection.

18. Willard W. Cochrane, "The Economic Research Service: 22 Years Later," *Agricultural Economics Research* 35, no. 2 (April 1983): 35, 29–38; Willard W. Cochrane, "Some Observations of an Ex-Economic Advisor: Or What I Learned in Washington," *Journal of Farm Economics* 47, no. 2 (May 1965): 457–59; Willard W. Cochrane, "The Role of Economics and Statistics in the USDA," *Agricultural Economics Research* 13 (3, July 1961): 69–74; Baker and Rasmussen, "Economic Research," 67; "Secretary Freeman Announces Reorganization of USDA Economics Services," Washington, February 24, 1961, FF XIB7, Agricultural Economics Research Agencies, 61–65, box 1.4/88, USDA History Collection.

19. Baker and Rasmussen, "Economic Research," 67; Cochrane, "The Economic Research Service," 30.

20. Cochrane, "The Economic Research Service," 29.

21. Baker and Rasmussen, "Economic Research," 65–66.

22. "Report and Recommendations of the 10th Meeting of the Economics Research

Advisory Committee, March 6–8, 1963, Washington, DC, FF XIB7, Agricultural Economics Research Agencies, 61–65, box 1.4/88, USDA History Collection.

23. *Looking Ahead: Summary Report of ERS Staff Conference, Front Royal, Va., May 6–8, 1965*, Economic Research Service, US Department of Agriculture, pp. 32–33, 38, FF XIB7, Agricultural Economics Research Agencies, 61–65, box 1.4/88, USDA History Collection.

24. "Program Evaluation Committee Report to the Administrator," Economic Research Service, U.S. Department of Agriculture, May 1965, FF XIB7, Agricultural Economics Research Agencies, 61–65, box 1.4/88, USDA History Collection.

25. "Program Evaluation Committee Report," 32 (quotations, p. 31).

26. Ibid., 49–50.

27. "Field Organization for Economic Research," ERS General Memorandum No. 38, June 10, 1965, FF XIB7, Agricultural Economics Research Agencies, 61–65, box 1.4/88, USDA History Collection.

28. Cochrane, "Some Observations of an Ex-Economic Advisor," 457.

29. Ibid., 457–59.

30. Frederick V. Waugh, "Should Universities Have a Monopoly on Brains?" *Journal of Farm Economics* 47, no. 2 (May 1965): 463.

31. Ernest W. Grove, "Mission Oriented Research," *Journal of Farm Economics* 47, no. 2 (May 1965): 462–63; Waugh, "Should Universities Have a Monopoly on Brains?" 463–64.

32. "A Working Paper Concerning Publicly Supported Economic Research in Agricultural Marketing," Economic Research Service, USDA, March 1968, FF XXIIA, Economic Research Service 1964–, box 1.4/105, USDA History Collection.

33. "Secretary Freeman Announces Reorganization of USDA Economics Services"; "Program Evaluation Committee Report to the Administrator," Economic Research Service, U.S. Department of Agriculture, May 1965, Appendix II, FF XIB7, Agricultural Economics Research Agencies, 61–65, box 1.4/88, USDA History Collection. Although it is not entirely clear from the records, the nearly six-hundred-person difference between the 1961 announced staffing numbers and the inventory of professional staff from 1965 is most likely the result of a combination of attrition in the field offices, some movement of positions into headquarters, and the number of full- and part-time support staff and student positions included in the 1961 count that were not part of the 1965 inventory.

34. "Program Evaluation Committee Report," 20–21; interviews with Davis, Cotner, and Marlow Vesterby, Andy Anderson, and Carmen Sandretto, August 9, 2011, former ARS and ERS economists, ERS 50th Anniversary Collection.

35. "Program Evaluation Committee Report," 22–25; interviews with Davis, Cotner, Vesterby, Anderson, and Sandretto.

36. "Program Evaluation Committee Report," 22, and appendix 2; interviews with Davis, Cotner, Vesterby, Anderson, Sandretto, Nelson Bills, December 12, 2012, former ERS and Cornell University economist, and Milton Ericksen and Edwin Young,

December 19, 2012, former ERS economists, ERS 50th Anniversary Collection.

37. Interviews with Davis, Cotner, Vesterby, Anderson, Sandretto, Ericksen, Young, and Bills; Kitty Smith, panelist, "USDA and ERS Leaders—Musings from the Past and Views on the Future," video recording of ERS 50th Anniversary Symposium "The Economic Research Service: Fifty Years of Excellence in Economic Research," ERS 50th Anniversary Collection; Baker and Rasmussen, "Economic Research," 67–68.

38. Interviews with Vesterby, Anderson, and Sandretto; transcript, Dr. Walter W. Wilcox interviewed by Thomas H. Baker, November 5, 1968, FF XIB7, Agricultural Economics Research Agencies, 66–71, box 1.4/88, USDA History Collection; Baker and Rasmussen, "Economic Research," 67.

39. Baker and Rasmussen, "Economic Research," 68–69; "Economic Research Service, Organization—Research Project Structure, 1975 Directory," Revised: November 1, 1974, FF XIH13 Economic Research Service (ERS) 1965–1976, box 1.5/23, USDA History Collection; "What Is the ERS Mission?" Draft, 4/18/72, FF XIB7 Review of ERS–1972, box 1.4/89, USDA History Collection, quotation on p. 2.

40. "The Natural Resource Economics Division," p. 4, review prepared for ERS Committee on Commercial Agriculture, May 31, 1972, FF XIB7 Review of ERS—1972, box 1.4/89, USDA History Collection.

41. "Economic Development Division: Description of Major Responsibilities," p. 4, FF XIB7 Review of ERS—1972, box 1.4/89, USDA History Collection; "Report on the Program and Activities of the Marketing Economics Division, ERS, Prepared for the Committee on Commercial Agriculture," pp. 9–10, FF XIB7 Review of ERS—1972, box 1.4/89, USDA History Collection.

42. "The Responsibilities and Program of the Farm Production Economics Division," pp. 7–8, review prepared for ERS Committee on Commercial Agriculture, May 31, 1972, FF XIB7 Review of ERS—1972, box 1.4/89, USDA History Collection; "Economic and Statistical Analysis Division, Major Responsibilities and Program of Work," p. 5, FF XIB7 Review of ERS—1972, box 1.4/89, USDA History Collection.

43. "Howard Hjort's Meeting with Economic Research Service, Wednesday, March 9, 1977," FF I.5 XIH13, ERS January–May 1977, box 1.5/23, USDA History Collection.

44. "ERS—Its Role, Work and Relationship to Others," [by John Lee], March 7, 1977, pp. 10–11, FF I.5 XIH13, ERS, January–May 1977, box 1.5/23, USDA History Collection.

45. Ibid., 12.

46. Ibid., 11–12.

47. "ERS: Status and Prognosis," 5–6, FF I.5 XIH13, ERS, July–December 1982, box 1.5/24, USDA History Collection.

48. "Looking Ahead: A View of ERS by Its New Top Manager," *Farmline*, May 1982; "ERS: Status and Prognosis," 6–7.

49. "ERS: Status and Prognosis," 8–9.

50. US General Accounting Office (GAO), *Report to the Secretary of Agriculture: Agricultural Economics Research and Analysis Needs Mission Clarification*, GAO/RCED 83–89, January 31, 1983, p. 1.

51. GAO investigators did not identify any of the individuals they interviewed by name.

52. GAO, *Report to the Secretary of Agriculture*, 22–23.

53. Ibid., 3, 22–24.

54. Ibid., 13.

55. Ibid., 12–16.

56. Ibid., 16.

57. John Lee, "The Mission and Program of the New Economic Research Service," February 22, 1983, pp. 12–13, FF I.5 XIH13, ERS, January–May 1983, box 1.5/24, USDA History Collection; Memorandum on Location Policy, John E. Lee Jr., Administrator, to ERS Staff, April 8, 1983, FF I.5 XIH13, ERS, June–November 1983, box 1.5/24, USDA History Collection.

58. Memorandum on Location Policy and ERS Research Capability, from Harry Ayer et al. to George Hoffman, June 24, 1983, FF I.5 XIH13, ERS, June–November 1983, box 1.5/24, USDA History Collection; interviews with Vesterby, Anderson, Sandretto, Cotner, Erickson, and Young; Memorandum on ERS Staff Location Policy, from George Hoffman to Harry Ayer et al., July 7, 1983, FF I.5 XIH13, ERS, June–November 1983, box 1.5/24, USDA History Collection.

59. Frederick D. Stocker, Professor, The Ohio State University, to Dr. Jerome M. Stam, Leader, State and Local Government Program Area, ERS, USDA, September 6, 1977, p. 5, FF I.5 XIH13, ERS, June–December 1977, box 1.5/23, USDA History Collection; Bill Lesher, panelist, "USDA and ERS Leaders," ERS 50th Anniversary Symposium, ERS 50th Anniversary Collection; interviews with Davis, Cotner, Vesterby, Anderson, Sandretto, Erickson, and Young.

60. Stocker to Stam, September 6, 1977.

61. Ibid.; Jerome M. Stam, "The State and Local Government Program Area in a Historical and Organizational Context," September 6, 1977, pp. 71–72, FF XIH13, Economic Research Service, June-December 1977, box 1.5/23, USDA History Collection; interviews with Davis, Cotner, Vesterby, Anderson, Sandretto, Erickson, Young, and Bills.

62. *Economic Research Service: Accomplishments in 1983*, pp. 2, 35, FF I.5 XIH13, ERS, December 1983, box 1.5/24, USDA History Collection; interviews with Vesterby, Anderson, Sandretto, Cotner, Erickson, Young.

63. *Economic Research Service in Transition*, p. 3, February 1985, FF I.5 XIH13, ERS, January–May 1985, box 1.5/24, USDA History Collection; Memorandum on Location Policy, April 8, 1983 AE—FF XIH13, Economic Research Service, June–November 1983, box 1.5/24, USDA History Collection; "The ERS Long-Term Plan," Working Draft, December 12, 1983, pp. 72–73, FF I.5 XIH13, ERS, December 1983, box 1.5/24, USDA History Collection.

64. "The ERS Long-Term Plan"; "Semiannual List of EAS, EMS, ERS and OE Employees on Committee," US Department of Agriculture, Economics Management Starr, December 1985, pp. 21–33, FF I.5 XIH13, ERS, June 1985–87, box 1.5/24, USDA

History Collection; Economic Research Service bimonthly newsletter, January/February 1986, p. 7, FF I.5 XIH13, ERS, 1986–87, box 1.5/24, USDA History Collection; John Lee and Kitty Smith, panelists, "USDA and ERS Leaders," ERS 50th Anniversary Symposium, ERS 50th Anniversary Collection; "ERS and the Land-Grant Universities," 47; B.F. (Bernard Freeland) Stanton, Audio O86A/B, USDA History Collection.

65. Interviews with Vesterby, Anderson, Sandretto, Cotner, Erickson, Young, and Bills.

66. Interviews with Vesterby, Anderson, Sandretto, Cotner, Erickson, and Young.

67. "ERS and the Land-Grant Universities," 47–57; Audio O86A/B, Meetings at the ERS Conference, April 4, 1991, box 8.2, USDA History Collection.

68. "ERS and the Land-Grant Universities," 51.

69. Ibid.; Hildreth, Audio O68A/B, USDA History Collection.

70. "ERS and the Land-Grant Universities," 50–52; Hildreth, Audio O68A/B, USDA History Collection.

71. "ERS and the Land-Grant Universities," 54–57; Sundquist, Audio O68A/B, USDA History Collection.

72. Question and answer period, Audio O68A/B, USDA History Collection; "ERS and the Land-Grant Universities," 50–51; Hildreth, Audio O86A/B, USDA History Collection.

73. "ERS and the Land-Grant Universities," 50–51; Hildreth, Audio O68A/B, USDA History Collection; interviews with Vesterby, Anderson, Sandretto, Cotner, and Ralph Heimlich, December 12, 2011, ERS 50th Anniversary Collection; Lee, "USDA and ERS Leaders," ERS 50th Anniversary Symposium.

74. "ERS and the Land-Grant Universities," 56–57; Sundquist, Audio O68A/B, USDA History Collection; interviews with Cotner, Erickson, and Young; author communication with Steven Crutchfield, assistant administrator, ERS, October 29, 2010.

5

The New Students

The GI Bill and Housing at Iowa State

DAVID L. HARMON

The onslaught of veterans returning from World War II profoundly affected land-grants. The GI Bill enabled servicemen to attend college, and the returning soldiers threatened to overwhelm these schools. Preparing campuses to house these veterans was a tremendous undertaking. Schools more than doubled in size. Majors, class size, and campus life were all impacted. Heating, lighting, and plumbing needed installation. Trenches needed to be dug, concrete needed to be poured, and structures needed to be framed. Housing these soldier students and their young families was particularly challenging. Colleges needed to build new dwellings and to revamp old ones. It was a significant task.

Harmon's chapter is a case study of one dramatic expansion. His focus on Iowa State points to the uniqueness of that school's situation. But it also highlights what lengths land-grants were willing to go simply to solve their own problems. Certain options were open to them. The schools weaved their ways through the various possibilities and the morass of red tape and regulation that accompanied them. In the end, they established temporary facilities that enabled them to meet the needs of the returning veterans. In characteristic land-grant fashion, Iowa State resolved the problem that it was forced to face.

✳✳✳

During World War II and after, land-grant colleges stepped up to meet the new challenges that were given to them. With dramatic growth in enrollment starting in fall 1945, housing all of the new students proved an immense task. Most university physical plants were unable, in their current condition, to handle the growth associated with returning veterans. Wartime had led the government to restrict many materials as well as to encourage industries to meet other demands innovatively. These restrictions continued through demobilization.

The impact of higher enrollment on colleges and universities due to the GI Bill of Rights proved to be only one factor administrators confronted. Many veterans returned to school married and with children. Fifty percent of Iowa State College's returning veterans were married.[1] University housing for married students barely existed in some schools. In other schools it did not exist at all.[2]

Iowa State College lacked the benefit of being near a major defense plant or military base, which as a part of reconversion simply transferred authority over much of their housing to local educational institutions. For example, the University of Wisconsin utilized units at nearby Camp Randall to house veterans, and the University of Michigan had nearby Willow Run. Like most land-grant institutions, Iowa State College instituted a program of infrastructural expansion to alleviate the strain on the university physical plant. In 1940, a year before America entered the war, universities and colleges spent $73 million on physical plant improvements. In 1946 spending reached $111 million, and in 1948, with all the soldiers home, the nation's schools spent $202 million on physical plant expansion. For Iowa State, this growth included a wide variety of structures. Housing units were paramount but temporary classroom and laboratory facilities were also built, as were additions to the power plant and the sewage treatment facility.

As was the case with virtually all land-grants, Iowa State's expansion involved national, state, local, and university agencies. The establishment of housing for married veteran students as well as the facilities necessary to meet their educational needs is evidence of these interconnected governmental associations. This chapter details the many actions required to implement a small portion of the larger readjustment strategy—that of Iowa State College providing facilities and equipment for veterans utilizing their GI Bill educational benefits.[3]

To address the immediate need of providing for veterans and their families, Iowa State first attempted to purchase surplus housing. The Federal Public Housing Administration (FPHA) in Chicago proved a likely source of such structures. Iowa State made inquiries to the FPHA in October 1945 and received some stock prior to approval by the administrative entities that directed Iowa State—the Iowa Board of Education and the state's attorney general. Students and families were actually living in this purchased housing—known as Pammel Court—prior to official college or State of Iowa approval. This initiative, undertaken simply through university channels, became de facto precedent; it set the stage for further action without state-sanctioned involvement.

The Iowa Board of Education authorized the housing purchases after the fact. The board was well aware of the desperateness of the situation and the fact that many universities and other entities were openly competing for these precious structures. For these reasons, it took bold action. It issued blanket permission for the college "to proceed with plans for securing trailers and houses that might be available . . . for temporarily housing married students."[4]

The board recognized that securing surplus housing was likely a stop-gap measure. There simply was not enough stock to meet demand. As a consequence, the board inquired into the legality of taking another course: erecting its own married student housing. The initial legal opinion the board received was negative and John M. Rankin, attorney general of Iowa, refused to reverse the decision. The board objected to the attorney general's refusal to sustain the board's position and employed counsel to fight his action. Iowa State College President Ralph Friley viewed the college's housing situation as desperate. He urged the board in early 1946 to act out of "necessity . . . for the good of the institution." The board concurred and willfully disobeyed the attorney general's decision, moving forward without state sanction. Within a few days it authorized Iowa State College to execute bailment contracts for students already living there and pressed the attorney general again to reverse himself. With the college squarely in the housing business, the attorney general had little recourse but to examine again his refusal to act. He had two options: arrest the board members or overturn his ruling of the previous year. On July 31, 1946, the attorney general reluctantly threw out his previous opinion and ruled that the board had the legal power to erect married student housing.

For Iowa State, the administrative battles had only begun. While the FPHA provided housing units and the school contemplated the construction of others, the college also needed to provide utilities and related services for all of these new domiciles. However, Iowa State could not contract with existing agencies because it was the de facto provider of these services:

water, sewage, garbage collection, road and walk maintenance, and electricity. This included the laying of mains, treating wastes, removing refuse, and the like. Extra capacity could not be secured without undertaking an extensive modification campaign to make the college's physical plant consonant with the technology used by the local government or private providers. The expansion of housing and educational facilities at Iowa State required the college to expand its own capacity; it needed to undertake a new round of facilities maintenance and utility service development.[5]

The FPHA regional office worked to secure housing for the college while the school prepared to accept and install the units. Iowa State had to contract not only for transportation but also for the entire disassembly and placement and assembly procedures. The federal government anticipated how costly that would be. The Lanham Act Amendment (December 31, 1945) provided reimbursement to colleges for costs already incurred for the "moving and converting" of housing units. For Iowa State, this meant reimbursement of approximately $50,000 since it had already brought in 150 housing units for married students.

Students moved in quickly. They occupied the first 36 units on January 3, 1946. This initial aspect of the housing project was all purchased through university funding. The first phase consisted of 69 standard trailers, 31 expansible trailers, 5 toilet trailers, 2 laundry trailers, and 1 office trailer. The remaining units included 17 one-bedroom and 33 two-bedroom units of the demountable type.[6]

The housing units were by no means comfortable accommodations, but the college was glad to get them. They were transported to Ames from three separate defense locations. From the wartime ammunition depot in Hastings, Nebraska, Iowa State College received 28 standard trailers, 8 expansible trailers, and 4 utility (expansible) trailers. An additional 41 standard, 23 expansible, and 4 utility trailers arrived from the Army Air Corps base located at Alliance, Nebraska, home of the 507th Parachute Infantry. The 50 demountable houses received from the Badger Ordnance Plant near Prairie du Sac, Wisconsin, required final setup in Ames and site restoration was needed at Badger.[7]

Each of these transfers was considerably more complicated than what might have been anticipated. The new trailers came with every accouterment. Foundations traveled with trailers. Hookups, many of which needed to be replaced to conform to the university's systems, also made the journey, as did even the most mundane things, such as clotheslines. Once positioned, and with running gear removed, each trailer was raised by jacks until it rested on a foundation.[8] Setup included repairs, cleaning and painting, and installing roads and walks, plumbing, wiring, garbage cans, dumpsters, and oil tanks. All of this work for these relatively few trailers cost the college $74,617.[9]

These fully loaded trailers had been initially constructed by the military to be grouped to maximize space; they were modular. Iowa State capitalized on their standardized sizes and shapes to erect a compact site for married student housing development on the outskirts of campus on what had been the polo field. This new subdivision became known as Pammel Court because it faced Pammel Drive, north of central campus.[10]

Getting and setting up these surplus trailers was only the tip of the iceberg—the college needed more housing immediately. The college wrote the Chicago FPHA office in February 1946 that of the "600 married veterans already registered to enroll in March for [the] first time [in college history]," 270 had children. The expeditious response by the FPHA in approving applications allowed the college's business manager, Boyne Platt, to announce in the *Iowa State Daily Student* on March 9, 1946, that delivery of "the second unit of 150 dwellings" would begin on March 21. Platt further noted that "the new units" consisted of "50 trailers and 50 two-family Quonset huts," many from Oak Ridge, Tennessee.[11] Working on a government-mandated "cost-plus-a-fixed-fee contract," the Kucharo Construction Company of Des Moines agreed on March 25, 1946, to erect the Quonset huts, which came from the navy base at Tacoma, Washington. Water and sewer lines needed to be dug to accommodate the new huts.

In accomplishing this massive undertaking, Iowa State eschewed an alternative, which would have been to privatize the space and units. Trailer parks, filled with mobile vehicles owned by occupants, were an anathema; they suggested that these returning heroes were being treated as second-class citizens. No matter how it appeared, veterans lived in student housing provided and maintained by the university. The gleaming (relative) newness of the aluminum structures led to Pammel Court being called Silver City. Others were less charitable, referring to it as "academic slums" and complaining about its "overcrowding, inadequate housing . . . [and] vestigial trailers." Yet the college remained the landlord as well as the purveyor of higher education. No matter how tattered the trailers might appear, veterans' housing remained part of the university proper.[12]

To maintain the fiction that veterans were treasured members of the student body and that the college took care of their and their families' needs, the university leased adjoining acreage to erect ever more "married student housing." Each of these standardized structures were symbols of modern life, the result of design experiments, scientific techniques, and advanced production methods. Each was shipped to Ames as soon as distributors collected enough inventory to meet the Iowa State order. Veterans sometimes did without, while at other times parts arrived well before competent personnel were available to install them.[13] But when these trailers/residences were finally up and running, they provided veterans' families with some of the amenities of modern life. Each house had a coal space heater—a necessity for Iowa winters—water heater, cooking stove, kitchen sink, and toilet. There even was a laundry to serve the new cohort.

Returning veterans overwhelmed campus facilities. Classroom space proved dear—so dear in fact that the university accommodated additional student-veterans by using an entire army encampment some twenty miles away. Designated Iowa State College Camp Dodge annex, the school leased the US Army Camp Dodge facilities to house more than 450 freshmen enrolled in engineering and science classes. Not only was the annex fully equipped to feed and house the students but arrangements for classrooms and staff were also made. While the annex operated for only one year, in that period of time 36 instructors educated almost 500 freshmen there. The temporary solution served the college well by alleviating the immediate postwar housing problem. This one-year postponement enabled the college to meet immediate housing needs and to secure extra classroom buildings. It also enabled Iowa State to complete the third, most involved phase of married student housing, which also proved to be the largest phase of veterans housing construction.[14]

This phase was to construct housing for 800 married veterans and 1,550 unmarried returnees. But government sources allocated the college only 1,036 family units and no dormitory units. At that point, Iowa State shifted course and asked specifically for 20 steel barracks to house the single men. Twelve of these enormous but spartan facilities were scheduled to be used precisely in that fashion but five were to become community houses or recreational centers including preschools, and three others were to serve as laundry buildings.

Timing continued to be an issue, as did unannounced substitution of housing stock. Governmental units sent whatever they had. Army barracks from Baton Rouge arrived unexpectedly as did POW barracks from

Concordia, Kansas. Iowa State had to hire construction crews to convert these units into usable—and desirable—domestic space.[15]

Construction materials proved to be very difficult to obtain, while miscellaneous components arrived at the college quite routinely. Furnishings and lavatory fixtures were generally transported in separate loads from Oak Ridge, Hastings, Alliance, Badger, and Baton Rouge. Boilers, water softeners, pressure water tanks, and pumps came from Iowa army bases. Still other components came to the college from the Federal Works Administration. The college regularly requested whatever surplus the FWA had.[16] The Federal Works Administration had been instrumental in remodeling classroom space and in securing nine temporary classroom and laboratory buildings from the Des Moines Ordnance Plant. Other Ordnance Plant–derived buildings, such as sentry houses, became telephone booths at the college.

The onslaught of human beings placed considerable stress on the recently enhanced infrastructure. Water works and a new sewage plant were built to serve the new population. The alteration and enlargement of the power plant proved especially expensive. A new steam generator and related equipment—turbo generator, switchgear, cooling tower, surface condenser, and so forth—consumed a significant part of the resettlement budget.[17]

The completion of the physical plant improvements and sewer operation upgrades signaled the beginning of the end of the construction phase of Pammel Court. With all of the additions and changes, the college physical plant—and indeed the college as a whole—was able to meet the increased demands placed on it by a dramatic increase in enrollment. Iowa State was very different in the late 1940s than it had been just five years earlier.

For Iowa State College, this translated into establishing married student housing as well as an unavoidable expansion of the college physical plant. Increased enrollment also demanded an increase in college staff, faculty, and related facilities. Iowa State College was but one of many institutions which, for the first time, had an enrollment of over ten thousand students and, also for the first time, included married student housing.

The Iowa State story was hardly unique. While the majority of land-grant institutions did not fare as well as Iowa State, postwar connections to the federal government grew in a wide array of areas including communications research with the University of California system, marine research at the University of Florida, and the famed Purdue University School of Aeronautics and Astronautics, which opened in 1945 and has graduated at least twenty-two astronauts including Neil Armstrong.[18]

It has often been said that the GI Bill "democratized education" and changed the culture of colleges in general. Some changes proved permanent including those to physical plants and in admission procedures, guidance and testing services, curriculum, pedagogy, and the relationship of American colleges and universities to the federal and state governments. In that regard, World War II impacted the United States in numerous ways. Some changes proved dramatically apparent while others have not been as obvious or as profound.[19]

NOTES

1. J. C. Schilletter, *The First 100 Years of Residential Housing at Iowa State University* (Ames: Iowa State University Press, 1970), 110.

2. For details on the legislation, procedures, support for and against increased veteran's appropriations, and appropriations for educational facilities in general, see Keith W. Olson, *The G.I. Bill, the Veterans, and the Colleges* (Lexington: University of Kentucky Press, 1974), especially 66–78.

3. Olson, *The G.I. Bill, the Veterans and the Colleges*, 66–67; *U.S. Statutes at Large*, v. 59, pt. 1, 79th Cong., 1st Sess., 1945, ch. 264, July 3, 1945 p. 383, and ch. 657, December 31, 1945, p. 674. See also the speech by Administrator of Veterans Affairs Omar Bradley to the Association of American Colleges in Boston, where he accounts for the enrollment "as of December 31, 1946 [of] more than two-and-a-quarter million veterans" in "education and training" facilities. The breakdown being about "one-half in higher education . . . one-fourth in other and one-fourth in on-the-job training." "Address by General Omar Bradley, January 14, 1947," University of Michigan Archives, Dean of Student Affairs (Bursley), Veterans Administration, 1946–49, Bentley Historical Library. Another act that also involved veterans in educational training programs, the Vocational Rehabilitation Act (Public Law 16), provided training for "veterans who have a service-connected disability . . . [constituting] a vocational handicap." For this study, these veterans will be considered as a part of the larger whole. It should also be noted that the Lanham Act and the Serviceman's Readjustment Act both included details that applied to other areas: defense-related housing and veterans benefits, respectively. For details on the Lanham Act, see the various amendments as found in *U.S. Statutes at Large* as well as the numerous Congressional Committee proceedings. For information on the full benefits package offered to veterans, see Public Affairs Press, *Going Back to Civilian Life: Official Information about the Privileges, Opportunities, and Rights of Returning Soldiers* (Washington, DC: GPO, 1944). See also "Letter from University Council to Dean Bursley dated December 13, 1945," which notes "houses for seventy-eight couples were moved from Willow Run Village to Ann Arbor and set up near the coliseum." University of Michigan Archives, Dean of Student Affairs, Student Affairs-Housing Committee 1942–55, Bentley Historical Library.

For the occupancy of the Willow Run facilities, see local newspapers for the period in question. For instance, University of Michigan veterans occupied 2,969 units at Willow Run in August 1946. *Ann Arbor News*, August 6, 1946.

4. Minutes, Iowa State Board of Education, 1945/46, published by the State of Iowa, Des Moines, November 2–3, 1945. These minutes are located in the University Archives, Iowa State University.

5. Ibid.; Dorothy H. Schrader, *History of Ames Municipal Government, Sewers* (Ames, Iowa, Iowa State University Press, 1965), 4–5. Schrader also notes that in January 1954, "final payment was made by ISC to the City for its share of the Treatment Plant cost. The total payment of $470,550 represented 39.62% of joint costs of the plant and interceptor." Also see *Report of the State Board of Education for the Biennial Period Ending June 30, 1948* (Des Moines: State of Iowa, 1949), 8, 431–32. *The Inventory of Improvements Other Than Buildings* notes the "sewage plant and connecting sewers installed jointly by the City of Ames 70%, and Iowa State College, 30%," which Schrader writes about her History of Ames (p. 432).

6. H. Summerfield Day, *The Iowa State University Campus and Its Buildings, 1859–1979* (Ames: Iowa State University Press, 1980), 373. Day cites the *Iowa State Daily Student*, January 3, 1946, for his estimate of 36 units. For a cost-to-date analysis (expenses incurred by the college prior to the December 1945 Lanham Act amendment authorizing reimbursement), see "Iowa State College Veteran's Housing Project" correspondence dated November 29, 1945, MSH, box 30.

7. Day, *The Iowa State University Campus and Its Buildings*, 373. See "Iowa State College Veteran's Housing Project" for information on the number of units transported. Details on the type of defense location were obtained through telephone interviews with Catherine Renschler at the Hastings Museum Library and with Joanna Hall of the Alliance Public Library.

A point to note here is the fact that highways in 1945 were not as wide as the standard road networks ribboning America today. The standard trailer of the period was at most eight feet wide and the housing units at Badger wider still. Indeed the "ten-wide" trailer of the 1950s proved to be a legal headache when interstate transport was required. Likewise, transporting the Badger units proved to be as complex.

8. "4000 Tires for 50,000 Units," *Architectural Record*, April 1942, p. 24; B. W. Schaefer to Mr. J. E. Dooley, December 2, 1945, Wheatland, Missouri, State Archives of Missouri History, (MSH), box 30.

9. FPHA Badger General Housing Manager, Otto J. Harm, to B. H. Platt, February 1, 1946, MSH, box 28; B. W. Schaefer to Otto J. Harms, February 26, 1946, MSH, box 28. Additionally, the final invoice attached to this letter indicates the Hastings and Alliance trailer data including Nebraska site location, government serial number, type, manufacturer, and conditional "remarks." For estimates and details on transportation, see J. D. Armstrong Company to Ben W. Schaefer, November 29, 1945, MSH, box 30; "Iowa State College Veteran's Housing Project."

10. Schilletter, *The First 100 Years*, 163–64; Day, *The Iowa State University Campus and Its Buildings*, 373.

11. B. W. Schaefer to Fred Kraft, telegram, February 4, 1946, FPHA, MSH, box 30; Quincy C. Ayres to Cmdr. Gene Spellman, February 9, 1946, MSH, box 30; "Pammel Court—New Village," *Iowa State Daily Student* 74, no. 106 (March 9, 1946): 1; Bergeron to Platt, May 27, 1946, MSH, box 29. This May 1946 document is the earliest document indicating that contracts for the Oak Ridge trailers had been secured in mid-February of that year. This document is important in that it shows that the whole process became more complicated and thus fulfilling the requests took much longer. Though Iowa State officials knew in February that they would receive the Tennessee units, delivery took another five months. Indeed, as the immediate postwar demobilization and readjustment strategies unfolded, more institutions scrambled to obtain housing or other facilities while further material shortages continually retarded the progress of those who did obtain facilities.

12. Alexander G. Ruthven, University of Michigan president, quoted in the *Michigan Daily*, January 19, 1946. Ruthven noted the policy to adopt temporary housing measures was necessary yet "greatly regretted." War Historian, box 15, Records 1941–1945, Bentley Historical Library; Rev. Le Roy S. Burroughs to daughter Marguerite, "Holy Monday, April 15, 1946," Papers of Le Roy S. Burroughs, Personal Correspondence, MS-223, Iowa State University Archives.

13. Norman Cherner, *Fabricating Houses from Component Parts* (New York: Reinhold Publishing Corporation, 1957), 125, 152. Additional details on the Quonset structures were obtained in telephone interviews conducted January 26, 1994, between the author and: Mr. & Mrs. Dick Seim of Ames, Iowa; Mrs. Pat Post of Ames, Iowa; and Mr. & Mrs. Alan Seim of Ottumwa, Iowa, all former residents of Pammel Court; W. E. Bergeron to Kucharo Construction Co., April 17, 1946, Kucharo Construction Company Notice to Proceed, MSH, box 28; FPHA to B. Schaefer, July 25, 1946, MSH, box 29; FPHA to Kucharo Construction Co., August 1, 1946, MSH, box 29; Hugh K. Crawford, Priorities Liaison Officer, FPHA, to B. H. Platt, September 20, 1946, MSH, box 29.

14. Schilletter, *The First 100 Years*, 118; Barbara Bailey, ed., *The Bomb, 1947* (Ames: Iowa State College Press, 1947), 218.

15. B. H. Platt to Orville Olmstead, Regional Director, FPHA, Chicago, July 13, 1946, MSH, box 28; Schilletter, *The First 100 Years*, 166; Notice to Bidders, July 23, 1946, and Hoak "Form of Proposal," August 17, 1946, MSH, box 30. The board minutes for May 12–13, 1947, state the contract was awarded August 29, 1946. Still, the board did not authorize Platt "to enter into a contract with" Hoak until the September 9–10, 1946 meeting as the minutes indicate. State Board of Education, Minutes, September 9–10, 1946, University Archives, Iowa State University; Specification for the Construction of Veterans Temporary Housing Project, July 12, 1946, MSH, box 28; "Veterans Housing Specification, National Housing Agency, Federal Public Housing Authority, Converted Army Barracks," January 8, 1946, MSH, box 28.

16. Schilletter, *The First 100 Years*, 165; J. D. Armstrong, Heavy Hauling Inc., to Ben Schaefer, July 17, 1947, MSH, box 28. For details on FWA involvement in demobilization (Title V), see *U.S. Statutes at Large*, v. 59, pt. 1, 79th Cong., 2nd Sess., August 8, 1946, chapter 917, Public Law 697, p. 958.

17. Iowa State Board of Education Minutes, June 30–July 1, 1947, University Archives, Iowa State University.

18. Day, *The Iowa State University Campus and Its Buildings*, 353, 371, 422, 439, 482.

19. H. Edward Humes, *Over Here: How the G.I. Bill Transformed the American Dream* (New York: Harcourt, 2006), 124–26; Glenn Altschuler, *The GI Bill: A New Deal for Veterans* (London: Oxford University Press, 2009), 83, 86–90; Milton Greenberg, *The G.I. Bill: The Law That Changed America* (New York: Lickle Publishing, 1997), 35, 44, 47, 56.

6

The Purposes of Higher Education

The Morrill Act and Military Science

Donald A. Downs

The Morrill Land-Grant Act demanded that its schools not exclude "military tactics." How that subject was broached was left to the states. Through much of the nineteenth century, states dabbled and tried various programs. World War I and the United States emergence on the international stage encouraged Congress to create some sort of national policy. Congress standardized and systematized mechanisms and techniques to teach military skills to future leaders; a regular military had become an important facet of America's international efforts, and it needed a standing, dependable cadre of officers to function well.

What became known as ROTC—Reserve Officers' Training Corps—emerged from that milieu. Through the Morrill mandate, the land-grants served as the primary venue for creating this uniform corps. While by no means a shotgun marriage, training the next generation of military leaders on land-grant campuses was not always smooth. The several decades after about 1950 were a remarkably contentious period. Never did the land-grants seem so central to the national defense. Questioning begot demonstrations, which by the 1960s yielded riots, violence, and other campus disruptions. Faculty members squared off against each other, as did students.

The situation calmed down after the Vietnam War, but military matters at land-grant universities continue to cause a kerfuffle. To Downs, the uneasy relationship between the military and the land-grants, formulated by the Morrill Act, is a benison, fully in line with the act's original purpose. ROTC programs at land-grants cement America's military as a democratic institution, not as the province of a self-selected elite, and one where its activities are closely scrutinized. Regular dispute and protest are the inevitable results.

✫✫✫

The Morrill Act's provision "and including military tactics" made the act the first national legislation to require a form of military education as a part of college instruction as a power. There were some precedents for such a position. In 1825, for example, the *New England Farmer* wrote about a proposal for the "Massachusetts Agricultural College," which would require instruction in military tactics and gymnastics.[1] But no specific military education was offered at American colleges—except West Point—until the Morrill Act. Over time, substantial military programs emerged out of the act's modest four words pertaining to military instruction. The act itself had provided little or no guidance regarding how to proceed. Nonetheless, the Morrill Act–spawned military programs became aligned with the act's general purposes and vision.

Two features stand out. First, military education took decades to develop. In the broadest sense, the implementation of the military provisions of the Morrill Act paralleled the nation-building process after the Civil War. That era's industrialization with its emphasis on more practical knowledge, a centralized administrative state, and the emergence of the nation as a power on the international stage contributed to the need for a more professional and centralized military force. Put simply, the growth of military education in land-grant institutions parallels the growth of professionalism in the United States.[2]

Second, though generally supported by university leaders and students, military education has been controversial throughout American history, and it remains so to this day. Indeed, the military clause remains unique among the Morrill Act's substantive educational provisions. Though the Morrill Act enjoyed substantial public support, many traditionalists questioned the act's emphasis upon more practical education, which they construed as detrimental to traditional liberal education. Over time, this critique would wither. Controversy regarding the military provision, however, proved longer lasting, as critics contended that military programs and liberal education do not mix.

The Morrill Act's Provisions and the Major Questions Concerning the Legislation

The Morrill Act had three major provisions. The first was to establish an endowment to support higher education. The second addressed the states' obligations to maintain funding for the enterprise. The third defined the type of educational goals to be furthered: "where the leading object shall be, without excluding other scientific and classical studies and including military tactics, to teach such branches of learning as are related to agriculture and mechanic arts, in such manner as the legislatures of the States may respectively prescribe in order to promote the liberal and practical education of the industrial classes in the several pursuits and professions of life."[3] Note that the inclusion of "military tactics" is not among the main purposes of the act, as it lies in the clause dealing with "other scientific and classical studies." That said, the inclusion was hardly an afterthought, for the Civil War was raging when Congress passed the act.

Much debate surrounded the politics, intent, and vision of the Morrill Act. As a major form of national legislation supported by numerous lawmakers and citizens, the act embodied many intents and aspirations, with supporters drawing on the thoughts of leading educational and economic thinkers of that time and earlier years. In addition, it built on previous legislation dealing with public land and education, such as the Northwest Ordinance of 1787. The act was also part of a larger package, for in 1862 Congress passed other major acts that also addressed economic expansion and the use of lands: the Homestead Act; the Emigrant Aid Act; and two transcontinental railroad acts. Topping off the legislative surge, Congress created the Department of Agriculture in 1862.[4] Thus the Morrill Act comprised part of a larger project of nation-building that accelerated in midcentury, as powerful national and international economic forces called for more scientific education and knowledge, and political forces favored a greater use of national power.[5]

The vagueness of the Morrill Act accompanied the breadth of its vision. The act did specify the nature or content of the types of education it required as a condition for its grants. But it left it up to the states to determine what the balance of practical and traditional liberal education would entail, and for decades they received little guidance from the act or the national government itself. The Morrill Act represented an experiment and the states would be the laboratories. That said, it is possible to glean some notion of the broader purposes of the act, most of which are also relevant to the act's military clause.

The purposes of the Morrill Act embraced two interconnected aspects: policy-oriented concerns both specific and more general in nature; and broader theoretical aspects related to visions of education and citizenship. Policy included the specific grants of land given on the condition of the fulfillment of the specified forms of education (however undefined). More generally and strategically, the act was intended to contribute to national wealth and progress by expanding higher education to new classes of citizens and by providing for more practical and scientific forms of knowledge suited to an age of utilitarianism, democratic sensibility, and growing concerns about America's status in the world community.

According to scholars, most proponents were primarily concerned with economic development and the status of America in the new industrial world order characterized by expanding international markets and commitments. For America to keep up, it needed to more effectively educate the middle and industrial classes, giving particular attention to scientific, technical, and practical knowledge. Economic development and status were Justin Morrill's predominant concerns. Morrill worried that soil erosion and deterioration would harm America's economic status in the world, and he hoped that the proper disposal of public lands would increase the nation's wealth. As researcher Kathryn Wade observes, "Morrill was concerned with the deterioration of the soil because it put the United States behind the agricultural productivity of England. In order to enlarge the productive power of the country, Morrill encouraged the scientific education of farmers and mechanics. Educating farmers and mechanics would enlarge the productive power of the United States and relieve the country from debts to creditors abroad."[6] In a speech before Congress in 1858, Morrill expressed dismay that "Other nations lead us, not in the invention and handling of improved implements, but in nearly all the practical sciences which can be brought to aid the management and results of agricultural labor. We owe it to ourselves to not become a weak competitor in the most important field where we are to meet the world as rivals."[7] Several other members of Congress joined Morrill in emphasizing economic development as a predominant objective of the act, with more practically oriented education serving as a means to that end. Supporters of the Morrill Act were also aware of the new type of university emerging in Europe, which served to advance more practical scientific and agricultural education.[8]

Some commentators conclude that the mid-nineteenth century was a turning point in educational thought, with more citizens and leaders questioning the validity of a predominantly classical liberal education and its emphasis upon pure mathematics, classic texts, and Latin. Other scholars have challenged this position, pointing out that earlier generations of Americans had valued such practical knowledge as scientific and vocational study along with traditional liberal education. Thomas Jefferson, James Madison, and George Washington favored the establishment of a national university or a national agriculture college, though such an institution did not come to pass, and Benjamin Franklin championed an education that would prepare one "for learning any business, calling, or profession."[9] The New York Society for the Promotion of Agriculture, founded in 1791, called for a more scientific and systematic approach to agriculture. And John Quincy Adams advocated public support of "scientific research and inquiry [directed toward] the improvement of agriculture, commerce and manufactures, the cultivation and encouragement of the mechanic and elegant arts, the advancement of literature, and progress of the sciences, ornamental and profound."[10] Scholars once believed that engineering schools did not exist in meaningful numbers until after the Civil War, but this contention, too, has been challenged by more recent research, as scholars have found numerous institutions that offered courses in engineering in the pre–Morrill Act period.[11] Thus the Morrill Act may not have been quite as path-breaking as some of its advocates have claimed. It expressly eschewed "excluding other scientific and classical studies and including military tactics," and its concern for practical and vocational scientific study was not entirely new. But the emphasis the act placed upon more practical education was new, along with the policy and financial tools it provided, as well as its egalitarian inspiration.

In addition to being a policy-oriented law in both more specific and general/strategic senses, the Morrill Act represented substantive visions of citizenship and education. Some supporters believed the act furthered egalitarian values, which included equal respect for the agrarian and mechanical classes and professions. In his seminal book written a few years after the act's centennial, Earle D. Ross called the higher education inspired by the Morrill Act "Democracy's College" for this and related reasons.[12] Many educational visionaries and practitioners influenced the thinking behind the Morrill Act, but I may only mention a few for the purposes of illustration.

Morrill himself spoke of the need to make college accessible to all citizens, including the "sons of toil." Senator James Harlan of Iowa (whose main concern was egalitarian) focused on "equal rights and representation." As Wade observes, "Judging from his remarks in the Senate, Harlan's vision for land-grant institutions might be succinctly articulated as educating the laboring classes so that they might rise in status and have representation and opportunities equal to that of the professional men of the country. His goal was to provide an education for the uneducated."[13] Harlan's vision harkened back to the ideas of the man whom many observers have considered the most influential intellectual father of the Morrill Act, Jonathan Baldwin Turner of Illinois College. Turner advocated a new system of education for the "industrial classes" in a speech he delivered in 1850 in which he presented his plan for an "industrial university." Turner's plan was supported by the famous *New York Tribune* journalist Horace Greeley, and was discussed in Congress in 1854. According to Turner, "All civilized society is, necessarily, divided into two distinct cooperative, not antagonistic, classes: a small class, whose proper business is to teach the true principles of religion, law, medicine, science, art, and literature; and a much larger class, who are engaged in some form of labor in agriculture, commerce, and the arts. For the sake of convenience, we will designate the former the professional and the latter the industrial class; not implying that each may not be equally industrious, the one in the intellectual, the other in their industrial pursuits."[14] Turner's plan echoed the egalitarian/utilitarian ideas of other pioneers in the expansion of education. Horace Mann, for example, envisioned common schools as "'great equalizers' designed to enforce and support the anti-aristocratic principles of the American dream."[15] We will see that the "anti-aristocratic" spirit was also an important aspect of the Morrill Act's "military tactics" provision. Growing out of the labor movement for mechanical education, the People's College of Havana, New York, and its president, Amos Brown, also embraced education for the industrial classes in the 1850s, emphasizing the working-class and scientific knowledge pertinent to mechanics and the arts. According to Wade, the college offered courses only in agriculture and mechanics, and did not clearly define what "mechanical education" meant: "It could mean anything from the education of engineers and architects to the training of machine operators and tradesmen."[16]

A final figure merits special attention, especially because of his connection to military-oriented education: Captain Alden Partridge. Partridge's theories of education presaged the military provisions of the Morrill Act and the

Reserve Officers' Training Corps that grew out of the seeds the act planted. A graduate of West Point in 1806, and one-time superintendent of that institution (he departed under controversy), Partridge was the founder of the first civilian military academy in American higher education, the American Literary, Scientific, and Military Academy, in 1819, which later changed its name to Norwich University. He was also the first person to propose the idea of land-grant higher education in the United States (Turner was the second). Partridge and Norwich championed an "American System of Education" that stood for a new conception of liberal education designed to foster a "constitutional republic": a combination of high-level civic knowledge; training in practical subjects that are conducive to the growth of national wealth (e.g., "agriculture, commerce, and manufactures"); and appropriate military training.[17] Partridge's notion of education and citizenship called for a well-rounded individual who would possess both liberal and practical knowledge, as well as an appreciation of the obligation of all citizens to bear the responsibility of national defense. This obligation was important for at least two reasons beyond the obvious practical need to defend the country from its enemies. First, because defense is the first responsibility of the state, citizens worthy of self-government will understand its significance and answer its call if need be.[18] Second, such citizenship protects republican principles because it guards against the encroachments of the military elite—a concern grounded in America's historical fear of a standing national army and, therefore, its commitment to the "citizen-soldier" ideal that stood as the remedy to this fear. According to Willard Lee Nash, "Opposed to a large standing army, [Partridge] felt that the country would do better to depend upon a trained citizenry which had been properly educated."[19] In Partridge's own words, "I am forced to the conclusion that in every republic the due cultivation of a proper military spirit amongst the great mass of the people and a general diffusion of military information are indispensably necessary for the preservation of liberty; and consequently that those republics which neglect these requisites, will eventually be driven to exchange their freedom for a form of government bordering at least on military despotism."[20]

Partridge's position echoed that of Jefferson, who also championed the citizen-soldier ideal: "We must train and classify the whole of our male citizens, and make military instruction a regular part of collegiate education. We can never be safe until this is done."[21] But Partridge placed military education in a broader context of liberal and practical education. According to Lee S. Harford, "He intended the military training at Norwich to 'constitute an appendage' to a cadet's civil education, only one element in a curriculum designed to educate young Americans for the dual role of the citizen-soldier: engineers, businessmen or teachers during peace and combat command-ers in the event of war. Along with the function of providing a reserve of trained officers for volunteer units and the militia, he expected the Norwich program to produce officers for the Regular Army as well."[22] Norwich Uni-versity was just the beginning of civilian military education in the United States, spawning the establishment of numerous other civilian military colleges.

Though conclusive evidence of Partridge's influence on Senator Morrill is lacking, circumstantial evidence persuasively supports a link. Morrill was acquainted with Partridge and resided only a few miles from him. In addi-tion, a business partner of Morrill's served on Norwich's board, and Morrill himself was asked to join the board, though he declined the offer. Beyond this connection, Partridge's theory of education is consistent with many of the aspirations of the Morrill Act mentioned earlier, including the inclusion of a wider class of citizens in higher education; the broadening of student bodies to include those with more practical education and interests; the belief that education should be useful in serving the public interest in addi-tion to respecting the traditional idea of knowledge as an end in itself; the egalitarian desire to foster equal respect for the middle and working classes; opposition to and fear of excessive elitism (the citizen-soldier ideal was con-sidered a major check on West Point and Annapolis); and the belief that the government and public should support such education in a meaningful way.

We should also note that at the same time, the military portion of the bill was distinct in its own respects. The wording places "military tactics" along with classical and scientific studies, which the act distinguishes from "branches of learning as are related to agriculture and mechanic arts." Though Norwich and its sister institutions attempted to pry military study and training away from their elitist origins, the Morrill Act's word-ing treated these educational enterprises as separate from agriculture and the mechanic arts. Second, and more important, after the exigencies of the Civil War, the military tactic requirement proved controversial in a way that has persevered to this day. And it is one thing to have military training in such a civilian institution as Norwich, which is designed to be a military school, and another thing to require such pedagogy in schools that are not preeminently military in nature. In a nutshell, Partridge's vision of military education could turn into dreaded militarism if not properly applied and contained.

The Military Provisions of the Morrill Act and Its Implementation before World War I

The Morrill Act was passed at the dawn of what Arthur M. Cohen calls the "University Transformation Era" in American history. In the seventy-five years after 1870, the number of students nationwide would swell from 63,000 to 1.5 million, and the number of faculty members from 5,500 to 150,000. Doctoral degrees mushroomed from zero to 3,300.[23] But whereas the mechanical and agricultural aspects of the Morrill Act grew with the burgeoning industrial and agrarian economies after the Civil War, the military provision languished, taking decades to have a meaningful impact. Indeed, it would not be until World War I that the military part of the Morrill Act would gain real traction. As with the other provisions of the act, the military section would become prominent when military necessity or convenience called for its implementation.

Before the Morrill Act, military instruction was conducted in either the two military academies (West Point and Annapolis) or one of the civilian military colleges (e.g., Norwich, Virginia Military Institute, Citadel). Though generally good at training officers—though many observers claimed that even these officers performed poorly in the earlier stages of the war—the academies could not produce the 20,000 or so officers the Union needed to wage successful battle. (West Point could provide only 1,500). Meanwhile, the local units of the militia had not performed up to expectations, and few leaders wanted to expand the military academies. A normative concern also accompanied the problem of numbers: the nation's traditional distrust of military professionals and a standing military, which comprised an important part of the citizen-soldier ideal. According to Michael S. Neiberg, "Like Partridge, [Morrill] offered the alternative of military training in civilian institutions as a means by which a democratic people could gain a competent officer corps without endangering their basic liberties."[24] Morrill was familiar with Norwich and the values behind the citizen-soldier ideal; in a similar vein, he was influenced by John Milton's thoughts in the *Tractate on Education*, in which the famous author wrote, "I call, therefore, a complete and generous education that which fits a man to perform justly, skillfully, and magnanimously all the offices, both private and public, of peace and war."[25]

The Civil War brought important historical tensions and forces to the fore: a greater need for military professionalism, which challenged the traditional commitments to civilian control of the military; and the citizen-soldier ideal. American citizens and leaders were deeply concerned about the need to beef up the military in this time of national crisis, but they continued to be dedicated to honoring and preserving the nation's traditional commitment to civil liberty and the appropriate distrust of a standing military. And as events would show, fighting the Civil War successfully obligated President Lincoln to stretch governmental power—especially executive power—beyond traditional limits, posing severe problems for civil liberty.[26] The Morrill Act addressed this tension by placing military instruction in land-grant civilian institutions. In so doing, the act created a third type of military instruction that resembled but also differed from the two preexisting models. The first type was represented by the two professional academies, West Point and Annapolis, military institutions that at the time downplayed the liberal arts in favor of instruction in military subjects and such sciences as engineering.[27] Second, civilian military colleges like Norwich emphasized liberal education more than the academies but were arranged along military lines. The new civilian land-grant institutions now constituted the third type of higher education institution: involved in military training but predominantly civilian in nature, with minor exceptions. The inclusion of the land-grants in the national scheme of military instruction would, over time, significantly shift the education of future officers in a civilian direction once the programs took on substance in the twentieth century.

Placing military instruction in nonmilitary civilian colleges was unprecedented national policy, though a military-civilian college nexus existed in several states. Georgia law, for example, had mandated that all men between the ages of eighteen and forty-five (except ministers) attend "military muster" a minimum of five times a year, a requirement that affected most students at the University of Georgia. "Muster days" became a cultural ritual involving entire communities throughout much of the South. According to one source, the militia drill associated with this ritual became "the earliest example of military training in American colleges."[28] By extending such exercises to land-grant colleges, the Morrill Act planted the seeds for what would become the thriving ROTC programs of the twentieth century. Neiberg, the leading historian of ROTC, pinpoints the legacy succinctly: "The crisis of the Civil War and its aftermath brought these two ideas [professionalism and commitment to the citizen-soldier ideal] together and eventually produced the modern antecedent to the twentieth-century ROTC program."[29]

The Morrill Act's passage came too late for land-grant military instruction to have a substantial effect on the war. The act's vagueness even precluded effective implementation for the next half century. Indeed, it remained unclear whether military instruction must be compulsory or not.[30] Furthermore, commitment to the military programs was generally lukewarm among the military, higher education, and the government until later in the century, when US involvement in world affairs and military matters became more prominent. (Throughout American history, the popularity of ROTC and its predecessor programs has been influenced by external political and military events, sometimes in straightforward ways, other times in more nuanced ways.)[31] But genuine commitment to the programs would have to await America's engagement in World War I, when historical necessities would once again shape the views of the stakeholders.

Objective observers who have studied the vicissitudes of the land-grant military programs between 1862 and World War I uniformly depict a desultory and ineffective national program. The lack of statutory guidance and carry-through on the part of the War Department and the Interior Department (which had administrative jurisdiction over the land-grants) "caused a great amount of confusion which existed for a long period of years in the various universities," according to Gene M. Lyons and John W. Masland.[32] In addition, "There was no organization and little enthusiasm for the training in the War Department. There was equally little agreement anywhere on the meaning of the Morrill Act itself."[33] At first the War Department did not even provide personnel to teach military tactics, so implementation depended upon individuals who happened to be on campus. Rutgers, for example, had an engineering professor from West Point in its employ who handled drill. The War Department modestly began to detail officers to the land-grants in 1866, but it would take forty years or more before it and Congress made fuller provisions for implementing the military clause of the act. Supplying of equipment—such as guns, ammunition, uniforms, instructional materials, space, and so forth—remained spotty. Even when Congress got around to furnishing more support, the military often resisted meaningful interaction or oversight. As Eddy observes, "an act of Congress does not always produce the desired results. Out of indifference, the military began its long-heard plea of poverty which would be repeated so many times in subsequent years. Though Congress gave its blessing to the provisions of officers, officers did not arrive."[34]

Early on the War Department distinguished between land-grant "military colleges" modeled roughly on West Point and Annapolis and those with less military emphasis. The former institutions were led by military officers, and their students lived in barracks, wore military uniforms during the day, and engaged in frequent drill exercises and tactical training. The military emphasis was notably less prevalent in most of the other land-grants. Cornell's story at the time appears ambiguous. Incorporated three years after the Morrill Act, Cornell was "at its beginning organized as a military school," according to Cornell historian Morris Bishop, hosting a school of military science designed to instill martial virtues in the students. But Andrew Dixon White, a pioneer in American higher education who served as Cornell's first president, was ambivalent about military education; he believed it worthwhile to impart certain virtues and to prepare Cornell students to "lead in repressing civil discord," but "his faith in human reasonableness, his detestation of social and intellectual discipline, his impatient utopianism, made him instinctively antimilitarist."[35] As of 1870, only three of the fifty-two "white" land-grant institutions presented clear examples of the military model: Clemson; the Agricultural and Mechanical College of Texas; and Virginia Agricultural and Mechanical College. From the beginning it was assumed (though, again, not specified in the law or regulations) that the programs would be mandatory for nonexempt male students. Consequently, compulsory programs became the uniform practice until 1923, when the Wisconsin legislature interpreted the Morrill Act to allow voluntary programs. This interpretation was later backed up by the US Supreme Court in a case involving the University of California, leading other schools to make the program voluntary. During the 1880–99 period some land-grants created four-year programs, whereas others offered programs of two years and three years.[36]

Faculty were generally lukewarm toward the programs, and until the 1890s, "the colleges attempted to reduce the requirement to a minimum necessary to comply with the vague mandate."[37] Drill was the predominant form of military instruction, with few offerings of courses in theory and tactics. But student, institutional, and governmental interest peaked in the last decade of the century as the United States emerged as a major power on the international stage, engaging in what historians have called "progressive imperialism" and colonialism, American style.[38] By then, colleges had striven to improve the programs in modest ways by teaching more than just drill, and students responded by enrolling in greater numbers, with the decade of 1888–98 witnessing 75,000 students taking at least one year of military instruction.[39] In addition, the War Department began to exercise closer oversight and contact in the later 1890s, including uniformly conducting inspections and treating all institutions on an equal basis. (Previous administration had been more haphazard and discretionary.) The department also increased the number of officers detailed to be instructors to between 100 and 110 in 1893. (It had detailed 29 in 1866, with incremental increases in subsequent years).[40] It also began to require that military instructors be given faculty status, enjoying the same rights and privileges as regular faculty members. (The fact that faculty were selected by the War Department rather than the civilian institutions created a new friction that has persisted to the present time despite reforms that arose in ensuing decades.)

This said, the programs still remained largely underdeveloped and non-rigorous compared to later programs, and Congress and the War Department continued to harbor indifference. Significantly, career opportunities for graduates were limited because the army and the state militias refused to recognize them with commissions. This pattern continued from 1900 to 1914: "Until World War I, military programs on campuses remained quite informal and inefficient. . . . However, the groundwork for such a system had been laid. A loose connection between the War Department and civilian institutions of higher learning had been established, and a preference for non-professional officers had become a consistent feature of American culture."[41]

Enter ROTC

As with most major wars, the Civil War's significance was greater than the military victory for the North. In addition to ending slavery, the war wrought profound changes in national consciousness, economic institutions and relations, and public administration and law. Among other things, the demands of the Civil War contributed to the development of a more centralized national state.[42] World War I was no exception to this historical truism. The reorganization of American armed forces in anticipation of the entry into the war was among the most important changes occasioned by the war.

Despite the improvements in the latter years of the nineteenth century, the decade prior to 1914 constituted one of the "lowest ebbs" for land-grant military programs.[43] Accordingly, in 1913 the Association of Land-Grant Colleges called on fellow institutions to pressure Congress to provide more uniform standards for instruction in military science and tactics. This move began to bear fruit when war broke out in Europe the following year. As in the early stages of the Civil War, national concern regarding preparedness provoked a congressional response. The 1916 Hay-Chamberlain bill—better known as the National Defense Act (NDA) of 1916—incorporated many of the proposals the association endorsed in the area of land-grant military instruction. Along with amendments in 1920 and 1924, the NDA created the basis upon which ROTC would operate in the collaboration between the government and civilian institutions of higher learning.

The NDA established "the essentials of military policy for the nation."[44] Among other things, the act created the three major components of the nation's military forces that have remained in effect to this day: the active duty forces; the National Guard (a reformed version of the state militia, constituting a compromise between national and state authority); and the organized reserves, which included the first official version of ROTC. The new ROTC program bestowed upon the War Department the power to create more uniform and complete programs in several respects: by standardizing the curriculum and equipment; by stipulating more hours for courses and the methods for teaching them; by requiring more substantive courses that would include classes in map reading, military history and law, basic tactics, marksmanship, camp sanitation, and drill; and by providing "commutation subsistence" at the government's expense. Neiberg depicts the creation of ROTC as a compromise measure with which the War Department, the regular forces, the National Guard, the states, and the citizenry could live. Funding was limited, however, and, as usual, the provision of instructors was less than hoped for, so schools rushed to compete for programmatic resources. Even "elite" schools that would rebel against ROTC in the 1960s vied to obtain programs because of the general collegiate commitments to patriotism and service. As Nash pointed out, ROTC was made available not only to traditional land-grant institutions but to private schools as well.[45] According to Neiberg, "Students at Bowdoin, Williams, Harvard, Princeton, Yale, and Dartmouth all circulated petitions asking to have an ROTC unit; all were approved, according to Neiberg."[46]

The War Department presented its plans for administering the ROTC programs in land-grants in the spring of 1917, and the land-grants responded that summer by submitting applications. But the exigencies of war soon complicated matters, as thousands of students withdrew from college in order to fight in the war. As in the Civil War, the necessities of national defense precluded relying upon the fledgling programs, so in the summer of 1918 the government suspended the land-grant program in favor of the Students' Army Training Corps (SATC). The SATC provided for direct War Department control of training, and campuses across the land became veritable armed camps that trained soldiers and conducted an array of war-related activities and research. Regular curricula were abandoned in favor of war-related training, "and courses were hastily improvised in order to meet the requirements of the War Department," leading to occasional friction between civilian institutions and the military.[47]

A couple of examples illustrate the nature of military instruction during the war. As in most land-grant universities, the military science program at Cornell waxed and waned in its popularity and quality before the advent of ROTC in the NDA of 1916. After Cornell's fledgling ROTC program was wrapped into the SATC, Cornell became in 1918 a military school. The university also hosted a variety of war programs, including a school of military aeronautics; radio engineers and aerial photographers; a naval training unit of 310 men; a Marines unit of 170 men; and an army trade school. The Cornell Medical College in New York City became the headquarters of the School for Military Roentgenologists.[48] According to Cornell's Army ROTC webpage, the university supplied more commissioned officers to the war effort than any other institution in America, including West Point (4,598). Two hundred sixty-four Cornellians died in the war.[49] The war left a mark on Cornell, enhancing the status of the sciences and leaving administrative reorganization in its wake.

Other Ivy League schools followed the Cornell pattern in the World War I period. Though not a land-grant institution, Yale, for example, initiated its own military program after the passage of the Morrill Act, and with the later passage of the NDA, it "immediately became involved [in ROTC] and because of its previous experience, it became the sole college to give field artillery training." When ROTC folded into the SATC, Yale faculty voted 38–0 to grant credit to the courses.[50] The university also pioneered the development of the Naval Aviation Force. At least 9,000 students and graduates served in the war effort, with 227 giving their lives. Overall, "Nearly the entire student body was enrolled in an informal military training course." As historian Gaddis Smith has pointed out that "ROTC was a problem from its inception in 1917" because of the less than stellar quality of its courses and instructors—a problem nationwide according to other scholars of ROTC: "A skeptical Yale College faculty acquiesced in granting course credit because President Arthur Hadley said it was the right thing to do."[51]

After the war, executives of the Association of Land-Grant Colleges and the War Department met in Baltimore to fashion a more formal plan to improve courses, equipment, and instruction. Writing at the time, Bizzell observed, "The result has been unusually satisfactory. The fact that at last a definite military policy had been established for the Nation, and clearly conceived objectives had been set up for military training, made it possible for the colleges to set about their task with a full understanding of what was expected of them."[52] This optimism was no doubt exaggerated, but Bizzell is right that the fledgling ROTC program was an improvement over the programs of previous decades. Though a national sense of isolationism, distrust of a standing military, and misgivings about military training on campus returned in the 1920s—spearheaded by the Committee on Militarism in Education, an anti–mandatory ROTC movement that was influential in the later 1920s and early 1930s—most colleges and universities accepted ROTC as a good thing, though with qualifications.[53] Despite tensions—both natural and circumstantial—and continued squabbles over resources and the extent of commitments, higher education remained in favor of ROTC for reasons of patriotism and a sense of service obligation. Neiberg mentions another reason: as universities and colleges moved away from their traditional religious moorings, educational leaders looked to secular programs that could instill a sense of duty, character, and discipline. Many leaders believed that appropriate military instruction could contribute to this goal.[54]

By the end of 1919, 135 institutions housed ROTC units, mainly consisting of two parts: a two-year mandatory program in which male students worked at least three hours per week; and a two-year voluntary advanced program for students who passed the requisite muster, which called for five hours of training each week. By this time, the army had standardized the curriculum to include the array of subjects mentioned earlier. Meanwhile, the antimilitarism movement of the 1920s challenged the mandatory nature of ROTC and questioned the fit between higher education and the military. Johns Hopkins, Princeton, the University of Wisconsin, the University of California, and some other schools experienced controversies over ROTC and moved to make ROTC noncompulsory. Before long, twenty-one schools had made military instruction voluntary.[55] For the most part, the antimandatory movement objected to making ROTC compulsory, not to the program's existence per se. That said, the movement constituted the first major protest movement against ROTC. Other movements would arise in later years. In addition to the controversy over mandatory enrollment, critics pointed to concerns that would become persistent issues for ROTC, including the quality of courses and instructors; the costs of the programs for the university; and the relative lack of institutional say regarding instructors and curriculum. The overarching concern is perhaps best expressed in Kipling's famous lament in *Barrack-Room Ballads and Other Verses*: "Oh, East is East, and West is West, and never the twain shall meet."

Except in such genuine national emergencies as the Civil War and the two world wars, the twain of the military and the university are as East and West. The moral charter of institutions of higher learning is centered on freedom of inquiry and dissent, whereas the charter of the military places much more emphasis upon hierarchical authority and obedience. To be sure, this distinction is predicated upon Weberian ideal-type models of each respective institution, so neither model adequately captures the actual subtleties and nuances of each complex institution. Nevertheless, the distinction is heuristically useful—and it has been politically salient in controversial times. The presence of the military in higher education poses a fundamental question about the presence of a nondemocratic institution in a democratic institution. Many naturally ask why a democratic institution should house a nondemocratic entity. This question echoes the very tension that lies at the heart of the Morrill Act more generally: the tension between the classic ivory tower conception of the university and the university as a place for the teaching of practical and useful knowledge. Farms and corporations, after all, are not democratic institutions either, but linking these institutions to universities was a central project of the Morrill Act. More broadly, is the proper function of university knowledge to understand the world, or to change it?[56] In the eyes of the Morrill Act's supporters, it is both.

World War II, the Cold War University, and the Vietnam Retreat

The exigencies of war after the attack on Pearl Harbor once again compelled the government to modify the ROTC program during World War II. The government lowered the draft age to eighteen, and university employees and students left campuses in droves to serve. Their exit posed a problem for universities and the military, which confronted a dearth of students and qualified officers, respectively. In response, the army turned to the Officer Candidate School (OCS) to produce officers, and the military forces formed new programs in 1943 to replace ROTC. These programs combined college education with military service, such as the navy's "V" Training Programs, the Naval Indoctrination Training School, and army programs under the umbrella of the Army Specialized Training Program. Once again, universities became veritable military instruction institutions.[57] Nonetheless, ROTC played a material role in preparing the United States to fight the war. Between August 1940 and the end of 1941, eighty thousand Organized Reserve Corps officers, most of whom hailed from ROTC, stepped up to duty, forming what Army Cadet Command historians Arthur T. Coumbe and Lee S. Harford call the "nucleus around which General [George C.] Marshall built the war-time Army." Indeed, Marshall declared that ROTC was the most important contributor to the officer mobilization the nation undertook (though the abilities that these officers attained were derived largely from real war experience and training, not ROTC itself; officers from OCS proved to be superior).[58] One hundred twenty thousand ROTC officers served as officers during World War II and the Korean War, thirty thousand of whom had graduated from the civilian military colleges.

As they had in World War I, institutions of higher learning became major centers of military training and war-related research during World War II—acts that transformed the very nature of higher education in ways consistent with the service orientation of the Morrill Act but also in ways that raised traditional academic eyebrows. As David Engerman writes, "World War II was the watershed moment for the involvement of federal agencies in university-based research."[59] After the war, America confronted a new historical circumstance. The nation was unable to retreat from substantial international engagement because of new obligations associated with its emergence as the leader of the free world and the concomitant rise of the Soviet challenge. Though proud of its prominence in world affairs, the nation was also uneasy about the new power it wielded. Reflecting on America's ascension to world-power status in the aftermath of World War II, Reinhold Niebuhr wrote, "We never dreamed that we would have as much political power as we possess today. . . . We were, as a matter of fact, always vague, as the whole liberal culture is fortunately vague, about how power is to be related to the allegedly universal values which we hold in trust for mankind."[60] For at least a decade, most Americans and universities agreed with the "Cold War Consensus," which accepted the need to maintain a military and a technological deterrence to the Soviet Union. But the tensions to which Niebuhr alluded would rise to the fore in the later 1960s.

The Cold War also gave birth to the so-called Cold War University, which continued the tradition of public service in both land-grant institutions and in private schools, though in a more controversial way. The ethic of the Cold

War University was service in the area of national defense and security, with ROTC constituting one foundation of this enterprise. The Cold War University involved dynamic relationships among universities, the government, private foundations, and corporations, each of which supplied large-scale funding through a complex web of interactions.

Though the Cold War University constituted an extension of the purposes of the Morrill Act, it was also sui generis in an important respect: its acceptance in the republic was dependent upon the vicissitudes of US foreign relations and defense policy. As is well-known, the Cold War Consensus unraveled as the prospects of the Vietnam War darkened, thereby throwing the Cold War University and ROTC into heated controversy. As might be expected because of the inherent controversies attendant to national defense policy and war—especially after World War II, when America found itself the new world leader assuming responsibilities far beyond its shores—no other areas of land-grant endeavor have proved to be so vulnerable or exposed to public controversy. War and defense are different animals from such policies as agriculture, engineering, and economics.

Historian Jeremy Suri has analyzed the constellation of factors that comprised the Cold War University in his book on Henry Kissinger, whose academic rise at Harvard epitomized the Cold War University. Though he does not mention the Morrill Act, Suri shows how the Cold War University embodied the broader purposes embedded in the Morrill Act. The "intellectual and institutional transformation from traditional scholarly detachment to contemporary political empowerment created the 'Cold War University,'" Suri observes. "The intentional blurring of the lines between academic and policy analysis, as well as scholarship and national defense, constituted the Cold War University." Noting the historical experiences of Jews such as Kissinger and other minorities who had suffered oppression at the hands of power, many pioneers of the Cold War University championed the values of liberal democracy while also valuing the role of the state in protecting the freedom and rights they cherished. (Kissinger himself maintained an uneasy philosophical balance between Kant and Hobbes.) The group of policy scholars Kissinger helped assemble at and around Harvard "identified themselves as defenders of the United States against extremes at home and abroad. For all their intellectual expertise they pursued research explicitly designed to serve practical and immediate government purposes, in the process protecting a liberal capitalist world. This was the overriding ethos of the Cold War University."[61] Kissinger drew inspiration from his Harvard mentor William Yandell Elliott, who helped Kissinger establish the famous International Seminar in 1950, which connected students and an extraordinary number of leading foreign policy analysts and practitioners. The seminar was a thread in the complex web of "Cold War networks" forged by Cold War University practitioners. Enjoying a prominent role in the Cold War policy community, Elliott envisioned the Cold War as "a struggle for national survival" that called for a stronger national defense. In Elliott's words, "the most elementary lesson of history: No power retains friends which is too weak to defend itself in will or war potential." Elliott's foreign policy realism called for political will to counter "the great mistake of liberalism," which is the belief "that there was [an] automatic character about the rights of people without an affirmation of values or a dedication to duty."[62] Liberal democracy's freedoms are not manna from heaven.

The Cold War University embodied Morrill Act principles on steroids, as an array of government agencies provided federal funds relating to defense, including the Department of Defense (DoD, which replaced the War Department in the 1947 reorganization of the national defense bureaucracy); the Office of Naval Research (ONR, established in 1946); the Atomic Energy Commission (AEC, founded in 1946); and the National Aeronautics and Space Administration (NASA, founded in 1958); the National Science Foundation (NSF, established in 1950) and the National Institutes of Health (NIH, founded in 1887) had broader missions, but their funding was "correlated with the Cold War." The NSF budget, for example, mushroomed from $100,000 in 1950 to $100 million in 1960, most of which went to university-related research. According to historian Matthew Levin, "By the late sixties, the numbers were even more dramatic, with universities spending three billion dollars on research in 1968, seventy percent of it funded by the federal government. . . . More than half of this came from defense-related agencies, including the AEC ($110,000,000), NASA ($129,000,000), and the Department of Defense ($243,000,000)." Another signal act was the National Defense Act of 1958, precipitated by the Soviet Union's launching of Sputnik in 1957. Although the majority of other outside funding went to natural scientists and language programs, social scientists also received support for interdisciplinary studies that had implications for the Cold War. The Rockefeller and Carnegie foundations disseminated funds for the first area-study programs, which had to do with the Soviet Union, and the Ford Foundation supplied funds for multidisciplinary studies of world regions. After Sputnik, the federal government unveiled the Title VI program, which furnished funds for area-studies programs.[63]

ROTC was part and parcel of this transformation for two essential reasons. First, the program was an integral aspect of a government-university partnership, which was an important element of the Morrill Act's vision. Second, ROTC is the modern embodiment of the citizen-soldier concept, which grew out of the vision of Partridge and Norwich. The program fared well during this period, with the military introducing some innovative new programs, such as the army's "Distinguished Military Graduate" program, which bestowed commissions in the regular army upon superior graduates. Cadet enrollment in the army programs grew to nearly 100,000 at 190 schools in 1955. At this time, 75–85 percent of all active duty army second lieutenants came from ROTC. By 1989, ROTC graduates would comprise almost 70 percent of the army's active field officers and nearly 60 percent of the generals.[64] The naval and air force programs—founded in 1926 and 1946, respectively—were also successful in similar respects. At the same time, however, the programs still tended to be less organized and centralized than many considered desirable. According to Harford, "The growing importance of the citizen-soldier to the active Army developed in spite of the ROTC's lagging management structure, which up until the mid-1960s administered the program in a very decentralized, haphazard manner."[65] True central standardization would not come until after the Vietnam War, with the establishment in the mid-1980s of Cadet Command centers in the respective services to oversee and systematize ROTC programs nationally. This reform was part of the military's broader effort to enhance its professionalism and reputation after suffering a decline in both areas during and after Vietnam.[66] Although beset by conflicts and problems endemic to the program (budget limitations, tensions with universities, the ebbs and flows of enrollments and the propensity to serve, etc.), Cadet Commands provided better regulation and oversight and strengthened the programs academically, making it easier for universities and colleges to accept a relationship in some form.[67]

The Cold War consensus began to crack in the later 1950s as a result of several factors, including the impact of McCarthyism, concerns about nuclear weapons and the arms race with the Soviets, questions regarding undue defense department funding on campus, and the equivocal results of the Korean War. In addition, the academic standards for faculty and students were becoming more rigorous and demanding, and some faculty members were becoming increasingly resentful or distrustful of ROTC with regard to the issues of quality and accountability that had accompanied the program since its inception. Concerns about the academic quality and accountability of ROTC programs engendered much give-and-take between higher education institutions and military leaders, leading to reforms that were designed to make ROTC more compatible with higher education. Intended to attract more high-quality students into the program, the 1964 ROTC Revitalization Act incorporated some major reforms after extensive congressional debate and horse trading that once again called Bismarck to mind. Among other things, the act created a new scholarship program, enhanced subsistence for cadets in the advanced course, and provided a modified curriculum option for students who decided to enroll in ROTC after their first or second year in school. This option allowed junior and community college students to join upon entering four-year colleges.[68]

Historians and political theorists have observed that reforms are often the harbingers of more radical change. Such was the case with the Revitalization Act, which was passed the same year as the Berkeley Free Speech Movement fired a shot heard around the academic world. Students around the country had already begun to express their discontent with higher education in protests against the quality of education, the lack of student academic freedom, and the presence of in loco parentis rules. In 1962, the Students for a Democratic Society wrote the famous Port Huron Statement, which stood as a latter-day declaration of independence from the pedagogical failings of the "multiversity," which embodied a bloated bureaucratic incarnation of the Morrill Act's aspirations. And 1964 was also the year of the Tonkin Gulf Resolution, which would propel the United States into the Vietnam War. What happened next is well-known: ROTC became a major target of antiwar protest in campuses across the land. Protesters physically attacked, and even destroyed, some ROTC establishments at many institutions in the late 1960s and early 1970s. ROTC commanders began to feel that they were living in an alien world—"an embassy on foreign soil," as one professor of military science put it.[69] The killings at Kent State in 1970 followed on the heels of the firebombing of an ROTC headquarters there, which, in turn, was a reaction to the disclosure of President Nixon's secret bombing of Cambodia.[70]

The anti–Vietnam War movement was the second important protest movement against ROTC in the nation's history, the first being the anti-militarism movement of the 1920s and 1930s. But the second movement was often more radical and violent than the first, depending on which institution was at stake. Whereas the first movement did not seek to abolish ROTC entirely, the more radical proponents of the second movement sought abolition, while also presenting a more thorough critique of American society to boot. As a result of the antiwar and antimilitary fervor engendered by the Vietnam War, several elite institutions, such as those in the Ivy League, either abolished ROTC or effectively barred it from campus. I say "effectively barred" because dispute reigns regarding the reasons for the programs' retreats. Were the programs terminated for academic reasons or because of the intense pressures exerted by antiwar protesters? New academic standards had been promulgated by many committees set up to reconsider ROTC, and the military refused to accept these in the cases under consideration. But it must be borne in mind that academic questions and concerns had always accompanied ROTC programs and that the committees that proposed the new standards often faced remarkable pressure. It is fair to say that both academic and political reasons were responsible but that political pressures were the most important cause.[71] According to Neiberg, as many as 88 programs left campus during this period. In a widely cited essay, military historian Peter Karsten has reported that 29 schools drove ROTC away between 1966 and 1970. The difference between these accounts could be explained partly by the fact that some schools lost multiple programs.[72]

Despite this trend in the upper echelons of higher education, most institutions and students remained committed to ROTC, even though enrollments fell during this period. And some schools, such as Boston College and Princeton, brought the program back a few years after dropping it, though in a watered-down form that made ROTC largely an extracurricular activity. Campus groups arose that favored returning ROTC, but they were usually countered by groups that reflected the views of the antiwar protesters of the 1960s. Then in the 1980s, a new objection arose.

DADT, ROTC's Comeback, and Concluding Thoughts

ROTC revived in the aftermath of Vietnam, but by the later 1980s it confronted a third protest movement: pro–gay rights advocates who opposed ROTC for discriminating against gays. This civil rights anti-ROTC movement prevented ROTC from returning to many campuses that had effectively barred it in the late 1960s, despite the renewal of pro-ROTC sentiment on many such campuses after the terrorist attacks of September 11, 2001. But this third opposition to ROTC lost its wind when President Obama signed the bill that abolished the "don't ask, don't tell" law in December 2010. As a result of this abolition, several schools brought ROTC back in some form, including Columbia, Yale, Harvard, and Stanford. Ilia Murtazashvili and I chronicle this process at length in *Arms and the University*.[73]

With the civil rights objection removed, the remaining criticisms of ROTC have to do with concerns about militarism—a concern left over from Vietnam and the earlier antimilitarism movement of the 1920s—and the lack of fit between the program's professional training and academic life. These concerns are, in essence, two sides of the same coin. In closing, let me address these concerns. First, ROTC can be justified as a proper extension of the Morrill Act's original aspirations. Military instruction was an explicit part of the original Morrill Act; more important, it is consistent with the purposes and aspirations of the Morrill Act, for it provides a form of practical education that addresses a vital aspect of national need. Indeed, national security is the primary obligation of the state. As John Jay wrote in *Federalist #3*, "Among the many objects to which a wise and free people find it necessary to direct their attention, that of providing for their safety seems to be first."[74] In addition, by setting future military officers side by side with civilian students and faculty, ROTC helps bridge the divisions among classes in America, another aspiration of the Morrill Act. Finally, having an appropriate military presence on campus contributes to the intellectual, experiential, and normative diversity of campus life. The Morrill Act itself is predicated on the productive friction engendered by the coexistence of practical, service, and theoretical education, and ROTC's presence on campus is a historically important aspect of this propitious balance and tension.

Notes

1. Willard Lee Nash, *A Study of the Stated Aims and Purposes of the Departments of Military Science and Tactics, and Physical Education in the Land Grant Colleges of the United States* (New York: Teachers College, Columbia University, 1934), 19.

2. This is a major theme in Stephen Skowronek, *Building a New American State: The Expansion of National Administrative Capacities, 1877–1920* (New York: Cambridge University Press, 1982). Skowronek devotes an ample section to military administrative development and its effect on the nationalization of administration. The theme is one of national advance, constantly checked by blowback from local and state interests. A similar theme (although with a stronger emphasis on libertarian philosophy) is found in Aaron Friedberg, *In the Shadow of the Garrison State: America's Anti-Statism and Its Cold War Strategy* (Princeton: Princeton University Press, 2000). See also Richard Franklin Bensel, *Yankee Leviathan: The Origins of Central State Authority in America, 1859–1877* (New York: Cambridge University Press, 1990). Bensel argues that the demands of the

Civil War contributed to the development of a centralized American state.

3. See in Gordon C. Lee, "The Morrill Act and Education," *British Journal of Education Studies,* 12 (1963): 26–27.

4. See Paul W. Gates, *Agriculture and the Civil War* (New York: Knopf, 1965), 263; Kathryn Lindsay Wade, "The Intent and Fulfillment of the Morrill Act of 1862: A Review of the History of Auburn University and the University of Georgia" (Master's thesis, Clemson University, 1965): 7.

5. See, e.g., P. M. Grant, T. G. Field, R. D. Green, and B. E. Rollin, "The Importance of Comprehensive Agricultural Education in Land-Grant Institutions: A Historical Perspective," *Journal of Animal Science* 78 (2000): 1684–89. On the drive toward nationalization on several fronts, see Skowronek, *Building a New American State.*

6. Wade, "The Intent and Fulfillment of the Morrill Act of 1862, 35.

7. Rep. Justin Morrill, US House of Representatives, 35th Cong., 1st Sess., *Congressional Globe* (April 20, 1858): 1693. See also Wade, "The Intent and Fulfillment of the Morrill Act of 1862," 36.

8. See Lee, "The Morrill Act and Education," 35–36.

9. Franklin's words were later echoed by Ezra Cornell, the founder of Cornell University, one of the leading land-grant institutions. Cornell's official motto is: "I would found an institution where any person can find instruction in any subject." Note, however, that Cornell has always remained committed to the traditional liberal arts, as famously exemplified in the life and values of its first president, Andrew Dixon White. See, e.g., Morris Bishop, *A History of Cornell* (Ithaca, NY: Cornell University Press, 1963).

10. Lee, "The Morrill Act and Education," 20–21.

11. See, e.g., Terry S. Reynolds, "The Education of Engineers in America before the Morrill Act of 1962," *History of Education Quarterly* 32, no. 4 (Winter 1992), 459–482.

12. Earle D. Ross, *Democracy's College: The Land-Grant Movement in the Formative Stage* (New York: Arno Press and the *New York Times,* 1969).

13. Wade, "The Intent and Fulfillment of the Morrill Act of 1862," 44.

14. Turner speech, in Mary Tuner Carriel, *The Life of Jonathan Baldwin Turner* (Urbana: University of Illinois Press, 1961), 138; Wade, "The Intent and Fulfillment of the Morrill Act of 1862," 50. See Ross, *Democracy's College,* 37–40.

15. Lee, "The Morrill Act and Education," 34; Ross, *Democracy's College,* 8–9.

16. Wade, "The Intent and Fulfillment of the Morrill Act of 1862," 55; Ross, *Democracy's College,* 24–27; Edward Danforth Eddy Jr., *Colleges for Our Land and Time: The Land Grant Idea in American Education* (New York: Harper and Brothers, 1956), 15, 34.

17. Wade, "The Intent and Fulfillment of the Morrill Act of 1862," 45; Gary Thomas Lord, "Alden Partridge's Proposal for a National System of Education: A Model for the Morrill Land-Grant Act. *History of Higher Education Annual* (1998): 13.

18. As John Jay wrote in *The Federalist #3,* "Among the many objects to which a wise and free people find it necessary to direct their attention, that of providing for their safety seems to be the first." *The Federalist Papers,* ed. Clinton Rossiter (New

York: New American Library, 1961), 42. The first twenty-nine of the eighty-five Federalist Papers are devoted to foreign affairs and national defense.

19. Nash, *A Study of the Stated Aims and Purposes*, 20.

20. Partridge, in Lee S. Harford, "A History of Officer Training at Civilian Military Colleges: 1819–1990," in Norwich Symposium on the Future of Military Colleges and ROTC, December 7, 1990, Washington, DC, p. 45. The symposium on Norwich and military education was published as the booklet in this citation.

21. Harford, "A History of Officer Training at Civilian Military Colleges," 46.

22. Ibid., 45.

23. Arthur M. Cohen, *The Shaping of American Higher Education, The Emergence and Growth of the Contemporary System* (San Francisco: Jossey-Bass Publishers, 1998), 101–2.

24. Michael S. Neiberg, *Making Citizen-Soldiers: ROTC and the Ideology of American Military Service* (Cambridge, MA: Harvard University Press, 2000), 20.

25. William Bennett Bizzell, "Military Training in the Land-Grant Colleges," Survey by the Department of the Interior, Bureau of Education, in *Land Grant College Education, 1910–1920*, ed. John C. Walton (Washington, DC: GPO), 65.

26. On Lincoln's embrace of the public necessity doctrine in war, see Daniel Farber, *Lincoln's Constitution* (Chicago: University of Chicago Press, 2003). Farber's book is part of a copious literature on this issue.

27. Today the academies provide excellent liberal education compared to what was offered in the past. Ironically, some contend that this fact is detrimental to the civilian-soldier ideal because it encourages the best officer material to go to the academies rather than to civilian institutions of higher learning.

28. E. Merton Coulter, *College Life in the Old South*, cited in William B. Parker, *The Life and Services of Justin S. Morrill* (Boston: Houghton Mifflin, 1924), 262. Both cited in James E. Pollard, *Military Training in the Land-Grant Colleges and Universities, with Special Reference to the R.O.T.C. Program* (Washington, DC: Association of State Universities and Land-Grant Colleges, 1962), 3.

29. Neiberg, *Making Citizen-Soldiers*, 19.

30. See Gene M. Lyons and John W. Masland, *Education and Military Leadership: A Study of the ROTC* (Princeton: Princeton University Press, 1959), 31.

31. For example, ROTC enrollment actually went up for quite a while when the Vietnam War became unpopular because it provided scholarship money and a better military option than the draft. Meanwhile, the National Guard also grew because President Johnson decided not to use the Guard in the war.

32. Nash, *A Study of the Stated Aims and Purposes*, 21.

33. Lyons and Masland, *Education and Military Leadership*, 31.

34. Eddy, *Colleges for Our Land and Time*, 92.

35. Bishop, *A History of Cornell*, 57, 170.

36. See Neiberg, *Making Citizen-Soldiers*, 30. The Supreme Court Case supporting this interpretation of the Morrill Act is *Hamilton et al. v. the Regents of the University of California*, 239 US 245 (1934).

37. Eddy, *Colleges for Our Land and Time*, 94.

38. Walter A. McDougall, *Promised Land, Crusader State: The American Encounter with the World since 1776* (Boston: Houghton Mifflin, 1997), ch. 5.

39. Eddy, *Colleges for Our Land and Time*, 93.

40. Nash, *A Study of the Stated Aims and Purposes*, 25.

41. Neiberg, *Making Citizen-Soldiers*, 22.

42. See Bensel, *Yankee Leviathan*. Bensel argues that the demands of the Civil War contributed to the development of a centralized American state. Drew Gilpin Faust makes a similar argument on several dimensions in *This Republic of Suffering: Death and the American Civil War* (New York: Knopf, 2008).

43. Eddy, *Colleges for Our Land and Time*, 163.

44. Bizzell, "Military Training in the Land-Grant Colleges," 67.

45. Nash, *A Study of the Stated Aims and Purposes*, 26.

46. Neiberg, *Making Citizen-Soldiers*, 24–27.

47. Bizzell, "Military Training in the Land-Grant Colleges," 68. On World War I's effect on universities, see Downs and Murtazashvili, *Arms and the University*, ch. 4.

48. Bishop, *A History of Cornell*, 425–36.

49. Cornell University, Excelsior Battalion US Army ROTC, Commissioning, http://armyrotc.cornell.edu/prospective_commissioning.shtml (accessed July 2010).

50. Brooks Mather Kelley, *Yale: A History* (New Haven: Yale University Press, 1974), 349–51; Marc Lindemann, "Storming the Ivory Tower: The Military's Return to American Campuses," *Parameters* 44 (Winter 2006–7): 46–47.

51. Gaddis W. Smith, "Yale and the Vietnam War," University Seminar on the History of Columbia University, October 19, 1999. Available at www.yale.edu/seas/GSmith_YaleandtheVietnamWar.pdf., 12–13; Arthur T. Coumbe and Lee S. Harford, *U.S. Army Cadet Command: The Ten Year History* (Fort Monroe, VA: Office of the Command Historian, US Army Cadet Command, 1996).

52. Bizzell, "Military Training in the Land-Grant Colleges," 70.

53. Roswell P. Barnes, with an introduction by John Dewey, *Militarizing Our Youth: The Significance of the Reserve Officers' Training Corps* (New York: Committee on Militarism in Education, 1927).

54. Neiberg discusses this "extracurricular stage," which followed the "religious stage" and "scientific stage" of higher education. See *Making Citizen-Soldiers*, 27.

55. Neiberg, *Making Citizen-Soldiers*, 42, 30.

56. Recall the classic debate between Marx and Hegel over the function of philosophy: is it to *understand* the world (Hegel) or to *change* it (Marx)?

57. See, e.g., Jennifer Seaton, "Dartmouth during World War II," http://www.dartmouth.edu/~library/rauner/archives/oral_history/worldwar2/history.html; adapted from an article by Seaton in *Dartmouth Engineer* (accessed July 2010).

58. Coumbe and Harford, *U.S. Army Cadet Command*, 18–19.

59. David Engerman, "Rethinking Cold War Universities: Some Recent Histories," *Journal of Cold War Studies* 5, no. 3 (2003): 80–95. "World War University" is discussed at length in Downs and Murtazashvili, *Arms and the University*, ch. 4.

60. Reinhold Niebuhr, *The Irony of American History* (New York: Charles Scriber's Sons, 1952), 69. See McDougall's portrayal of the tension between America as a moral beacon (the City on a Hill) and a leader in world affairs in *Promised Land, Crusader State.*

61. Jeremy Suri, *Henry Kissinger and the American Century* (Cambridge, MA: Harvard University Press, 2007), 93, 97.

62. Elliott to Paul Nitze, Policy Planning Staff, US State Department, December 11, 1950, and Transcript of William Elliot and Henry Kissinger in Elliot's Contemporary Political Theory Seminar 204 at Harvard University, March 21, 1955. Quoted in Suri, *Henry Kissinger and the American Century,* 112–13. Nitze was one of the leading national architects of Cold War containment and nuclear deterrence. He often engaged in a love-hate relationship with Princeton's George Kennan, the father of the containment policy who began to question the policy in later years. See Nicholas Thompson, *The Hawk and the Dove: Paul Nitze, George Kennan, and the History of the Cold War* (New York: Henry Holt, 2009).

63. Much of the information in this paragraph is from Levin, "Cold War University" (PhD dissertation, University of Wisconsin-Madison, 2009), 57–58, 64–65; and Engerman, "Rethinking Cold War Universities." See also Robert A. McCaughey, *Stand Columbia: A History of Columbia University in the City of New York* (New York: Columbia University Press, 2003), 365.

64. See Harford, "A History of Officer Training at Civilian Military Colleges," 48.

65. Ibid.

66. On the military's successful effort to restore morale and public respect after Vietnam, see David C. King and Zachary Karabell, *The Generation of Trust: How the U.S. Military Has Regained the Public's Confidence since Vietnam* (Washington, DC: American Enterprise Institute Press, 2003). See also Andrew J. Bacevich, *The New American Militarism: How Americans Are Seduced by War* (New York: Oxford University Press, 2005).

67. On the rise and administration of the Army Cadet Command, see Coumbe and Harford, *U.S. Army Cadet Command*; and Arthur T. Coumbe, Paul N. Kotakis, and W. Anne Gammell, *History of the U.S. Army Cadet Command: The Second 10 Years, 1996–2006* (Stillwater, OK: New Forums Press, 2009).

68. Much of the discussion in this section is drawn from Neiberg, *Making Citizen-Soldiers,* chs. 1 and 2. Other sources include Coumbe and Harford, *U.S. Army Cadet Command,* ch. 1.

69. Neiberg, *Making Citizen-Soldiers,* 113.

70. There is a copious literature on the campus antiwar movement and ROTC, much of which is discussed in *Arms and the University,* ch. 5.

71. The abandonment of ROTC by the Ivies and other elite schools, as well as its return to some schools in 2011, is discussed at length in *Arms and the University,* chs. 5–8. I borrow the term "effectively barred" from Professor Allan Silver, the Columbia University sociologist and humanist who has played a significant role in bringing ROTC back to Columbia University in recent years.

72. Neiberg, *Making Citizen-Soldiers*; Peter Karsten, "Anti-ROTC: Response to Vietnam or 'Consciousness III?'" in John P. Lovell and Philip S. Kronenberg, *New Civil-Military Relations: The Agonies of Adjustment to Post-Vietnam Realities* (New Brunswick, NJ: Transaction Books, 1974), 114.

73. Downs and Murtazashvili, *Arms and the University*, ch. 5–8.

74. John Jay, *Federalist #3*, in *The Federalist Papers*, 42.

7

Taking Off

National Security, Identity, and Aerospace Engineering at Land-Grant Universities, 1957–1972

Erinn McComb

Land-grant universities participate in virtually every facet of American life. Foreign policy is no exception. Land-grants provide for the common defense and promote the general welfare. Those endeavors include adapting new scientific principles to war and defense. Indeed, in the twentieth century, the best defense often seemed to be a great offense. Nowhere was that philosophy more rigorously applied than during the Cold War. The American objective was to win the war but to keep it cold. A full-blown physical conflagration was almost certainly nuclear war and unspeakable devastation.

Department of Defense and other research found a welcome home on many land-grant campuses. There faculty pursued research to give America vaunted superiority in military matters as well as others that symbolized military, scientific, and technological might. This research did not go unchallenged, however. Students and even some faculty questioned whether it was healthy for universities to be inextricably intertwined with American foreign affairs. A struggle for the soul of the university ensued. The status quo generally became the ultimate victor.

***

In his 1961 farewell address, President Dwight Eisenhower warned of a growing "military-industrial complex." He feared not only that such a complex might be a harbinger of "misplaced power" but also that in "free universities . . . a government contract becomes virtually a substitute for intellectual curiosity." Eisenhower went on to caution that "The prospect of domination of the nation's scholars by Federal employment, project allocations, and the power of money is ever present."[1]

Even before Eisenhower's speech at the height of the Cold War, aeronautical and aerospace engineering were central components of American military and industrial strength in both the public and private sectors. Universities, especially land-grant institutions, had been indispensable to innovations in the field since the birth of modern flight in 1903. By World War I, the federal government recognized their strategic military importance. The relationship between aeronautics and national security grew exponentially on the eve of World War II. So much so, argues Deborah Douglas, that during the war the federal government bypassed state legislators, granting money and contracts "directly to universities, departments, and even professors." Douglas maintains that this omnipresent and "not-so-invisible hand" reinforced the "norm," if not the purpose, of the nineteenth-century Morrill Act.[2] Similarly, Amy Bix contends that the federal government's Engineering, Science, and Management War Training program, which operated at universities throughout the country, "underlined the significance of engineering training to modern America's military readiness and industrial strength." This growing "military-industrial-academic complex" continued into the Cold War with a general consensus in Washington that "Technology had helped America win the war, and technology was a requirement to maintain the peace."[3] The narrative of the military-industrial-academic complex persisted into the turbulent 1960s as universities debated their role in national security and how that role might conflict with academic freedom.[4]

The American backlash from the October 4, 1957, flight of the first Soviet satellite, Sputnik, encouraged Big Science in both industry and the classroom. To overcome the perception of American failure in science and technology in the wake of the Soviet Union winning the opening salvo of the Space Race, Congress passed the National Education Defense Act in 1958. The flood of government funding for the hard sciences added to an already engorged military-industrial-academic complex. Universities, including land-grant institutions, worried about the survival of academic freedom as their engineering departments were transformed into arsenals of national security.[5] John L. Rudolph argues that "questions of democratic capability became increasingly relevant, and, in the political climate of the time, this meant educational programs that would ensure the survival of democracy in the face of the Soviet ideological challenge." In essence, hard science programs were not just about science; American science and technology needed to "reinforce American democratic values."[6] Universities found themselves caught in a pendulum swing between raw military prowess and the depiction of American ideals.

Not everyone saw a contradiction between military power and democratic values. After arranging to surrender to US forces at the end of World War II, Dr. Wernher von Braun, who had designed and built Nazi Germany's V-2 rocket, quickly became a key figure in America's postwar space program. He preached that the "Soviet challenge" required more than just "generals and statesmen." Speaking at the University of Florida in 1959, von Braun exhorted that the Space Race "is by no means restricted to military technology." Rather, "It goes far beyond the realms of politics and armies. . . . The struggle involves ever[y] facet of our civilization, every part of our society: religion, economics, politics, science, technology, industry and education." Von Braun's solution was "not anti-Communism, but the belief in God and the dignity of the individual."[7] To win the Space Race, Americans, especially those in aerospace engineering departments, needed to emphasize American culture and ideology as a contrast to Soviet communism.

Political scientist Joseph Nye's framework of hard power/soft power helps illustrate the paradoxes aerospace engineering departments encountered during the Space Race as they began to receive increased government funding and gain influence. Nye defines hard power as military and economic might, or "strength through war," and soft power as "cultural attraction" and "ideology."[8] According to Nye, cultural and ideological soft power came in the form of "democracy, personal freedom, upward mobility, and openness," all of which were crucial American values to win the Cold War.[9] During the early Space Race, aerospace engineering education was part of a larger public discourse that forced land-grant institutions to come to terms with their responsibility to American national security. However, as von Braun has pointed out, national security during the Cold War was twofold. National security was not the creation of hard power missiles alone but also a cultural and ideological battle that demanded American universities promote soft power through the peaceful exploration of space, academic freedom, democratic technology, urban development, environmentalism, and, especially, individualism.

While universities and departments professed to be institutes focused on the soft power of academic freedom and individuality, aerospace engineering programs, among other disciplines, received funds from the Department of Defense (DoD), raising serious questions and concerns about the ability of universities to project a democratic identity. The idea of American universities as representatives of American democracy was not a twentieth-century phenomenon. In the late 1850s, Vermont representative Justin Smith Morrill envisioned land-grant schools that would "promote the liberal and practical education of the industrial classes in the several pursuits and professions in life."[10] Not having the funds to receive an education himself, Morrill championed the ability of the "industrial classes" to have access to higher education.[11] Since the passage of the Morrill Act, historians have emphasized its soft power nature, especially its "democratic" ideals of educating all classes of Americans.[12] However, looking at the act in a different way reveals that, in their history and purpose, land-grant institutions were not completely detached from hard power politics and certainly not national security. Signed into law during the Civil War, the act mandated that these schools should not exclude the "classics" and "military tactics."[13]

In the political climate of the 1860s, Congress understood the importance of a military education. Some land-grant schools, such as Auburn and Purdue, continued the Morrill Act's ROTC military education requirement into the 1970s.[14] However, by the advent of Cold War aerospace engineering, controversy over hard power geopolitics surrounded the ROTC requirement as faculty and administrators increasingly questioned their roles in national security and educating their students about "good citizenship."[15] Through the paradoxes of peace and military strength, the identity of aeronautical engineering education programs was in conflict and morally suspect. Aerospace engineering programs struggled to champion soft power academic freedom while navigating the role of defense research in aerospace engineering education.

The Massachusetts Institute of Technology (MIT) is an excellent example of the paradoxes faced by American universities during the Cold War. MIT has played a leading role in flight education in the United States, but its accomplishments are not without controversy.[16] At the center of the hard power/soft power debate was one of the hallmarks of MIT's Department of Aeronautics and Astronautics, the Instrumentation Laboratory, established in 1932 by department head Charles S. Draper. Researchers at the laboratory spent most of World War II working on radar systems for the military. By the end of the war, MIT emerged as the largest American nonindustrial defense contractor with seventy-five contracts totaling $117 million for national security research.[17] Furthermore, the Korean War brought with it the need for improved air defense. In 1951, in conjunction with the air force, MIT built the Lincoln Laboratory. In its first decade, engineering majors worked on SAGE (Semi-Automatic Ground Environment), essentially a "nationwide network of radar and antiaircraft weapons linked with digital computers."[18] The project highlighted the multidisciplinary work that reflected Cold War engineering education, both civilian and military. However, fears of a growing dependence on military funding escalated. In November 1952, MIT vice president Julius Adams (J. A.) Stratton claimed that MIT's faculty had been "infected by Washington war fever."[19] A year later, MIT president James Killian acknowledged that MIT "recognized an inescapable responsibility" to "national security." However, he hoped that the faculty and administration could find a "balance" so as to not "detract from our educational program."[20]

The launch of the first Soviet satellite brought Killian to the White House in his new role as the head of the Presidential Science Advisory Committee (PSAC), and MIT pressed forward into the Space Age despite Stratton's warnings.[21] Sputnik compelled the School of Engineering to reexamine their curriculum, adding more requirements for classes dealing with jet propulsion, space vehicle systems, automatic control, and vertical takeoff. Two years later, MIT's Department of Aeronautics officially changed its name to the Department of Aeronautics and Astronautics.[22] The department took on projects that were largely interdisciplinary and multidisciplinary. The complexities of automatic controlled spaceflight made it customary for aerospace engineers to work side by side with physicists, mathematicians, and engineers of all disciplines. Professors needed to ensure a curriculum that was above and beyond applied science and theory. Faculty and students alike needed "to develop and use theory to the greatest possible extent."[23] These bigger and more powerful weapons were not only dangerous but expensive. To aid the institute, outside funding was necessary, and in the geopolitical climate of the Cold War, the federal government continued to be an excellent provider. Draper knew the drill, commenting in 1959 that "Aeronautics and Astronautics at M.I.T. as it now exists has been very strongly influenced by sponsored research carried out under government sponsorship."[24]

MIT's hard power research program was astounding. The Space Race created a deluge in MIT government contracts and jobs. Writing in 1958 in the aftermath of Sputnik, MIT's dean of the School of Engineering, C. Richard Soderberg, reported that MIT aeronautics was "responding with characteristic vigor to the challenge of the space age."[25] Stuart W. Leslie points out that most of MIT's research during this time was for the benefit of the military. Draper's Instrumentation Lab "had a $12.9 million budget—$9.8 million from the Navy (the lion's share for the Polaris missile guidance system) and $3.1 million from the Air Force (the lion's share for the Titan II missile guidance system)." Leslie adds that "virtually the entire $14.6 million department research budget came from DOD." But it did not end there. Fifty-nine out of the department's 104 graduate students were on leave from the military engaging in "special (sometimes classified) courses in weapons systems, instrumentation, propulsion, or aerodynamics."[26]

Other land-grant universities also benefited from space exploration. Alabama Polytechnic Institute's (API) rocket and jet propulsion class (AE 415) opened as early as the 1950–51 academic year.[27] In March 1951, API president Ralph Brown Draughon remarked that in the struggle for science and technology education, "This Nation is engaged in a silent but, nonetheless, serious struggle of such gravity that the current Korean War, as deadly as it is, must be considered a minor incident."[28] In accord with building American technological supremacy, aero engineering grew substantially during Brown's presidency. After Sputnik, in 1959, AE 415 became a required course as opposed to an elective.[29] In 1960, API officially changed its name to Auburn University.[30] In the 1961–62 academic year, the Department of Aeronautical Engineering transitioned into the Department of Aerospace Engineering. That same year, Auburn offered Space Propulsion Systems (AE 428) as an elective.[31] Funding at Auburn also intensified. The School of Engineering saw an increase from roughly "$35,000 in 1957 to more than $320,000 in 1961." Auburn's aerospace department received contracts from the air force, the Army Guided Missile Agency, the National Aeronautics and Space Administration (NASA), and the National Science Foundation (NSF).[32] In December 1962, Auburn's engineering department announced that graduate aerospace engineers would be able to take advantage of a new cooperative education program in conjunction with NASA's Marshall Spaceflight Center.[33] Finally, Auburn created a master's program in aerospace engineering to meet the demand for hard power rocket engineers at Redstone Arsenal in Huntsville, Alabama, in 1961.[34]

Purdue also recognized the importance of the university to national defense. In 1940, Purdue's dean of engineering, Andrey A. Potter, argued that the United States "must meet this competition [World War II] by more scientific and technological knowledge. . . . Higher education, particularly in science and technology, is also a major essential in our military defense."[35] Purdue created highly successful World War II training courses for American soldiers, and by the Cold War, Purdue was ready to meet the Soviet challenge. In the fall of 1957, Purdue introduced aerospace engineering courses that covered terrestrial and extraterrestrial flight, rockets, and orbital mechanics.[36] Administrators argued the following year that if "the US is to remain a great power, it must lead the world in the science and technology of defense."[37] From a military standpoint, to lead the world in science and technology, Purdue, like other land-grant institutions, counted military officers among its ranks of graduate students. In fact, in the fall of 1962, Purdue designed an aero master's program specifically for US Air Force Academy graduates. Federal funding in Purdue's aeronautical engineering program soared in the late 1950s. The aerospace research budget at Purdue rose from $24,079 in 1955–56 to $57,383 in 1959–60. Departmental research was funded by the Air Force Office of Scientific Research, NASA, the Army Ballistic Missile Agency, McDonnell Aircraft Corporation, NSF, the Army Signal Corps, the Purdue Research Foundation, and the Purdue Engineering Experimental Station.[38]

Sputnik helped bring not only fat government contracts for research, but, as the National Defense Education Act intended, it also encouraged students to enter math, science, and engineering disciplines. But during the glut of hard power funding in aerospace engineering, universities, on paper at least, fought to maintain their soft power image of academic freedom and individualism in the face of Soviet crash programs and collectivism. For instance, while giving the January 1958 convocation address at Nebraska Wesleyan University, Senator Carl T. Curtis (R-NE) advocated that within the American educational system, the major goal "should never be by mass education—rather, it should be the education of each individual in our society." Protesting "assembly line" schools, he argued that "America is a land of individuals . . . capable of thinking for themselves. . . . We should never undervalue the individual. . . . The age of space is the age of the individual."[39]

Soft power academic freedom and the individual were not only basic beliefs put forth in the Morrill Act but also, as von Braun described, "antidotes" for the expansion of communism.[40] In his first year as president of MIT, J. A. Stratton, in his 1959 annual report, lashed out against the "comparison of the process of mass production in industry with the education of human beings." Stratton argued "that the cultivation of the individual is our single goal, the sole reason for our being."[41] That same year, C. Richard Soderberg demanded that the direction of MIT's engineering "increase the opportunities provided for students to develop self-reliance in thought and action, with emphasis on originality, creativity, judgment, perseverance, and awareness of human relationships."[42] There was real concern in the engineering field about the loss of soft power in individual initiative in the wake of massive DoD funding. For example, an editorial in the *Auburn Engineer* expressed fears of overcrowded engineering classes. The National Society of Professional Engineers (NSPE) cautioned that engineering majors were already at an all-time high, warning that "an artificial stimulation to further increase enrollments in engineering will severely handicap institutions that devote adequate attention to the capable students." The society warned that universities needed to stress "quality rather than quantity."[43]

Emphasis on individuality within engineering programs continued. In his 1962 presidential address, Stratton hailed the Department of Aeronautics and Astronautics' "Project Laboratory" requirement for developing "independence of action" and "self-reliance." Much like the 1862 Morrill Act intended, the department stressed that education in both engineering and the humanities led to "good citizenship."[44] Two years earlier, Auburn also maintained that the "central importance" of land-grant institutions was not "vocational training" but rather an "academic and cultural" cache. The 1960 Auburn curriculum highlighted the importance of the Morrill Act with its accentuation of "good citizenship and the good life."[45] In 1962, Auburn's new Master's in Aerospace Engineering emphasized "flexibility and individual" research.[46] Aerospace engineering programs attempted to balance hard power missiles with soft power individuality. But universities were not alone; their messages of individualism and democracy increased in the private sector of aerospace engineering.

An article appearing in the *Auburn Engineer* boldly proclaimed that the American "missile program" represented "Democracy at Work" through its reliance on free enterprise. The article suggested that "there is no better illustration of this concept than in the many diverse corporations combing to work on one project." Not only were companies competing with each other, but they were also joining forces to "rally to the cause of world peace and lending our support to the desire for economic harmony."[47] To fight an ideological and cultural war with the Soviet Union, the field of aerospace engineering looked not for mere cogs or drones but for individuals to enhance not only a democratic image of aerospace engineering but also, one could argue, the soft power of the United States.

For engineers, scientists, and mathematicians seeking to break into Cold

War space technology, *Aviation Week* and *Aero/Space Engineering* were the go-to magazines. Within their pages, companies such as Goodyear Aircraft touted their "respect for individual thought and effort."[48] Likewise, Avro Aircraft Limited advertised that its projects "give engineering people unexcelled opportunities to utilize individual ingenuity, initiative, imaginations, and creative qualities." The company frequently applauded "individual ideas and accomplishments."[49] In its advertisement for a thermodynamicist, General Electric (GE) wanted an "individual contributor."[50] In December 1956 Hayes Aircraft Corporation, supplier of parts for the Army Ballistic Missile Agency at Redstone Arsenal, suggested that "the human element" was as important as "atomic energy."[51] Curtiss-Wright boasted that their engineers' "individual efforts and accomplishments are quickly recognized."[52] Convair-Fort Worth marketed their company as "Best individual effort . . . best combination of ideas."[53] Likewise, the Aerospace Corporation wanted to not only build an air force science-industry team but have "the men of Aerospace marshal individual talents for the full exploration and assessment of advanced concepts, selected for significant potential."[54] In 1962, Fairchild Stratos Corporation professed to be part of a new "growing boldness and vision" that cultivated "true technical excellence which comes from talented individuals and small elite groups rather than massive mediocrity." The company offered "recognition and reward of top individual contributors who are challenged and stimulated to truly professional creativity."[55] A Du Pont advertisement said that careers at the company were "tailored to the individual."[56] Similarly, Martin Orlando wanted "Individuals with inventive talents and a desire for a challenging career."[57] The aerospace field wanted rugged individualists, men in control. Exercising individuality in space and in engineering symbolized the very best of American culture over Soviet communism.

This individual initiative, creativity, and engineering teamwork at MIT's Instrumentation Lab helped complete the Apollo Guidance Computer in 1963. The event was a cause for celebration, but the invention only highlighted the push and pull between hard power/soft power at American universities. That same year, Stratton acknowledged the "serious questioning" over the institute's "major organized projects and big laboratories, with a flow of Federal funds, and a network of communications and ties to Washington." Stratton encouraged group projects, large laboratories, and teamwork but pleaded "that in our cultivation of group activities we do not neglect the individual."[58]

In 1966, his final year as president, Stratton maintained that the "crisis" facing universities was how to continue academic freedom in an age of "new science of new economics, of new politics—in sum, of a totally new world." Professors needed to know when to engage in "isolation" and when to engage in "worldly entanglements." Stratton argued that the purpose of MIT as an instrument of "public welfare and service" was "a concept inherent in the original idea of the land-grant college." But both he and MIT struggled to draw lines between the land-grant mission, good citizenship, and national security. Stratton remarked that mass government funding for military projects distorted the identity of the university. He pleaded with his faculty and staff to remember that the "special role" of the university was to "offer a haven and an intellectual climate in which the highly creative, highly individual scholar can fruitfully pursue his own course in his own way." He wanted an environment in which a faculty member or student could "strike out intellectually upon his own." Stratton knew the national security realities of hard power, but he also stressed that soft power culture and ideology were just as essential to the survival of democracy, both domestic and international.[59]

Soft power concerns emerged at both Purdue and Auburn as the two universities saw declining numbers of engineering students. Between 1968 and 1973, Purdue's engineering majors dropped from 5,244 to 4,215. A. F. Grandt Jr., W.A. Gustafson, and L. T. Cargnino argue in *One Small Step: The History of Aerospace Engineering at Purdue University* that soft power environmental concerns led to the declining numbers as students feared that spaceflight caused pollution.[60] Beginning in 1969, Auburn president Harry M. Philpott said that his university needed to address the "serious social conflicts" of American society. While he noted that Auburn was "spared" the "disruptive behavior" experienced at northern universities, he and the administration were engaging in talks concerning the contribution of land-grant universities to society, especially in regard to pollution.[61] In order to use the land-grant universities as instruments to help solve societal problems, in 1970, President Philpott proposed the creation of the Center for Urban and Regional Planning and a Human Rights Forum.[62] Similarly, in 1970–71, Auburn's School of Engineering cited "changing national priorities based on societal needs" for the school's introduction of new courses that emphasized "environmental quality."[63] Despite dropping numbers, writing in 2004, John E. Cochran Jr., head of Auburn's aerospace engineering department, noted that Auburn saw a benefit for the students in that smaller enrollment numbers meant more intimate classes.[64] In 1971, Philpott praised smaller class sizes and the benefits of "individualized instruction."[65] As Purdue and Auburn integrated soft power environmental and societal problems into their academic mission, protests erupted at institutions in the Northeast.

Tensions at MIT came to a head in 1969 as troop involvement in Vietnam escalated and DoD funding clashed with an increasingly aware, intellectual, and liberal student and city population. The Department of Aeronautics and Astronautics had been under attack from students and faculty since 1966. By 1969, protestors jeeringly labeled MIT the "Pentagon East" or "Pentagon on the Charles." Historian Stuart W. Leslie notes that "With $119 million in military research contracts for fiscal 1968, MIT ranked first among university defense contractors, with twice the total of second-ranked Johns Hopkins and seven times more than fourth-ranked Stanford," which held the dubious distinction among protestors as the "Pentagon of the West."[66] Protests against DoD funding began with the faculty. In March 1969, the *New York Times* reported that a group of physics faculty members had been meeting throughout the semester for a "discussion on the uses and misuses of scientific knowledge."[67] Moreover, the chair of engineering, Raymond L. Bisplinghoff, expressed "a growing concern for human and societal problems in contrast to the heavy engagement of earlier years in the narrow, sophisticated problems posed by the nation's military and space programs." MIT's faculty forced the institute to focus more on soft power through fixing "man-made environmental problems."[68]

As the American dream of conquering the moon swiftly became a reality, MIT's classified research projects and military funding continued to face scrutiny as Americans conquered the moon in 1969. In previous academic years, the navy, air force, army, and NASA had heavily subsidized the Instrumentation Lab. In 1969, Rene H. Miller, chair of the Department of Aeronautics and Astronautics, wrote that the lab endured "strong attacks from students and several faculty groups, including speeches, handouts, and picketing with threatened occupation of some Laboratory facilities which disrupted normal work during a period of some two months."[69] MIT's public image was at an all-time low. However, demonstrating the power of peaceful protest, dissent at MIT was mild compared to that at Columbia, Harvard, or Wisconsin.

On March 4, 1969, demonstrations led by the Science Action Coordinating Committee (SACC) commenced. Classes were canceled not only at MIT but also at Yale and Cornell as a result of anger over the "Misuse of Science."[70] At MIT, the SACC objected to "cooperative education courses with the defense industry." They wanted "an end to academic credit for classified research and theses, an end to 'war related research,'" and favored "the establishment of new, 'socially constructed' priorities for Lincoln Laboratory and the Instrumentation Laboratory." A month later on April 22, fifty students led by SACC rallied at the Instrumentation Lab to protest the Poseidon missile guidance research.[71] The students released a statement demanding that "M.I.T. must end its symbiotic relationship with the Defense Department. We must fight to reduce the power of the defense establishment."[72] The protestors' mission was clear: they wanted MIT to discontinue hard power research in favor of soft power research.

Campus unrest continued as the institute examined its hard power/soft power identity. On May 7, 1969, MIT suspended classes to give students and faculty an opportunity "to discuss the military, social and educational problems" after receiving complaints that MIT's laboratories were "neglecting other more socially orientated problems, such as poverty, overpopulation and education." The university offered a series of seminars and as many as a thousand students and faculty participated. Among discussions on military research, students and faculty talked about the Vietnam War, draft dodging, pollution, urban problems, and education. At a mass meeting in Kresge Auditorium, the paradox of the hard power/soft power dichotomy reached its climax when the institute's president, Howard W. Johnson, asked, "How do we best respond to society's interests?" and "How do we meet our responsibilities?"[73]

Johnson "formed a 22-man committee to reexamine the relationship between the institute and the two laboratories." The committee met until the following October. In the meantime, MIT did not accept any new classified projects, nor did it interrupt any present projects. The *New York Times* reported that the professors appeared "divided" on the issue. For instance, professor of physics Bernard T. Field "objected to secret research as long as the two laboratories were part of the educational process at M.I.T.," commenting, "I would draw the line on classified research involving substantial numbers of students and faculty." While Field warned of the growing number of classified research projects on campus, Jack P. Ruina, vice president for special laboratories, worried that "If universities severed all ties with the Defense Department 'the country would be left in the hands of the professional military and industrial group.'" Walter A. Rosenblith, professor of electrical engineering and chairman of the faculty, echoed this concern when he warned that "for M.I.T. simply to cast these things out on the waters is not in any sense responsible."[74]

Demonstrations, specifically against research for the navy's Poseidon Missile, continued to plague the Department of Aeronautics and Astronautics' Instrumentation Lab. In October 1969, students and outsiders prepared for peaceful protests. The SACC, MIT Students for a Democratic Society (MITSDS), and the November Action Committee (NAC) led the demonstrations. The campus was inundated with petitions, candlelight vigils for peace, and faculty meetings. The Instrumentation Lab geared up for potential break-ins, the administration took legal precautions to protect itself from threats of violence, and general trepidation fell over the campus as the students and outside protestors prepared for what was known as the "November Action."[75]

On November 3, President Johnson attempted to calm the situation by announcing the decision of the faculty and administration. He said, "It is our policy now to exclude secret research from the campus. No classified theses are being prepared." Turning to the importance of soft power, he said that MIT was "currently engaged in a test of the proposition of whether we can move some technological capacity of our two off-campus laboratories to the problems of domestic and civil life." But Johnson was not happy. He admonished the NAC for threatening violence and the freedom of the university. Protestors were not satisfied either, demanding that the institute break all ties with the laboratory.[76]

On November 4, a thousand people gathered on campus in peaceful protests against defense projects. *New York Times* reporter Robert Reinhold claimed that the protesters from the SACC spilled over from previous protests at Harvard. NAC demonstrators placed Vietcong flags outside the student center, admonishing MIT for its "imperialistic actions." At Rogers Hall, students "chanted, 'Ho, Ho, Ho Chi Minh, N.L.F. Is Going to Win.'"[77] Other organizations from outside the university, such as the women's liberation organization Bread and Roses, showed support by denouncing "male chauvinism and its links to domestic and foreign imperialism."[78] Reinhold wrote that fearful "Scientists quickly bolted their laboratory doors" and noted that the demonstration turned almost "jovial" as both sides claimed victory.[79]

Three hundred fifty protestors clashed with police the next day. Demonstrators were "restrained, with only brief outbursts of clubbing." During these protests, one hundred faculty members met to continue the discussion on military research at the university. A *New York Times* article reported that not only did the majority of the faculty disapprove of DoD projects, but they felt research for the defense department did not "add to our security, but undermine[d] it."[80] Demonstrations died down until the following spring.

On May 20, 1970, MIT announced that it would sever ties with the Instrumentation Lab. The institute argued that the Poseidon Project was an "inappropriate" undertaking of the university. However, MIT retained the Lincoln Laboratory and the lab's $65 million in DoD contracts. The university released a statement saying that a "new independent corporate entity" would take over the Instrumentation Lab in one year.[81] The department decided that "classified projects will be avoided when this is possible and security restrictions will be minimized in all ways possible. It is agreed that when adequate support is available, civilian projects will be given preference to military unless an overriding national emergency exists."[82] The press reported that Professor Draper "retired" that same year, despite his claims that he had been forced out. Investors renamed the lab the Charles S. Draper Laboratory.[83] When Draper left, the laboratory's budget was $54 million, approximately the total of all other MIT laboratories combined, excluding, of course, the Lincoln Laboratory.[84]

In the late 1960s, aerospace engineering departments had been vilified as hard power arsenals of national security. With the conquest of the moon completed and with aerospace engineering's identity tainted by its long association with the military, the American public discourse questioned its relevance and necessity. Aerospace engineering programs around the country needed to find a new mission and a new identity as manned spaceflight transitioned from a national security crash program to the moon to the space shuttle program, which the *Washington Post* referred to jokingly as a $6 billion "taxi service."[85] Aerospace engineering shifted from the conquest of space to the routinization of spaceflight. Layoffs in aerospace engineering had been steadily increasing since the mid-1960s. According to a 1967 *New York Times* article, the war in Vietnam and a "stalemate" over the appropriate role of federal funding sent a group of aerospace engineers into "defeatism."[86] News of a dying field permeated the public discourse. More than half a million aerospace employees lost their jobs between 1967 and 1971. In July 1972, military aerospace writer Frank Macomber argued that the shuttle program alone could not accommodate the previous numbers of aerospace engineers. Unemployment and a questionable future forced the American Institute of Aeronautics and Astronautics to ask, "'Is aerospace engineering obsolete?' According to Macomber, most of the members voted 'yes.'"[87]

The Ohio State University (OSU) rejected these claims. The College of Engineering's dean, Harold Bolz, and Director of Engineering Placement Richard Frasher maintained that the field of aerospace engineering "wasn't that bad. . . . Many of the people dismissed were given the name 'engineer' but were not actually performing engineering jobs." However, at OSU, engineering enrollment numbers had dropped 20 percent in the previous two years. Neither man had a substantial explanation for the downturn. While both were adamant that they would not alter their "admissions requirements," they attempted to bolster enrollment by focusing on soft power. The department commenced a campaign to recruit minorities and women, demonstrating to the world the culture and ideology of democracy within the United States. Bolz said that more women were necessary in engineering because "if more women had been 'involved in these types of decisions in the past, maybe we could have avoided some of the problems we are now facing.'"[88] Even though they unfairly assigned gender roles to hard and soft power by blaming the decisions of war on men and placing the care of soft power in the hands of women, OSU and other land-grant institutions forged ahead into the post-Apollo era.

Despite protests during the previous decade, the number of students in MIT's Department of Aeronautics and Astronautics continued to climb into the 1970s. The department even experienced a 30 percent increase in enrollment from 1977 to 1978. That same year the department commenced a "five-year plan" to upgrade its facilities. Department Chair Rene H. Miller was optimistic, suggesting that while "Rocket propulsion and space propulsion have passed through a period of low interest," they were "expected to grow appreciably in the near future." In the late 1970s, aeronautical and aerospace research stayed at a steady $4-6 million, and the department's five divisions of instrumentation and fourteen laboratories remained among the best in the country. Miller went on to report that the now independent Draper Laboratory continued to support nearly half the graduates in the department's popular division of Instrumentation, Guidance and Control. The Division of Mechanics and Physics of Fluid greatly added to domestic soft power through its partnership with the Boston's Children's Hospital under the National Institutes of Health's sponsorship of spinal research.[89]

In the shuttle era, Ronald Reagan's 1984 Strategic Defense Initiative (SDI) and the January 1986 Challenger explosion caused a surge in aerospace enrollment and research. Amid hard power satellites and the dangers of space, as OSU envisioned, aerospace engineering programs turned to soft power through the enrollment of minorities and women. In 1978, twenty sophomore coeds entered MIT's School of Engineering, thus raising female enrollment 198 percent from what it had been in 1973.[90] In 1983, MIT's School of Engineering formed an affirmative action committee whose purpose included pinpointing "problems facing minorities and women in the School and to formulate positive actions." The school also "offered 'special' positions for outstanding women or minority faculty candidates."[91]

Despite the new soft power image, hard power certainly remained. By 1988, the *Chronicle of Higher Education* still ranked MIT as "the number one non-profit Department of Defense contractor in the nation" with "$407.6 million in DoD contracts, outdoing second runner-up Johns Hopkins University by $52.7 million." Daniel J. Glenn has pointed out that the 1988–89 *MIT Bulletin* states, "'Draper Laboratories maintains a relationship with the Institute that permits students to engage in joint research activities' and enjoy 'its unique contribution to the Institute's education program.'"[92] By 1993, MIT appeared to have scaled back its DoD funding. That year, MIT launched the Lean Aerospace Initiative (LAI), comprising "the US Air Force, the Massachusetts Institute of Technology (MIT), labor unions, and defense aerospace businesses." The institute's president suggested that LAI was necessary owing to "declining defense procurement budgets collided with rising costs and military industrial overcapacity promoting a new defense acquisition imperative: affordability rather than performance at any cost."[93]

CONCLUSION

The historic impact of land-grant institutions on geopolitics is tremendous. The inclusion of military tactics in the Morrill Act created a connection between land-grant universities and national security. Airpower during the world wars created a union between federal government funding and aeronautical engineering education. Pundits questioned this relationship and its threat to the image of American democratic education in the post–World War II era even before the launch of Sputnik. However, with the shock of the satellite and the technological and military capabilities of the Soviet Union, the DoD pumped more money into universities. Aerospace engineering departments had a dual image as they remained split between soft power peaceful exploration of space and hard power missiles. The hard power image became too much for faculty, students, and the general public in the late 1960s. In an interesting bottom-up approach, protestors forced a major university to cut ties with a highly respected academic laboratory.

Land-grant aerospace engineering departments currently hold a middle ground between hard and soft power, but the need for research dollars from defense industries is ever present. Purdue's School of Aeronautics and Astronautics receives 45 percent of its funding from the DoD, 20 percent from the NSF, and about 15 percent from NASA.[94] Similarly, MIT's department continues to receive funding from the DoD and the Draper Laboratory. MIT remains highly respected throughout the world. In terms of soft power, MIT was recently the only academic institution picked by NASA to design a bigger, faster, more fuel-efficient commercial jet liner. Focusing on soft power, the "D8 Double Bubble" promises to generate greener commercial airplanes by 2035.[95] Overall, the future of aerospace engineering education raises more questions than answers. Soft power in aerospace engineering certainly prevails as environmental concerns, international cooperation, and curiosity continue, but the goals of aerospace engineering remain unclear. As India, China, South Korea, Iran, Pakistan, Russia, and Japan vie for a place in the heavens, aerospace engineering departments at land-grant universities will continue to wrestle with a hard power/soft power dichotomy as they search for new identities and responsibilities for national security in the twenty-first century.

NOTES

1. President Eisenhower, "Military-Industrial Complex Speech, Dwight D. Eisenhower," the Avalon Project, Yale University, http://avalon.law.yale.edu/20th_century/eisenhower001.asp (accessed August 28, 2012). In his speech, military-industrial complex is spelled "militaryindustrial complex."

2. Deborah Douglas, "The End of 'Try and Fly': The Origins and Evolution of American Aeronautical Engineering Education through World War II," in *Engineering in a Land-Grant Context: The Past, Present, and Future of an Idea*, ed. Alan I Marcus (West Lafayette, IN: Purdue University Press, 2005): 77–78.

3. Amy Sue Bix, "Engineering National Defense: Technical Education at Land-Grant Institutions during World War II," in *Engineering in a Land-Grant Context*, ed. Marcus, 119; Jack H. Nunn, "MIT: A University's Contribution to National Defense," *Military Affairs* 43, no. 3 (October 1979): 123. For more on the "military-industrial-academic complex," see Stuart W. Leslie, *The Cold War and American Science: The Military-Industrial-Academic Complex at MIT and Stanford* (New York: Columbia University Press, 1993), 2. See also J. William Fulbright, "The War and Its Effects: The

Military-Industrial-Academic Complex," in *Super State: Readings in the Military-Industrial Complex*, ed. Herbert I. Schiller (Urbana: University of Illinois Press, 1970): 171–78.

4. For further historiography on American universities during the Cold War, see David A. Wilson, ed., *Universities and the Military*, a special issue to *The Annals of the American Academy of Political and Social Sciences* (March 1989): 502

5. John L. Rudolph researches the incorporation of scientists into the "national security arsenal" in *Scientists in the Classroom: The Cold War Reconstruction of American Science Education* (New York: Palgrave, 2002): 5.

6. Ibid., 10.

7. Dr. Wernher von Braun, "The Struggle of the Future" (paper presented to the University of Florida, May 8, 1959), NASA Historical Reference Collection, https://mira.hq.nasa.gov/history/ws/hdmshrc/all/main/DDD/42490.pdf/ (accessed October 20, 2012), 2, 15. Dr. von Braun became the director of the Marshall Spaceflight Center in Huntsville, Alabama, in 1960. For more information on von Braun's career in both Germany and the United States, see Michael J. Neufeld, *Von Braun: Dreamer of Space/ Engineer of War* (New York: Vintage, 2007).

8. Joseph S. Nye Jr. introduced "soft power" in *Bound to Lead: The Changing Nature of American Power* (New York: Basic Books, 1990), 193. He broadens his ideas on the subject in *The Paradox of American Power: Why the World's Only Superpower Can't Go It Alone* (New York: Oxford University Press, 2002) and in *Soft Power: The Means to Success in World Politics* (New York: Public Affairs, 2005).

9. Nye, *The Paradox of American Power*, 11.

10. "Morrill Act," *An Act Donating Public Lands to the Several States and Territories Which May Provide Colleges for the Benefit of Agriculture and the Mechanic Arts*, July 2, 1862, http://memory.loc.gov/cgi-bin/ampage?collId=llsl&fileName=012/llsl012.db&recNum=534 (accessed June 10, 2012), 503–5.

11. Coy F. Cross, *Justin Smith Morrill: Father of the Land-Grant Colleges* (East Lansing: Michigan State University Press, 1996), 78.

12. For the term "democratic" pertaining to the Land-Grant Act, see Harvard professor W. K. Jordan's quote in *After 100 Years: A Report by the State of Vermont Morrill Land-Grant Centennial Committee*, as quoted in Cross, *Justin Smith Morrill*, 77. Morrill himself pointed to the democratic use of the land in his speech "Bill Granting Lands for Agricultural Colleges," delivered April 20, 1858, in which he suggests that such "public lands . . . should be considered a common fund for the use and benefit of all." For this quote, see Cross, *Justin Smith Morrill*, 81.

13. "Morrill Act," 503–4.

14. See *The Auburn University Bulletin, 1970–1971* (Auburn, AL: Auburn University, 1970), 144, Auburn University Libraries, Ralph Brown Draughon Library, Department of Special Collections & University Archives (hereafter cited as RBD AUA). Purdue University Army ROTC, "Purdue University Army ROTC History," Purdue University, http://www.purdue.edu/armyrotc/overview/history.php (accessed October 20, 2012).

15. Charles S. Draper, "Department of Aeronautics and Astronautics," *Massachusetts Institute of Technology Bulletin: President's Report Issue, 1962* (Cambridge, MA: Massachusetts Institute of Technology, 1962), 78, http://dome.mit.edu/handle/1721.3/59044 (accessed August 9, 2012).

16. Leslie, *The Cold War and American Science*, 2. See also Fulbright, "The War and Its Effects," 171–78.

17. Leslie, *The Cold War and American Science*, 14. Leslie also points out that the second- and third-largest nonindustrial defense contractors were Caltech and Harvard, receiving $83 million and $31 million in contracts, respectively.

18. Ibid., 35.

19. As quoted in ibid., 34.

20. As quoted in Nunn, "MIT: A University's Contributions to National Defense," 124.

21. James R. Killian, *Sputnik, Scientists, and Eisenhower: A Memoir of the First Special Assistant to the President for Science and Technology* (Cambridge, MA: MIT Press, 1977).

22. The Department of Aeronautics and Astronautics is first introduced in the *Massachusetts Institute of Technology Bulletin: President's Report Issue, 1959* (Cambridge, MA: Massachusetts Institute of Technology, 1959), 20, http://dome.mit.edu/handle/1721.3/59041 (accessed August 9, 2012).

23. Charles Stark Draper, "Department of Aeronautics and Astronautics," *Massachusetts Institute of Technology Bulletin: President's Report Issue, 1959*, 84–85.

24. As quoted in Leslie, *The Cold War and American Science*, 77. It should be pointed out that most departments did away with the name "aeronautics" in favor of "aerospace," but MIT was one of a handful that kept the aeronautical identity. Doing away with the name "aeronautics" actually became a point of contention at Purdue. For more information, see A. F. Grandt Jr., W. A. Gustafson, and L. T. Cargnino, *One Small Step: The History of Aerospace Engineering at Purdue University* (West Lafayette, IN: Purdue University Press, 2010), 152.

25. C. Richard Soderberg, "School of Engineering," *Massachusetts Institute of Technology Bulletin: President's Report Issue, 1958* (Cambridge, MA: Massachusetts Institute of Technology, 1958), 63, http://dome.mit.edu/handle/1721.3/59040 (accessed August 9, 2012).

26. Leslie, *The Cold War and American Science*, 77. Other labs that benefited from military contracts were the Navy Supersonic Laboratory, whose $1.5 million budget came from the army and the navy, as well as the Aeroelastic and Structures Research Laboratory.

27. *The Alabama Polytechnic Bulletin, 1950–1951* (Auburn: Alabama Polytechnic Institute, 1951), RBD AUA.

28. Quoted in Alumni Legislative News Letter, "Letter No. 1, July 10, 1959," Presidential Office Records (Alumni Association), RBD, AUA.

29. *The Alabama Polytechnic Bulletin, 1958–1959* (Auburn: Alabama Polytechnic Institute, 1959), 169, RBD AUA.

30. Auburn University, introduction to *Glomerata*, 1960.

31. *The Auburn University Bulletin, 1961–1962* (Auburn, AL: Auburn University, 1962), RBD AUA.

32. John E. Cochran, "Aerospace Education and Research at Auburn University," in *Aerospace Engineering Education during the First Century of Flight*, ed. Barnes McCormick, Conrad Newberry, and Eric Jumper (Reston, VA: American Institute of Aeronautics and Astronautics [AIAA], 2004), 242. For information on Auburn's research contracts from 1958 to 1972, see *The Annual Report of Auburn University to the Board of Trustees* (Auburn, AL: Auburn University), RBD AUA.

33. Bill White, "The Master of Science Program in Aerospace Engineering," *Auburn Engineer*, December 1962, 18.

34. Gene I. Maeroff, "100 Protestors Seize Library at Cornell," *New York Times*, April 28, 1972; "Cornell Decides to Give Up Its Aeronautical Laboratory," *New York Times*, January 22, 1968; "Cornell Plans to Sell its Research Center to EDP Technology," *New York Times*, September 22, 1968; David Bird, "State Challenging Cornell's Attempt to Sell Space Lab; Cornell is Trying to Sell Space Lab," *New York Times*, November 8, 1968; "Charges Traded on Cornell Lab; Contract for Military Study Stirs Campus Debate," *New York Times*, November 21, 1968; and Pete Neal, Associate Aeronautical Engineer, Cornell Aeronautical Laboratory, "Lab Sale by Cornell," *New York Times*, December 2, 1968.

35. As quoted in Bix, "Engineering National Defense," 108.

36. Grandt, Gustafson, and Cargnino, *One Small Step*, 133.

37. *Purdue University Bulletin: Annual Report of the President, 1958* (West Lafayette, IN: Purdue University, 1959), 22.

38. Grandt, Gustafson, and Cargnino, *One Small Step*, 174–75, 134–37, 171.

39. Senator Curtis of Nebraska, convocation address at Nebraska Wesleyan University, "The Individual in the Age of Space, January 20, 1958," inserted by Senator Roman L. Hruska (R-NE), *Cong. Rec.*, 85th Cong., 2nd sess., 1958, 104, pt. 4, 1797–98.

40. Von Braun, "The Struggle of the Future," 2.

41. J. A. Stratton, "President's Report," *Massachusetts Institute of Technology Bulletin: President's Report Issue, 1959*, 10, 11.

42. C. Richard Soderberg, "School of Engineering," *Massachusetts Institute of Technology Bulletin: President's Report Issue, 1959*, 86.

43. Editorial, *Auburn Engineer*, December 1957, 3.

44. *Massachusetts Institute of Technology Bulletin: President's Report Issue, 1962* (Cambridge, MA: Massachusetts Institute of Technology, 1962), 10, 78, http://dome.mit.edu/handle/1721.3/59044 (accessed August 9, 2012).

45. Auburn University, introduction to *Glomerata*, 1960.

46. White, "The Master of Science Program in Aerospace Engineering," 18.

47. R. L. Schuiling, "Missiles: A United States Program of Free (?) Enterprise," *Auburn Engineer*, November 1957, 10.

48. Goodyear Aircraft, advertisement, *Aviation Week*, October 1, 1956, 107.

49. Avro Aircraft Limited, advertisement, *Aviation Week*, December 3, 1956, 118.

50. General Electric, advertisement, *Aero/Space Engineering*, June 1958, 128.

51. Hayes Aircraft Corporation, advertisement, *Aviation Week*, December 3, 1956, 7.

52. Curtiss-Wright, advertisement, *Aero/Space Engineering*, July 1958, 87.

53. Convair-Fort Worth, a Division of General Dynamics, advertisement, *Aviation Week; Including Space Technology*, April 20, 1959, 118.

54. Aerospace Corporation, advertisement, *Aero/Space Engineering*, January 1962, 79.

55. Fairchild Stratos, advertisement, *Aero/Space Engineering*, March 1962, 86.

56. Du Pont, advertisement, *Auburn Engineer*, November 1962, 21.

57. Martin Orlando, advertisement, *Aviation Week and Space Technology*, June 3, 1963, 93.

58. *Massachusetts Institute of Technology Bulletin: President's Report Issue, 1963* (Cambridge, MA: Massachusetts Institute of Technology, 1963), 4, 23–24, http://dome.mit.edu/handle/1721.3/59045 (accessed August 9, 2012).

59. *Massachusetts Institute of Technology Bulletin: Report of the President for the Year Ending June 30, 1966* (Cambridge, MA: Massachusetts Institute of Technology, 1966), 3, 7, 19, 20, http://dome.mit.edu/handle/1721.3/59047 (accessed August 9, 2012). That same year, students at Cornell railed against their university's aeronautical laboratory's hard power image. In response, the university attempted to sell the lab to a private company, EDP Technology, but the state of New York objected to the sale. Unrest directed at the lab remained on campus from 1966 until 1972, with the students demanding the immediate cessation of all war-related research at the Cornell Aeronautical Laboratory and a commitment to end the Reserve Officers Training Corps. The aeronautical laboratory was originally built in Buffalo by Curtiss-Wright for World War II research and donated to the university in 1946. Throughout its history, the lab experienced great technological success, but its $1.5 million project on counterinsurgency in Thailand caused the greatest controversy. For more information on the Cornell Aeronautical Laboratory, see Gene I. Maeroff, "100 Protestors Seize Library at Cornell," *New York Times*, April 28, 1972; "Charges Traded on Cornell Lab; Contract for Military Study Stirs Campus Debate," *New York Times*, November 21, 1968; Pete Neal, Associate Aeronautical Engineer, Cornell Aeronautical Laboratory, "Lab Sale by Cornell," *New York Times*, December 2, 1968; "Cornell Decides to Give Up Its Aeronautical Laboratory," *New York Times*, January 22, 1968; "Cornell Plans to Sell Its Research Center to EDP Technology," *New York Times*, September 22, 1968; and David Bird, "State Challenging Cornell's Attempt to Sell Space Lab; Cornell Is Trying to Sell Space Lab," *New York Times*, November 8, 1968.

60. Grandt, Gustafson, and Cargnino, *One Small Step*, 166, 163. Most aerospace engineering programs and the industry itself saw declining numbers; this was due to bloated numbers of engineers and the decline of the Apollo program.

61. *The Annual Report of Auburn University to the Board of Trustees, 1968–1969* (Auburn, AL: Auburn University, 1969), President Philpott's letter and page 12, RBD AUA.

62. *The Annual Report of Auburn University to the Board of Trustees, 1969–1970* (Auburn, AL: Auburn University, 1970), RBD AUA.

63. *The Annual Report of Auburn University to the Board of Trustees, 1970–1971* (Auburn, AL: Auburn University, 1971), 11, RBD AUA. Auburn also canceled its mandatory two-year ROTC requirement beginning in the 1970–71 academic year. See page 15 and *The Auburn University Bulletin, 1970–1971*, 144. It should be noted that even though Auburn discontinued its two-year ROTC requirement and enrollment numbers dropped 50 percent, the ROTC program remained popular among male and female students. MIT canceled its ROTC program in the 1958–59 school year. For more information, see *Massachusetts Institute of Technology Bulletin: Presidential Report Issue, 1958*.

64. Cochran, "Aerospace Education and Research at Auburn University," 244.

65. *The Annual Report of Auburn University to the Board of Trustees, 1970–1971*, 5.

66. Leslie, *The Cold War and American Science*, 235.

67. Robert Reinhold, "Scientists Halt Work for a Day, Troubled Over Role in Research," *New York Times*, March 5, 1969; *Massachusetts Institute of Technology Bulletin: Report of the President, 1969* (Cambridge, MA: Massachusetts Institute of Technology, 1969), 54, http://dome.mit.edu/handle/1721.3/59050 (accessed August 9, 2012).

68. *Massachusetts Institute of Technology Bulletin: Report of the President, 1969*, 45–46.

69. Ibid., 85.

70. Walter Sullivan, "Strike to Protest 'Misuse' of Science; Researchers at M.I.T., Yale, and Cornell Plan a Day's Stoppage on March 4," *New York Times*, February 6, 1969.

71. Leslie, *The Cold War and American Science*, 235. See also Dorothy Nelkin, *The University and Military Research: Moral Politics at M.I.T.* (Ithaca, NY: Cornell University Press, 1972), 58–59.

72. Robert Reinhold, "M.I.T. Professors Applaud Curb on Military Research Contracts," *New York Times*, May 1, 1969.

73. Robert Reinhold, "M.I.T. Suspends Classes for Campus Discussions," *New York Times*, May 8, 1969.

74. Reinhold, "M.I.T. Professors Applaud Curb on Military Research Contracts."

75. Greg Bernhardt and Duff McRoberts, "Institute Braces for November Action; Petitions Circulate as Week of Protests Nears," *The Tech*, October 31, 1969; Alex Makowski, "GA Sanctions Civil Action," *The Tech*, October 31, 1969; Greg Bernardt, "I-Labs, MIT Plans Defense," *The Tech*, October 31, 1969; Steve Carhart, "Faculty Meetings Planned," *The Tech*, October 31, 1969.

76. "Text of Statement Made by M.I.T. President to Faculty Meeting," *New York Times*, November 4, 1969.

77. Robert Reinhold, "1,000 Stage a Peaceful Protest against War Research at M.I.T.," *New York Times*, November 5, 1969.

78. "NAC Rallies 650 to March on CIS, I-Labs, and Offices; Kabat and SACC Avert Possible Occupation of Johnson's Office," *The Tech*, November 5, 1969.

79. Reinhold, "1,000 Stage a Peaceful Protest against War Research at M.I.T."

80. Robert Reinhold, "Police Disperse Demonstrations at M.I.T. Lab," *New York Times*, November 6, 1969.

81. Robert Reinhold, "M.I.T. Will End Relationship with a Research Laboratory," *New York Times*, May 21, 1970. Reinhold purports that other universities that had closed similar research facilities included Columbia, George Washington, and American University. The Instrumentation Laboratory was named the Charles Stark Draper Laboratory in 1970, and in 1973, the lab cut ties with MIT, becoming an independent, not-for-profit organization. See Draper Laboratory, "History," http://draper.com/history.html (accessed August 20, 2012).

82. *Massachusetts Institute of Technology Bulletin: Report of the President, 1969*, 85.

83. Dr. Charles S. Draper maintained in the press that he was "fired" as head of the Instrumentation Laboratory. See Associated Press, "Scientist Draper Says: 'I Was Fired,'" *Abilene Reporter-News*, October 17, 1969. See also "M.I.T. Union Files Draper Grievance," *New York Times*, October 18, 1969.

84. Leslie, *The Cold War and American Science*, 77.

85. "Von Braun and Colleagues Designing Space Shuttle," *Washington Post*, July 25, 1969.

86. Lawrence Davies, "Aerospace Group Hits 'Defeatism'; Association Says Strategy of Stalemate Hurts Technology," *New York Times*, March 16, 1967.

87. Frank Macomber, "Aerospace Engineering Gets 'Obsolete' Label," *Big Spring Herald*, July 4, 1972.

88. Robert Puhr, "Engineering Shortage Anticipated [in] '73," *Ohio Lantern*, May 17, 1973.

89. *Massachusetts Institute of Technology: Report of the President and the Chancellor, 1977–1978* (Cambridge, MA: Massachusetts Institute of Technology, 1978), 197–200, http://dome.mit.edu/handle/1721.3/59059 (accessed August 9, 2012).

90. Ibid., 186. Minority enrollment grew 60 percent from 1973 to 1978.

91. *Massachusetts Institute of Technology: Reports to the President, 1983–1984* (Cambridge: MA: Massachusetts Institute of Technology, 1984), 113, http://dome.mit.edu/handle/1721.3/59065 (accessed August 9, 2012).

92. Daniel J. Glenn, "MIT Research Heavily Dependent on Defense Department Funding; A Crack in the Dome," *The Tech*, February 28, 1989, http://tech.mit.edu/V109/N7/glenn.07o.html (accessed September 2, 2012). The article suggests that 78 percent of the institute's research funding came from the federal government. Draper Laboratory was fiftieth runner-up, receiving $164.7 million in DoD contracts. Glenn also suggests that the four years of protests "had little impact on MIT's ties to Draper."

93. *Massachusetts Institute of Technology: Reports to the President, for the Year Ended June 30, 2002* (Cambridge, MA: Massachusetts Institute of Technology, 2002), 198.

94. Dr. Tom Shih, head of the School of Aeronautics and Astronautics, Purdue University, e-mail message to the author, November 1, 2012.

95. Morgan Bettex, MIT News Office, "MIT-Led Team Designs 'Green' Airplane; Would Use 70% Less Fuel than Current Models," *MIT Media Relations*, May 17, 2010,

http://web.mit.edu/press/2010/green-airplanes.html (accessed September 2, 2012). The potential aircraft is to be quieter, use 70 percent less fuel, and emit 75 percent less NO(x) into the atmosphere. See also "MIT's Double-Bubble Design," CNET, May 18, 2010, http://news.cnet.com/2300–11386_3–10003481–5.html (accessed September 2, 2012). See also NASA, "The Double Bubble D8," http://www.nasa.gov/topics/aeronautics/features/future_airplanes_gallery2.html (accessed September 2, 2012). The Double Bubble is designed to fit 180 passengers and replace the Boeing 737-800. It not only has a "wider cabin" but also has "three side-by-side turbofan engines."

Part Three

Modern Food, Modern Society

Twentieth-century Americans believed that the making of a better tomorrow begins today. That was the modernist creed. A better future could be engineered. It could be manufactured. It could be created. It merely took decisive action in the present to overcome some perceived obstacle.

That article of faith dominated land-grants. It provided a potent justification for action and an equally valid reason to reject inaction. An unacceptable present simply was intolerable. Fixing what was wrong required little more than modifying the status quo to lead to a more favorable outcome.

At the heart of this assumption rests a simple cause and effect. Planned action undertaken now will produce a predictable result in the future. However, that model is much too simplistic. Almost everything is much more complicated and complex than straightforward cause and effect. Interrelationships, interdependencies, hierarchies, and inequities characterize ordered systems, social and otherwise. Action in the present is almost certainly going to produce unanticipated consequences or affect segments of society or a project differentially. Sometimes those unexpected outcomes prove far more enduring and meaningful than the question that gave rise to the initial act.

8

Fruit Cocktail, Rations, and By-Products

The University of California-Berkeley and Modern Food

STEPHANIE STATZ

Statz tells a fascinating story of how scientists at one land-grant university—the University of California—sought to create a use for surplus grapes to assist its grape growers. Their act helped pioneer something far greater: the entire prepared food industry. On its most basic level, this chapter is about land-grants seeking to "solve" a problem for their stakeholders, a characteristic obligation of these schools. The resolution was prescient; the University of California's fruit initiative paralleled the rise of consumer culture in America generally. Canned and frozen products almost immediately became staples of American life. Access to fruits and vegetables no longer depended on local growers; they came from industrial farms a continent away. Menus could be varied. Dinners took less time to prepare, and daily shopping trips became a thing of the past for a growing single-family, homeowning suburban population. In a very real sense, California's land-grant scientists participated in a general redesign of American society.

***

Commodities are often taken for granted and groceries are no exception. Consumers focus on price and health benefits, and little else. Almost never do they treat the products as the consequence of historical processes. Yet these foodstuffs are the explicit result of historical decisions, choices, and forces: state development, business trends, and, especially, for this study, the fundamental role land-grant university scientists played. America's land-grants have been and continue to be essential to how and what Americans have eaten in the past and what we eat today.

In the 1920s, California fruit canners faced a dilemma: they had more grapes, pineapples, and peaches than they could sell, as fresh or processed fruit. They were the victims of their success. The fruit market boom of the 1910s had encouraged Northern California growers to plant more orchards. Canneries proliferated to create a secondary market for the fruit but that only led to more growers establishing more orchards. Additionally, Californians' nineteenth-century investments in pineapple canning in Hawaii were also booming; national pineapple marketing campaigns increased consumption on the East Coast and large yields on the islands created even more fruit every year. Grape growers encountered a different problem: Prohibition threatened California's vineyards, and even raisin packers could not use all the grapes grown.

Canners were already packing cans with whole and sliced peaches, pears, and pineapples, but they needed new ways to pack the fruit to attract more customers. In response to the national prohibition on alcohol manufacture, Berkeley's College of Agriculture changed the focus of its Department of Viticulture and Enology from grape growing and wine producing to fruit products in general. The newly reconfigured department's fruit products lab took on the canners' problem. Creation of fruit cocktail in 1923 was the most conspicuous immediate result. The laboratory has been providing solutions for canners, farmers, driers, and vintners ever since.

The University of California, Berkeley's vital role in the development of food processing provides an example of the far-reaching impact of the Morrill Land Grant Act in America. The canners, driers, and packers of the Golden State often had turned to the University of California for help in solving industry-wide problems from field to factory. Scientists at land-grant universities tackled the many predicaments faced by food processors in addition to pursuing fundamental agricultural and food science research. This dual thrust contributed in many ways to the creation of modern food-processing industries in the West to meet the needs of industrialized society in the nineteenth and twentieth centuries.

While food processing has been around for millennia, people have applied technology that emerged during industrialization to modernize the methods to do so over the last two hundred years. Finding, producing, and storing food has been a time-consuming task throughout human history. Although humans need food regularly to survive, in most climates nature provides much of her bounty only at certain times of the year. It takes extensive knowledge of the local environment to be able to survive as a hunter-gatherer. Agriculture mitigated the problem with regular food production, and development of food preservation methods enabled humans to take full advantage of the agricultural abundance.[1]

Humans have preserved food for millenia. Evidence suggests that in 12,000 BC Egyptian tribes dried fish and poultry. Like agriculture, food preservation depended on climate. Different climates encouraged the development of different preservation methods. The heat of the Mediterranean has made it possible for Sicilian fishers to dry their catch and distribute it throughout Europe for centuries. Cod fishermen in the Northern Atlantic experienced a less advantageous climate, and alternatively filled their ships' hulls with salt, allowing the fish to dry as the fishermen returned to Europe.[2] Dependence on nature's whims made humans vulnerable. By the later eighteenth century, Europeans tried to overcome this dependency by applying science to food preservation.

Nicholas Appert, often known as the father of modern canning, was one of the earliest food scientists to use scientific techniques to solve the problems that industrialization and imperialism revealed. Working in France in the turbulent last decades of the eighteenth century, he was a chef and confectioner fascinated by food preservation. He searched for a way to preserve foods in a way such that they would remain closer to their original texture and flavor. Appert's successful experimentation with fruits, vegetables, and meats led to canned beef stew, which he later sent out with the French navy for three months to test for durability and palatability. Appert focused on vegetables and stews stored in glass jars in small batches. The products were so delicious that they impressed finicky, influential French gourmand Grimod de La Reyniere, who gave his blessing to the process.[3]

Modern canning, the most technologically advanced food preservation method of the nineteenth century, was born from a combination of entrepreneurship and science. Appert's methods crossed the English Channel when British entrepreneur Peter Durand took the Frenchman's process of canning, changed the packaging to tin cans, and patented the concept in England. Tin cans made the product sturdier to ship within Britain's industrialized nation and across its empire.[4] Appert's procedures combined with Durand's innovations first emerged in the United States in the 1830s when Americans began their own canning companies rather than rely on imports.

Although food science began outside of the university, during the early twentieth century it became a thriving field of study. In America, the study of food science almost always occurred at land-grant universities, and companies and government agencies used resultant research to increase production and improve product quality. Land-grants became one of the various ways the government supported industry and contributed to the production of processed foods. Additionally, all levels of government sought to regulate the food processors.[5]

American industrialization and urbanization lengthened the amount of time that food needed to travel from field to table. In the late nineteenth and twentieth centuries, the food supply network that began with farmers and ended in the family kitchen included processors, brokers, grocers, and wholesalers. Producer-to-consumer pathways went from simple, direct exchanges to a complex web so difficult to unravel that most consumers are unaware of how many hands touch their food before purchase. These new pathways rendered urban consumers dependent and uncertain about the quality of food. In the years after 1900, a number of mechanisms emerged that made consumers more secure in the salubrity of their purchases; the state, through supporting the research universities, increasingly played a large role in developing them. The story of the University of California is an excellent example of a land-grant university supporting industrial food processing.

The University of California-Berkeley opened its doors in 1869 as a land-grant college with ten faculty members and forty students. When Eugene Hilgard became a professor of agriculture in 1873, he insisted on the intellectual importance of the college and believed that with proper nurturing the college could make many scientific as well as technical contributions. He was actively involved in national discussions about agricultural science and still managed to keep in touch with the needs of local farmers.[6] Hilgard recruited and promoted scientists for his mission. As part of the faculty at Berkeley, Dr. William Vere Cruess helped solve some of the most disruptive issues that confronted the young California food-processing industries in the early twentieth century. Cruess worked closely with major food producers to further the science of fruit and vegetable processing. Wine making and olive production were his specialties, but over time, his interest in commercial food production provided crucial information on production techniques, varieties, and other issues to all food processors. Cruess and other American food scientists improved existing products and turned waste into profits by helping create new marketable items, such as baby food and fruit juices.

Cruess was born on a farm in 1886 in San Miguel, California, only a few years before the fruit boom that occurred in the state. He obtained a B.S. in chemistry from the University of California, located in Berkeley, in 1911 and a PhD from Stanford in 1931 specializing in zymology (study of fermentation). During his undergraduate studies, he assisted Dr. Frederic Bioletti, a specialist in wine and grapes. This experience helped convince him to take on a career in food science and introduced him to the most important leaders in the California wine-, olive-, and fruit-processing industries. Employed with the University of California-Berkeley from 1911 to 1965, his research interest in processing fruits often led him out of the laboratory and into the factories and fields.[7] This was not common among most early food scientists; most of them stayed in the lab.

Cruess was passionate about improving fruit products from the field to the table. This led to his involvement, during his long career, with all of the major fruit-processing groups in California: fruit canners, driers, olive processors, and winemakers. While some scholars may question his objectivity because he was working with industry, for Cruess, his work with canneries was a reciprocal relationship. He was able to gain access to huge amounts of information from canneries and orchards that would have been very difficult for him to obtain otherwise. While Berkeley did develop two fine agricultural experiment farms, at Davis and Riverside, it took decades. During Cruess's early years of research, facilities for full production research were not available.[8] Businesses that consulted him gained valuable expertise in improving production and overcoming problems as company research labs were not common during this time. This arrangement also allowed resource sharing in newer, developing regions and industries. He took the knowledge he gained and passed it on to future cannery managers and executives who attended the University of California. By publishing in science journals, he was able to pass along research to the scientific community. Thus, from his perspective, he was creating a better, safer, more reliable food supply for America.[9]

Cruess was intimately involved in Berkeley's expansion of research from viticulture to include other fruits and food processing. Within the Fruit Products Lab, the dramatic increase in production led scientists and canners to accentuate efficiency and scientific management as they profited from economies of scale. Production of more consistently shaped and sized fruit was critical to mechanization both on the farm and in the factory. Standardization of canned products and grading of raw materials proved to be contentious, much-discussed topics among canners and growers. Growers were anxious to make sure they sold as much of their crops as possible in this new climate, but in an era priding itself on standardization and consistency, not all peaches were the same quality or garnered the same price at market.[10]

Probably the most widely adopted product to come out of the Fruit Products Lab was fruit cocktail. Scientists created this delicious combination of diced peaches, diced pears, grapes, pineapple chunks, and maraschino cherry halves in the lab as an experiment in fruit by-product use and grape use. It resulted when canners and food scientists in the fruit products lab searched for uses for the lower-graded fruit to provide additional markets for canners. The item "fruits for salad" already existed, but the larger slices of fruits in the product necessitated higher-graded fruit. Lower grades often tasted like higher grades, though they were not as perfectly formed, thus dicing was a way to use misshapen peaches and pears. The addition of heavy sugar syrup to fill the can hid any lack of flavor that might have been an issue.[11] H. E. Gray, a small cannery in San Jose, produced the fruit cocktail on a small scale. When the product turned out to be successful, other canners picked it up and began producing increasingly larger packs of fruit cocktail.

During this time, the fruit products lab also worked on creating more efficient fruit dehydrators. The earliest fruit dryers in California used big ovens to make the prunes, raisins, and apricots that became popular products from the state, but this method limited their production quantities. In the late nineteenth century, fruit driers discovered that the sun dried fruit more efficiently than the oven. Food processors used this method for decades. Floods in the 1920s destroyed a season's worth of prunes and raisins that were sitting outside, and driers were desperate to find a way to produce high quantities again without being dependent on nature. The result was a technical solution: heated fruit driers that were better suited for large-scale production than were the old-fashioned ovens.[12]

Cruess also worked with the olive industry in helping establish the processing procedure for green olives, which before that time was not economically feasible in California. The benefit of selling pickled green olives in addition to ripe black olives was that olive growers could use more of their crop. His work took him to Spain, where he met with olive growers and processors to discover new varieties, how the Spanish olive industry operated, and how they handled particular problems, such as olive discoloration and processing time. After their introduction to the American olive market, green olives became a successful product for the olive industry.[13]

In 1942, the Institute of Food Technologists gave one of its most prestigious awards, the Nicholas Appert Award, to Dr. William Cruess for lifetime achievement. During his career, Cruess had advanced the field through research and teaching. Cruess took the knowledge he gained working with food processors and passed it on in many ways. Teaching at Berkeley was one way he could disseminate what he had learned by working in his lab and with the industry. Cruess wrote a definitive textbook titled *Commercial Fruit and Vegetable Products*, which was first published in 1924 and updated four times by 1958. His classes included lessons on production and the scientific analysis of a canned product. One detailed lecture took students through a number of experiments in determining the quality—or lack thereof—of a product. Cruess was an active writer, publishing in academic journals, USDA bulletins, and extensions newsletters. One of his colleagues wrote a summary of his publications through 1960 and discovered a total of five books and 895 publications of various forms.[14] Through his many publications for extension programs and USDA bulletins, he sought to educate the public as well as the industry by explaining the various methods of canning and preservation. Home economics teachers, home canners, and extension agents wrote to him for advice, and the archives containing his correspondence are thick with answers to their questions. The canning bulletins he wrote became vital during the campaign for home canning during World War II. This aspect of his career demonstrates his personal dedication to teaching and food safety.[15]

Frozen foods became a popular research topic in university labs in the early twentieth century. Interest in freezing foods first focused on meat. The discovery of procedures for flash freezing fruits and vegetables improved palatability, creating another avenue for preserving fresh produce. Like fruit juices had been years before, frozen juice concentrate became a product that increased the efficiency of fruit producers and increased the amount of fruit the producers could purchase from growers. Frozen juice concentrate was a product of efficiency, much like other fruit juices and nectars. Frozen vegetables were superior in taste and texture to canned or dried vegetables. The consumer frozen food market did not become very substantial until the 1950s because freezers were not common home appliances until then, and even refrigerators had small freezing spaces. Electrification intensified access by World War II, and home designs in the postwar housing boom had higher square footage to accommodate a larger refrigerator or freezer and more outlets to support electric appliances. However, the study of freezing food began decades before in food science laboratories. The study of freezing fruit began in the 1920s, and the largest hurdle to producing frozen foods was creating a consistent product. Scientists could freeze fruit, but it often had an off-flavor and when thawed had an undesirable consistency. Clarence Birdseye's method of flash freezing finally solved many of the problems food scientists had been working to overcome for years and gave life to what was to become the most popular food-processing method of the twentieth century.[16]

While some scientists at the university worked toward making a better product in the factory, others contributed by perfecting the raw materials entering it. Agricultural science was vital to the food processors as it provided expertise for field and orchard creation and maintenance. Scientists discovered varieties of peaches, pears, cherries, apples, chilies, asparagus, tomatoes, and oranges, for example, that would be best for processors. Different varieties were ready to harvest either earlier or later during the summer; by choosing and recommending those that would extend the length of the harvest, agricultural scientists gave farmers and processors more time to harvest and process the crops, which was extremely valuable during the chaotic harvest and packing season. Crop studies had been part of the research agenda since the university's beginnings. Hilgard arranged for practical demonstrations and short courses for farmers in addition to formal academic research. Berkeley's agriculture and food scientists published their research in the *Hilgardia*, a compendium of findings specific to California's agricultural needs.[17]

In addition to solving problems of disease, such as San Jose scale, or pest infestations, agricultural scientists at Berkeley studied the varieties of deciduous fruits, olives, and asparagus to isolate varieties most suitable for specific processing. As canners mechanized their plants, machines replaced people, taking over the tasks of peeling fruit, dicing pears, pitting peaches, and stemming asparagus. Processors sought consistently shaped fruit that was also attractively colored and good tasting, which was quite a demand. This is why clingstone peach varieties became more prominent than freestone peach varieties in Northern California. The clingstone peach had a firmer texture, allowing it to make the journey through the cannery and into the can with less damage.[18]

The Giannini Foundation of Agricultural Economics was another avenue of intersection between agribusinesses, food processors, and the university. Amedeo Peter Giannini, a San Jose native and successful produce dealer in Santa Clara County, established the Bank of Italy in San Francisco in 1904. The bank helped many middle-class depositors, such as growers and small businessmen, operate in Northern California by providing credit. Founded in 1931 with a \$1.5 million gift in honor of Giannini and housed at the university, the foundation used the research capabilities of the university to solve local problems and provide growers and farmers with knowledge they could use in production. Although the number of intended beneficiaries of this research was small initially, the research was often applicable in many other regions. The foundation's researchers published studies in top-ranking agricultural journals on a wide variety of topics including fruit and nut production in wartime, the demand for various types of deciduous fruits, transportation costs, and the cost of waste reduction. The work of the Giannini researchers remained relevant for decades. For example, during the 1930s the foundation studied what variables affected the prices of raw fruits. The researchers' analysis was important for growers associations and canners as they tried to make annual negotiations between canners and growers more predictable.[19] Because of government support of scientific research through the creation of land-grand universities, scientists became essential contributors to the development of food-processing industries. University scientists provided solutions to industry problems and trained generations of future scientists, company managers, and government employees. Their involvement also calmed consumers' fears and provided legitimacy to an industry that once had a reputation for questionable quality.

University scientists were also involved in developing regulations for the food-processing industries. Philosophies of laissez-faire and individualism of the nineteenth century faded as industrialization, unfettered capitalism, and urbanization contributed to social turmoil and public health crises. While the federal government had assisted developing markets in the nineteenth century, it rarely regulated them or protected consumers. Following a strict constitutional interpretation, most politicians and lawmakers left the job of protecting citizens largely to the individual states. This situation proved to be a problematic aspect of federalism as businesses grew larger and routinely crossed state lines. Individual states rarely coordinated their regulation of industry, and when they did, they did so ineffectively.

Similar to other Progressive Movement activities and ideas, the Pure Foods Movement originated in the 1870s from women's concerns about industrially processed food products. Many women organized to promote the creation of regulation that would protect their families from tainted foods. Agricultural chemists, such as Harvey Wiley, were also key supporters of the movement. Their efforts, along with those of others, culminated in the Pure Food and Drug Act of 1906 and the subsequent creation of the Food and Drug Administration (FDA). The FDA sought to protect the food supply and ensure purity through inspection of production systems. The agency tested chemicals to determine if they were too poisonous to use in food and promoted descriptive labeling of ingredients. Originally the FDA was part of the US Department of Agriculture (USDA). However, there was an implicit contradiction in this partnership. The USDA's mandate was to expand agricultural markets and food production while the FDA regulated food production. Despite the potential conflict, the USDA also protected the food supply through inspection of food and agricultural facilities. Both agencies became increasingly involved in the canneries during the twentieth century to the benefit and frustration of cannery owners, particularly given its origins. However, in the early twentieth century a gap existed between the FDA's authority and its ability to carry out its mission because of a lack of funding. State governments often had to cover the gap for the sake of public health.[20]

An example of the complex relationship between scientists, industry, and regulatory agencies is the botulism scare in the olive industry in the early twentieth century. Cruess researched the use and processing of olives to help the industry. In 1919, reports started coming in of deaths attributed to canned ripe olives from California. The food poisoning outbreak came at a time when Americans were still reconciling themselves to trusting canned foods. Even though canned food had become commonplace by this point in the United States, consumers still questioned such foods' consistency of quality. The fear of canned olives spread quickly, and public health officials in some states, such as Michigan, banned all canned foods made in California from entering their state. The loss of $70,000 weekly was devastating for California's canners and they, collaborating with the National Canners' Association and Canners' League of California, put together a research team to investigate the outbreaks. Cruess, along with epidemiologists Karl F. Meyer and Ernest Dickson, played an important role in helping put scientific principles discovered by the epidemiologists into practice in the canneries. The ultimate result was the creation of the California Cannery Inspection Board, which had authority over all food processors that used pressure cookers. Inspectors reporting to the board received training to detect damaged or improperly prepared canned foods so as to determine the cause of the spoilage. They inspected factories for cleanliness and the quality of raw materials. Serving on the board were leaders from the largest companies in the state and an appointee by the California Board of Health. Meyer served as the appointee for many years.[21]

The associative state emerged during the late nineteenth century as a way to temper the chaotic economy created by industrialization and the growth of large corporations without creating many strong regulatory agencies. Underlying this form of government-business relationship was the idea that industries or companies could be more efficient and interact better with the national economy if they worked together voluntarily, increased communication, and supported research in science and technology. In addition, the role of the government was to provide support to industry without creating overly complex and rigid regulation.[22] Thus government agencies, such as the USDA, reached out to industries and encouraged the creation of trade associations and other formal and informal groups to disseminate information and undertake research that would improve the efficiency of the agricultural and food-processing industries.[23] Canners' trade organizations received assistance from the University of California-Berkeley that helped them increase the quality and variety of their products and create new markets.[24] Land-grant colleges, agricultural experiment stations, and extension programs created opportunities for USDA and land-grant college scientists to collect and disseminate information to food industries.[25]

The emerging field of food science also contributed to creating the modern army. The role of food and supply logistics during war is often lost among biographies of heroes, the intricacies of international politics, and cutting-edge weapons technology. Often the most necessary common things in life are easy to forget about until they are gone, such as clean air, adequate food, and drinkable water. But all of these things become priceless in wartime. One key element of the study of the history of wartime logistics is food science. In American history, war has been a catalyst for innovation in the food industry. Frozen foods, freeze-drying, and canning trace their roots back to experiments in feeding the military. Another key element in provisioning troops was the art of getting sustenance to the frontline. It depended vitally on the geography on which the battle was taking place. Reaching the trenches of World War I, setting up food stations on captured Pacific Islands, or following soldiers from the beaches of Normandy to

Germany each presented unique environmental challenges; feeding thousands or millions of men of varied backgrounds in these different environments was not easy, especially while the enemy targeted supply lines.

Berkeley food scientists, such as William Cruess and his colleague Emil Mrak, assisted the distributor of army rations and supplies, the Quartermaster Corps. During World War I, the army took the first steps to alter its food distribution system by centralizing purchasing and creating combat and emergency rations in a more scientific way. This was in part a result of complaints about rations provided to troops during the Spanish-American War. Trench warfare had also forced the Corps to rethink how food was packed and distributed. The Quartermaster Corps created the Subsistence School and a research laboratory after the war to continue studying the nutrition required by soldiers and logistics for providing balanced nutritional rations to soldiers, especially in combat situations.[26]

During World War II, university food scientists helped the Quartermaster Corps in the ongoing development of rations and the distribution of food during the war. The work required an understanding of nutrients and calories, the specialty of food scientists. Cruess, for example, served in the Guinea Pig Program, testing and tasting the various rations. More complex and better nutrition for soldiers in combat emerged as a result, greatly altering military fare and its distribution between World War I and World War II. Combat rations for soldiers in World War I were a pound of canned meat, corned beef or a slab of bacon, sixteen ounces of hard bread, sugar, coffee, and some salt. By World War II, the C-ration included a Meat Unit (M-Unit), which could be pork and beans, meat and vegetable hash, or meat and vegetable stew. It also included a Bread Unit (B-Unit), which included hard bread, coffee, sugar, and a chocolate fudge bar, candy, or fruit cocktail. The C-ration was a huge step forward in nutrition. K-rations had smaller packaging so that paratroopers could fit them in their pockets. The ration included summer sausage, canned meat, crackers, cheese, candy, and chocolate. Emergency kits designed for the air force included rations specific to tropical or arctic situations.[27]

In the 1940s, California's food processors played a vital role in supplying food for American soldiers and allies. Getting nutrition and calories to the soldiers at the front was vital. Food scientists worked with the military to develop the most nutritious, inexpensive, and portable food options. Cruess and his colleagues worked on two major projects during this time. One was a nutrition research project that sought to create the best rations possible.

The other major research focus was dried vegetables. Canners had studied dehydration of fruits extensively in the 1920s, but dehydrated vegetables were in much less demand commercially then; canned vegetables were superior in taste and texture. The pressing need of war brought dried vegetables back into California food scientists' labs. Although vegetables were not Cruess's specialty, they were an important product of California. The scientists in the lab modified fruit-drying machines to make them more efficient at drying large lots of vegetables and capable of producing a better tasting product. With their knowledge of food chemistry, the scientists were able to develop products to meet to the Quartermaster General's needs.[28]

After the war, food processers entered a new era of product development and expansion. Once again, expertise provided by land-grant university scientists was essential. Even though the field had matured by midcentury, new issues emerged. The food science departments at land-grant universities had trained thousands of food scientists to work outside the university with government agencies and food processors. Many food processors or trade associations had created their own food science laboratories in the 1950s, staffed by food scientists trained at universities such as Berkeley. Even midsize canner/grower cooperatives in California, such as Tri Valley Packing Association, had their own product development team employing food scientists.

Food and agricultural science studies at Berkeley grew to such a degree by 1950 that the departments moved to a second campus. In 1951, the food science department, along with much of the Department of Agriculture, moved to the Davis campus, which once served as the university farm. The University of California-Davis became an independent university only eight years later and quickly emerged as a national leader in food science. UC-Davis had the advantage of plenty of room to grow, administrative dedication to food and agricultural science, and location. The campus was over sixty miles northeast of the main campus, which was closer to the Central Valley, the heart of Northern California's agricultural production.[29]

In this period, the university continued to provide valuable expertise in the orchard. During the introduction of mechanical harvesting of food crops in the 1950s and 1960s, the University of California scientists contributed valuable advice. The interest in mechanical harvesting of fruit crops in California emerged from the method's success in Hawaii. Pineapple harvesting began in the 1950s, and the success of pineapple farmers encouraged California's canners and growers to try the method with other crops. The end of the bracero program in 1964 encouraged mechanical tomato harvesting, which was a huge success. Shortly after, peach growers turned to mechanical harvesting. Agricultural scientists at UC-Davis helped develop machinery and select varieties best suited for mechanical peach harvesting.[30]

In the mid-twentieth century, canners faced another problem: cannery waste disposal. Population growth, increase in the quality and span of public health regulation, and environmental awareness led to numerous restrictions on food processors' options for disposing of waste. Food processors created millions of tons of green waste each day during the peak processing season. Where was it all to go? Waste disposal possibilities depended on the cannery's location and the products the factory produced. Vegetable wastes could become animal feed. Canneries located near water sources often dumped their waste in the water, expecting the dilution power of the water to carry it away or disperse the mass into smaller pieces until it disintegrated or an animal ate it. Factories located far from water sources often dumped their waste on land in private dump sites.[31]

Most often, food processors received assistance from the College of Agriculture for improvement of production and solving particularly difficult problems, but after World War II, other departments also contributed to solving the waste problems faced by the food-processing industry. Sanitary engineers and biologists were vital in creating technical solutions and providing quantified definitions of purity. Sanitary engineers helped create filtration systems to separate the solids from liquids to preserve water resources. Wet sewage disposal in Santa Clara County was difficult because of dramatic population growth and suburban building, and an innovative solution to cannery waste disposal was to try to create a product from the fruit sludge. Processors often sold vegetable wastes for cattle feed, thus canners and food scientists began to experiment with the concept on fruit wastes. The National Canners Association (NCA) Western Regional Research Laboratory in Albany, California, and the Canners League of California (CLC) experimented with the conversion of pear waste to feed molasses and dried feed pulp. In 1949, the NCA lab and the CLC had worked with the University of California Agricultural Experiment Station in Davis to see if the products were palatable to cows and sheep. After successful experimentation feeding it to livestock, the scientists pushed the project past its original focus on pear experimentation and tested the procedure with other fruit cannery waste, such as peaches and tomatoes. The concept was exciting for everyone involved and attracted local media attention.[32]

After agricultural scientists successfully converted pear waste in the laboratory, several Santa Clara County canners invested in a new company, Pacific Biochem, which promised to make the processing of pear waste into cow feed profitable. While the theory was sound, there were a number of production and marketing problems with Pacific Biochem. Canneries produced waste, and the San Jose Scavenger Company delivered it to the factory. Unfortunately, Pacific Biochem could not process most of it because of management's inability to bring the factory to full production, and the San Jose Scavenger Company had to take the waste to Newby Island instead. In the end, the canners paid disposal fees rather than receiving a return on their investment in waste processing. Also, the San Jose Scavenger Company drivers dripped the wet garbage on their routes to the factory and the nearby disposal site. The waste spilled from the trucks generated nuisance complaints from people living along their routes, resulting in health department reprimands to Pacific Biochem, the canners, and the hauling company. After a few years of intermittent operation, the amount of product made proved inadequate to cover operational costs. While the concept worked in the experimentation phase, the management could not make the plant profitable, and the company ceased operations in 1955 in debt. However, a company in Oregon succeeded a few years later in using pear waste to produce byproducts, proving the concept could be financially successful.[33]

In the 1970s, extension services helped Santa Clara County Canners develop a huge composting operation on 2,300 acres. Extension researchers first tested the concept of composting sludgy fruit cannery wastes on a very small scale. The Santa Clara County Canners Association created the Cooperative for Environmental Improvement (CEI). A brochure about the company's startup claimed CEI's purpose was to meet the environmental and economic needs of Santa Clara County. After formally setting up the company, President Harvey Lancaster searched for a site for the project and selected 2,300 acres on the Santa Clara and San Benito county line. The company began hauling cannery waste from the 1970 pack to the leased land. Trucks brought the cannery waste to the compost site, and bulldozers spread it over the land evenly to dry. The company let the first layer dry for a couple days. Then CEI workers disked the waste into the soil, allowing the microorganisms to break down the waste and create carbon dioxide, water, and humus. The first year, CEI received 67,251 cubic yards of material from the Santa Clara County Canners and the San Benito County Canners. They processed 98,742 cubic yards a year two years later. The site also became a place to dispose of surplus or unusable products. For example, the California Prune Growers Advisory Board dumped 2,585 tons of prunes at the site in 1970.[34]

Canners were pleased with the results of the experiment because they had found a reliable way to removing waste for which they received good press and that benefited others. The public health departments of Santa Clara County and San Benito County were spared the struggle over cannery waste disposal for a few years. Both counties kept watch over the process to ensure CEI management handled the waste properly because composting on such a large scale can have dangerous results if neglected.

The University of California agricultural experiment stations also watched the operations and conducted experiments on part of the acreage to determine the maximum amount of waste the earth would bear. In some experiment stations projects, the scientists successfully composted four times as much waste as CEI had used on the large-scale composting site. Farmers also had something to gain from composting. The chosen site's soil was alkaline, and the waste was mostly acidic. Experiment administrators hoped the introduction of waste would create balanced humus, improving the soil for planting. The first plantings in the soil of the compost experiment grew normally, and in some cases, the plants thrived in the cannery waste compost soil.[35]

As the composting project was also an agricultural extension experiment, the knowledge gained from it became part of the national agricultural scientific community. A description and analysis of the experiment appeared in several scientific publications. Sharing the results of experiments allowed other canning communities and companies across the United States to learn from the experiment and assess the risks involved in such an operation. Small food processors in the Midwest and East faced many of the same pressures as California's canners, such as waste disposal and suburbanization, and the publication of the results of the experiments of communities with more resources, such as northern California, gave them information they could not have afforded to discover themselves.[36]

The Morrill Act and succeeding acts that created the land-grant universities and extension programs had far-reaching impacts. One example of this is the way land-grant universities changed the lives of many Americans through advancements in the food-processing industry. While food preservation methods, such as drying, salting, and fermentation, were thousands of years old, tools that emerged during industrialization drastically altered the methods of food processing and distribution, creating a modern food-processing system. Factories increasingly preserved the food most people consumed, and less food was processed in the home. Land-grant universities were a fundamental part of this transition, and food scientists were partly responsible for modernizing food processing. While traditional preservation methods depended on environment, modern canned food was made in a factory that would reproduce the same product in any environment whether humid, dry, hot, or cold. Canned food was extremely useful in an era of industrialization and imperialism because so many people moved to foreign environments and needed a dependable food source.

The work of scientists such as William Cruess demonstrates the impact of the Morrill Land Grant Act. His invaluable work led the University of California-Berkeley to become very involved in the quickly growing food-processing industry in California in the early twentieth century. Scientists following Cruess's example worked out the problems of mechanical harvesting of peaches, pears, and tomatoes from orchard to canning line. Cruess is one of the many food scientists who emerged in the early twentieth century as part of the creation of a commercial, industrial food supply in America. Though his career was exemplary, it illustrates the growing role of university food scientists. The transformation of America's food system played a key role in the nation's modernization. Studying the food system reveals the rapidity of national changes in urbanization and manufacturing.

Land-grant universities provided valuable research for the public, growers, and food processers. While some trade associations and major companies created their own research and development labs by the 1920s, many companies were unable to afford such an expense until after World War II. They relied on the university scientists to help them solve problems. For example, prior to World War I, large companies such as the California Packing Corporation, later known as Del Monte, were unique; most fruit canners were small to midsized companies. Smaller canneries in California could never have financed a research and development department to provide the kind of valuable information that came from Berkeley and UC-Davis. The knowledge and expertise the university provided gave smaller and midsized canners research and information they needed to compete against large companies such as California Packing and helped prevent monopoly in the industry.

While the food scientists at land-grant universities developed methods that benefited local agricultural communities and food processors, as well as the military, their publications and interactions with other food scientists spread their findings around the globe and contributed to a broader understanding of food science. Land-grant universities also trained thousands of students to be food scientists who could work for the government, private research labs, and universities.

While many land-grant universities in the United States contributed to food-processing industries in one way or another, examining the University of California-Berkeley provides a deeper understanding of how one university contributed to a critical national industry. California became the western center for many food-processing industries, which became an integral part of the state's economy. Thus the university contributed to the development of a larger national industry while helping shape regional economies as well.

While such food science research was advantageous for the industry, some criticized the work of the university scientists. The intricate web modern food processors spun from the field to the table became too complex for most consumers to follow. Critics argued the industrial food system separated people from the environment so much that consumers no longer knew where their food was grown or processed. In the same region that was home to many fruit and vegetable processors, Alice Waters opened Chez Panisse in 1971, a restaurant that celebrated the local foods of Northern California. She argued that fresh foods prepared simply with minimal processing were better for people and the community. Waters and like-minded colleagues helped start the local foods movement, calling for sustainable agriculture and simple foods. While canned and processed foods have many valuable uses, as for the military and for emergencies, nutritionists have concerns about the health consequences for those who are dependent on them.

The food-processing industry concentrated the activities of preservation from thousands of homes into one location. As a result, the regions in which food processors operated supplied the crops, labor, and fossil-fuel energy, and they had to deal with waste disposal. Industrial, intensive agricultural methods preferred by land-grant scientists included irrigation, pesticides, and transformation of land that was not commercially productive. For much of the twentieth century, these lands were wetlands and deserts. California's wetlands are part of the Pacific flyway and support millions of birds. As people transformed the land to produce a profit, vital spaces for these species disappeared. Industrial food also contributed to the development of a high-energy food supply dependent on fossil fuels for production and preservation.

Criticism of industrial food production and food science has led to industry changes. One can now find organic processed foods with minimal additives that represent a different philosophy of resource use than was dominant through much of the twentieth century. Unfortunately organic food is still too expensive for all Americans to eat exclusively. Some food scientists and agricultural scientists are now starting to address some of the flaws of the industrial food system the land-grant universities helped build. Given the flexibility of the system, perhaps land-grant university scientists will take leadership in the twenty-first century as they did in the twentieth century and reorient America's food supply down a more sustainable path.

NOTES

1. Sue Shephard, *Pickled, Potted, and Canned: How the Art and Science of Food Preserving Changed the World* (New York: Simon and Schuster, 2000).

2. Kenneth Pomeranz and Steven Topik, eds., *The World That Trade Created: Society, Culture, and the World Economy, 1400 to the Present,* 2nd ed. (Armonk, NY: M. E. Sharpe, 2006); Mark Kurlansky, *Salt: A World History* (New York: Penguin, 2003); Shephard, *Pickled, Potted, and Canned.*

3. Shepherd, Pickled Potted and Canned.

4. Ibid., 226–40.

5. My analysis of the runs of *Canning Age* and *Western Canner and Packer* revealed the constant interaction between universities such as Berkeley, Oregon State University, and University of Wisconsin.

6. Patricia A. Pelfrey, *A Brief History of the University of California,* 2nd ed. (Berkeley: University of California Press, 2004); Ann Foley Scheuring, *Abundant Harvest: The History of the University of California, Davis* (Davis: UC-Davis History Project, 2001), 3–9; Kevin Starr, *California: A History,* 1st ed., A Modern Library Chronicles Book 23 (New York: Modern Library, 2005), 108.

7. Ruth Teiser, "A Half Century in Food and Wine Technology: An Interview with William V. Cruess," interview transcript, UC-Berkeley Regional Oral History Office.

8. W. V. Cruess, *Commercial Fruit and Vegetable Products: A Textbook for Student, Investigator and Manufacturer,* 2nd ed. (New York: McGraw-Hill, 1938); Scheuring, *Abundant Harvest.*

9. Teiser, "A Half Century in Food and Wine Technology."

10. "Canners' League of California 1917 Annual Meeting Notes," 1917, box 61, folder 2, Special Collections, University of California-Davis; "Canners' League of California 1918 Annual Meeting Notes," 1918, box 61, folder 2, Special Collections, University of California-Davis; "Fifteenth Annual Meeting of the Canners' League of California," 1919, box 61, folder 2, Special Collections, University of California-Davis; "Annual Meeting of the Canners' League of California 1920," 1920, box 61, folder 10, Special Collections, University of California-Davis.

11. Sherman Leonard, "Dr. William V. Cruess: His Contribution to the Canning Industry," n.d., box 6, folder 62, Special Collections, University of California-Davis; Cruess, *Commercial Fruit and Vegetable Products*, 168–72.

12. Teiser, "A Half Century in Food and Wine Technology," 80–93.

13. Ibid., 57–67; "Manuscripts & Printed Material," 1965, 1915, box 1, folder 48 through box 7, folder 11, William V. Cruess Collection, Special Collections, University of California-Davis.

14. Leonard, "Dr. William V. Cruess."

15. "Manuscripts & Printed Material."

16. Shephard, *Pickled, Potted, and Canned*; Shane Hamilton, "The Economies and Conveniences of Modern-Day Living: Frozen Foods and Mass Marketing, 1945–1965," *Business History Review* 77, no. 1 (Spring 2003): 33–60; Cruess, *Commercial Fruit and Vegetable Products*; Teiser, "A Half Century in Food and Wine Technology."

17. California Agricultural Experiment Station, *Hilgardia* (Berkeley: California Agricultural Experiment Station, n.d.).

18. Cruess, *Commercial Fruit and Vegetable Products*.

19. Daniel A. Sumner, "Giannini Economics and Agricultural Supply in California," May 3, 2006; H. J. Stover, *An Analysis of the Prices Received for Canned Peaches by Canners in California: Seasons 1922–23 through 1934–35*, Giannini Foundation of Agricultural Economics, June 1935; Trimble R. Hedges and Warren R. Bailey, *Appraisal of California Agricultural Capacity Attainable in 1955*, Giannini Foundation of Agricultural Economics, June 1952; R. L. Adams, *Seasonal Labor Needs for California Crops in Alameda*, Giannini Foundation of Agricultural Economics, October 1936; all located in Giannini Reports, Bioscience Library, University of California-Berkeley.

20. Oscar Edward Anderson, *The Health of a Nation: Harvey W. Wiley and the Fight for Pure Food* (Chicago: University of Chicago Press, 1958); James Harvey Young, *Pure Food: Securing the Federal Food and Drugs Act of 1906* (Princeton: Princeton University Press, 1989); Lorine Swainston Goodwin, *The Pure Food, Drink, and Drug Crusaders, 1879–1914* (Jefferson, NC: McFarland, 1999); Mitchell Okun, *Fair Play in the Marketplace: The First Battle for Pure Food and Drugs* (DeKalb: Northern Illinois University Press, 1986); Marc T. Law, "The Origins of State Pure Food Regulation," *Journal of Economic History* 63, no. 4 (December 1, 2003): 1103–30.

21. Karl F. Meyer, "Historical Background Cannery Inspection State of California Department of Public Health," n.d., California State Library. See also Cannery Inspection Board Papers, California State Archive, R 384.070.

22. Louis Galambos and Joseph A. Pratt, *The Rise of the Corporate Commonwealth: U.S. Business and Public Policy in the Twentieth Century* (New York: Basic Books, 1988).

23. Historian David Hamilton argues that the USDA played a vital role in the formation of the associative state because the scientists working in the growing number of specialized departments, such as the Bureau of Chemistry, were influential in forming early associations related to their fields and training scientists to work for corporations and trade associations.

24. David E. Hamilton, "Building the Associative State: The Department of Agriculture and American State-Building," *Agricultural History* 64, no. 2 (Spring 1990): 207–18; David M. Hart, "Herbert Hoover's Last Laugh: The Enduring Significance of the 'Associative State' in the United States," *Journal of Policy History* 10, no. 4 (1998): 419–44.

25. Hamilton, "Building the Associative State"; R. Douglas Hurt, *American Agriculture: A Brief History*, 1st ed. (Ames: Iowa State University Press, 1994), 190–220; Wayne David Rasmussen and Gladys L. Baker, *The Department of Agriculture*, Praeger Library of US Government Departments and Agencies, No. 32 (New York: Praeger, 1972), 3–87; Clayton A. Coppin, *The Politics of Purity: Harvey Washington Wiley and the Origins of Federal Food Policy* (Ann Arbor: University of Michigan Press, 1999); Anderson, *The Health of a Nation*.

26. John C. Fisher and Carol Fisher, *Food in the American Military: A History* (Jefferson, NC: McFarland, 2011), Kindle edition, location 2121–2124.

27. Ibid., location 2113–2120, 2328–2615; "Awards & Certificates," 1965 1925, box 9, folder 6 through box 11, William V. Cruess Collection, Special Collections, University of California-Davis.

28. Teiser, "A Half Century in Food and Wine Technology," 94–115.

29. Scheuring, *Abundant Harvest*.

30. "At Calpak's Peach Receiving Stations They're Delivering the Goods," *Del Monte Shield*, September 1953; "Are We Headed for Crisis on the Farm? Part 1," *Del Monte Shield*, August 1964; "Are We Headed for Crisis on the Farm? Part 2," *Del Monte Shield*, September 1964.

31. Paul A. Shaw, "Pollution Control Work of the California State Division of Fish and Game," *Sewage Works Journal* 12, no. 5 (1940): 947–53; Cruess, *Commercial Fruit and Vegetable Products*; Wm. J. O'Connell, "California Fruit and Vegetable Cannery Waste Disposal Practices," *Sewage and Industrial Wastes* 29, no. 3 (March 1, 1957): 268–80; W. S. Everts, "Disposal of Wastes from Fruit and Vegetable Canneries," *Sewage Works Journal* 16, no. 5 (September 1944): 944–46.

32. United States Department of Agriculture, "USDA Press Release about San Jose Waste Disposal Experiment," January 24, 1952, box 36, folder 45, California League of Food Processors Collection, Special Collections, University of California-Davis; M. A. Clevenger, "Pilot-Plant Research on Cannery Waste Pays Off," *The Canner*, November 5, 1949; M. A. Clevenger, "Pilot-Plant Research on Cannery Waste," *Western Canner & Packer*, November 1949.

33. Box 55, folder 41, Waste Disposal 1951; box 36, folder 46, Waste Disposal Tersini Plant Sale 1952; box 36, folder 53, Tersini Plant Sale; box 21, folder 59, Tersini Plant Sale 1955, all in California League of Food Processors Collection, Special Collections, University of California-Davis. These folders are filled with notes on the meetings of the Waste Disposal Committee, many of which discuss the functioning of the plant. In these notes, cannery executives, managers, trade association leaders, and other engineers discuss and problem-solve the various technical difficulties with the large-scale processing of pear waste.

34. "Cooperative for Environmental Improvement, Inc.: A Santa Clara County Canners Food Residuals Disposal Association D-2613," n.d., California League of Food Processors, Special Collections, University of California-Davis; A. D. Reed et al., "Soil Recycling of Cannery Wastes," *California Agriculture* 27, no. 3 (March 1973): 6–9.

35. "Cooperative for Environmental Improvement."

36. Reed et al., "Soil Recycling of Cannery Wastes"; William N. Helphinstine, "Using Cannery Wastes on Forage Cropland," *California Agriculture* 30, no. 9 (September 1976): 6–7.

9

"Waist Deep in the Big Muddy"

Land-Grant Social Scientists and Modernity from the Country Life Movement to the Cold War

HAMILTON CRAVENS

This chapter focuses on a prime land-grant objective: to use science to engineer a better society. That practical aspect of the land-grant experience holds that knowledge readily applied inevitably produces manifest blessings. While that is an important premise, it is also brimming with hubris. It presumes that experts can use social science to design social systems and situations that are markedly better than what preceded them. It replaces community control and even assent with professional dictate.

The case laid out by Cravens is far starker. It concentrates on one particular group of people—rural dwellers—and discusses some of the land-grant universities' attempts to make them modern. These universities had the best of intentions; they wanted to improve the lives of rural people. But their approach went far beyond that. They in effect replaced the lives of rural folk. They substituted modernity and its discontents for rural life and its problems. Destruction of precious rural traditions and customs became collateral damage, the inevitable consequence of a "better" existence. A lack of circumspection accompanied this land-grant-led initiative. The schools pursued that policy under the guise of a method so profound and above reproach as to brook no rational objection. Science rigorously and relentlessly applied would drag rural America into a far better place: the twentieth century.

But that was not all. Land-grant university professors took the model they applied to rural America and, during the height of the Cold War, exported it to the Third World. Confronted by the blessings of modernity, it was argued, developing and unaligned nations would reject communism and choose to affiliate with the cause of the free world.

The irony is that many Americans and others from the 1960s on saw that initiative as anything but free. To these men and women, it was nothing more than a blatant and ignorant attack on local traditions and practices, one that promised to destroy the cultures that it had planned to save.

***

I.

In April 1966, *Ramparts* magazine published a sensational exposé of Michigan State University's efforts to support the anti-communist, repressive government of Ngo Dinh Diem in South Vietnam. *Ramparts'* writers charged that this seemingly innocuous land-grant institution—an upstart "cow college" indeed—had included in its advisors to Diem's autocratic regime experts from its own faculty who aided and abetted that regime's actions against dissidents and operatives from Communist North Vietnam.[1] Michigan State had also enmeshed within its South Vietnam mission interrogation officers and spies from the Central Intelligence Agency to facilitate the mission and enforce its will upon persons they deemed regime opponents. The university had created the Michigan State University Group (MSUG) in 1957, even before the Eisenhower administration had set up its "nationalist" candidate, Diem. The MSUG funneled federal funds through standing university faculty departments in the applied social sciences to support the mission in South Vietnam. The MSUG thus had on its Vietnam roster faculty from several departments, including political science, economics, public administration, and police science. Several individuals on the police science roster were actually Central Intelligence Agency operatives operating under faculty cover. Through the MSUG personnel, technical advice and support were provided to the Diem regime, which included not merely instruction on how to set up a modern government, institute land policies, and rural pacification but also to train the regime's secret police in effective—that is, brutal—interrogation methods. Millions of federal dollars went through the MSUG to supply Diem's government with the tools of autocratic governance. Through its police administration department, the

MSUG transferred, with federal support, all manner of weapons, ammunition, handcuffs, and other instruments of dissident pacification to the Vietnam police forces being trained through its contract with the country. All of this was intended to make South Vietnam a Westernized, *modern* bulwark against communism's expansion into Southeast Asia. Perhaps the most sensational charge the *Ramparts* writers made was that the Central Intelligence Agency had clandestine operatives on the MSUG payroll spying in Vietnam and assisting in the pacification of the population. The magazine's editors closed with the tart question, "What the hell is a university doing buying guns anyway?"[2] In a couple of respects, the *Ramparts* article was old news. For one thing, President Diem had canceled the MSUG contract in 1962. He was angered that a handful of MSUG professors had complained about his repressive regime. Two Michigan State professors had previously tattled on Diem's regime in the *New Republic*. By 1965 at least one book had been published in the United States whose authors foreshadowed much of the *Ramparts* article's criticisms. An important monograph published in 1998, long after *Ramparts'* demise, outlined the MSUG mission and its actions in precise detail.[3]

Nor was tardiness the only defect in the *Ramparts* piece. Lack of historical knowledge about "cow colleges," not to mention a more general historical insight, further clouded the *Ramparts* writers' views. These Bay Area writers and sophisticates, who liked their whiskey and good times, were quite ignorant of the Morrill Land Grant Act that established the land-grant college system in 1862, in the heat of the American Civil War. The organic act may well have outlined an impossible mandate for the land-grant colleges' curricular offerings in the nineteenth century; everything but the proverbial kitchen sink was thrown into the mix—the industrial, agricultural, scientific, and socioeconomic disciplines; the classics and liberal arts; and military science and tactics.[4] It is true that the routine participation of the land-grant schools in national foreign policy came only with the national security crisis that began with the Japanese attack on Pearl Harbor and continued even after the collapse of the Soviet Union a half century later. In the century after the Morrill Act's enactment, these curricular offerings were established and institutionalized on a national basis. By World War I or so the land-grant colleges were sustaining instruction and research in the rural social science disciplines, such as agricultural economics, rural sociology, and home economics.

Timing matters. When Michigan State's "Vietnam Adventure" ended in

1962, most Americans were focusing on the threat of nuclear war with the Soviets, as the Cuban missile crisis that year illustrated. President Johnson escalated the nation's military effort to hundreds of thousands of conscripts and volunteers fighting in the jungles, deltas, and skies of that war-torn, unhappy nation. American interventions in neutral or nonaligned nations, either through civilian or military "technical assistance," from the administration of President Eisenhower onward numbered in the several dozen in any given year.[5] It is likely that the *Ramparts* article helped spark the growing antiwar movement on college campuses and other venues in the mid- and late 1960s. The Civil Rights and antiwar movements eventually tore the nation apart and splintered the fragile national political consensus that had held the nation together ever since the Japanese attack on Pearl Harbor in 1941.[6]

What were the implications of these developments for American social scientists and their pursuit of federal contracts and grants and greater professional opportunities? Clearly social scientists had involved themselves in public policy debates, especially since the New Deal. One thing was certain: if Americans needed any public evidence of the alliance between American social scientists and the national government's interventions in nonaligned nations, the Project Camelot affair in June 1965 provided it. Project Camelot's goal was to study social conditions in Chile to develop a social scientific model that could "predict" the conditions under which a Marxian war of national liberation might be prevented and a Western, modernized state friendly to US foreign policy interests established. When Camelot became an international scandal—a public relations disaster—the Johnson administration canceled it. Perhaps ironically, the administration and its successors continued to support some forty or fifty other similar projects at a time well into the future.[7]

To reiterate the question the *Ramparts* editors posed: "What the hell is a university doing buying guns anyway?" It is a long story and a good example of how human affairs twist and turn, often with unintended consequences. Usually the originators, as was the case here, have the best of intentions; had they lived long enough, they might have been amazed at, or even horrified by, these later developments. Briefly put, after about 1890 or so, academic social scientists bandied about notions of how to create a modern, that is, ideal, not traditional, urban or rural *community*. The contribution of the rural social scientists to this discourse is far less well-known than that of the urban social scientists. The land-grant rural professoriate—the agricultural economists, the rural sociologists, and the home economists—played a vital role in working out notions and even models of a modernized community. That idea, of a *modern* rural community, with transportation links for farmers and other rural denizens, with up-to-date schools, with a wholesome and stable family environment, with modern community necessities and amenities, including fire and police protection, libraries, mercantile establishments, and, above all, community amity and comity leading to community harmony—what contemporary German social scientists and philosophers called *Gemeinschaft* (community) rather than *Geschellschaft* (society)—seemed the way to bring antiquated, traditional rural or peasant societies into the modern age—and painlessly, too, was the hope. This was a kind of reform social Darwinism, an evolutionary model of social progress that would work in any traditional or rural society.[8]

And, indeed, in the early twentieth century, the Tuskegee Institute, with Booker T. Washington at the helm, became involved with imperial Germany in an overseas development project in Germany's new colony of Togoland, acquired in 1889. German officials contemplated what to do with Polish seasonal agricultural workers in East Prussia, and they saw in the New South cotton crop system a way to control both the Polish peasants in imperial Germany and the natives in Togoland. With the ardent assistance of Tuskegee apparatchiks, Togoland became modeled, as much as was possible, after the American South, which meant, in Togoland, the complete uprooting of indigenous society, economy, and polity, which had worked well for the people there for many generations, and the attempt to reorganize Togoland as a cotton-producing region, with male heads of households, no multiple marriages, and each family assigned to a single plot of land and shown how to produce cotton. In this Tuskegee officials worked very hard to transplant the American South to German Togoland. So this was perhaps the first example of a land-grant institution providing technical assistance to a foreign nation, in this case the Kaiserreich, which, of course, the United States helped defeat in World War I.[9]

By World War I, America had emerged as a world power in all the sciences, including engineering and the social sciences. Its intellectual resources now mattered even more than Europe's. State and federal support boosted budgets for state universities whether land-grant or not. Said institutions learned how to cultivate constituents and client populations for additional resources, material and human. By then there were the new foundations, such as Russell Sage, Carnegie, and Rockefeller, to supply resources to support the social disciplines. All of these developments helped to create technocratic and modernized society, economy, and polity.[10] America's mushrooming universities strongly emphasized research as well as teaching among the faculty, and support and research in industry were crucial, too. And so was the contribution of government—state governments but also the federal government. Each state had a public university for the liberal arts and sciences, and, thanks to the first and second Morrill land-grant acts, every state had at least one college or university dedicated to the practical subjects—agriculture, engineering, home economics, and agricultural economics. Beginning in 1887, the federal government enacted a series of laws that strengthened the land-grant institutions and, through the US Department of Agriculture (USDA), became a powerful ally—and cash cow—of the land-grant institutions. The Hatch Act (1887) permitted scientists as well as experts in farm management to be appointed to the colleges and create the institutions' agricultural experiment stations.[11] The Adams Act (1906) ruled that only scientists could teach or do research in the sciences at these schools.[12] The Smith-Lever Act (1914) established cooperative extension, so that college scientists could bring the latest research to their rural constituents. The Smith-Hughes law (1917) provided federal support for agricultural vocational education.[13] Relevant for our purposes was the Purnell Act (1925), which legitimated and funded the installation of the social sciences in the land-grant colleges—initially meaning agricultural economics, rural sociology, and home economics but also the social scientific sides of such technical disciplines as nutrition, statistics, crop management and pricing, and so forth.[14] And many land-grant institutions began to develop major programs in the chemical, physical, mathematical, and biological sciences as well.[15] The Smith-Lever Act carried forth the Tuskegee initiative, for it permitted agricultural experiment station officials in the eleven former states of the Confederacy to serve African Americans, first, by including all farmers in their services, and second, in Texas at least, by enabling African Americans to become extension agents through the Negro Division of the Texas Agricultural Experiment Station. White officials supervised African American agents and lower officials. Now money flowed to African American farmers and agents, under the watchful eye, to be sure, of white bosses in the larger extension system. The Texas Negro Division became involved in international projects, especially during World War II and the Cold War, not unlike the problematic Tuskegee project, and, according to the division's expert historian, this pattern was repeated by many of the other extension services. The Texas Negro Division was dissolved in the 1960s.[16]

These developments went hand in hand with larger cultural ideas or ideologies about the value of science and applied expertise as well as the goodness of the American nation. An ideological consequence of the rise of science and of technical knowledge generally was the widespread acceptance by Americans in many walks of life of what is known as scientific positivism—the idea that science depicts natural and social reality and is absolutely true. Thus absolute truth can be discovered in nature and culture. And since there can be absolute truth, the promises of contemporary technology, such as the automobile, the radio, and the airplane, validated that concept. It was increasingly accepted in American public discourse that the problems of society, as well as of nature, could be resolved through an engineering point of view in which one used many different kinds of expertise to solve problems. Thus the idea of "social technology" arose in the early twentieth century.[17] And positivism among the scientists gave many other Americans the confidence that truth would set them free and allow them to be triumphant. As the great scientist Albert Einstein famously insisted, God does not play dice with the universe. The other cultural notion went along with America's rise as a nation to world power—that America was a force for good in the world, what Abraham Lincoln termed the last, best hope of mankind.[18]

Such cultural attitudes helped shape and redefine technical ideas in the land-grant social disciplines by the 1920s. The Country Life movement helped modify a national political discourse about rural life and what to do about it along the lines of the professional academic, rather than the farm protest leader or orator. Of special concern and note were the declining fortunes of white farmers from economic, political, and even social perspectives. Prices of commodities rose and fell, but mostly fell, property taxes increased, and shippers charged increasingly substantial fees to get goods to market, or at least to processors. City folk exerted more and more influence in local, state, and national politics, thus diverting public attention and tax dollars away from the hard-pressed countryside. Those who settled the arid Great Plains, beyond the Missouri River, found conditions there for farming and community-building challenging. Gradually many Americans realized that future progress in the countryside would require science and technology to achieve national dreams of endless progress, growth, and a modern civilization there—and elsewhere in the nation, for that matter.

On August 10, 1908, President Theodore Roosevelt appointed a Commission on Country Life, largely in response to the constant complaint of country folk that their lot in life needed repair, reform, and updating. Liberty

Hyde Bailey, pioneering landscape architect, dean of the agricultural college of the state of New York at Cornell University, and a noted, prolific scientist and effective administrator and public man, chaired the commission. Six other prominent Americans, including Henry C. Wallace, Walter Hines Page, and Gifford Pinchot, also served. Bailey strongly believed, and his colleagues agreed, that the answer to the country life problem was the development and application of the rural social sciences, meaning the triad of agricultural economics, rural sociology, and home economics. Agricultural economists would study prices and production to advise farmers on how to get the most profit from their efforts and, in general, on how to manage their farms and their finances. The rural sociologists would study the problems in rural society, including questions of demography, land use, social isolation, and community-building, and how to make social and cultural institutions in the countryside modern, up-to-date, and efficient. The home economists would help the farmer's partner, his wife, with all the challenges of creating a wholesome family and home life that would support farm and promote community. The commission conducted an ambitious social survey, with thirty public meetings at which farmers and their wives from forty states and territories attended for long discussions of problems and suggestions for their solution. In addition, more than half a million printed circulars found their way into farmers' mailboxes, with even more detailed questions, and approximately 120,000, slightly more than one-fifth, came back. USDA clerks prepared the results for the commission's use. Roosevelt submitted the commission's final report to Congress in early 1909, just weeks before his term ended.[19]

The sixty-page report was a call to arms: create an efficient national *system* of the countryside, including agriculture. In this new *system*, all the elements of the whole, which were disparate and differed from one another, would be unified in a centralized hierarchy of expertise, knowledge, and competence, each group grasping the true principles of its sphere of operation. The countryside would be organized like the modern corporation— or any other aspect of contemporary society.[20] Bailey was the commission's spokesman and the leader of the Country Life movement. Ultimately the people in the country had to solve their economic, social, political, and cultural problems themselves. But with a typically Progressive reform approach, they could accept a helping hand from state and national government, chiefly through the agricultural colleges: their scientific and technical expertise, and their knowledge as dispensed through extension agencies, supported in part through the USDA's activities and policies.[21] The Country Life Commission, and Bailey in particular, insisted that this partnership between government, national and state, and the country folk would enable the people on the land to produce better crops, get better prices for their commodities, create cooperative institutions for their own development, understand and improve their local institutions and societies, develop a more sound and supportive home life for family and community, and become as advanced a civilization as that in the nation's cities and towns. As Bailey put it, to achieve the proper state of efficiency in the country, it was critical to develop the agriculture and thus advance the country life "by organizing the work of all the agencies on a systematic plan, so that an orderly development may be secured." In other words, it was essential to create an orderly *system* of the many distinct and separable elements of the countryside as had occurred in industry and the large cities. By definition, such a system was efficient, orderly, based on expertise, and hierarchical. That was how contemporary society worked. Rural people were too individualistic, too atomized: this was their downfall. This pertained to all aspects of rural existence, from husbandry to education to public health and economic prosperity.[22] Bailey urged the development of the rural social sciences—agricultural economics, rural sociology, and home economics.

What about agricultural economics? Agricultural economists had the longest history of the three types of rural social scientists. They studied many aspects of farm economics, including commodity prices, the costs of production, how cheap or dear land was, how to manage a farm, and the impact of soil conditions on farm prosperity. Throughout the nineteenth century agricultural economists, as well as economists more generally, shifted their gaze from production to consumption, from *value* to *demand*. They embraced one of the two main schools of nineteenth-century economics. For the classical, laissez-faire economists, disciples of Jean-Baptiste Say, David Ricardo, John Stuart Mill, and many others, the market transaction between individual buyers and sellers was the fundamental paradigm. For the *institutional* economists, those who ascribed to the theories of Max Weber or John R. Commons, the institutions and socioeconomic histories of each nation were most important, for they embraced, defined, and regulated the many markets of the national economy. Land was, in both versions, absolutely fundamental. It represented wealth and was even counted as capital in the early to mid-nineteenth century. By the early twentieth century, agricultural economists at such universities as Wisconsin and Harvard were combining the theory of the firm with developing theories of marketing and organization, or classical economics, now dubbed "neoclassical economics,"[23] with bits and pieces of institutional economics—that is, elements of both schools.

What agricultural economists imbibed from these schools by the mid-1910s was their interest in commodity pricing and land values, for which they had quantitative data. From this they aspired to calculate demand and consumption. The conversion of the nineteenth-century reform discipline of statistics into the twentieth-century technical, applied branch of mathematics, occasioned by the seminal work of work of Francis Galton, Karl Pearson, George Udny Yule, and R.A. Fisher in Britain and by the practical work of such men as Luther Burbank, Henry C. Wallace, Raymond Pearl, and the growing number of agricultural experiment station geneticists working with plants and animals, led, by the 1910s, to the prospect of a scientific agriculture in which quality of stock could be attained and the relation between supply and demand could yield a good living to the farmer and sufficient food and other agricultural crops to the nation. In 1909 Henry C. Taylor founded the first department of agricultural economics at the University of Wisconsin; he also published the field's first text, *An Introduction to the Study of Agricultural Economics*. He championed rigorous scientific farming. The "close dependence of the farmer upon physical and social conditions which are subject to variation from year to year, make it impossible for him to manage his work by rule of thumb. He must follow general principles rather than specific rules," he wrote. Taylor invoked the concept of *system* when he declared that the development of commercial agriculture had brought farmers "into close economic relations with those engaged in other industries."[24] John D. Black, who earned his doctorate at Wisconsin in 1918, started the nation's second department of agricultural economics, at the University of Minnesota, the next year. Soon agricultural colleges everywhere followed suit.

Agricultural economists sought to make agricultural economics an applied field of the discipline of economics, with a definite, problem-solving engineering perspective. And it was agricultural economists who were among the first in their discipline to meld the new statistics and the available quantitative data from American farms into what was to become econometrics after World War II. The promise of econometrics, not fully realized until after 1945, was that the economist could, with the relevant variables, predict the future with sophisticated mathematical models. Such models would guarantee progress. And what were the tools of progress? Belief in American institutions and American science and technology— often called good old American know-how, that is, American nationalism and scientific positivism. The USDA had been keeping track of agricultural statistics—including market prices—since 1863, and its bureaucratic satraps and titles kept evolving with larger and larger mandates and more funds until 1923, when such functions were combined into the Bureau of Agricultural Economics (BAE) with expanded responsibilities and staff—and Taylor as bureau chief. The USDA's professionals supplied these statistics to the agricultural colleges and thus to the public and to various interest groups, including farmers. And, in 1919, the agricultural economists had created their own professional association, the American Farm Economic Association, and were publishing the *Journal of Farm Economics*.[25] In the 1920s and 1930s many agricultural economists suggested ways of rescuing farmers that would violate or distort neoclassical economics, such as the industrial tariff had for manufacturers. Hence there was a definite political coloration to agricultural economics—as there was to laissez-faire neoclassical economics, for that matter.[26]

Rural sociology grew out of both sociology and agricultural economics. In the institutional context, both sociologists and agricultural economists helped nurture the fledgling discipline. Just as the first generation of academic sociologists were often progressive reformers, such as Edward A. Ross at the University of Wisconsin or Robert E. Park at the University of Chicago, so were their emerging colleagues in rural sociology. And many of the first generation of academic sociologists were reformers, Protestants, and favorably disposed toward the development of rural sociology.[27] Rural sociology had particular antecedents in various late nineteenth-century reform movements, notably the Grangers and the Populists, but clearly Bailey and his Country Life Commission and movement gave rural sociology an enormous boost, a ringing endorsement for its installation in academic and governmental institutions, especially in the USDA and agricultural college nexus. Much of the Country Life Commission's mandate enumerated various improvements in the social as well as economic conditions of rural life, including not merely stimulating economic prosperity but also education, public health, and the knitting together of town, village, and country into distinct, coherent *communities*. The ultimate hope was that through the methods and concepts of modern science and technology, rural folk would experience a better quality of life and the disorganized and dysfunctional countryside would achieve a level of civilization comparable to that of the nation's great cities.[28]

Two important trailblazers of rural sociology were John M. Gillette and Charles J. Galpin. Both had credentials as Protestant reform ministers who moved into and founded their discipline. Gillette started instruction in rural sociology at the University of North Dakota in 1907 and produced the first textbook in the field, *Rural Sociology* (1913). He had a handful of doctoral graduates in 1928 take an appointment at the University of Iowa. Although he published several important works in the field, his influence was within academe. Gaplin had a larger and different impact. He founded rural sociology at the University of Wisconsin. Galpin came to Madison as the university's Baptist preacher in 1905. In 1911 he established teaching and research in rural sociology in the economics department. There he produced a score of doctoral graduates who went on to teach and do research at land-grant institutions. He also published several influential works. In 1915 he completed the field's first experiment station bulletin, a county study, a demographic census of a rural community.[29] Galpin also wrote *Rural Life* (1918), in which he outlined the field, based on his own work and that of his many doctoral graduates and research assistants. He constructed a conceptual tool of rural life: the *borough*, which combined a discrete group of farms and their commercial center—usually a nearby village. This tool was essential, he believed, for the proper reconstruction of county life. Only through modern science, and with tools such as this, would the traditional countryside be converted into a modern *community* that was as functional as a neighborhood in a modern city.[30]

In 1919 Henry C. Taylor, Galpin's Wisconsin colleague, joined the USDA in Washington as chief of the Office of Farm Management, the department's research unit, which became in 1923 the Bureau of Agricultural Economics (BAE). He hired Galpin to work for him as head of the new Division of Farm Population and Rural Life in "the sociological phases of rural life."[31] In the succeeding years Galpin organized many research projects. By gaining access to the rural schedules for the 1920 census, he obtained much grist for his research mill. He also initiated cooperative research projects on rural social life with six land-grant institutions in 1920—the agricultural colleges in New York, Iowa, Montana, Nebraska, Wisconsin, and West Virginia. He added more every year. The basic idea was to initiate rural sociological research rapidly; he guided such projects with a light hand. The larger theme was that facts could be gathered to build a coherent, modern rural *community* out of the muck and mire of traditional rural society. Thanks to Galpin's leadership and resources, the field of rural sociology grew rapidly: many programs in rural sociology were established at agricultural colleges, as well as a professional society, the Rural Sociology Society, and a journal, *Rural Sociology*, apart from the sociologists, in 1937.[32]

Home economics was the third leg of Bailey's tripod, or *system*, of rural scientific disciplines that would uplift and modernize the *community* in the American countryside. Its existence predated the Country Life movement, if not precisely Bailey himself. Home economics began as a woman's reform movement with the publication of Catherine Beecher's *The American Woman's Home* (1870), a statement of how to manage systematically the many different and distinct aspects of home life, including meal preparation, cleaning, the laundry, managing the children, and other matters of "domestic" or home science. To be a wife and a mother was to be an expert, a professional in contemporary terms.[33] In the 1880s and 1890s the land-grant colleges began offering courses, programs, and even degrees in home economics. Home economics meant the science of maintaining the home—cooking, cleaning, and child nurture—domestic science and modernized family life rolled into one field of study and practice.

A critical issue in home economics was human nutrition. There was a growing competition between two groups of nutritional chemists, one led by men, the other by women, aided by male allies: businessmen. Tsar of the first group was Wilbur O. Atwater, chemistry professor at Wesleyan University and head of the USDA's office of experiment stations. He gathered about him an international network of chemists. To Atwater belongs the distinction of inventing the scientific theory of the calorie; he and his associates applied the concepts of thermodynamics to human nutrition. They measured how many calories it would take a particular species or race to exert a certain amount of energy or work. Different races used different amounts of energy—useful information indeed to entrepreneurs who wished to squeeze the greatest amount of work for the lowest amount of compensation. Atwater's competitor was the tsarina of the female chemists, the energetic, formidable Ellen Swallow Richards, officially a lowly instructor in chemistry at MIT but in reality a highly respected expert in certain chemical tests of water and industrial wastes, which gave her access to wealthy New England entrepreneurs. She and her female allies wished to break the male stranglehold over the prestigious appointments and handsome fees available in the booming field of American chemistry science—and industry. Richards and her allies inserted themselves into the scientific conversation on human racial nutrition of the 1890s and early 1900s that Atwater and his colleagues were then leading to gain a foothold in chemical science and the chemical industry.

In the end, Atwater rebuffed Richards and her troops. Richards had been a major player at the famous Lake Placid conferences from 1899 on that launched the home economics profession. After licking their wounds they returned to home economics, where they had been laying the groundwork for home economics as a scientific profession since the first Lake Placid conference in 1899. They hobnobbed with their feminine colleagues as stalwarts of home economics and as proficient women chemists, whose credentials would boost the field's scientific stature. The larger point of home economics, as distinct from mere domestic science, was to professionalize all aspects of home management, to make the woman in the home as much of a professional as her husband was at work in the field, at the factory, or at the office.[34] In 1907 Atwater died, ironically enough of stomach cancer. His allies continued their dominance of chemistry in the academy and the industry. They became professors of chemistry, a high and mighty masculine science of chemical theory and commercial application. When home economics came into existence in the land-grant institutions, it was a thoroughly feminized academic subculture, albeit with all the professional attitudes common to that era's notions of expertise, and it included, not food chemistry, located in the departments of chemistry, but human nutrition, an applied social technology from which women nutritionists borrowed scientific work from male professors of chemistry to apply to home economics.[35]

Bailey had his tripod, his *troika*. He argued that farming was "a co-partnership . . . between a man and a woman. . . . The home is on the farm, and a part of it," he wrote. Both women and men have important responsibilities in the countryside. Just as the farming business had to be reorganized— that is, modernized, remade from its traditional forms and structures—so did the home. But this was a partnership in the community as well as on the farm. The rural community of the future had to be held together by the wives as well as the husbands, by the farmers' spouses no less than the farmers themselves. Through the three rural social sciences, the transition from the dysfunctional traditional countryside into a functional, modern agrarian *community*—an up-to-date *system*—would take shape.[36] Or, at least, that was what Bailey and his allies were hoping for.

In 1932 Roderick D. McKenzie, a well-respected urban sociologist at the

University of Chicago, published what was to become a classic in his field, *The Metropolitan Community*. He defined the city as an organic, holistic network, in which the whole was different from or greater than the sum of its parts. And the parts of the whole were a dynamic, interacting whole; any change in any element, no matter how apparently insignificant, could have incalculable effects on the whole, perhaps sufficient to trigger enormous changes in that whole. "Just as communities within the metropolitan region have a certain degree of independence and local identity, yet are closely bound within the economic and the cultural network of the central city," penned McKenzie, "so the regional communities themselves are independently in many things, yet are part of a national and international economy."[37] How different was this perspective from that of *system*: this was *network*, or a system of systems. The search for the modern, as distinct from the traditional, community had changed.

Planning was hardly an innovation in American institutions during the interwar years. Especially with the merger movement of the 1890s and 1900s, corporations found planning essential to their manifold operations. One of the fruits of the contemporary urban reform movement was the impetus for cities to hire planners to help them with their problems, and this spread to the states in the 1910s and early 1920s. Yet planning outside the private sector was controversial; it seemed subversive to conservatives, especially after the Bolshevik Revolution and the Soviet state's planned socialist programs. Yet the USDA, especially under the leadership of Henry A. Wallace, forged ahead with planning; actually the New Deal, at least for Wallace and Roosevelt, was about planning for many aspects of collective American life.

In the 1930s and 1940s the USDA got into hot water for championing planning for the agricultural economy. At first, all seemed well. The department had created the BAE in 1923; as late as 1930, fewer than one hundred agricultural economists worked there, but a decade later more than 750 did. With Franklin Roosevelt's electoral triumph in 1932, the department's political coloration turned from right-center to center-left. Henry A. Wallace, son of Henry C. Wallace, who had been secretary of agriculture in the early 1920s, became Roosevelt's secretary of agriculture, and he turned the BAE into the central planning agency to coordinate the "action agencies" within the department. He gathered around him a coterie of like-minded advisors, who wanted such things as production control and other measures to "cure" the countryside and its farmers and other rural denizens of economic, social, and even political disadvantages. In the 1930s, despite occasional reverses for the New Deal's agricultural reforms, overall its programs found their place in the federal system, and there were some distinctive New Deal successes at building modern communities. An early example was the Tennessee Valley Authority (TVA), established in 1933 by Congress during the "hundred days" of relief legislation. The TVA was a federally owned corporation, intended to provide flood control, electricity, and modern amenities for that impoverished area of the South. It had quite an impact on the region, promoting cheap electric power, restoring soil fertility, creating industry and commerce, and bringing, in general, the benefits of modernization to the Upper South.

Under the leadership of FDR's economic advisor, Rexford Guy Tugwell, who headed the Resettlement Administration (RA) from 1933 until he resigned in 1937, planning was the main thing—although there was always conservative opposition. The RA's most expensive, and celebrated, accomplishment was the construction of three "garden cities" as de facto suburbs in Maryland, Ohio, and Wisconsin, providing holistic communities where residents could live, work, and play. Its successor, the Farm Security Administration (FSA), attempted to carry on with the RA's resettlement of the rural poor where their chances at a better life would be markedly improved through buying unprofitable farms and establishing subsistence homestead communities. The RA founded thirty-four such communities. In 1938, after considerable intellectual fermentation in both the land-grant colleges and in the USDA from the stock market crash onward, New Deal AAA officials called a conference in early July 1938, at Mount Weather, Virginia; they invited representatives of the land-grant institutions and experiment stations to thrash out the general outline for implementing planning for the nation's agricultural industry, leading to cooperation between the department and the land-grant colleges for several years.[38] It was the demand for war work, whether on the battlefield or in the defense industry, that brought the rural poor, African American as well as white, out of the countryside and into a modicum of decent living, but not affluence.[39]

Mordecai Ezekiel, a close confidant of Wallace and Tugwell and a gifted statistical agricultural economist, published a most interesting book, *Jobs for All through Industrial Expansion* (1939), in which he extended the idea of national planning from the countryside to the industrial and commercial economies.[40] His scheme resembled that of the farm program, with perhaps inspiration from the Populist idea of the sub-treasury scheme, under which the government would buy up all the nation's crops and sell them at advantageous prices when the market was favorable. The point was to bring production and employment into balance. The apposite federal agency would plan to expand demand for goods and services, purchase them, thus creating many more jobs, and hold these goods and services from the market until the right time, and meanwhile the millions of unemployed Americans would find jobs again and their employers would make higher profits. It was, in short, what is today called a "win-win" proposal. Ezekiel posed a long list of questions about his scheme and how it would work, always answering in a reassuring and confident manner that this was modernized capitalism, not socialism or fascism. Doubtless this did not endear the tribe of agricultural economists or the department to their conservative critics. Indeed, from 1940 on, with FDR and Wallace preoccupied with the 1940 election and then with the war and its aftermath, the department's critics grew in power and helped shut down the left-leaning programs and agencies in the USDA.[41]

Rural sociologists and agricultural economists worked closely together in these years. Indeed, often they were even institutionally as well as intellectually close. This was true of the rural sociologists in many land-grant institutions and also in the BAE's Division of Farm Population and Rural Life. Galpin headed the division until he retired in 1934. And Galpin promoted the field as much as he could. In 1931, with two colleagues, he published a three-volume anthology of rural sociological articles from many countries, thus demonstrating that rural sociology was an internationally established science.[42] As an administrator, Galpin sought to expand the scientific knowledge of rural sociology by sponsoring cooperative studies with the agricultural colleges and by using the US Census and other materials by his colleagues. He pushed certain lines of investigation, especially standard-of-living studies, farm labor, rural social organization, and demography. But there were limitations on what could be investigated. Some were difficulties of method and theory within the discipline, such as inadequate statistics or lack of agreement on basic sociological concepts. Others were external. Congressmen suspicious of expertise or simply left-liberal ideas of social engineering could interfere with the budget, as could their constituents, especially representatives of agribusiness firms or the American Farm Bureau Federation. Certain topics were politically risky; if a research team poked its nose into, say, relations between southern white planters and their African American or white tenants, trouble aplenty brewed. Often there were fireworks. And for many potential areas of investigation, such as studies of farmwomen, rural health, and industries in the countryside, the achievements were sketchier, even rare.

Galpin retired as division head in 1934; the unit was small during his tenure, numbering five staff and annual appropriations of $34,000. Carl C. Taylor succeeded Galpin. Taylor had a PhD in sociology and got in trouble while teaching at North Carolina State for challenging racial segregation there. Hence he retreated to the division. Even more than Galpin, Taylor pushed investigations and publications that would address the issue of how to create a modern rural community based on scientific principles—those of the social as well as the natural sciences. With the so-called Second New Deal in 1935, the division won larger appropriations, more staff, and bigger budgets; its growth skyrocketed and was proportional to that of the BAE. Secretary Wallace enthusiastically supported rural sociology and agricultural economics. With Wallace's anointment of the BAE as the department's central planning agency in 1938 and the Mount Weather Agreement, also in 1938, the division's mandate was now emphatically to develop planning, into the indefinite future, for all aspects of rural life for the people who lived and worked there. Thus country and county land-use planning came under the division's supervision.

These were heady times for the likes of Carl Taylor and his colleagues in the land-grant network of universities, colleges, experiment stations, and requisite professional organizations. They compiled various community studies, such as one of Greene County, Georgia, which made clear the oppressive texture of white–African American relations there. They also studied the often miserable conditions of farm laborers, some of which occasioned hostile comment from conservative quarters. There was also division work on the Columbia River Basin Irrigation Project, in central Washington state, in which Grand Coulee Dam, which the Interior Department's Reclamation Bureau originated, was to provide for the conversion of high desert land into an irrigated modernized rural paradise, after the fashion of such enterprises in California and Utah. The division's work began in 1939 and soon aroused criticism because of its left-liberal reputation for democratic social planning for the new communities. In 1942 Congress stopped all planning activity in the USDA, thanks to the opposition from the American Farm Bureau Federation, many county extension agents, food processors, and others who fretted that the USDA policies would undermine and upset large landowners and agribusiness firms. Thus the notion of community was firmly implanted in American social science. There were even rural sociological research projects in foreign lands to modernize rural communities, such as those in postwar Japan and Argentina in the 1940s.[43]

Of the growing number of academic centers of rural sociology, probably the leader was Cornell's—and Bailey's hand in the appointment of its head was obvious. Bailey lured Dwight Sanderson to come to Ithaca in 1918 to develop a department of rural sociology. Sanderson had a highly successful and productive career as an economic entomologist for two decades, and before coming to Ithaca he had taught at several land-grants, including Maryland, Delaware, New Hampshire, Texas, and West Virginia; he even was a dean. In 1915 he became interested in rural social life and he did graduate work in that field at the University of Chicago before moving to Cornell. Sanderson was more of a positivistic scientist than was Galpin, reflecting the stiffening of positivism and the "unity of science" movement within scientific circles then. Thus in a rigorous study of rural health problems in three nearby townships, after reviewing all the evidence, with appropriate tables and charts, Sanderson had a cursory public policy conclusion: that the people there might be better-off with a county health department both financially and for the sake of their health.[44]

In 1937, Sanderson published *Research Memorandum on Rural Life in the Depression*, under the auspices of the Social Science Research Council. Although he insisted that it was too early to tell whether the Depression had altered the basic structures and institutions of rural society, it was also obvious that he thought a good deal of rehabilitation and reform of rural life were essential to improving the nation's welfare.[45] In 1942 he published a text, *Rural Sociology and Rural Social Organization*, in which he outlined his positivist views of the field. He carefully distinguished between the science of rural sociology and the social technology of rural social organization. A science of rural sociology, to be a science, had to have a unique point of view. A social technology, as with rural social organization, was a synthesis of many different fields of knowledge—truly the conception of an engineering perspective. In the rest of the book, he explained the social taxonomy of rural social organization, as befitted a former biologist, including biological organizations, the family, and spatial organizations, including neighborhoods, villages, communities, regions, and districts, institutional organizations, meaning churches, schools, and various governmental agencies, interest groups, such as farmers' organizations, and then he discussed how rural social organizations related to the larger society. This was a far more elaborate and positivistic conception than that of John Gillette, a reformer and herald of rural sociology, or even of Galpin.[46] Until Sanderson retired in 1943, he had many doctoral graduates, even more than Galpin, and he made rural sociology into a distinct field of study, going much further than Galpin—actually by applying the underlying assumptions of group conflict and assimilation of the "urban" Chicago school of sociology to the countryside, with parallel theoretical concepts, statistics and other research methods, and the like. With Sanderson as with Galpin—and Gillette, for that matter—the entire goal of rural sociology was the improvement of the quality of rural life—or, in other words, the development and modernization of the countryside *community*: the adoption of public health, public education, civic participation, and other such social goals of twentieth-century reform.[47]

In the interwar years the home economics movement spread to colleges and secondary schools throughout the nation. Young girls and coeds alike took classes in all aspects of home management as a profession: infant and child care, sewing, efficiently managing the home, designing and preparing wholesome, nutritious meals, raising children, and relating to the neighborhood and the community. In these decades, the college-trained home economists found professional opportunities in the workforce as teachers, professors, managers of institutional kitchens, and researchers; they also advocated for corporations that produced domestic products and were able to find technical professional appointments in the federal government and in the states. From the 1920s to the 1940s, home economics was a growing field with many career opportunities for the college educated.[48]

In these three decades a potentially energizing development for home economics was the insertion into certain universities, by philanthropic fiat, of the social science of child development and the social technology of parent education. Psychologists had studied the mental and physical growth of children as a way of understanding the adult mind. Clark University president and psychologist G. Stanley Hall coined the term "genetic psychology," meaning how the mind or consciousness evolved from the lowliest paramecium to those sitting at the apex of the evolutionary pyramid, rational white European and American men. In his magnum opus, *Adolescence*, and in his many talks to child study groups, he stressed, as had the great Sigmund Freud, the importance of early infancy and childhood in shaping the adult mind and personality.[49] Hall trained many of the next generation of child psychologists, who, by the 1920s, thanks to the widespread adoption of the

Binet-Simon scaled test of intelligence, occupied a critically important niche in psychology at large.

At this point philanthropists intervened. In 1918 John D. Rockefeller Sr. donated more than $70 million to form a charity, the Laura Spelman Rockefeller Memorial (LSRM), to honor his late wife, with the vague mandate to uplift and improve the lives of women and children. For several years the LSRM's trustees handed out sums to apposite local charities, but they desired a more imaginative use of the money, which they got, in spades, when they hired psychologist Beardsley Ruml as chief program officer and he hired a young New York economist, Lawrence K. Frank, to head up a new program in child study and parent education. After several years of investigation, interviews, and conversation, Frank, with Ruml's enthusiastic encouragement, created a plan to build, and then insert, an entire professional scientific subculture of scientific child study and efficient, modernized parent education at several universities, including Yale, the Teachers College of Columbia University, and the universities of Iowa, Minnesota, and California. In each case, the psychology departments looked the philanthropic gift horses in the mouth, so the LSRM negotiated a separate child study or welfare institute on each campus with an institutional president.

Ultimately the colleges or departments of home economics became the institutional home for child study and parent education; most psychologists in colleges of arts and sciences found such female intrusion unacceptable. The home economists found the LSRM's plans entirely digestible; they welcomed emphasis on family life education as a contribution to a modern, wholesome community. The LSRM's idea in each grant was to create a statewide organization, a research center, such as the Child Welfare Research Station at Iowa, which would train undergraduates and graduates; then a family life program, complete with research access to children in a laboratory school, within the college of home economics at the land-grant school, in this case Iowa State College; and, finally, a department at the state teachers college, in this instance the Iowa State Teachers College, which would train young women how to teach parent education. The specific institutional arrangements varied from state to state; LSRM officials were careful not to tread on too many toes. But the outline of an entire academic professional subculture, in this case organized around a discipline that was just being formed intellectually, was nevertheless eminently clear. Through this *network* of professional institutions, researchers would uncover the true facts and principles of child development in the modern *community*, and

at a much larger phalanx of public land-grants, various types of professionals would disseminate these new facts and principles through extension
bulletins, classes, special conferences, radio programs, motion pictures,
talks at service clubs, and the like. In this way the correct methods of childhood nurture and socialization would be understood, and this modern,
up-to-date knowledge could then contribute to the full conception of the
modernized *community*. Like the other land-grant social sciences, this new
field was imbued with the twin ideas of scientific positivism and American
patriotism.[50]

In the postwar years, thing were not so rosy for home economics. For one
thing, corporations tended to take over the role of the home economists as
advocate, not to say shill, of their products, thus undercutting home economists' cultural authority and professional stature. Of the three "rural" social
sciences, home economics was, by then, only partly located in the rural land-
grant colleges. Home economics had spread to many colleges and universities in cities, far beyond the countryside, as well as to secondary schools,
where their courses often became "dead end" affairs in training to be a wife.
As an astute historian of home economics recently pointed out, home "economists found themselves in a[n] odd situation having done 'a good job' of
training women for wifehood and not a good enough job convincing everyone else that housework was a serious profession."[51]

This is not to say, by way of conclusion, that in any important sense the
Country Life movement or its products, the land-grant social sciences discussed here, had anything to do in a direct or causal sense with Project
Camelot, with the Michigan State University kerfuffle, or any other American Cold War operations. What the social sciences of the first half of the
twentieth century did do was provide tools, conceptual and methodological,
that the decision makers of national foreign policy in the Cold War appropriated for their toolboxes. The idea that one could create, from the chaos of
traditional rural life, even of a peasant world, a modernized, stable, Westernized community, with entrepreneurial values implanted by proper childhood nurture, community organization, and political leadership, was clearly
available for Cold War intellectuals, such as the MIT economist Walter W.
Rostow, as well as for the advisors of presidents from Truman to Nixon.[52]

And, indeed, high government officials did drink this heady brew of
modernization in the immediate post–World War II years. As President
Harry Truman and his advisors contemplated worsening relations with the
Soviet Union in 1946 and 1947, especially with regard to Soviet penetration

into Greece and Turkey. They also feared that such penetration would destabilize Western Europe. It also might lead to war with the Soviets. Thus they adopted a rigid, hardnosed attitude toward the Soviet Union and, at the same time, celebrated American superiority—American exceptionalism with militarized rhetoric. President Truman went before Congress in March 1947 and made a major speech outlining what has become known as the Truman Doctrine. He made four basic points to American foreign policy, which included full support for the United Nations and its affiliated organizations, as well as foreign economic aid (the Marshall Plan), and negotiation of a North Atlantic mutual defense pact (NATO), which came about in 1949 concurrently with the establishment of the Federal Republic of Germany out of the French, British, and American occupation zones. The fourth point was "a bold new program for making the benefits of our scientific advances and industrial progress available for the improvement and growth of underdeveloped areas."[53] Truman insisted that the modernized societies of the world had a special responsibility to uplift and modernize said undeveloped areas, to help them achieve freedom, prosperity, and new ways of living—Western ones, to be sure. Truman insisted that this would not be a new imperialism but development according to democratic (and Democratic) fair dealing.[54]

Private philanthropy was already well versed in such endeavors, as in the Mexican Agricultural Project, created and financed by the Rockefeller Foundation, which sought to make Mexico a country that could sustain its food supply and, at the same time, to make it a food-exporting country through the development of wheat, corn, and livestock programs. Norman Borlaug, a graduate of land-grant schools, namely the Iowa State College and the University of Minnesota, and later of Green Revolution fame, worked on the wheat program in the early to later 1940s.[55] Yet there were often many slips between the cup and the lip. As one enterprising historian has outlined, extension agents from Utah State University, in Provo, spent the years 1950–54 in Iran, attempting to help Iranian farmers modernize their practices. It did not turn out well. Iranian farmers did not adapt to the Utahans' suggestions. They liked things the way they were.[56]

An example of how these notions had percolated into a seemingly highly scientific work was *The Achieving Society* (1961) by Wesleyan University psychologist David C. McClelland, which demonstrated how mothers with particular values of child rearing would raise sons who would go on to become entrepreneurs in underdeveloped or Third World countries and be part of the pro-Western political and economic elite.[57] In 1966, Lucien W. Pye, a political scientist colleague of Rostow's at MIT, published *Aspects of Political Development*, a work that spelled out the full-blown theory of how the West—meaning the United States and its allies—would fight national wars of liberation, with armies that would if necessary transform unstable "traditional" societies in revolutionary ferment into stable Western-style political democracies with capitalist economies. Pye was a key player in the Social Science Research Council's Committee on Comparative Politics, an important incubator of such grand visions.[58] Clearly notions of development and modernization largely originated within the social sciences. They espoused not only technology transfer from West to East (or North to South) but also modern, Western democratic society's central elements. In a recent, excellent book Michael Latham has reminded us that these strategies of the Cold War from the American side always meant what he dubs the "right" kind of revolution, what we Americans have legitimated, not what others, especially those with darker skins, might have preferred.[59]

NOTES

1. Warren Hinckle, Robert Scheer, and Sol Stern, "MSU: The University on the Make," *Ramparts* 4 (April 1966): 11–22. Peter Richardson, *A Bomb in Every Issue: How the Short, Unruly Life of "Ramparts Magazine Changed America* (New York: The New Press, 2009) is an able, popular account of the magazine's colorful history.

2. Hinckle, Scheer, and Stern, "MSU: The University on the Make," 22.

3. Robert Scigliano and Guy H. Fox, *Technical Assistance in Vietnam: The Michigan State Experience* (New York: Praeger, 1965). John Ernst, *Forging a Fateful Alliance: Michigan State University and the Vietnam War* (East Lansing: Michigan State University Press, 1998) is the indispensable monograph.

4. *Act of July 2, 1862, Public Law 37-106* (Washington, DC: GPO, 1862).

5. George C. Herring, *America's Longest War: The United States and Vietnam, 1950–1975*, 3rd ed. (New York: John Wiley and Sons, 1996) is a standard history of that war.

6. See Kenneth J. Heineman, *Campus Wars: The Peace Movement at American State Universities in the Vietnam Era* (New York: New York University Press, 1993), a thoughtful and thorough account.

7. Irving L. Horowitz, *The Rise and Fall of Project Camelot: Studies in the Relationship between Social Science and Practical Politics* (Cambridge, MA: MIT Press, 1974) is a standard account. For more recent views, see Juan Jose Navarro, "Cold War in Latin America: The Camelot Project (1964–1965) and the Political and Academic Reactions of the Chilean Left," *Comparative Sociology* 10 (2011): 807–25.

8. See Eric Goldman, *Rendezvous with Destiny: A History of Modern American Reform* (New York: Knopf, 1952) for the idea of reform social Darwinism.

9. See Andrew Zimmerman's brilliant, deeply researched, and very disturbing monograph, *Alabama in Africa: Booker T. Washington, the German Empire and the Globalization of the New South* (Princeton: Princeton University Press, 2010). See also Zimmerman, "A German Alabama in Africa: The Tuskegee Expedition to German Togo and the Transnational Origins of West African Cotton Growers," *American Historical Review* 110 (2005): 362–98.

10. On the growth of state government, see Jon C. Teaford's excellent, succinct book, *The Rise of the States: Evolution of American State Government* (Baltimore: Johns Hopkins University Press, 2002); for why the Rockefellers, at least, supported social science research, see David L. Seim, *Rockefeller Philanthropy and Modern Social Science* (London: Pickering and Chatto, 2013).

11. Alan I Marcus, *Agricultural Science and the Quest for Legitimacy: Farmers, Agricultural Colleges, and Experiment Stations* (Ames: Iowa State University Press, 1985) is the standard work on the genesis of the Hatch Act. The Hatch Act is printed in US Secretary of State, *U.S. Statutes at Large*, Sess. II, ch. 314 (Washington, DC: GPO, 1887): 440–42.

12. Charles E. Rosenberg, "The Adams Act: Politics and the Cause of Scientific Research," *Agricultural History* 38 (January 1964): 3–12.

13. P. A. Grant, "Senator Hoke Smith, Southern Congressmen, and Agricultural Education, 1914–1917," *Agricultural History* 60 (April 1986): 111-122.

14. *U.S. Statutes at Large* (Washington, DC: GPO, 1925) Title 43, ch. 308: 970–90.

15. Among many accounts, probably still the best on the history of the land-grant institutions is Merle Curti and Vernon Carstensen, *The University of Wisconsin*, 2 vols. (Madison: University of Wisconsin Press, 1948).

16. Debra A. Reid, *Reaping a Greater Harvest: African Americans, the Extension Service, and Rural Reform in Jim Crow Texas* (College Station: Texas A&M University Press, 2007), 145–76 and passim.

17. John M. Jordan, *Machine-Age Ideology: Social Engineering and American Liberalism, 1911–1939* (Chapel Hill: University of North Carolina Press, 1994).

18. Hamilton Cravens, "Column Right, March! Nationalism, Scientific Positivism, and the Conservative Turn of the American Social Sciences in the Cold War Era," in *Cold War Social Science: Knowledge Production, Liberal Democracy, and Human Nature,* ed. Mark Solovey and Hamilton Cravens (New York: Palgrave Macmillan, 2012), 117–36; Jessica Wang, *American Science in an Age of Anxiety: Scientists, Anticommunism, and the Cold War* (Chapel Hill: University of North Carolina Press, 1999).

19. US Senate, 60th Cong., 2nd sess., *Report of the Country Life Commission: Special Message from the President of the United States Transmitting the Report of the Country Life Commission,* Document No. 705 (Washington, DC: GPO, 1909), Illinois Institute for Rural Affairs, Western Illinois University, www.iira.org/clc (accessed February 19, 2013).

20. A sophisticated discussion of the age of system may be found in Alan I Marcus and Howard P. Segal, *American Technology: A Brief History* (San Diego: Harcourt, Brace, and Jovanovich, 1989), part 3, as well as in the next note.

21. An excellent, unsentimental conception of "typical" Progressive reform attitudes is Samuel P. Hays's brilliant *Conservation and the Gospel of Efficiency: The Progressive Conservation Movement, 1890–1920* (Cambridge, MA: Harvard University Press, 1959).

22. L. H. Bailey, *The Country-Life Movement in the United States* (New York: Macmillan, 1911), 73, www.forgottenbooks.com.

23. Thorstein Veblen, the celebrated American critic of economic theory, coined the term "neoclassical economics" to describe laissez-faire economists who accepted the doctrine of marginal utility, a post-1870s concept.

24. Henry C. Taylor, *An Introduction to the Study of Agricultural Economics* (1909; New York: Macmillan, 1911), 5, 8.

25. C. Ford Runge, "Agricultural Economics: A Brief Intellectual History," Center for International Food and Agricultural Policy, University of Minnesota, Working Paper WP06–01, June 2006, pp. 1–9 et passim, ageconsearch.umn.edu/13649/1/wp06–01.pdf (accessed February 27, 2013). The paper also has a useful bibliography.

26. Joseph Dorfman, *The Economic Mind in American Civilization*, vols. 4 and 5, 1918–1933 (New York: Viking, 1959): 579–82, 625–30.

27. See, for example, John M. Gillette, *Constructive Rural Sociology* (New York: Sturgis and Walton, 1917).

28. Bailey, *The Country-Life Movement in the United States*, 201–20. Harlan P. Banks, "Liberty Hyde Bailey, 1858–1954," National Academy of Sciences, *Biographical Memoirs* (Washington, DC: National Academy of Sciences, 1994), 3–32, is a convenient sketch; I used www.nasonline.org/publications/\biographical-memoirs/memoir-pdfs/bailey-liberty-h.pdf (accessed February 19, 2013).

29. Charles J. Galpin, *My Drift into Rural Sociology: Memoir of Charles Josiah Gilpin*, Rural Sociological Monographs (Baton Rouge: Louisiana State University Press, 1938), 23–26.

30. Charles J. Galpin, *Rural Life* (New York: The Century Company, 1918), 66–100, especially 98–100.

31. Galpin, *My Drift into Rural Sociology*, 36.

32. Olaf L. Larson and Julie N. Zimmerman, *Sociology in Government: The Galpin-Taylor Years in the United States Department of Agriculture, 1919–1953* (University Park: Pennsylvania State University Press, 2003), 29–44 and passim.

33. Catherine Esther Beecher, *The American Woman's Home: Principles of Domestic Science as Applied to the Duties and Pleasures of Home: A Textbook for the Use of Young Ladies in Schools, Seminaries, and Colleges* (New York: J. B. Ford, 1870).

34. Emma Siefrit Weigley, "It Might Have Been Euthenics: The Lake Placid Conferences and the Home Economics Movement," *American Quarterly* 26 (1974): 79–96; Mary Hinman Abel et al., "The Home Economics Movement in the United States," *Journal of Home Economics* 3 (1911): 323–427.

35. Hamilton Cravens, "Establishing the Science of Nutrition at the USDA: Ellen Swallow Richards and Her Allies," *Agricultural History* 64 (Spring 1990): 122–33.

36. Bailey, *The Country-Life Movement in the United States*, 85; Megan J. Elias, *Stir It Up: Home Economics in American Culture* (Philadelphia: University of Pennsylvania Press, 2008), 18–61, a useful account.

37. Roderick D. McKenzie, *The Metropolitan Community* (1932; New York: Russell and Russell, 1967), 313.

38. Richard S. Kirkendall, *Social Scientists and Farm Politics in the Age of Roosevelt* (Columbia: University of Missouri Press, 1966), 157, 160, 164, 168, 172, 173, 178, 196, 201.

39. I have drawn much of my account of agricultural economics from Kirkendall's excellent book, *Social Scientists and Farm Politics in the Age of Roosevelt*.

40. Mordecai Ezekiel, *Jobs for All through Industrial Expansion* (New York: Knopf, 1939).

41. Kirkendall, *Social Scientists and Farm Politics in the Age of Roosevelt*, 191–261.

42. Pitrim A. Sorokin, Carle C. Zimmerman, and Charles J. Galpin, eds., *A Systematic Source Book in Rural Sociology*, 3 vols. (1931; New York: Russell and Russell, 1965).

43. Larson and Zimmerman, *Sociology in Government*, 43–269.

44. Dwight Sanderson, "A Survey of Sickness in Rural Areas in Cortland County, New York," *Cornell University Agricultural Experiment Station, Memoir 112*, March 1927 (Ithaca, NY: Published by the University, 1927), 27.

45. Dwight Sanderson, *Research Memorandum on Rural Life in the Depression, Bulletin 34* (New York: Social Science Research Council, 1937), 151–58.

46. Dwight Sanderson, *Rural Sociology and Rural Social Organization* (New York: John Wiley and Sons, 1942), 10–22, 212–785.

47. Larson and Zimmerman, *Sociology in Government*.

48. Elias, *Stir It Up*, 18–99.

49. G. Stanley Hall, *Adolescence: Its Psychology, Anthropology, Sociology, Sex, Crime, Religion, and Education*, 2 vols. (New York: D. Appleton, 1904). Dorothy Ross, *G. Stanley Hall: The Psychologist as Prophet* (Chicago: University of Chicago Press, 1972) is the standard biography of Hall.

50. Hamilton Cravens, *Before Head Start: The Iowa Station and America's Children* (Chapel Hill: University of North Carolina Press, 1993). See also, Cravens, The Triumph of Evolution. American Scientists and the Heredity-Environment Controversy 1900-1941 (Philadelphia: University of Pennsylvania Press, 1978).

51. Elias, *Stir It Up*, 103.

52. Walter W. Rostow, *The Stages of Economic Growth: A Non-Communist Manifesto* (Cambridge: Cambridge University Press, 1960); Nils Gilman, *Mandarins of the Future: Modernization Theory in Cold War America* (Baltimore: Johns Hopkins University Press, 2003).

53. As cited in Alonzo L. Hamby, *Beyond the New Deal: Harry S. Truman and American Liberalism* (New York: Columbia University Press, 1973), 354.

54. In addition to Hamby, *Beyond the New Deal*, see John Lewis Gaddis, *The United States and the Origins of the Cold War, 1941–1947* (New York: Columbia University

Press, 1972), 282–362, which is a standard account of the origins of the Cold War policies of the United States.

55. Of course the Rockefeller family, through Nelson Rockefeller as FDR's assistant secretary of state for Latin America, dug out German and British spies and investments in the region, thus preparing the postwar years for Rockefeller commercial interests to fill the economic vacuum there. National security and corporation profits went hand in hand. See David H. Price, *Anthropological Intelligence: The Deployment and Neglect of American Anthropology in the Second World War* (Durham: Duke University Press, 2008), 107–14, a deeply researched account.

56. See Jessie Embry, "Point Four, Utah State University Technicians and Rural Development in Iran," *Rural History* 14 (2003): 99–113.

57. David C. McClelland, *The Achieving Society* (New York: The Free Press, 1961).

58. Lucien W. Pye, *Aspects of Political Development* (Boston: Little, Brown, 1966).

59. Michael E. Latham, *The Right Kind of Revolution: Modernization, Development, and U.S. Foreign Policy from the Cold War to the Present* (Ithaca, NY: Cornell University Press, 2011). See also Volker R. Berghahn, *America and the Intellectual Cold Wars in Europe: Shepard Stone between Philanthropy, Academy, and Diplomacy* (Princeton: Princeton University Press, 2001).

Part Four

The New Agriculture

For much of their existence, agricultural colleges acknowledged no disjunction between increasing crop yields and the condition of rural America. Greater yields promised more money for farmers and lower prices for consumers. Wealthier farmers meant more prosperous communities. Land-grants did recognize that rural life paled in some ways when compared to urban life, but that did not dissuade them from changing course. The schools continued to press for an agriculture that was more productive and that required fewer farmers, larger farms, and greater investment in agricultural inputs and machinery.

Not everyone outside the land-grant universities recognized similar correlations in similar ways. Questions were raised about the relationship between farms and farmers and between both and rural life. As significant, questions surfaced in some quarters over exactly what agricultural colleges should be. What should they do? Who were their "true" stakeholders? Could the various interest groups dependent on agricultural colleges be homogenized? What were the obligations of agricultural colleges to future farmers and rural communities?

Each of these questions generated diverse responses, gained support from varied constituencies, and engendered controversy. But while each question reflected a particularistic perspective, demanding that land-grants revamp visions or missions was not one of them. Land-grants had long been called on to change course as client groups tried to impose agendas on them. Invariably the schools managed to mollify criticism by adopting new programs or tasks. And inevitably other groups organized to protest the new plans. Whether these latter groups were successful or not rested less on the merits of their argument than on their political acumen.

10

"Havens for Golf-Turf Science"

New Agrarians and the Land-Grant Legacy

MELISSA WALKER

Many social critics have long carried on a love-hate relationship with land-grant university agriculture. To some, land-grant agriculturists have slavishly privileged large-scale agriculture. That bias has led to the death or disability of rural communities, polluted ground water, caused tremendous erosion, and produced unhealthy and unhealthful crops. Others have championed the universities, claiming that they have made two blades of grass grow where one had before, supplied bountiful harvests, and kept food costs low. At the heart of this contention has been the application of agricultural science and who determines what science to seek and apply and for whom.

What is fascinating about the debate is that critics sometimes strive to make their case by arguing that land-grants have deviated from their Morrill Act roots. They claim the Morrill Act was class legislation; its goal was to produce and teach the knowledge necessary to enable the nation's yeomanry to thrive, nothing more. Others see it more globally, as a means to democratize education and knowledge. Opening higher education to the children of the working classes provided them with the talents and skills necessary to become the next generation of leaders in a wide variety of fields, while the professorate made and applied discoveries that would transform American work and life.

A critique of the virtues and vices of the modern age undergirds the debate and provides a true demarcation. Walker's chapter focuses on a new group of commentators. This group of reformers does not want to do away with the modern age but to modify it. And they see in land-grant universities the power to fuel and spread that improvement throughout the land.

✷✷✷

In 1930, a group of writers and philosophers affiliated with Vanderbilt University published a manifesto titled *I'll Take My Stand: The South and the Agrarian Tradition*. The authors, who came to be known as the southern agrarians, denounced encroaching modernity, urbanization, and industrialization. They declared, "The theory of agrarianism is that the culture of the soil is the best and most sensitive of vocations, and that therefore it should have the economic preference and enlist the maximum number of workers."[1] More than forty years later in a work titled *The Unsettling of America: Culture and Agriculture*, farmer and writer Wendell Berry launched a critique of industrial agriculture that echoed many of the themes in *I'll Take My Stand*. In the decades since, other farmers, writers, activists, and philosophers have joined Berry in an increasingly vocal critique of the mechanized, specialized farming methods that dominate world food and fiber production today. One of this group, legal scholar Eric Freyfogle, dubbed the critics the "new agrarians."[2] Other leaders in the resurgence of agrarian thought include Ohio writer and farmer Gene Logsdon, formerly a writer and editor with Farm Journal; biologist and Kansas Land Institute founder Wes Jackson; California classics scholar and farmer Victor Davis Hanson; historian Brian Donahue; journalist Michael Pollan; and philosophers Paul Thompson, Norman Wirzba, Ronald Jager, and many others.[3]

A number of common threads emerge in the new agrarian critique of today's food system. They share a conviction that modern industrial agriculture is destructive and unsustainable. They advocate sustainable farming practices, wise land use, and environmental protection. Another central principle is that, in Berry's words, "Eating is an agricultural act," and as a result, agrarianism must be the concern of everyone, not just the few remaining farmers.[4] The new agrarians maintain that consumers must bear much of the responsibility for restoring agrarian values to the center of American life. As Eric Freyfogle puts it, "The product cycle, from earth to consumer good to waste, traces not just lines of dependence and causation, but also lines of responsibility. Agrarians believe that those who buy products are morally implicated in their production, much as those who discard waste items are morally involved in their final end."[5] Most of all, like their 1930s counterparts, the new agrarians conceptualize "agriculture as a countercultural ideal to industrial modes of production," in the words of historian James E. McWilliams.[6]

The new agrarians also share a conviction that adopting a comprehensive agrarian worldview can have cultural and spiritual benefits for the nation and its citizens. Agrarians argue that farming is a way of life that limits the alienating effects of modern postindustrial society, and they insist that culture, agriculture, and environmental health are intrinsically linked. Norman Wirzba says, "What makes agrarianism the ideal candidate for cultural renewal is that it . . . [is] a deliberate way of life in which the integrity and wholeness of peoples and neighborhoods, and the natural sources they depend upon, are maintained and celebrated."[7] Echoing Thomas Jefferson, the new agrarians argue that the concept of the free citizen is rooted in yeomen farming and that agrarian values are vital to the health of US democracy. Victor Davis Hanson says, "The farmer's understanding of man and society in our present age is absolutely critical to the survival of democracy as we once knew it."[8]

The new agrarians blame greedy agribusiness corporations, USDA policymakers, and misguided farmers for the development of the industrial farming system, but they reserve some of their most scathing criticism for the land-grant universities that were created under the auspices of the Morrill Act. Wendell Berry accuses land-grant universities of having utterly failed in their mission to aid "the preservation of agriculture and rural life." In fact, many new agrarians argue that land-grant universities, instead of assisting farmers, have actually contributed to the decline of the small family farm and rural communities.[9]

Berry launched the critique of land-grant universities in 1977 with his book *The Unsettling of America*. In a chapter titled "Jefferson, Morrill, and the Upper Crust," he contrasts Thomas Jefferson's mistrust of a manufacturing economy and belief in broad liberal education with Representative Justin Morrill's acceptance of an industrial economy and vision for practical education. Berry wrote that Morrill lacked "Jefferson's complex sense of the dependence of democratic citizenship upon education. . . . Morrill . . . looked at education from a strictly practical or utilitarian viewpoint." Berry believes that Morrill intended that land-grant universities would serve the best interests of farmers and local communities. Morrill, says Berry, intended to "promote the stabilization of farming populations and communities and to establish in that way a 'permanent' agriculture, enabled by better education to preserve both the land and the people."[10]

The land-grant universities failed to carry out these intentions, according to Berry. Instead, he says, they promoted "an *impermanent* [emphasis his] agriculture destructive of land and people." Berry attributes this failure in part to Morrill's vision of practical education, which Berry characterizes as "the lowering of the educational standard from Jefferson's ideal of public or community responsibility to the utilitarianism of Morrill." Berry admits that Morrill's vision reflected "a shift of public values," but he refuses to accept that such a shift and the resulting emphasis of land-grant universities was either inevitable or appropriate. Instead, he says that the land-grants have eroded Morrill's vision further, reducing "liberal and practical to practical and then for 'practical' they substituted 'specialized.'"[11]

To Berry's chagrin, the rise of land-grant universities resulted in the professionalization of the land-grant professoriate, and therein lies much of the problem. Instead of being locally controlled and responding to the needs of local communities, as Berry insists that Morrill intended, land-grant universities became part of the national higher education apparatus. Colleges of agriculture "orient themselves within the university rather than within the communities they were intended to serve," he says, adding that over the decades, "The standard of their [land-grant universities'] purpose has shifted from usefulness to careerism." Berry says, the "careerist professor is by definition a specialist professor."[12]

Specialist professors focus on research, and in Berry's view, most modern agricultural research is conducted without regard for its economic consequences. For example, in 1984, Berry wrote, "It is still perfectly acceptable in Land Grant universities for agricultural researchers to apply themselves to the development of more productive dairy cows without considering at all the fact that this development necessarily involves the failure of many thousands of dairies and dairy farmers." The reason for research that disregards the interests of farmers? Berry accuses the land-grants of being in bed with chemical and machinery companies. Instead of conducting research on small-scale technologies and methods to address the problems faced by independent family farmers, the land-grants have conducted research that promotes industrial agriculture. Agribusinesses, Berry argues, have co-opted the research mission of land-grant universities, funding and promoting research that helps the corporations themselves develop new products for profitable markets. At the behest of agribusiness, land-grants have focused on using science and technology to increase agricultural productivity at the expense of farmers, culture, and the land. In the end, he laments, "The tragedy of the Land Grant acts is that their moral imperative came finally to have nowhere to rest except on the careers of specialists whose standards and operating procedures were amoral. . . . Their work thus inevitably serves whatever power is greatest. That power at present is the industrial economy."

Berry reserves his most scathing criticism for the colleges of agriculture housed within land-grant universities. He maintains that these colleges have failed in what he sees as their main mission—that of educating the next generation of family farmers: "The education of the student of agriculture is almost as absurd, and it is more dangerous [than academic careerism]: he is taught a course of practical knowledge and procedures for which uses do indeed exist, but these uses lie outside the purview and interests of the school. The colleges of agriculture produce agriculture specialists and 'agribusinessmen' as readily as farmers."[13]

Berry summarized much of his early thinking on the failures of land-grant universities in his 1986 essay, "A Defense of the Family Farm." Acknowledging that many individual faculty members had dedicated their lives to the service of rural people, he nonetheless concluded, "One hundred and twenty-four-years after the Morrill Act, ninety-nine years after the Hatch Act, seventy-two years after the Smith-Lever Act, the 'industrial classes' are not liberally educated, agriculture and rural life are not sound or prosperous or permanent, and there is no equitable balance between agriculture and other segments of the economy. Anybody's statistics on the reduction of the farm population, on the decay of rural communities, on soil erosion, soil and water pollution, water shortages, and farm bankruptcies tell indisputably a story of failure."[14] Building on his critique, a few years later Berry quoted the 1887 Hatch Act, which created the agricultural experiment station system affiliated with land-grant universities, to explain his disdain for colleges of agriculture: "The colleges of agriculture . . . [which] have presided over the now nearly completed destruction of their constituency—the farm people and the farm communities—are now scrambling to ally themselves more firmly than ever, not with 'the rural home and rural life' that were, and are, their trust, but with the technocratic aims and corporate interests that are destroying the rural home and rural life. This, of course, is only a new intensification of an old alliance."[15]

Other agrarians have offered similar critiques of land-grant universities though less often and with less depth and vitriol than Berry. Gene Logsdon, for example, echoes Berry's indictment of agricultural colleges that have aligned themselves with the interests of agribusiness and "become havens for golf-turf science" instead of serving the needs of farmers.[16] Wes Jackson has blamed the land-grant system and the Agricultural Extension Service for the development and promotion of soil-destroying, high-efficiency forms of till agriculture. Jackson agrees that careerism shaped the outlooks of agricultural researchers because it motivated them to build on existing knowledge—the risk-free route to academic success—rather than strike out in bold new directions. Jackson adds that throughout the mid- to late twentieth century, the nation's cheap oil policies also played a role, encouraging agricultural researchers to look in directions that involved the use of fossil fuels to power farm equipment or manufacture fertilizers. Jackson agrees with Berry that the land-grant system tends to devote the lion's share of its attention to farmers (and agribusinesses) with money at the expense of the small family farm. Finally, to Jackson, the largest failing of the land-grant system is that it takes a "slot machine" approach to dispensing knowledge instead of tailoring research and advice to conditions on an individual farm. The result has been the nationwide promulgation of methods unsuited for all regions.[17]

Another critic of the land-grant system is Victor Davis Hanson, a California fruit and raisin producer and a classics scholar. Hanson indicts the entire USDA establishment, linking experiment stations and extension work to land-grant universities. In his book *Fields without Dreams*, Hanson offers a prescription for arresting the "decline of the American yeoman." His first suggestion is to eliminate the USDA "root and branch." Hanson also advocates getting rid of state and local farm agencies. He writes, "The growth in size of the Department of Agriculture is commensurate with the decline of the family farmer; such is the nature of all similar government entities devoted to agricultural development, from Pharaoh's to Montezuma's." As evidence of the misalignment of land-grant resources to the reality of the needs of individual farmers, Hanson cites the University of California's expansion of agricultural field stations even as nearby farms declined, and California State University-Fresno's construction of impressive complexes devoted to viticulture and fruit production when prices for those commodities were "at an all-time low." Like Berry and Jackson, Hanson believes that the misalignment of resources is the result of an unholy alliance of corporate interests with the land-grant system. As he puts it,

"This is no accident, but the logical coalescence of corporate, government, and university moneys."[18]

Agronomist Greg Vaughan has lodged a more recent entry in the litany of critiques of the colleges of agriculture within land-grant universities. In his blog "Agrarian Ideas for a Developing World," he wrote in 2010 about his ambivalence about his own agricultural education at the University of Illinois. He said, "At UIUC I had learned a lot about the technical side of farming, but it was a very industrial focus. . . . The main problem with the agriculture education at UIUC was the lack of farmers. It seems that the UIUC goal was to increase gross agricultural productivity, and not necessarily to improve life for farmers. We looked at agriculture in terms of plants, soils, insects, fungi, pollution, economics, international trade, but never in terms of the farmers. During my four years studying agriculture at U of I, I never talked to any farmers, never analyzed a real farm. Even when we talked about farming systems, or sustainability, it was always in terms of plants, soil, the ecosystem, and sometimes large-scale economics, but never about the viability of a given farm." Vaughan concluded, "It's truly a sickly science that doesn't ever come in direct contact with its subject."[19]

In recent years, some agrarians seem to have muted their critique. This may be due in part to land-grant universities' response to the growing interest in sustainable agriculture. Most land-grant universities now have ongoing research on sustainable agriculture and organic farming.[20] It may also be due to the budding partnerships between land-grants and some of the new agrarians. For example, Wes Jackson's Land Institute has developed good working relationships with agricultural researchers at a number of midwestern universities.[21]

In contrast to the broad condemnations of many new agrarians, Frederick L. Kirschenmann, himself a farmer, philosopher, and land-grant university employee (he is a fellow at the Leopold Center for Sustainable Agriculture at Iowa State University), has offered a recent and more nuanced critique of the land-grant system. Recognizing that land-grant universities have evolved as the society in which they are embedded has grown and changed, Kirschenmann argues that land-grants are caught in a "peculiar set of circumstances, partly due to the social changes that have transpired over the last several decades." He says that the original goals of the Morrill Act were undermined by "the industrialization of America [which] demanded a more labor-efficient agriculture to 'free' people from the 'drudgery' of agriculture so that they could work in industry. . . . In response to this new social demand, our Land Grant universities devoted significant research to developing a constant stream of new technologies that required less labor on the farm, reducing the need for people in our rural communities." Today, Kirschenbaum says, "Government officials, agribusiness firms, and farmer commodity groups still largely operate out of the old paradigm of maximizing production with as little labor as possible in order to compete in the global economy. Land Grant universities are following suit by pursuing one-dimensional research that allows farmers and agribusiness industries to meet that singular goal."[22]

If some agrarians have recently muted their criticism of land-grant universities, Wendell Berry has refined and honed his critique over the years. By the first decade of the twenty-first century, Berry had moved beyond criticizing land-grant universities to launch a scathing critique of the entire higher education system. In 2007, he delivered a commencement address at Bellarmine University in which he attacked research universities. He asserted that higher education has become a "debased commodity" whose "purpose is now defined by the great and the would-be-great 'research universities.'" He says that research universities "no longer make even the pretense of preparing their students for responsible membership in a family, a community, or a polity. They have repudiated their old obligation to pass on to students at least something of their cultural inheritance. The ideal graduate no longer is to have a mind well-equipped to serve others, or to judge competently the purposes for which it may be used. Now, according to those institutions of the 'cutting edge,' the purpose of education is unabashedly utilitarian."[23]

Berry reserves his harshest criticism for institutions that emphasize science, technology, engineering, and mathematics education. These courses, he says, are "called, with typical ostentation of corporate jargon, STEM. . . . The course of study called STEM is in reality only a sort of job training for upward (and lateral) mobility. It is also a subsidy granted to the corporations, which in a system of free enterprise might reasonably be expected to do their own job training. And in the great universities even this higher job training is obstructed by the hustle and anxiety of 'research,' often involving yet another corporate raid on the public domain."[24]

Berry's analysis of the shortcomings of American universities both anticipated and echo recent criticisms that—combined with economic forces and technological change—have precipitated a public crisis in confidence in the nation's higher education system.[25] In a 2009 essay in *Progressive*, Berry lamented, "Education has been oversold, overbuilt, over-electrified, and made more expensive. Colleges have grown into universities. Universities have become 'research institutions' full of under-taught students and highly accredited 'professionals' who are overpaid by the public to job-train the young and to invent cures and solutions for corporations to 'market' for too much money to the public. And we have balanced this immense superstructure, immensely expensive to use and to maintain, upon the frail stem of the land economy which we conventionally abuse and ignore."[26]

In 2009, Berry publicly announced that he was pulling his papers from his alma mater and former employer, the University of Kentucky, in protest of the university's decision to accept a $7 million donation from Wildcat Coal Company, a company notorious for the destructive surface mining that Berry has long railed against. The University of Kentucky is a land-grant institution, and Berry linked much of his explanation for the decision to pull his papers to his belief that land-grant universities are failing to fulfill their original mission as outlined by the Morrill Act. But he went further. In an interview in *Science Insider* titled "Writer Wendell Berry Takes Aim at the Modern Research University," Berry explained the reasons for his decision, one he characterized as a "family dispute" because of his long ties to the university as alumnus and professor. He said, "I think [the university] has gone astray first with its long emphasis on research instead of teaching. If you promote research, which can be quantified, and make it the paramount issue with promotion and tenure and salary raises, then you diminish the standing and importance of teaching necessarily, which can't be quantified. . . . Administrators have to find a way to reward professors for teaching." He decried the university's announced goal of becoming a top-20 research university, saying, "The issue for me is that the University of Kentucky has a mandate to look after the country people and the rural landscapes. [It is] promoting a research agenda that is without standards. Will it do harm to our people here, or will it be of some use? I can't discover that there is any such standard by which the effectiveness or usefulness or beneficence of the research can be judged. They're going to take the [research] grant money and do what they are asked to do with it."

Berry explained that the university's acceptance of the Wildcat Coal gift was only the "last straw" in his fraught relationship with his alma mater and former employer. The university had previously infuriated him by selling surface mining rights and engaging in cutting a tract of unlogged forest that it had owned and managed for decades. He explained, "They [the university] dealt very poorly with those who opposed the project and wanted to talk to them about it. I was a member of the opposition. Then the issue of the Wildcat Coal Lodge came up. I have been an opponent, in my writing and in other ways, of surface mining. . . . The university has never taken a stand on the issue, . . . but when they accepted a $7 million gift from the coal industry and named their dormitory the Wildcat Coal Lodge, that meant that they had explicitly come out as an ally of the coal industry. That meant I can't be an ally of the university anymore, obviously."[27]

For agricultural historians, land-grant employees, policymakers, and lay-people alike, the challenge is to fairly assess the new agrarian critique of land-grant universities. We know that many of the agrarians' critiques are substantive and accurate. The link between agribusiness firms and funding for agricultural research at land-grant universities is well established. In the 1980s when the USDA made its first efforts to allocate funding for sustainable farming research and education, the result was an outcry from agribusiness corporations and powerful industrial farming trade groups like the Farm Bureau. Farm Bureau officials called the proposed low-input sustainable agriculture (LISA) programs the "low income sustainable agriculture." During that same decade, the agribusiness lobby succeeded in stalling several efforts to fund education for farmers that would reduce their use of chemicals.[28]

Even as USDA and land-grant universities have devoted a growing but still small share of resources to research on sustainable agriculture, the level of corporate research funding is growing. In the spring of 2012, the environmental group Food and Water Watch released a new report revealing that almost one-quarter of the money spent on agricultural research at land-grant universities comes from corporations, trade associations, and foundations while less than 15 percent of research funding comes from the USDA. The report notes that "This funding steers Land Grant research toward the goals of industry. It also discourages independent research that might be critical of the industrial model of agriculture and diverts public research capacity away from important issues such as rural economies, environmental quality and the public health implications of agriculture." In language reminiscent of Berry's, the report goes on to say, "Private-sector funding not only corrupts the public research mission of Land Grant universities, but also distorts the science that is supposed to help farmers improve their practices and livelihoods. Industry funded academic research routinely produces favorable results for industry sponsors."[29]

For my part, I cannot help but feel that the agrarian critique of land-grant universities is unfair. First, many of the new agrarians, Berry and Jackson among them, are products of land-grant universities and owe much of their own professional and vocational success to the education they received at land-grant institutions. Second, the critics, especially Berry, seem to be reinterpreting or selectively interpreting the intent of the Morrill Act. The act dictated that proceeds from the land-grants should be invested in endowments that would support at least one college in each state "where the leading object shall be, without excluding other scientific and classical studies, and including military tactics, to teach such branches of learning as are related to agriculture and the mechanic arts, in such manner as the legislatures of the States may respectively prescribe, in order to promote the liberal and practical education of the industrial classes in the several pursuits and professions in life."[30] Berry conveniently ignores the provisions for scientific and classical studies and for the "liberal and practical education of the industrial classes in the several pursuits and professions in life." From its beginning, the Morrill Act was intended to provide a broad-based liberal education for students aspiring to many professions, not simply agricultural pursuits.

Moreover, the agrarians seem to hold land-grant institutions to different standards than any other educational institutions. The agrarian insistence that land-grant universities should have continued to fulfill Morrill's original vision without any adaptation to meet the demands of the modern economy and society strikes me as being as unhelpful as the proposals of politicians who want to interpret the Constitution by the narrow rubric of "original intent." Land-grant universities, like the culture in which they are embedded, must evolve to fit the circumstances of that culture. Why ignore the aspirations of today's students to conform to some narrow vision of the land-grant mission? Why condemn the land-grant professoriate for professionalization when every other white-collar occupation has professionalized and specialized over the past century? Why dismiss STEM education out of hand when indeed the tools of science are some of the most powerful for creating a case for sustainable agriculture? The agrarians seem to cling to a static view of culture, but culture is never static. The challenges of changing our food production system are indeed systemic, and they have to be addressed at a macrolevel. Individual land-grant universities cannot achieve the change that Berry and his new agrarian friends are advocating, and neither can land-grants collectively change our agricultural system without meaningful changes in our federal food and agricultural policy. We are engaged in a national conversation about how our food is produced and what we eat. That conversation can provide impetus for change—if that conversation is sustained and if proponents of change can wield some political influence.

Notes

1. Twelve Southerners, *I'll Take My Stand: The South and the Agrarian Tradition* (Baton Rouge: Louisiana State University Press, 1977), p. xlvii.

2. One of the first to call these social critics the "new agrarians" was one of their own: legal scholar Eric T. Freyfogle in *The New Agrarianism: Land, Culture, and the Community of Life* (Washington, DC: Island Press, 2001). See also Wendell Berry, *The Unsettling of America: Culture and Agriculture* (San Francisco: Sierra Club Books, 1977).

3. Gene Logsdon, *At Nature's Pace: Farming and the American Dream* (New York: Pantheon Books, 1994) and *You Can Go Home Again: Adventures of a Contrary Life* (Bloomington: Indiana University Press, 1998); Wes Jackson, *New Roots for Agriculture*, foreword by Wendell Berry (1980; Lincoln: University of Nebraska Press, 1985); Victor Davis Hanson, *Fields without Dreams: Defending the Agrarian Ideal* (New York: The Free Press, 1996); Victor Davis Hanson *The Land Was Everything: Letters from an American Farmer* (New York: The Free Press, 2000); Brian Donahue, *Reclaiming the Commons: Community Farms and Forests in a New England Town* (New Haven: Yale University Press, 1999); Eric T. Freyfogle, *Agrarianism and the Good Society: Land, Culture, Conflict, and Hope* (Lexington: University of Kentucky Press, 2007); Norman Wirzba, ed., *The Essential Agrarian Reader: The Future of Culture, Community, and Land* (Lexington: University Press of Kentucky, 2003); Ronald Jager, *The Fate of Family Farming: Variations on an American Idea* (Hanover, NH: University Press of New England, 2004); Michael Pollan, *The Omnivore's Dilemma: A Natural History of Four Meals* (New York: Penguin, 2006).

4. Norman Wirzba, introduction to Wendell Berry, *The Art of the Commonplace: The Agrarian Essays of Wendell Berry*, edited and with an introduction by Norman Wirzba (Emeryville, CA: Shoemaker and Hoard, 2002), xv–xvi.

5. Freyfogle, *Agrarianism and the Good Society*, 107.

6. James E. McWilliams, *Just Food: Where Locavores Get It Wrong and How We Can Truly Eat Responsibly* (New York: Little, Brown, 2009), 8.

7. Norman Wirzba, "Introduction: Why Agrarianism Matters—Even to Urbanites," in *The Essential Agrarian Reader*, 5.

8. Hanson, *The Land Was Everything*, 2.

9. Wendell Berry, *The Unsettling of America*, 155. See note 2 above.

10. Ibid., 144–47.

11. Ibid., 147.

12. Ibid., 147–48.

13. Ibid., 158.

14. Wendell Berry, "A Defense of the Family Farm," in *Bringing It to the Table: On Farming and Food* (Berkeley, CA: Counterpoint, 2009), 40.

15. Wendell Berry, "Economy and Pleasure," in *The Art of the Commonplace*, 210.

16. Logsdon, *At Nature's Pace*, 76.

17. Jackson, *New Roots for Agriculture*, 85–87.

18. Hanson, *Fields without Dreams*, 277.

19. Greg Vaughan, "The Morrill Act and Agrarian Philosophies," 2010, http://agrarianideas.blogspot.com/2010/08/agrarian-philosophies-and-morrill-act.html (accessed July 5, 2012).

20. For a sampling of some of these programs, see "Sustainable Agriculture Activities at Land-Grant Universities," National Institute of Food and Agriculture, USDA, March 18, 2009, http://www.nifa.usda.gov/nea/ag_systems/in_focus/sustain_ag_if_lgu.html (accessed July 21, 2012).

21. See, for example, the list of research partners in Jackson's "50-Year Farm Bill," in Wes Jackson, *Consulting the Genius of Place: An Ecological Approach to a New Agriculture* (Berkeley, CA: Counterpoint, 2010), 178.

22. Frederick L. Kirschenmann, *Cultivating an Ecological Conscience: Essays from a Farmer-Philosopher* (Lexington: University Press of Kentucky, 2010), 74-75, 325.

23. Wendell Berry, commencement address at Bellarmine University, 2007, http://www.bellarmine.edu/studentaffairs/graduation/berry_address/ (accessed July 6, 2012).

24. Ibid.

25. Media accounts of the crisis in higher education have abounded since the 2008 financial crisis and recession led to massive cuts in state funding for higher education and a growing concern that American colleges and universities are delivering an increasingly expensive, but less valuable, product than ever before. For a cogent distillation of the critique, see "Not What It Used to Be," *The Economist*, December 1, 2012, 29–30.

26. Wendell Berry, "Inverting the Economic Order," *Progressive* 73 (September 2009): p. 25.

27. Eli Kintisch, "Writer Wendell Berry Takes Aim at the Modern Research University," *Science Insider*, June 24, 2010, http://news.sciencemag.org/scienceinsider/2010/06/writer-wendell-berry-takes-aim.html (accessed July 7, 2012). Berry went on to say, "This is a heartbreaking thing for me. The university is an alma mater. I have two degrees from the University of Kentucky. I taught there. They have honored me. I have friends there; I have friends that are currently teaching there. And so this is a break that feels to me like a family disruption."

28. See, for example, "Organic-Farming Study Irks Fertilizer Industry; An Unusual Protest by Agribusiness Lobby," *Washington Post*, March 17, 1988; "Small Grant Stalls $44 Billion Agriculture Bill; Attempt to Advance Use of Less-Toxic Chemicals Runs Afoul of Conventional Adherents," *Washington Post*, October 22, 1989; "Appropriations

Bills Transferred to Fast Track; Some Controversial Amendments Removed," *Washington Post*, November 16, 1989; John Ikered, "Sustainable Agriculture: It's about People" (paper presented at Sustainable Agriculture Seminar, sponsored by Bowling Green University, Bowling Green, Ohio, November 17, 2001), http://web.missouri.edu/ikerdj/papers/SusAgpeople.html (accessed July 22, 2012).

29. Food and Water Watch, "Public Research, Private Gain: Corporate Influence over Agricultural Research," April 2012, http://documents.foodandwaterwatch.org/doc/PublicResearchPrivateGain.pdf (accessed July 28, 2012). Gary Holthaus has pointed out that land-grant universities often conduct research that creates trade-related intellectual property—patents on plants—that prevents farmers from saving seeds. Holthaus, *From the Farm to the Table: What All Americans Need to Know about Agriculture* (Lexington: University Press of Kentucky, 2009), 222.

30. Morrill Act of 1862, transcript available at http://www.ourdocuments.gov/doc.php?flash=true&doc=33&page=transcript (accessed December 11, 2012).

11

The Sustainable Agriculture Movement and Land-Grant Universities

A Contentious History

ROBERT C. MCMATH

Walker's essay outlines the debate for the heart and soul of the modern land-grant university. McMath provides a potent history of one of the many battles within that contest. His focus on the idea of sustainability as a social movement simplifies the matter by reducing the question to interactions between land-grants and sustainability proponents. It demonstrates that a fundamental premise of the Morrill Act remains vibrant. Land-grants persist as exquisitely sensitive institutions, responsive to the demands of governments and shareholders. Social movements invariably impact land-grants—sometimes even their missions—as they continually grapple with change.

Despite the pressure exerted on land-grants, they always find resolution in the same place. Expertise and a cadre of its practitioners remain a staple of land-grant universities. In the case of sustainability as a social movement, the key is introducing into land-grants experts with a vision different than that that had preceded it. The means—science—remained the same but its new promoters held quite different intellectual underpinnings.

***

The relationship between sustainable agriculture and America's land-grant institutions has produced two conflicting narratives. One goes like this: Sustainable agriculture is a popular movement among farmers and ranchers that promotes "ecologically sound, economically viable, and socially responsible" practices.[1] But the movement has been rebuffed by land-grant institutions committed to industrial agriculture in which increased production is *the* goal, regardless of what it may do to our ecology and society. The other narrative goes like this: The land-grant system led the development of a science-based system of agriculture that increased productivity beyond the wildest dreams of our forebears. But in recent years land-grant institutions have come under attack from environmental extremists seeking to impose their schemes on them and on American agriculture, thereby threatening the productivity and earnings of American farmers.

Rather than trying to convince you that one or the other of these narratives is true, I want to situate both in their historical context and recast this struggle as the story of a social movement—sustainable agriculture—and its contentious relationship with land-grant colleges, experiment stations, and the cooperative extension service.

The historical roots of land-grant institutions, dueling forms of agricultural production, *and* social movements are to be found in the early nineteenth century, framed politically by the presidency of John Quincy Adams, the emergence of the Whig Party, and, for the purposes of the subject at hand, the election of Justin Morrill to Congress from Vermont as a Whig in the 1850s. All three were part of a powerful cultural milieu that can be described as "the culture of improvement."

As historian Daniel Walker Howe notes, "'Improvement,' in its early nineteenth-century sense, "constituted both an individual and collective responsibility, involving both the cultivation of personal faculties and the development of national resources."[2] Rapid advances in science and technology produced revolutions in transportation, communication, and agriculture that transformed the way people lived and worked and instilled confidence in humankind's ability to create lasting progress. Adams and Henry Clay laid out a plan for achieving this goal, and Morrill and a young Whig congressman named Lincoln shared the faith of these statesmen that science-based progress could transform the lives of ordinary Americans.[3]

Leading American agriculturalists, following in the footsteps of their British cousins,[4] helped shape the culture of improvement. Steven Stoll describes a "loose movement" for improvement among scientific agriculturalists that stretched from Maine to Mississippi by the 1830s.[5] Through agricultural journals and societies they spread a gospel of intensive agriculture based mainly on the use of manures and cover crops to replenish the soil.

Many of these scientific agriculturalists, particularly in the seaboard states, were already experiencing crises of soil depletion, and the Panic of 1819 triggered an economic crisis in commercial agriculture. In this frightening new environment, "Improvement" was essential for the survival of farmers' livelihood and communities.

In early nineteenth-century America the practice of agricultural improvement was closely coupled with a set of values or a worldview now known as "agrarianism," a word derived from the Latin *agrarius*, meaning "pertaining to the land." Unlike the culture of improvement, early American agrarianism is associated not so much with the Whigs as with their opposite number, the political descendants of Thomas Jefferson. Drawing on the works of the eighteenth-century French Physiocrats, Jefferson and his contemporaries espoused the idea that wealth comes from the land, and therefore farming is the foundational profession. From this perspective farming is not simply a means of making a living but is a way of life, grounded in the land itself, the wellspring of home and community. In agrarian thought working the land was a source of security and independence (what nineteenth-century Americans called a "competency," in the sense of self-sufficiency capable of supporting a family), and even a source of virtue. As Jefferson wrote in his *Notes on the State of Virginia*, "Those who labour in the earth are the chosen people of God, if ever he had a chosen people, whose breasts he has made his peculiar deposit for substantial and genuine virtue."[6]

Statements like this one from Jefferson have given agrarianism a bad name, and historical essays on agrarian rhetoric by Richard Hofstadter and others have led to the conclusion that those who talk about farming and the land in moral terms are just pining for a lost status in American society, a mythic arcadia that will never return.[7] To accept such a simplistic judgment is to misunderstand the condition and state of mind of farmers from Jefferson's day to our own who are at risk of losing "competencies" built up by families over generations, whether it be a Populist going bust in Georgia, a Dust Bowl wheat farmer walking away from an Oklahoma farmstead, or an Iowa corn grower facing the loss of a highly capitalized five-generation farm in the 1980s. Over many generations and for millions of Americans, self-sufficiency *on the land* was the source of home and security and beyond that a central element of what it meant to be a citizen and to be a *man*. Over time the gendered and sometimes racialized aspect of agrarianism has faded, but its core meaning still has the power to persuade.

Beginning in the early nineteenth century, the culture of agrarianism and the culture of improvement combined to form a powerful means of self-understanding and purpose in America. But "improvement" based on manure was labor intensive and required large herds of well-fed cattle. As such, it was beyond the reach of most farmers and antithetical to the slash-and-burn system of the frontier (a system, by the way, that was often at odds with the values of agrarianism). The national conversation about improving worn-out farmland shifted dramatically in the 1840s when advances in agricultural chemistry led to the commercialization of nitrate and phosphate fertilizers. These innovations are commonly associated with the dissemination in America of works by the German chemist Justus von Liebig, particularly his *Familiar Letters on Chemistry and Its Relations to Commerce, Physiology, and Agriculture* and *Chemistry in Its Application to Agriculture and Physiology*.[8] Commercially available minerals did not immediately replace manure as the preferred means of enhancing worn-out or poor soil, but the gospel of chemistry seemed to offer easier means of making soil more productive, if not of preserving it for future generations.

Paralleling this chemical revolution was a mechanical revolution (more accurately an "evolution") in the harvesting of small grains, most importantly in the invention and improvement of the mechanical reaper and related technologies attributed to men like Cyrus McCormick and Obed Hussey. In the same decade John Deere patented the steel plow that would allow the native grasses of the American West to be plowed up for planting. Without these mechanical innovations the rapid development of the western wheat belt would have been impossible,[9] but because of them the very ecology of the Plains suffered long-term disruption.

The age of improvement is symbolized as much by the reaper as it was by the telegraph and the steam engine. Though they emerged from the same culture of improvement as scientific agriculture based on enriching *and* preserving the soil in one place, the chemical and mechanical advances briefly described here would lead American commercial agriculture in a very different direction in the decades that followed.

The age of improvement was also the incubator for the land-grant system, which came of age amid the post–Civil War industrial revolution. The absence of southerners in Congress in 1862 cleared the way for passage of Morrill's land-grant bill and also of legislation to create the transcontinental railroad system. The war stimulated industrial and urban growth and increased demand for labor-saving devices in agriculture. The form of agricultural production that dominated the post–Civil War era and *shaped* the land-grant system was *shaped* by Liebig and McCormick,[10] not by the champions of intensive and sustainable farming.

In the time it took to complete the land-grant system of colleges, experiment stations, and cooperative extension between 1862 and 1914, "new" or "industrial" agriculture waxed, and "improving" or "sustainable" agriculture waned, as experts within and without the land-grant institution strove to make farming more efficient (i.e., more productive). This trend continued,[11] and following World War II, what I will hereafter call "conventional" agriculture[12] became fully entrenched in the land-grant universities (LGUs). This close relationship was confirmed in the 1960s with the success of Norman Borlaug's Green Revolution, which brought input-intensive farming, extensive monoculture, and the land-grant model of agricultural extension to many developing nations and seemingly validated the efficacy of conventional agriculture. During the Nixon presidency federal support for maximizing production for export and the mantra of "get big or get out" were passed along to farmers through the land-grant system.

During the first century of the land-grant colleges the knowledge and practices of sustainable agriculture waned but did not disappear. For example, in the 1880s University of California entomologists developed an integrated pest management system for use in the state's citrus industry.[13] And as Mark D. Hersey has shown, the disciplines of ecology and agricultural science, which emerged from common nineteenth-century roots, maintained a healthy relationship in land-grant institutions and elsewhere until the narrowing of disciplinary specialization forced them apart in the 1920s.[14]

Before and during the ecological disaster that befell the Great Plains in the 1930s, some ecologically minded agronomists and soil scientists within land-grant institutions challenged the prevailing production methods in the wheat belt. One was Harlow L. Walster, dean of the School of Agriculture at North Dakota State University. For much of the 1930s Walster also served as director of extension and director of the experiment station in North Dakota, and he was also the author of a leading textbook on soil science. In 1938 he wrote:

> Our approach to some of the fundamental problems in production in the Great Plains has been, from [the] beginning of settlement, that of a rather blind faith in machinery, and with little or no faith in biological science. This is well illustrated by the early adherence to the fallacious notion that "rain follows the plow" and the continuing fallacious

notion that we can be saved by some new tillage implement. Improved tillage implements are helpful but they are not the complete answer. The answer to the problems of the Great Plains lies in a more complete ecological approach. More people must come to understand human ecology, plant ecology, and animal ecology. When we understand the Great Plains "ekos," the environment of its people, its plants, its animals, we shall be able to deal with the Great Plains intelligently.[15]

Walster penned these words for a federal report on drought conditions on the Great Plains after governmental responses to the crippling drought had already come to be dominated by mechanical solutions focused on tillage, plus cover crops and shelter belts. In 1938 Walster was challenging the prevailing strategy of Soil Conservation Service scientists and their local extension service partners in the Great Plains, particularly in the Dust Bowl region of the southern plains, where much of the federal effort was focused. But when FDR's Department of Agriculture first began to assess the Dust Bowl crisis that decimated crop and livestock production in parts of Oklahoma, Kansas, Colorado, Texas, and New Mexico, a much wider range of options was under consideration, at least among some senior officials including Rexford Tugwell, Lewis Gray, M. L. Wilson, and others.[16] These USDA leaders shared a faith in public land-use planning and aggressive federal intervention to address what they believed was a man-made disaster that followed the "great plow-up" of Plains grasslands. In their view erosion caused by wind, drought, and inappropriate cropping practices on the Plains and erosion caused by water and poor cropping practices elsewhere in the nation could only be reversed through systematic land-use planning and federal intervention.

The planners found allies among the ranks of academic ecologists, including Frederic Clements, Paul Sears, and Carol Saur, along with ecologically minded agronomists and soil scientists like H. L. Walster. This group explained the Dust Bowl, and the accompanying invasion of insect and animal pests, not in terms of nature or divine retribution but of agricultural practices that had disrupted the region's ecological balance. For them, re-creation of a state of equilibrium in the Great Plains ecosystem was the only solution, but, like the planners, at least some of them understood that this would require massive federal intervention on behalf of land reform that could challenge traditional American property rights and would most certainly challenge the paradigm of conventional agriculture.

The federal conservation program that was actually implemented on the Great Plains and supported by land-grant institutions was massive by historical standards, but much less ambitious than what the planners and ecologists had advocated, and far more compatible with conventional agriculture. Historian Donald Worster contends that in the 1930s "there were enough suggestions made by scientists to comprise, if one brought them together, a program for farming by ecological principles,"[17] and he lays much of the blame for the failure to implement such a program at the feet of the ecologists themselves, who failed to reckon with the challenges of creating such a program and a "new land ethic" alongside the prevailing economic values and conventional cropping methods. To be sure, most scientists and academicians are far better at envisioning transformational systems than persuading ordinary citizens to implement them, but I believe Worster underestimates the challenges of implementing radical change among people who had been drawn to this region by the promise of success through conventional commercial agriculture and who were, sometimes literally, fighting for their lives. It was a challenge that the modern movement for sustainable agriculture would confront four decades later.

The eventual triumph of conventional agricultural practices and values in the New Deal farm program over ecologically grounded practices and values was probably never in doubt. In hindsight, this triumph confirms that sustainable agriculture had largely lost whatever place it once had within the land-grant community and USDA. Consequently, the campaign for sustainable agriculture that emerged in the 1970s mainly started outside the land-grant system and other parts of the US Department of Agriculture. Of necessity, champions of sustainable agriculture developed alternative narratives of improvement and methods of production, as well as alternative vehicles for mobilizing support. And it used these stories and organizing techniques to challenge the strategic direction of the land-grant system. In other words, modern "sustainable agriculture" had the hallmarks of a social movement.[18]

What do I mean by "social movement," and how do movements work? For thousands of years human beings have joined forces with others of like mind to effect one sort of change or another. But social movements, in something like their present form, first appeared in the late eighteenth and early nineteenth centuries in Western Europe and then in the United States. The antebellum agricultural societies mentioned earlier are examples, or at least precursors, of social movements. The spread of printing and literacy, coupled with the development of voluntary, or specialized, associations helped create what Sidney Tarrow has called "communities of print and association." They provided new and effective structures through which aggrieved people could engage in "contentious politics" with national governments and other centers of power.[19] Modern social movements mobilize people with shared grievances to seek redress by means that are, in some sense, political. Movements are a form of "contentious politics" for effecting changes within powerful institutions. To understand a social movement we must assess the conditions under which it emerges and examine the ideas and arguments through which participants "frame" their objectives. Then we must discover the cultural resources (familiar forms of disseminating ideas and mobilizing people) that they bring to bear to win support for their cause. Finally, we must follow the dynamic relationship between the movement and those centers of power with which it is in contention, in this case the land-grant system, the US Department of Agriculture (USDA), and associated food-processing and agribusiness firms.[20] Here, in brief outline, is how such an analysis of the sustainability movement might look.

In the late 1970s the United States found itself in economic crisis, suffering simultaneously from high inflation and high unemployment. For American farmers, the situation was compounded by the federal embargo of agricultural products to the Soviet Union, sharp increases in interest rates, and a spike in oil prices that revealed the Achilles' heel of conventional agriculture: its dependence on petroleum-based inputs. Farmers who had long been on a treadmill trying to reduce costs while increasing yield now faced the prospect that their profit margins would disappear altogether and they would be forced out of farming.

At the same time, the national mood was shifting from one of unquestioning faith in experts to a growing distrust of those whose expertise had seemingly failed, whether it was economists who predicted unending growth or scientists who promised that the chemicals we depend upon were safe, effective, and affordable. Two distinct and widespread concerns about the unintended consequences of scientific innovations upon the environment had actually emerged more than twenty years earlier. One concern stemmed from the mounting evidence that radioactive fallout from aboveground testing of thermonuclear bombs by the United States and the Soviet Union had dispersed widely from the test sites and posed grave threats to the human food chain and to human health. The other grew out of the initial findings that widely used chemical pesticides were having harmful effects on the environment and on human health.

In 1962 Rachel Carson put the two threats together in her best-selling book, *Silent Spring*, drawing an explicit analogy between the threats of radioactive fallout and the widespread use of pesticides.[21] Both, she said, were unseen killers. Contrary to the claims of her critics, Carson did not advocate a complete ban on pesticides but rather a more discriminating use of them. Carson sharply attacked manufacturers and scientific institutions that had developed and promoted the indiscriminate use of pesticides such as DDT without careful regard for their potentially harmful consequences. Those she criticized directly included the USDA. Although LGUs were not singled out specifically for criticism in *Silent Spring*, many within those institutions felt the heat. Interestingly enough, a good deal of the evidence Carson used to critique the department's pronouncements and programs of spraying "indiscriminately from the skies" came from studies conducted by land-grant institutions, including several from Auburn University and the Alabama Experiment Station.[22]

Those whom Carson challenged responded with ferocious attacks on her and her findings, but eventually most of her claims were borne out.[23] More immediately, *Silent Spring* made a powerful impact on public opinion and set in motion the modern environmental movement and inspired many young people to "put ecological concepts into action."[24] By the 1970s, some of them were pioneering the new fields of agroecology and conservation biology, and some producers of farm products were joining them in reevaluating the costs and benefits of heavy reliance on pesticides.

A decade and a half after *Silent Spring* appeared, concerns about environmental degradation continue to grow and, along with the economic crisis facing farmers, fueled a sustainable agriculture movement whose core participants made their living from or were in touch with commercial agriculture and often had connections with the land-grant system. This group included, even from the beginning, some personnel from within the LGUs, state experiment stations, and extension services. Emerging at the same time as the growth of the wider environmental movement, sustainable agriculture naturally attracted some environmentalists with no direct ties to production agriculture.[25]

The sustainable agriculture movement was framed by stories from people who lived with the economic, ecological, and social crises facing rural

America, many of whom had read widely in the philosophical literature of conservationism and environmentalism and drew inspiration from it. Organizationally, the movement consisted of loosely connected local, state, and regional networks led by farmers, farm journalists, and agricultural professionals, some of whom were employed by land-grant institutions. No single organization controlled or dominated "sustainable agriculture."

The breadth of the movement almost defies definition, and some have argued against trying. But most participants would probably agree that sustainable agriculture would be "ecologically sound, economically viable, and socially responsible."[26] While many could agree on these broad goals, the precise definitions of each and the means proposed for achieving them varied widely. Some movement participants insisted on organic practices, while others advocated *limiting* the use of chemical inputs to the greatest extent possible. Some would tolerate no genetically modified organisms (GMOs) but others would make use of them to achieve goals of sustainability, and so forth. By multiple means and with different emphases movement leaders and participants shared their own experiences of a crisis in conventional agriculture and of apparent successes with sustainable methods. They developed alternative or parallel models for agricultural education, research, and extension. And they charged the land-grant system and the USDA with being unresponsive to their needs and to the health of the land itself.

How did farmers and people associated with farming move from fear or anger to participation in a movement focused on a strategy that would require individual producers to abandon or modify many of the practices of conventional agriculture? The economic and environmental conditions of the times pushed many into receptiveness to new ideas, and by the late 1970s early adopters of sustainable practices, along with other *thought leaders* in agriculture, put forth stories, arguments, and descriptions of alternative cropping practices based on ideas already validated in the United Kingdom and the United States. Simultaneously, they developed alternative educational networks for disseminating these practices, thus implicitly or explicitly challenging the orthodox ideas and practices of the land-grant system. As one advocate later recalled, "the greatest obstacle to ecologically informed alternative practices has not been a shortage of ideas; it has been a dearth of practical educational alternatives—also known as "extension"—to help producers learn about them."[27]

Critiques of the land-grant system like this one drew not just on personal experiences but also on several books published in the 1970s that achieved iconic status among early supporters of sustainable agriculture and other environmentalists and social justice advocates with no connection to the production of food and fiber. Two were particularly influential. The first was *Hard Tomatoes, Hard Times* (1973) by Texas gadfly and former state commissioner of agriculture Jim Hightower. The subtitle of Hightower's book, *A Report of the Agribusiness Accountability Project on the Failure of America's Land Grant College Complex*, telegraphs his message. The other was *The Unsettling of America: Culture and Agriculture* (1977) by naturalist, essayist, farmer, and latter-day agrarian philosopher Wendell Berry. Both authors took dead aim at the land-grant institutions' role in developing technologies that were of value to large-scale agriculturalists and agribusinesses. Berry, and to a lesser extent Hightower, also challenged the environmental stance of the land-grant/agribusiness network. Berry's influence among advocates of sustainable agriculture has persisted, and he has lived long enough to become godfather to the local food movement. Hightower's influence has waned. Although Hightower was satirical, and possessed a wicked wit, his leftist politics probably wore thin with most farmers, even when some of them agreed with his criticisms of the land-grant institutions.[28] In 1990 Hightower was defeated for reelection as agriculture commissioner by a young Republican challenger named Rick Perry.

The sustainable agriculture movement first gained traction not simply because of its own criticism of the land-grant system and its embrace of critics like Hightower and Berry but also because it articulated a positive vision of an alternative future. In "framing" their movement, sustainability pioneers made the case that amid the multifaceted crisis facing American farmers, conversion to a new system of agriculture could be ecologically sound, economically viable, and socially responsible. Their case absolutely had to include facts on the ground—convincing evidence that the new system could turn a profit and provide effective alternatives to the chemical solutions of conventional agriculture, and it had to have the science necessary to back up that evidence. But it also had to include appeals to a trustworthy and familiar set of values that gave meaning and purpose to their actions. The framing of sustainable agriculture included a powerful articulation of the vision and values some now call "the new agrarianism."[29]

The vision and values undergirding the sustainable agriculture movement descended, in modified form, from Jeffersonian agrarianism. Many of the twentieth-century thinkers who presaged the modern movement drew upon that tradition, explicitly or implicitly. In *The Holy Earth* (1915) and other works Liberty Hyde Bailey, dean of Cornell's College of Agriculture and chair of Theodore Roosevelt's Country Life Commission, endorsed environmental stewardship and affirmed a spiritual relationship between humans and the land. Sir Albert Howard, the "patron saint of organic farming,"[30] took a similar approach decades later in *An Agriculture Testament* (1943). In that same year Lady Eve Balfour, another British pioneer of organic farming and an early leader in the international organic movement, published *The Living Soil*, which echoed the holistic and reverential tone of earlier works.[31]

The interdependence among flora, fauna (including humans), and the land expressed in these various works was a major theme of the new agrarianism and connected it to the systems thinking of agroecology. Aldo Leopold, the father of wildlife ecology, was a key intellectual figure in the rise of environmentalism and particularly of environmental ethics. He was certainly the pioneer in environmental ethics who paid closest attention to agriculture, as evidenced by this aphorism: "There are two spiritual dangers in not owning a farm. One is the danger of supposing that breakfast comes from the grocery, and the other is that heat comes from a furnace."[32] Leopold's collection of essays, *A Sand County Almanac, and Sketches from Here and There* (1949), became a core document (some would say sacred text) for the sustainable agriculture movement. His notion of a "land ethic" as laid out in that book reflected both the appreciation for the natural world that he developed in his native Iowa and his familiarity with earlier writers in the new agrarian tradition: "A land ethic changes the role of homo sapiens from conqueror of the land-community to plain member and citizen of it. It implies respect for his fellow members and also respect for the community itself. . . . A thing is right when it tends to preserve the integrity, stability, and beauty of the biotic community. It is wrong when it tends otherwise."[33]

The cluster of ideas articulated by Leopold and others gave actual and potential participants in sustainable agriculture a "lens" through which to see themselves as part of a struggle to restore the proper order of things, as well as to improve their livelihood. But how do you actually get that message across to folks who can't spend all day reading books? Making the case sometimes took the form of individual "testimonies" about an epiphany, a realization that the production methods of conventional agriculture were no longer economically or ecologically viable and no longer able to sustain the social fabric of rural communities. The testimonies were "conversion stories"—not religious conversion, though religious and ethical values often played a role, but conversion on the land from one system of production to another.

Here is one such story about the promise and the difficulty of converting to sustainable or organic farming in the 1970s. Fred Kirschenmann grew up on a North Dakota farm that his parents had started in 1930, just before the great drought struck the plains. His father understood that "the Dust Bowl was not just about the weather but about the way farmers farmed," and to prevent such disaster from crippling his farm again, "caring for the land became his top priority."[34] Fred left the farm to study philosophy and theology (including taking a PhD in philosophy from the University of Chicago) and enjoyed an academic career as a professor and administrator. But when his father suffered a heart attack in 1976 he returned to manage the family's 3,500-acre grain and livestock operation. Farming conditions, conversations with his student and organic farming pioneer David Vetter, and his own philosophical/theological perspective persuaded Fred to take the plunge. But when he started the transition in 1977, "the concept of sustainability was not yet in the public domain, nor had I heard of it. I also was unaware that a special market existed for organic production. I was motivated entirely by the fact, brought to my attention by my former student David Vetter[,] that well-managed organic farms could dramatically improve soil quality."[35] If Kirschenmann's background was atypical of sustainability pioneers, his initial reaction revealed a fear that was all too common: "The beginning was lonely. No one else was doing what I was doing. No neighbor had left a budding career in higher education to undertake the task of managing a farm in an isolated area under difficult economic conditions. Converting a farm from accepted, conventional, chemical, agribusiness management practices to an organic farm was unheard of in the area. Organic agriculture was derided by ag experts, frowned upon by the United States Department of Agriculture, and ridiculed by many farmers. . . . [T]here was no one with whom to check my perceptions."[36]

Modern farmers are of necessity innovators, and in the development of conventional agriculture in the first half of the twentieth century land-grant institutions had been a major source of on-farm innovation. But, as Kirschenmann's experience illustrates, in the early days of sustainable agriculture (and to a lesser extent today), most land-grant professionals were skeptical of the new model and loath to embrace it. To be sure, the rhetorical "framing" of the movement featured a narrative of more uniformly negative attitudes among land-grant personnel than the facts warranted, and there were always exceptions like Dean Walster of North Dakota State and researchers at the University of California-Davis who helped Doug Hemly and his family develop "ecologically informed strategies" for blending controlled use of pesticides with predatory insects to control the codling moth in their pear orchards.[37]

Nevertheless, the early development of "practical educational alternatives" was largely a grassroots effort that emerged outside the land-grant system. The sustainable agriculture pioneers were not entirely without exemplars and supporters in the private sector, the most important of which was the Rodale Institute in rural Pennsylvania. The institute (originally known as the Soil and Health Foundation) was founded in 1947 by organic farming advocate J. I. Rodale with profits from his Rodale Press, itself a major source of books and magazines on organic practices for cropping and soil improvement. Although some within the LGU community challenged Rodale's science and his claims for success, in the early days of the sustainable agriculture movement Rodale and later the Rodale Institute demonstrated practical methods of soil improvement and provided seed funds for educational programs on sustainability.[38]

By the late 1970s pioneers of the sustainable agriculture movement were beginning to establish their farmers' institutes, field days, and other collaborative vehicles for sharing and spreading the new message, with or without assistance from the Rodale Institute, LGU specialists, or other exemplars. These new alternative forms of extension popped up across the country, often launched by community innovators and their neighbors. Doug Hemly's fellow California fruit growers observed what was happening in his orchards and worked together to develop an integrated pest management system. Iowa corn farmers observed Dick and Sharon Thompson's low-till system and created the Practical Farmers of Iowa to spread the word. And Wisconsin dairy farmers, organized as the Ocooch Grazers Network, shifted toward a system of intentional rotational grazing. Pioneering organizers and sympathetic observers contrasted this movement-based collaborative learning model with what they considered to be the extension service's expert-driven demonstration model.[39] Energized by the "dearth of practical educational alternatives," they created their own.

Some of these grassroots efforts looked beyond demonstration projects toward the creation of complex research and extension organizations that could develop and disseminate new forms of ecosystem agriculture appropriate for specific locales. None of these new organizations was more ambitious, or more radical, than the Land Institute that Wes and Dana Jackson established on a patch of tallgrass prairie near Salina, Kansas, in 1976. Wes, a fourth-generation Kansan, had earned a PhD in plant genetics at North Carolina State University before founding one of the nation's first academic programs in environmental studies at California State University-Sacramento. Influenced by the writings of Aldo Leopold, Liberty Hyde Bailey, and Wendell Berry, and after observing a tallgrass preserve in Kansas on a field trip with his California students, Wes left his tenured academic position and with Dana (herself an advocate for social aspects of sustainability) founded the Land Institute with the goal of using nature's own methods to develop an alternative to annual monoculture production of grains, legumes, and other plants. Jackson believed that system he called "perennial polyculture" could, in time, produce locally suitable strains that retained the hardiness and strong root systems of native plants while producing seeds that matched those of hybrid annuals.[40]

Since the late 1970s the Land Institute's research team has made progress toward this hugely ambitious goal, but a commercially viable perennial polyculture remains far in the future. In the meantime, "Land," as its adherents call it, has documented the relative costs of conventional grain production on the Kansas prairies and systems that reduce or eliminate the need for chemical inputs and mechanical power. It has also trained a cadre of interns and graduate students who are continuing the research and educational missions of the institute across the nation and around the world.

Creation of these and other alternative educational systems at the grassroots are examples of what students of social movements call "modular repertoires"—organizing techniques that can be modified and transferred from one setting to another to create and grow a movement.[41] Earlier examples include the Farmers' Alliance's adaptation of the Methodist circuit-rider system for its own organizing in the 1880s and the John Birch Society's variation on Tupperware parties in suburban homes that won converts in the 1950s. Other examples of modular repertories to promote sustainable agriculture included new magazines and journals for practitioners and scientists and new research and extension facilities such as Wes and Dana Jackson's Land Institute and the Practical Farmers of Iowa.

At the same time, and in tandem with the farm-based movement, sustainable agriculture began to develop a larger and more focused presence within some LGUs. Agroecology emerged as a new discipline at the intersection of ecology and agronomy, and its practitioners saw it as the emerging scientific framework for sustainable agriculture. Grounded in ecological systems theory and the social values of applied agricultural research, agroecology addressed all three of the broad goals of sustainable agriculture: that it be ecologically sound, economically viable, and socially responsible.[42] While agroecologists were a small minority among LGU scientists, they were part of a growing international network of scientists, extension works, and farmers stretching from Asia and Europe to Latin America. But support for sustainable agriculture within the LGUs was by no means limited to agroecologists. Growing numbers of horticulturalists, agricultural economists, and specialists from across the life sciences began to incorporate sustainability into their teaching and research.

Although many still considered sustainable agriculture to be a fringe movement, by the late 1980s and early 1990s it was becoming part of an emerging new "mainstream" in American life and thought, fed in part by growing awareness of and actions to address environmental issues, including recurring problems of soil erosion as well as chemical pollution. In 1989 a committee of the National Research Council (NRC), with heavy representation from LGU faculty and administrators, published a study titled *Alternative Agriculture* that endorsed many goals of sustainability.[43] But the report was more than just a catalyst for change. It was also a sign of significant shifts in public opinion and with the agricultural establishment about sustainability in general and sustainable agriculture in particular. *Alternative Agriculture* turned out to be the first of several such reports from the NRC that provided substantial data and increasingly specific recommendations, the most recent being *Toward Sustainable Agricultural Systems in the 21st Century* (2010).

Beginning in the 1980s, LGUs and the USDA responded to changing conditions with what might be considered a form of co-optation, endorsing some of the less controversial aspects of sustainability while downplaying others that implied systemic change. The relationship between the sustainable agriculture *movement* and the LGUs also changed in subtle ways as more agricultural professionals associated with the movement opted to pursue their goals from within the system with at least some prospect of securing the resources needed to achieve those goals.

What resources? Between 1985 and 1990 Congress passed significant agricultural-environmental legislation with real budget implications.[44] The Food Security Act of 1985 included major land conservation programs, the Appropriate Technology Transfer for Rural Areas project (ATTRA), and some funding for research and education on sustainable agriculture. Congress authorized and the USDA established modest funding for research and education through two programs, first the Low-Input Sustainable Agriculture program (LISA), authorized by Congress under the 1985 act, and its much better funded successor, the Sustainable Agriculture Research and Education program (SARE), which provides competitive funding for research, demonstration, and educational projects within each of its four regions.[45] And in 1990 Congress passed the Organic Foods Production Act, which established national organic certification standards. Movement participants took heart from these developments in the legislative and policy realm, but some also noted that goals for sustainable agriculture were framed in legislative language that began with increasing farm profitability coupled with expanding capacity to feed the world's nine billion, put environmental quality in second place, and described societal change in only the vaguest of terms.[46]

When Congress set in motion a process to replace state and regional organic standards with a national standard, many organic producers and processors feared it would lead to a dilution of standards and the rapid consolidation of organic processing and marketing under the control of very large food-processing firms. Both have proven to be true, but for complex reasons. Even before the first draft of the national standard was released in 1997, organic production, processing, and marketing of "organic" foods was viewed as a lucrative niche market, and large integrated processing companies were buying up independent organic firms. Large processors were guaranteed a major presence on the National Organic Standards Board, but efforts to include GMOs among the nonorganic substances allowed in certified organic products may have resulted from a softening of opposition to GMOs within segments of the sustainable agriculture movement as well as from the wishes of Big Food.[47]

Since the 1990s sustainable agriculture has gained a larger presence in LGUs, although organic and sustainable initiatives still represent only a small fraction of LGU activities and budgets. How may we account for this changed relationship between a movement and a powerful set of institutions that had so recently viewed each other as the archenemy? In addition to shifts in public opinion (increasingly reflected in corporate strategies and federal policies), specific changes in the relationship between the movement and institutions included the following:

1. *Growing student and faculty interest in sustainability and sustainable agriculture.* This increased interest reflected an important generational shift, with a cohort of mid-career agricultural scientists who came of age during the early days of the environmental movement, and also with increasing numbers of young women pursuing degrees in the biological sciences, including agricultural sciences.

2. *Some reintegration of agroecology and ecology and rapprochement between agroecology and agronomy, soil science, and crop science.*[48] One LGU faculty member notes that this integrated approach to agroecosystems has been driven by genetically modified crops as much as by alternative methods such as organic, permaculture, and polyculture.

3. *Some shifting of the movement away from attacks on LGU research priorities toward what some see as a greater emphasis on building "an alternative locally based food system involving more direct linkages . . . between farmers and consumers."*[49]

4. As mentioned previously, *co-optation of sustainability by the LGUs and USDA.* This is usually a sign that a movement poses significant challenges for dominant institutions, but to some extent the co-optation has been mutual, based on a shared realization that to feed the world's nine billion we need every tool in our toolbox.

One measure of sustainable agriculture's impact within LGUs is the growth of courses and degree programs in agroecology and sustainability, research and extension centers dedicated to these subjects, and student farms that practice sustainability and support farm-to-table programs. Fifteen LGUs now offer interdisciplinary or transdisciplinary degree programs in sustainable agriculture or agroecology, while nineteen offer undergraduate concentrations and/or minors. Eleven LGUs currently operate student farms with a sustainability focus, along with thirty-five other colleges and universities, and at least thirteen LGUs have multidisciplinary research centers focused on sustainable agriculture.[50] Educational programs in sustainable agriculture and student farms now have a growing organization of their own, the Sustainable Agriculture Education Association, which at the end of 2012 had 203 members, including many faculty members and students from land-grant institutions.[51]

At some universities, including Iowa State University, North Carolina State University, and the University of California-Davis, these three programmatic innovations are highly synergistic, with LGU personnel participating in more than one. Educational programs, research/extension, and student farms are characterized by a focus on systems approaches, including in some cases the use of agroecology as the core discipline, and a high level of experiential learning as opposed to passive, teacher-focused learning. The latter reflects not only their origin in the sustainable agriculture movement but also the influence of educational theories ranging from the active learning approaches propounded by John Dewey over a century ago to the social constructivist theories applied by some today.[52] The author of a new study of the student farm movement makes the case for experiential learning in jargon-free terms, noting that while there are many arguments in favor of student farming, "at their most basic level, they come down to this: it's good for students to put down their books (or close their computers) occasionally, and get outside, to get some exercise, to put their hands in the earth, to learn how to wield a spade. Having a student-run farm or garden on campus enables universities to demonstrate their commitment to environmental ideals while letting students explore how those ideals might be applied in the real world."[53]

These sustainability programs within LGUs are attracting scholarly attention, and there is a growing body of research on them. But we need to know more about them before we can assess their scope and impact with any degree of confidence. That said, in general, these programs appear not to be well integrated into the mainstream activities of the land-grant institutions, despite federal support through SARE and other sources that has allowed some to flourish.[54] And while more faculty members and students in LGUs are gravitating toward sustainable agriculture programs, the institutions themselves and USDA funding in general are still focused on the agenda of conventional agriculture and increasingly on the "molecularization" of agricultural research and the corresponding shift to partnerships with biotechnology firms.[55] On the other hand, these sustainability programs and other niches within universities and colleges provide sustainability advocates a base of operation and potential for expanding the conversation with international partners than a stand-alone movement could ever provide. Furthermore, the growth of what we might call a "movement culture" of sustainability within LGUs could lay the groundwork for future collaboration between LGUs and sustainability-minded corporations and government agencies.

The relationship between social movements and the power centers with which they contend is dynamic, and the sustainable agriculture movement and America's land-grant institutions are no exception. Sometimes changes in one come in response to actions of the other, but both are changing in response to powerful forces and events in the global and national arenas.

Consider the well-documented challenges facing the land-grant institution in recent years, including the impact of the molecular revolution in agricultural science and the concomitant control of much of this new knowledge by biotechnology firms, the long-term decline in federal Hatch funding and other forms of support for agricultural research, uncertainty about federal agriculture funding in general, and the decline in state funding for higher education. Add to that the withering criticisms leveled at the land-grant system and "big agriculture" over the last half century, first by environmental and social justice advocates and now by elements of the rapidly growing but still ill-defined food movement. The challenge to the LGUs from the sustainable agriculture movement is only one manifestation of declining public support for the overall federal agriculture program.

For its part, despite the policy and funding shifts of the past quarter century, the sustainable agriculture movement still finds itself largely out of the loop with massive federal agricultural programs developed over the past eighty years and only marginally integrated into the mission and programs of the land-grant institutions. Today's sustainable agriculture movement, both within and outside of the land-grant system, finds itself in an interesting position relative to forces shaping the LGUs, particularly the overall decline in public funding and the simultaneous rise of proprietary research partnerships with biotechnology firms. One could add to that the growing "extension" role of the biotech firms that own the patented agricultural materials plus the shifting attitude of Big Food toward sustainability. So *what might become of the movement in the coming years, and what might its relation be to the land-grant institutions?*

For social movements that achieve any level of success in their struggle with centers of power there comes a moment when the movement faces a fork in the road. Should it stick to its full agenda without compromise and seek complete victory over its foes, or should it work to maximize its impact by making allies wherever it can and seek to be part of collaborative solutions to the problems it was created to address?[56] The sustainable agriculture movement is at such a juncture today. For some the goal has been to transform the land-grant institutions, making ecology the core scientific discipline, the spread of sustainable practice the core mission of cooperative extension, and transformation of the social order an ultimate goal. But for other participants the goal of the movement has been to create alternative institutions of education, research, and extension that develop and disseminate sustainable practices with the intention that the land-grant system would ultimately embrace these alternative practices as part of its overall mission, thus returning to what these advocates consider the original land-grant vision.[57]

I believe that the latter course of action will prevail. Certainly many sustainability advocates inside and outside of the land-grant institutions are already working to that end, and they have reason to believe that time is on their side. The generational shift previously described, some movement in their direction by administrators and faculty members in colleges of agriculture, the previously noted challenges facing LGUs today, and the twin prospects of declining supplies and increased cost of fossil fuel and the rise of global warming all suggest the likelihood of major changes ahead in the land-grant system. Sustainable agriculture is well positioned to play a more central role within that system. Let me offer two scenarios through which the sustainable agriculture movement may increase its impact by working through and with the land-grant system.

The USDA's SARE program suggests one such scenario. SARE is organized to provide research grants through four regional branches, each administered through a land-grant university in the region. Despite its limited funding, SARE has already had significant impact in some parts of the country, and as one close observer notes, "The SARE research programs in the North Central Region have provided substantial direction for designing and improving future farming systems that will be profitable, environmentally sound, and socially viable."[58] SARE research projects tend to focus on the needs of small and medium-sized farms and treat participating farmers and ranchers as a major source of knowledge, not simply as passive recipients of expert knowledge. In this regard its operations look very much like the alternative research and extension programs developed over the past decades as core activities of the sustainable agriculture movement. The solutions to on-farm and community problems coming out of this research involve production practices, soil fertility, integration into alternative marketing systems such as local food movements and Community Supported Agriculture (CSA) programs, and other issues. Some solutions simply provide the means for making conventional practices more efficient (i.e., reducing fertilizer application rates), while others point to substitutions (i.e., cultivation rather than herbicides), and some, in the tradition of Wes Jackson's Land Institute, aim toward major redesign of agricultural systems. In a sense, these projects are advancing ecological systems-scale agriculture research and making it publicly available at a time when mainstream research conducted within the LGUs is increasingly molecular and proprietary. Jackson himself suggested the complementarity of the two when he was asked in 2011, "What emerging trend do you think will shake up how food is raised?" Jackson responded with an appeal for collaboration between traditional plant breeders and molecular geneticists in combining field and laboratory research: "Looking at molecules is to look downward in the hierarchy. Often overlooked, but of equal importance, is the necessity to look upward in the hierarchy of the sciences to the ecosystem level, which makes ecology/evolutionary biology of greater importance to agriculture."[59]

Cooperative extension already for over a decade had considerable involvement in SARE projects, including one model program that involves a partnership of the Iowa Cooperative Extension, the Leopold Center for Sustainable Agriculture at Iowa State University, and the Practical Farmers of Iowa. Since its creation in 2008, the National Institute of Food and Agriculture (NIFA), successor to the Cooperative State Research, Education, and Extension Service, has given sustainability a higher priority for funding of projects across its area of responsibility, thus increasing the opportunities for making sustainability a much more integral part of the land-grant system.[60]

A second scenario through which the sustainable agriculture movement (or at least the broad movement *culture* that is increasingly visible within LGUs) could increase its impact begins with the growing pressure on LGUs from Big Food, the giant corporations that dominate the processing, aggregation, distribution, and sale of food products. As suggested earlier, biotechnology firms, including producers of genetically modified seed, have already assumed some of the role played by the LGUs in research and extension. Now consumer-serving food companies have become deeply concerned about the safety and security of the food they handle and the concomitant liabilities and risks to their reputations, arising domestically and internationally. Within the past few years, corporate concerns about these threats have begun driving sustainable agriculture practices from production to point of sale.

As corporations increase pressure on suppliers and producers to document the safety and security of agricultural products, reduction of environmental impacts, and humane treatment of workers, pressures mount on LGUs to help suppliers and producers meet these demands. Although the LGUs as a whole are not well prepared to meet these challenges quickly, the demands of Big Food may force them to move expeditiously in the directions that the sustainable agriculture movement began demanding of them over three decades ago. If so, the alternative methods developed by the movement and now maturing within and in partnerships with the LGUs could prove crucial.

When the Chinese revolutionary leader Zhou Enlai was asked whether he believed the French Revolution had been a success or a failure he replied, "it is too soon to tell." A better question to ask about a movement, but also one that may take many years to answer, is "what has been its impact?"[61] Like all movements, the sustainable agriculture movement did not spring up in a vacuum. It resonated with earlier movements centered on care for the land and for the creation of "competencies" on the land using renewable resources. It emerged alongside of and in partnership with the larger environmental movement and a widespread but amorphous distrust of big government and big science. More recently it has made common cause with the emergent food movement of which Michael Pollan is one of many spokesmen.[62]

Acknowledging the interconnected forces at work in the last three or four decades to effect change in American agriculture and in the land-grant universities, what can we say now, in a preliminary way, about the impact of the movement for sustainable agriculture? Without question, it has convinced many farmers and ranchers to convert from or modify their use of conventional production methods, though today the percentage of food and fiber produced using some form of sustainable practice is still relatively small. The movement also began a public conversation about the proper role of land-grant universities in American life that resembled but was more focused than the critique of LGUs emanating from environmentalists and other critics of corporate science and technology.

Today, even many of the movement's strongest critics of LGUs are partnering with like-minded LGU professionals and students, and much of the movement's energy and direction is coming from people within American LGUs. While corporate and political forces will likely play a greater role in moving the land-grant institutions and the USDA in general toward a more systematic focus on sustainability than will the movement described in these pages, the movement for sustainable agriculture and the "practical educational alternatives" that it created have helped create the context within which such a shift could occur.[63]

NOTES

1. John Ikerd, "On Defining Sustainable Agriculture," North Carolina Sustainable Agriculture Research and Education Program, http://www.sutainable-ag.ncsued/onsustainableag.htm (accessed July 19, 2012). For their helpful insights and wise counsel, the author wishes to thank Marty Matlock, Curt Rom, Jennie Popp, and Mike Vedya, all of the University of Arkansas, as well as Damien Parr of the University of California-Davis.

2. Daniel Walker Howe, *What Hath God Wrought: The Transformation of America, 1815–1848* (New York: Oxford University Press, 2007), 244.

3. Coy F. Cross II, *Justin Smith Morrill: Father of the Land-Grant Colleges* (East Lansing: Michigan State University Press, 1999), 51. Abraham Lincoln revered Clay as "my beau ideal of a statesman." Daniel Walker Howe, *The Political Culture of the American Whigs* (Chicago: University of Chicago Press, 1979), 272.

4. For an excellent local history of this transatlantic exchange, see Brian Donahue, *The Great Meadow: Farmers and the Land in Colonial Concord* (New Haven: Yale University Press, 2004): "My contention is that colonial agriculture in Concord was an ecologically sustainable adaptation of English mixed husbandry to a new, challenging environment. Mixed husbandry combines livestock and tillage into a single integrated system whereby, among other things, the stock fertilize the crops by recycling or transferring nutrients. As far as I can tell, farming in colonial was not extensive. It did not rely on fresh land, or on long fallows, as its primary source of continued fertility. Instead, it rested upon *husbandry*—on the careful balance and integration of diverse elements across a varied and difficult landscape" (xv).

5. Steven Stoll, *Larding the Lean Earth: Soil and Society in Nineteenth-Century America* (New York: Hill and Wang, 2002), 24.

6. Thomas Jefferson, *Notes on the State of Virginia*, Query 19, in Thomas Jefferson *Writings* (New York: Literary Classics of the United States, 1984), 290–91.

7. Richard Hofstadter, *The Age of Reform: From Bryan to FDR* (New York: Vintage, 1955). See especially chapter 1, "The Agrarian Myth and Commercial Realities," and chapter 2, "The Folklore of Populism."

8. Margaret W. Rossiter, *The Emergence of Agricultural Science: Justus Liebig and the Americans, 1840–1880* (New Haven: Yale University Press, 1975), 28–46. Rossiter argues that Liebig's *Familiar Letters on Chemistry and Its Relations to Commerce, Physiology, and Agriculture* (1843) had a greater impact on American farming practices than his now better-known work, *Chemistry in Its Application to Agriculture and Physiology* (1840).

9. Alan L. Olmstead, "The Mechanization of Reaping and Mowing in American Agriculture," *Journal of Economic History* 35 (June 1975): 327; John Nader, "The Rise

of an Inventive Profession: Learning Effects in the Midwestern Harvester Industry," *Journal of Economic History* 54 (June 1994): 397–408; Wesley F. Buchele and Graeme R. Quick, *The Grain Harvesters* (St. Joseph, MI: American Society of Agricultural Engineers, 1978). According to the interpretation now widely accepted by historians, mechanical innovation in early America was driven much more by tinkering and incremental improvements by many hands rather than by the genius of a few individuals.

10. I am using these names as shorthand for the innovations that had many fathers.

11. David Danbom may be correct to argue that "[b]y 1930 the industrialization of agriculture was assured," but not until the postwar era was it fully realized and recognized as a cornerstone of the land-grant system's mission. David B. Danbom, *The Resisted Revolution: Urban America and the Industrialization of Agriculture, 1900–1930* (Ames: Iowa State University Press, 1979), 138.

12. In recent years even the naming of these two agricultural systems has become part of the war of competing narratives. I will use "conventional" and "sustainable" as terms generally acceptable to the champions of the systems to which they refer.

13. Keith Douglass Warner, *Agroecology in Action: Extending Alternative Agriculture through Social Networks* (Cambridge, MA: MIT Press, 2007), 46.

14. Mark D. Hersey, "'What We Need Is a Crop Ecologist': Ecology and Agricultural Science in Progressive-Era America," *Agricultural History* 85 (Summer 2011): 316. Hersey rightly suggests that "the co-evolution of ecology and agronomy suggests that the agrarian wing of the Progressive conservation movement merits more than a perfunctory nod to [Liberty Hyde] Bailey and the Country Life Movement."

15. Quotation from Donald Worster, *Dust Bowl: The Southern Plains in the 1930s*, rev. ed. (New York: Oxford University Press, 2004), 201. Biographical information from "Finding Aid to the Dean Harlow L. Walster Records," North Dakota State University Institute for Regional Studies and University Archives, http://library.ndsu.edu/repository/bitstream/handle/10365/4476/Walster,DeanHarlowL.pdf (accessed November 21, 2012).

16. This account of federal responses to the Dust Bowl draws heavily on Worster, *Dust Bowl*. See also Pamela Riney-Kehrberg, *Rooted in Dust: Surviving Drought and Depression in Southwestern Kansas* (Lawrence: University Press of Kansas, 1994); R. Douglas Hurt, *The Dust Bowl: An Agricultural and Social History* (Chicago: Nelson-Hall, 1981); Randal S. Beeman and James A. Prichard, *A Green and Permanent Land: Ecology and Agriculture in the Twentieth Century* (Lawrence: University Press of Kansas, 2001), 24–32; and Wayne D. Rasmussen, *Taking the University to the People: Seventy-five Years of Cooperative Extension* (Ames: Iowa State University Press, 1989), 100–102.

17. Worster, *Dust Bowl*, 203.

18. Others have treated sustainable agriculture in the United States as a form of social movement. See, in particular, Neva Hassanein, *Changing the Way America Farms: Knowledge and Community in the Sustainable Agriculture Movement* (Lincoln: University of Nebraska Press, 1999).

19. Sidney Tarrow, *Power in Movement: Social Movements and Contentious Politics*, 2nd ed. (New York: Cambridge University Press, 1998), 43–53; Charles Tilly, "Social Movements and National Politics," in *Statemaking and Social Movements: Essays in History and Theory*, ed. Charles Bright and Susan Harding (Ann Arbor: University of Michigan Press, 1984), 297–317; Charles Tilly, "Britain Creates the Social Movement," in *Social Conflict and the Political Order in Modern Britain*, ed. James E. Cronin and Jonathan Schneer (New Brunswick, NJ: Rutgers University Press, 1982), 21–51.

20. The characterization of social movements outlined here is drawn primarily from the works cited in the previous note and Doug McAdam, Sidney Tarrow, and Charles Tilly, *Dynamics of Contention* (Cambridge: Cambridge University Press, 2001); and Donatella della Porta and Mario Diani, *Social Movements: An Introduction*, 2nd ed. (Malden, MA: Blackwell, 2006).

21. Rachel Carson, *Silent Spring* (Boston: Houghton Mifflin, 1962, 6–7, 208–9. The analogy appears throughout the book. See also William Sounder, *On a Farther Shore: The Life and Legacy of Rachel Carson* (New York: Crown, 2012), 290–92.

22. Carson, *Silent Spring*, 154–72. "Indiscriminately from the Skies" is the title of the chapter in which most of these references appear.

23. Gino J. Marco, Robert M. Hollingsworth, and William Durham, eds., *Silent Spring Revisited* (Washington, DC: American Chemical Society, 1987); Mark L. Winston, *Nature Wars: People vs. Pests* (Cambridge, MA: Harvard University Press, 1997).

24. Carson, *Silent Spring Revisited*, 3–11; Warner, *Agroecology in Action*, 26. Warner provides a useful summary in his opening chapter, "Rachel's Dream: Agricultural Policy and Science in the Public Interest."

25. My focus on people associated with production agriculture in one way or another is somewhat arbitrary, but while I understand the role played by environmentalists and other interested parties outside the agricultural economy who had strong philosophical and even spiritual interests in sustainable agriculture, it seems to me that they were more of a resource for than the drivers of the movement.

26. Ikerd, "On Defining Sustainable Agriculture," 1–2, 4. Ikerd specifically excludes "those who do not accept agriculture as a legitimate human activity." He is professor emeritus of Agricultural & Applied Economics at the University of Missouri. Compare this definition by rancher and philosopher Fred Kirchenmann: sustainable agriculture must be "ecologically restorative, socially resilient, and economically viable." "A Brief History of Sustainable Agriculture," Science & Environmental Health Network, *The Networker* (May 6, 2010), 2, http://www.sehn.org/Volume_9–2.html (accessed May 6, 2010).

27. Warner, *Agroecology at Work*, 3.

28. Frederick H. Buttel, "Ever since Hightower: The Politics of Agricultural Research Activism in the Molecular Age," *Agriculture and Human Values* 22 (Spring 2005): 277–78.

29. The literature on this subject is large and growing, but see in particular Eric T. Freyfogle, ed., *The New Agrarianism: Land, Culture, and the Community of Life*

(Washington, DC: Island Press, 2001); and Paul B. Thompson, *The Agrarian Vision: Sustainability and Environmental Ethics* (Lexington: University Press of Kentucky, 2010).

30. Beeman and Prichard, *A Green and Permanent Land*, 41.

31. http://ladyevebalfour.org/ (accessed September 11, 2012).

32. Quoted in Thompson, *The Agrarian Vision*, 20.

33. Aldo Leopold, *A Sand County Almanac, and Sketches from Here and There* (1949; New York: Oxford University Press, 1987), 262.

34. Frederick L. Kirschenmann, *Cultivating an Ecological Conscience: Essays from a Farmer Philosopher*, ed. Constance L. Falk (Lexington: University Press of Kentucky, 2010), 8.

35. Ibid., 99.

36. Ibid., 27.

37. Warner, *Agroecology at Work*, 9.

38. William Lockeretz, ed., *Organic Farming: An International History* (Cambridge, MA: CAB International, 2007), 51, 56; "The History of the Rodale Institute," http://www.rodaleinstitute.org/about_us (accessed May 6, 2012).

39. Warner, *Agroecology at Work*; Charles A. Francis, Raymond P. Poincelot, and George W. Bird, eds., *Developing and Extending Sustainable Agriculture: A New Social Contract* (New York: Haworth Food & Agricultural Products Press, 2006); Hassanein, *Changing the Way America Farms*.

40. For a quick introduction to the Jacksons and the Land Institute's development, see Scott Russell Sanders, "Learning from the Prairie," reprinted in *The New Agrarianism*, ed. Freyfogle, 3–15; Beeman and Pritchard, *A Green and Permanent Land*, 126–29; and Emily Q. Hazzard, "A Conversation with Wes Jackson, President of the Land Institute," *Atlantic Monthly* http://www.theatlantic.com/international/archive/2011/03/a-conversation-with-wes-jackson-president-of-the-land-institute/72927/#disqus_thread (accessed June 17, 2015); and various entries in the Land Institute's website at http://www.landinstitute.org (accessed June 13, 2012).

41. Tarrow, *Power in Movement*, 38–41.

42. Practitioners of agroecology put a greater emphasis on social responsibility than did many participants in the movement. The term "agroecology" was coined in Mexico by scientists who developed it as an alternative to the chemical-intensive framework of the Green Revolution. Mexican practitioners of agroecology employed ethnobotanical approaches in opposition to high-input practices. Warner, *Agroecology in Action*, 27; Stephen Gliessman, *Agroecology: Ecological Processes in Sustainable Agriculture* (Boca Raton, FL: CRC Press, 1997).

43. National Research Council, Committee on the Role of Alternative Farming Methods in Modern Production Agriculture, *Alternative Agriculture* (Washington, DC: National Academies Press, 1989). Thirteen of the seventeen members of the committee, including the chair, were faculty members and/or administrators at land-grant institutions.

44. The following description of legislation is drawn primarily from Beeman and Prichard, *A Green and Permanent Land*, 158–61.

45. Beeman and Prichard, *A Green and Permanent Land*, 160–61; http://www.sare.org (accessed June 2, 2012).

46. The current version of the SARE website outlines SARE's "3 Pillars of Sustainability" as "*Profit* over the long term, *Stewardship* of our land and water, and *Quality of life* for farmers, ranchers, and their communities." http://www.sare.org/ (accessed December 2, 2012).

47. Philip H. Howard, "Consolidation in the North American Organic Food Processing Sector, 1997 to 2007," *International Journal of Sociology of Agriculture and Food* 16, no. 1 (2009): 13–30.

48. Stephen R. Gliessman, *Agroecology: The Ecology of Sustainable Food Systems*, 2nd ed. (Boca Raton, FL: CRC Press, 2007), unpaginated preface to the second edition. The collaboration between agroecology and the core agricultural sciences that Gliessman describes has been taking place at the level of professional societies and the publication of monographs and journal articles.

49. Buttel, "Ever since Hightower," 280.

50. Agricultural Research Service, National Agricultural Library, *Educational and Training Opportunities in Sustainable Agriculture*, 20th ed. (Maryland: National Agricultural Library, 2012); "Student Farms in the US and Canada," Sustainable Agriculture Education Association, 2012, http://sustainableaged.org/Resources/StudentFarmDirectory/tabid/85/Default.aspx (accessed July 25, 2012); "Academic Programs," Sustainable Agriculture Education Association, 2012, http://sustainableaged.org/Resources/AcademicPrograms/tabid/86/Default.aspx (accessed July 2, 2012).

51. Kim Niewolny, personal communication with the author, December 29, 2012.

52. Ryan E. Galt, Damian Parr, Julia Van Soelen Kim, Jessica Beckett, Maggie Lickter, and Heidi Ballard, "Transformative Food Systems Education in a Land-Grant College of Agriculture: The Importance of Learner-Centered Inquiries," *Agriculture and Human Values*, June 23, 2012, http://link.springer.com/article/10.1007%2Fs10460–012-9384-8#page-1 (accessed July 2, 2012); C. A. Francis, N. Jordan, P. Porter, T. A. Breland, G. Lieblein, L. Salomonsson, N. Sriskandaraja, M. Wiedenhoeft, R. DeHaan, I. Braden, and V. Langer, "Innovative Education in Agroecology: Experiential Learning for a Sustainable Agriculture," *Critical Reviews in Plant Sciences* 30, no. 1–2 (2011): 226–37; Damian Michael Parr, "Student Farmer-to-Student Farmer" (PhD diss., University of California-Davis, 2009).

53. Laura Sayre, "The Student Farm Movement in Context," in *Fields of Learning: The Student Farm Movement in North America*, ed. Laura Sayre and Sean Clark (Lexington: University Press of Kentucky, 2011), 2–3.

54. Funding, the mother's milk of research and education, is difficult to determine for programs specifically focused on sustainable agriculture. But one *partial* measure of public and private funding in this field comes from an organization called Sustainable Agriculture and Food Systems Funders (SAFSF), whose goal is "to increase

support and funding for organizations that (i) promote sustainable food production; (ii) link to concerns about sustainability of our food system; and/or (iii) connect food production with issues of environmental stewardship, diet and health, and viability of rural communities." The SAFSF survey does *not* include all federal funding, including funding specifically for studying organic farming system. In 2003–6 (the last year for which SAFSF has provided data), the organization reported contributions of $213.6 million, with $62 million coming from USDA-Cooperative State Research, Education, and Extension Service (much of it passed along through SARE grants) and $53.6 million coming from the W. K. Kellogg Foundation. These funds are strategically important for sustainable agriculture, but they pale into insignificance alongside other governmental and corporate funding for agricultural education, research and development, and extension. www.safsf.org (accessed October 11, 2012). The 2006 report is found at http://www.safsf.org/documents/Ag Report Update 8–08.pdf.

55. Buttel, "Ever since Hightower," 280.

56. For one historical example of this debate within a movement, see Robert C. McMath Jr., *American Populism: A Social History* (New York: Hill and Wang, 1993).

57. The latter approach is spelled out in great detail based on the recent history of movement/land-grant interaction in Charles A. Francis, Raymond P. Poincelot, and George W. Bird, eds., *Developing and Extending Sustainable Agriculture: A New Social Contract* (New York: Haworth Food & Agricultural Products Press, 2006).

58. Charles A. Francis, "Future Multifunctional Rural Landscapes and Communities," in *Developing and Extending Sustainable Agriculture*, ed. Francis, Poincelot, and Bird, 329. The following discussion draws heavily on this essay and the volume of which it is a part.

59. Hazzard, "A Conversation with Wes Jackson."

60. "NIFA Fact Sheet," May 22, 2012. For more detail from the NIFA website, see http://www.crees.usda.gov (accessed July 19, 2012).

61. For an outstanding application of this question to twentieth-century movements in the United States, see Edwin Amenta, *When Movements Matter: The Townsend Plan and the Rise of Social Security* (Princeton: Princeton University Press, 2006).

62. See Michael Pollan, *The Omnivore's Dilemma: A Natural History of Four Meals* (New York: Penguin, 2006) and *In Defense of Food: An Eater's Manifesto* (New York: Penguin, 2008).

63. The relationship among movements, public opinion, and mission-focused federal agencies in modern America has not received the scholarly that it deserves. A major exception focusing on the early days of the modern era is Elisabeth S. Clemens, *The People's Lobby: Organizational Innovation and the Rise of Interest Group Politics in the United States, 1890–1925* (Chicago: University of Chicago Press, 1997).

12

Teaching Agricultural History at Land-Grant Institutions

R. Douglas Hurt

By creating and perpetuating a highly successful nationwide knowledge production and transmission system, the Morrill Act and subsequent legislation transformed American agriculture. That narrative has been especially vigorous since the 1970s. Recombinant DNA and other technologies seem to have converted farming from something farmers did into life science applied to the soil.

Hurt's essay ironically demonstrates just how extensive the idea of a vast transformation was. To modern-day college students, it rendered the agricultural past to the dustbin of history. Teaching about agricultural history before the transformation seems irrelevant, at best quaint or anachronistic. That transformative event provided a schism between the new and the old. Studying agriculture post-transformation seemed ahistorical; it seemed like common events, not an apt subject for historical investigation.

Hurt notes that even as universities disclaim interest in agricultural history courses, their offerings include numerous facets of the subject en passant. The tremendous change in farming practice has led many to declare its history moot, but questions of rural life and living persist. Communities struggle with change in all its manifestations. These issues continued to draw attention from land-grant academics and frequently spark disputes. That contemporary land-grant university faculties and students have embraced the notion that agriculture has been so radically and fundamentally transformed shows just how pervasively persuasive that Morrill Act narrative has been. Rural life remains an apt subject of concern, but now it rests in sociology, political science, and human ecology departments, departments that deliberately ignore or reject the past.

✲✲✲

The 150th anniversary of the Morrill Act presents an excellent opportunity to study the teaching of agricultural history at land-grant institutions. Justin Smith Morrill envisioned institutions of higher education that would teach students to "feed, clothe, and enlighten the great brotherhood of man." If one expands the "brotherhood of man" to include women, the teaching of agricultural history helps meet his goal of enlightening those who attend land-grant institutions so that they might learn and lead productive and meaningful lives. More specifically, Section 4 of the Morrill Act authorized the creation of land-grant institutions "to promote the liberal and practical education of the industrial classes in the several pursuits and professions in life." A liberal education certainly means the inclusion of history courses, and it should include the study of agricultural history. Students at land-grant institutions and more than a few of their professors apparently could benefit from an agricultural history course. At the University of Florida plant scientist Ida Altman reported that "The subject is neglected," and she had to prod the task force charged with preparing a Morrill Act anniversary celebration to remember the historical context in which the university was founded.[1]

The history of American agriculture as a recognized field of study dates from the early twentieth century. In 1914, Louis B. Schmidt apparently taught the first agricultural history course in the United States at Iowa State College. Since that time the teaching of agricultural history has occurred unevenly at best. In 1985, Monroe Billington, professor of history at New Mexico State University, investigated whether anyone taught agricultural history at land-grant institutions. He surveyed seventy-four such universities founded under the Morrill acts of 1862 and 1890 and those created by amendments to that legislation. He found that the land-grant institutions essentially ignored the teaching of agricultural history. The responses to his survey indicated that fifty-six institutions did not offer such a course, while forty-four institutions had never offered a course in agricultural history. Twelve institutions had dropped it for lack of student interest or qualified faculty to teach it or as a result of curriculum revision. At the institutions where a department of history offered an agricultural history course about half the respondents said that its future looked bright, but half reported a bleak prospect for its continuation. Five institutions reported that the future of the course ranged from good to excellent or firm and secure. One respondent, however, cogently noted that the course at his institution was "less likely to stay alive over the next generation." Others reported a "murky" or "uncertain" future and that student interest remained "limited" and doubtful. Agricultural colleges did not seem interested in supporting the course with its majors.[2]

Billington concluded that "agricultural history as a teaching field in the nation's institutions of higher learning is barely alive" because over three-fourths of the land-grant institutions did not offer it. No institution planned to offer an agricultural history course if it was not currently taught. Where instruction occurred, its existence remained precarious. Billington concluded that historians did not consider agricultural history a "respectable teaching field." Given the absence of trained agricultural historians, he warned that if others did not retool and teach the subject the result would be "the essential death of agricultural history as a teaching field in the nation's institutions of higher learning."[3]

In order to learn about the state of agricultural history as a teaching field today at land-grant institutions nearly thirty years after Billington conducted his survey, I contacted the chairs or heads of the respective departments of history, consulted departmental web pages, corresponded with faculty who might have a recollection about agricultural history offerings in the past, and researched selected histories of the land-grant colleges and universities. I surveyed fifty-six land-grant universities that were founded under the authorization of the Morrill Act of 1862 and its amendments. I, too, discovered that today agricultural history is seldom taught anywhere. Only five departments of history at these institutions currently teach agricultural history in some fashion. I also surveyed the eighteen historically Black land-grant institutions that date from the Second Morrill Act of 1890. Agricultural history is not taught and apparently never has been taught at those institutions. I did not survey the twenty-nine Indian institutions supported by the Equity in Educational Land-Grant Status Act of 1994, which brought them into the system.[4]

Some department chairs recommended that I contact their agricultural colleges because agricultural history courses might be taught there. This response indicates several things. First, their departments have little contact with agricultural colleges. Second, they do not know what is taught beyond their own college curricula. Third, they apparently do not care whether an agricultural history course is taught beyond their history departments.

Or, in the words of one chair at a historically Black land-grant university who spoke for many departments at all land-grant institutions: "If it was [taught], it had to be long, long ago." Some department chairs reflected that if agricultural history had ever been offered in their departments it had not been taught within memory, meaning at least two decades and in one case not during the previous forty-five years. The reasons why agricultural history is not taught at the land-grant institutions also reveal a good deal about curriculum, professional training, and urbanization as well as demographic change. Some respondents confessed that no one on the faculty was a member of the Agricultural History Society. This comment in itself tells us much about the state of the field for both teaching and scholarship for agricultural history as a self-identifying category.[5]

Most respondents, however, could not recall whether anyone had taught a stand-alone course in agricultural history. Some respondents speaking for the department said that they did not intend to offer such courses. This response is deceptive, however, because several departments reported that they planned to offer courses titled "Food in History" or "Rural History," none of which can be taught, of course, without discussing a variety of issues related to agricultural history. Many respondents also reported that their faculty discussed some agricultural history topics in their survey and specialty courses, particularly environmental history. The agricultural history taught in the survey courses, however, tends to be superficially covered with passing references to slavery, the Homestead Act, sharecropping (but not necessarily tenancy), Populism, and New Deal agricultural policies, the latter usually regarding the Agricultural Adjustment Act of 1933, Resettlement Administration, and Farm Security Administration. Environmental issues related to agriculture have not yet been adequately included in survey textbooks, if at all.[6]

The problem is, in part, that few historians profess any knowledge or interest in agricultural history. If they have any, it usually involves, for example, specific knowledge about some aspect of social, immigration, race, or gender history. But they do not have much general knowledge about agricultural history. This can be explained for several reasons. First, the United States is an urban nation. More people live in the towns and cities than in the countryside, particularly on farms, and their interests are seldom agricultural. Second, the historical profession focuses on issues that, even if they are not urban, are not necessarily perceived as agricultural. The training of PhDs in history seldom involves coursework, research, or dissertations in agricultural history, even broadly conceived. Many scholars, historians included, have written dissertations and published books, articles, and essays in the field, some may be members of the Agricultural History Society, but most do not teach courses in agricultural history because of a perceived lack of student or personal interest.

This is not to say that agricultural history has not been taught at land-grant institutions where it currently does not constitute part of the curriculum. No one at Cornell University, for example, has taught agricultural history for thirty years. Between 1903 and 1913 George Lauman apparently taught an agricultural history course in the College of Agriculture at the request or at least with the support of Liberty Hyde Bailey, who served as dean of the college. G. P. Colman reports that Lauman "collected much source material . . . but few students." Colman attempted to revive the course during the early 1960s as the college historian, but the faculty in the Department of Agricultural Economics "dismissed the subject as useless." During the 1980s when a dozen students petitioned to have the dean reinstate the course, Colman and Gene Erikson, chair of the Department of Rural Sociology, offered it but the course ended after a single term because only three students enrolled. Paul Wallace Gates never taught the course.[7]

Cornell is interesting in another aspect. Although I only asked whether agricultural history had been taught or was being taught in the department, to which the answers in this case essentially were "perhaps" and "no," the department apparently did not know or did not choose to report that Margaret Rossiter, the Marie Underhill Noll Professor of the History of Science in the Science and Technology Studies Program, taught a course titled "Agriculture, History, and Society: From Squanto to Biotechnology" as an American studies course. Many considerations are, no doubt, involved when decisions are made to offer agricultural history courses beyond departments of history.[8]

Agricultural history as a stand-alone course has not been taught at the University of Wisconsin since Morton Rothstein departed for the University of California-Davis, where he served as the editor of *Agricultural History*. Allan Bogue did not teach the course but he incorporated "a lot" of agricultural history in his Western history course. At North Dakota State University David Danbom taught the "History of Rural America" for many years. Occasionally he also taught "US Agricultural History" and "World Agricultural and Rural Systems." When he retired, however, these courses were not continued. At Colorado State University, the Department of History offered agricultural history during the 1940s and 1950s. From 1938 through 1941, Robert G. Dunbar taught "Social History of American Agriculture." In 1942 he changed the title to "History of American Agriculture." Dunbar also taught "History of Agricultural Institutions" from 1945 through 1947. Several years later, from 1955 to 1959, John C. McKinnon taught "History of American Agriculture" and from 1949 to 1959 "History of Irrigation in the United States." After his death in 1959 these courses were not taught again at Colorado State. At another western institution, William Rowley once taught the course for two or three years at the University of Nevada-Reno, but he transformed it into "American Environmental History." The Department of History at Washington State University at one time offered "American Agriculture and Rural Life," but it has not been taught since the fall of 2007 when the instructor retired. The department chair did not "anticipate it being offered again in the near future." At Montana State Tom Wessel regularly taught agricultural history, but when he retired, the department no longer offered it for lack of faculty expertise.[9]

At the University of Kentucky David Hamilton taught an agricultural history course twice under the auspices of a Kellogg Foundation grant, after which other duties required his attention. Mary Wilma Hargreaves, a past president of the Agricultural History Society, however, integrated agricultural history into her two-semester sequence on US economic history and Thomas Clark did so as well in his southern history courses. At the University of Minnesota, Rodney Loehr, a Fellow of the Agricultural History Society, along with Phil Jordan, another agricultural economist, taught agricultural history but the course was not continued after they retired in the 1970s. At Michigan State Thomas Summerhill once taught a special topics course titled "America's Rural Past," but no one has offered it regularly and "only as special topics and rarely."[10]

To the south at Auburn University president Bradford Knapp advocated the teaching of agricultural history course during the 1920s, but it is not clear whether anyone taught it. In the immediate post–World War II years, probably during or after 1948, the department offered a course titled "History of Agriculture" that covered the period from "ancient times to the present." It was taught for one quarter, but reportedly "the Ag School found no use for it, and it quickly disappeared." This statement is troubling because the course was offered by the department of history. Perhaps the agricultural college did not recognize these credit hours in history for its degree programs. Aaron Shapiro, however, began offering a course titled

"Agriculture and Forest History" as a special topics course on an occasional basis beginning in 2008. In 2012 the department prepared to make it a regular course with an independent number.[11]

At Virginia Tech Tom Dunlap taught the course after his arrival in 1975. The earliest catalog for the department dates from the 1981–82 academic year, and it lists a course titled "American Agriculture since 1865." At some point it became "History of American Agriculture," and Dunlap taught it regularly until he left Virginia Tech in 1991. Thereafter, a faculty member in one of the agriculture departments taught the course until the fall of 2007, after which he retired. The repeated response that the few agricultural history courses offered were discontinued upon the death or retirement of the instructor indicates that an older generation of historians taught these courses and that little interest followed them as their departments hired in other areas.[12]

This response implies several things. The discipline of history has changed. Areas of interest come and go. If agricultural history was once popular, it no longer remains a compelling teaching field, and these courses have faded from memory and apparently the written record. Today social, political, and gender history courses, among others, capture the most attention. Although agricultural history is, or at least can be, part of these subject areas, few historians consider it central to their subdiscipline. This is important because, as Joëlle Rollo-Koster, chair of the Department of History at the University of Rhode Island, reported, "many of us do agricultural history even though we do not call it as such." She identifies the issue as one of "historiographical proportion." For her, "the term agriculture is not used but the methodology is." She, for example, spends three weeks on the eleventh-century agricultural revolution in her course titled "European Middle Ages." The specialist in ancient history covers agricultural history when discussing slavery and the Gracchi of Rome as do the Americanists in their courses on the eighteenth and nineteenth centuries. Rollo-Koster contends that "the interesting questions that used to be categorized in agricultural history are now covered by environmental historians." Moreover, she rightfully argues that the followers of the Annales School do agricultural history even though they do not call it as such as do scholars of environmental and social history. "So," she writes, "it is all a question of historiography."[13]

The teaching of agricultural history in some fashion at the University of Rhode Island reflects how the subject is taught at other institutions where Europeanists, Americanists, and Asianists cover agricultural history to some extent in their courses. At Rhode Island a course on industrialization includes discussion of the market economy, meatpacking, ranching, and the fast-food lifestyles of contemporary American culture. Another faculty member responded that s/he talked quite extensively about rice growing and slash-and-burn agriculture and other topics related to agricultural history. In a related manner, since the early 1990s, Penn State has offered a course titled "The American Food System: History, Technology, and Culture." It is cross listed with the Department of Nutrition. Sally McMurry reported that "When it was first taught, the ag. college was not too enthusiastic about it. . . . [I]n this year's class (2012) there are no students from the ag. college."[14]

These responses, however, can give those who care about the teaching of agricultural history some hope and comfort that it is indeed taught in some fashion and context. At Mississippi State University, for example, where agricultural history also has not been taught as a stand-alone course, the department recently created a course titled "Rural History" in the hope of attracting more students than if it titled the course "Agricultural History." Jeannie Whayne at the University of Arkansas also taught agricultural history as a "special topics" course, and she planned to have it on the books for regular offering by the 2013–14 academic year. In addition, agricultural history as a stand-alone course remained secure at Iowa State, Kansas State, and Purdue universities. At Kansas State Homer E. Socolofsky taught the course in the 1960s, and Bonnie Lynn-Sherow continued that tradition. A two-semester survey course and graduate seminars in agricultural history also have been taught regularly at Iowa State University by James Whitaker, Doug Hurt, and Pamela Riney-Kehrberg and several graduate students since the 1970s.[15]

Beyond the departments of history at the land-grant institutions, it is worth noting that agricultural history is occasionally taught in other departments where such courses may be overlooked because they are not taught in history departments but agricultural economics or rural sociology departments. The Department of Rural Sociology at Ohio State University provides an example. There, the department offers courses titled "Women in Rural Society" and "Sociology of Agriculture and Food Systems." In 2006 Debra Reid, an agricultural historian and faculty member at Eastern Illinois University, began teaching "History of Agriculture in Illinois since 1860" for the College of Agriculture, Consumer and Environmental Science at the University of Illinois. In 2012 she transformed it into an online course and offers it regularly with the primary enrollment of agriculture and engineering students. At the University of Missouri the Department of Agricultural Education offers a course titled "Orientation to Agricultural History." At Purdue University in addition to the course "History of United States Agriculture," offered by the Department of History, the College of Agriculture offers an Honors Seminar to incoming freshmen and the organizing theme often is historical. During the fall semester of 2012, the "seminar" with some ninety students strong considered the historical implications of drought.[16]

But no one should assume that because agricultural history is seldom taught as a stand-alone course that the subject is not taught at the vast majority of the land-grant universities because students are not interested in the subject. They are. The real question is, which students? Agriculture majors often show a great deal of interest in the course. When such courses help meet humanities or core requirements, enrollments are not a problem. This is understandable because agriculture majors want to study a history that relates to their chosen fields as well as learn more about their agricultural past, particularly if they do not come from or have work experience on farms. Agriculture majors are far different from a century ago when a degree in "agriculture" meant a general survey of many subjects. Today the agriculture colleges offer a wide variety of specialty degrees, such as animal science, agribusiness, landscape design, turf science, agronomy, agricultural education, horticulture, plant genetics, and soil and crop management. Nonagriculture majors often are interested in agricultural history if they have or had grandparents or relatives who lived on a farm, or because they considered it a curiosity.

Today land-grant institutions are more popular among students than they have been in decades. At these institutions the tuition is lower than at private universities, at least for in-state students, and the job-oriented focus on science, engineering, and agricultural specializations that range widely have attracted more students than ever before. Invariably, core and major curriculums require a certain number of credit hours in the humanities, and history courses often constitute part of the menu for selection. If agricultural history courses are not included on these lists, students still find agricultural history courses educational and highly desirable. This is of consequence because undergraduate agriculture students have dramatically increased in numbers at many land-grant institutions and many, if not most, of those students are not from farm backgrounds.[17]

The field of agricultural history, of course, has changed over the years— or rather the interests of agricultural historians have changed over time— and we should expect it to continue to change. To the extent that agricultural history is taught at land-grant institutions today, it tends to be offered as part of technology, social, and environmental history courses. In the past, the emphasis in agricultural history was institutional, political, social, and economic. Environmental history as agricultural history may strengthen the subject for teaching and research, but agricultural history per se already has been established as a poor cousin. In this survey one department reported that for a recent environmental job search, two candidates had dissertations that were judged agricultural history, and they were rejected as not significant to the field. Although the strength of those candidates and their dissertations may well have merited rejection, the suggestion that agricultural history was not part of the main focus of environmental history indicates problems of identification and for research and publication. Some university presses, for example, that once had a distinguished reputation for publishing important works in agricultural history now only consider the subject if it can be cast as environmental history.[18]

Although this discussion has related to the teaching of American—or U.S.—agricultural history, only Mark Tauger at West Virginia University apparently teaches a course on world agricultural history at a land-grant institution. He has done so for more than a decade, and he has published a book on that subject titled *Agriculture in World History*. Today, land-grant institutions increasingly require an international component for their majors. A course in world agricultural history, if it could be counted as part of the core or general education requirements for students, might be well received.[19]

With the economy was volatile during the recent past, public and private institutions have hired fewer assistant professors in various fields of history, and the immediate future does not bode well for the expansion of history courses, let alone the offering of agricultural history. If the teaching of agricultural history at the land-grant institutions increases it probably will depend on the faculty already employed in the departments of history, although this statement does not preclude the potential offering of such courses by new hires. But the important issue to remember is that agricultural history as a field has been remarkably adaptable and inclusive of other subfields.[20]

In 1914, for example, Louis B. Schmidt urged scholars to study agriculture history to help government officials provide solutions to problems that were becoming increasingly economic rather than political. Schmidt believed historians had given too much attention to political, military, and religious history, and he considered the economic history of agriculture a new and exciting subject for historical inquiry. Schmidt recognized the limitless topical nature of such work, because so little had been done. He urged historians to investigate land, immigration, tariff, currency, and banking policy as well as organized labor, corporate regulation, slavery, and the influences of agriculture, broadly conceived, on the development of national life.[21]

Schmidt called on the first generation of professionally trained historians, who intended to make history more useful and relevant and whose interests often involved economic causation, to interpret the present "in light of economic and social evolution." Schmidt wrote, "Viewed in one way the history of the United States from the beginning has been in a very large measure the story of rural communities advancing westward by the conquest of the soil, developing from a state of primitive self-sufficiency to a capitalist and highly complex agricultural organization." Clearly he had been influenced by the frontier thesis of Frederick Jackson Turner, who saw the American experience continually remade as settlers moved west across the continent. In the best tradition of the ancient Greek historian Polybius, Schmidt also expected the economic history of American agriculture to provide useful lessons for the present. He believed that "Government action involving agricultural interests should be based on a broad knowledge of rural economic history" and that agricultural history was "indispensable to a correct understanding of much of our political and diplomatic history." Fundamentally, the study and teaching of agricultural history provided lessons of cause and effect in American history. In many respects Schmidt foresaw the emergence in the distant future of what would be called the new rural history. He contended that agricultural history should be "viewed not in the strict or narrow sense, but in the broad sense so as to include the whole life of the rural population, the influences which have affected its progress and the influence its progress has in turn had on the course of events." The result, Schmidt believed, would lead to "a well-balanced history of our nation."[22]

Whether Schmidt also urged his colleagues, peers, and other historians to follow his example and teach agricultural history courses remains unknown, but many scholars, often not historians, accepted his challenge to make agricultural history a research field, and it has enjoyed considerable, often decadal or at least generational, change ever since. Schmidt and those who followed him believed that agricultural history should be broad, that is to say, using the context of the twenty-first century, interdisciplinary and transnational. This approach resonates today and enables agricultural historians not only to practice their craft in a most productive and significant manner but also to integrate agricultural history into courses not specifically designated for that subject matter. This is important because most scholars who teach about agricultural history in some fashion are not agricultural historians. Yet those scholars who come to agricultural history from other fields and disciplines indicate the vibrancy of the field that dates from the early twentieth century when Schmidt began teaching the course at Iowa State.

Indeed, many scholars who pursued agricultural history during the early twentieth century were not historians by training or even academics. Rodney H. True, the first president of the Agricultural History Society, was a botanist, and Lyman Carrier, the first secretary-treasurer, an economist. Economists, rural sociologists, biologists, librarians, and journalists, many of whom were employed by the United States Department of Agriculture, also joined the society, whose modest purpose was "To stimulate interest, promote the study and facilitate the publication of researches in the history of agriculture"—a goal that remains unchanged today. At first economists constituted the largest group in the Agricultural History Society after its founding on February 14, 1919, at the Cosmos Club in Washington, DC; they dominated the organization until 1945, after which historians constituted the largest disciplinary group. This early demographic membership by discipline also tells us much about the teaching of agricultural history at the college and university level, because many of these early scholars taught the subject within the context of their own disciplines and not as members of departments of history.[23]

The multidisciplinary and later interdisciplinary interests of those who study American agricultural history, for both teaching and research, however, have kept the field amorphous and unstructured, although much of the published work has emphasized economic and political affairs. Indeed, American agricultural history remains a field where the definition of it has been vague and its boundaries limitless, particularly with the emergence of the new rural social history as a subfield during the 1970s and now environmental history in the early twenty-first century. Even so, agricultural historiography (and its teaching as reflected in survey textbooks) has made its greatest contributions to understanding the American experience in eight major areas: (1) land policy, including tenancy; (2) the South for slavery and tenancy; (3) agricultural organizations, particularly the People's Party; (4) the development of commercial agriculture; (5) government policy; (6) rural social history; (7) migrant labor; and (8) women's history. Whether environmental history develops as a similar subfield of agricultural history remains to be seen, but the future for the teaching of agricultural history at land-grant institutions may be with environmental history.[24]

Today agricultural history remains as diffuse in its teaching and topical emphasis as it did at the formal founding of the field with the organization of the Agricultural History Society. Historians, geographers, economists, sociologists, political scientists, anthropologists, and others teach and write agricultural history. By so doing, they help provide interdisciplinary perspective to explain the past. But the interdisciplinary diversity of the field remains both a strength and a weakness. It is beneficial to the field because a variety of scholarly disciplines have provided valuable perspectives about the past from many vantage points for nearly a century. The result has been an important interdisciplinary consideration of a host of topics—science, technology, production, marketing, government policy, religion, race, class, gender, the family, and the environment—in relation to American agricultural history. The weakness has been that these scholars often do not see themselves as part of a coherent whole, that is, as agricultural historians. Put differently, many people teach or write about agricultural history, but they do not consider themselves agricultural historians. Their work often remains isolated in their own subdisciplines, such as labor, social, economic, political, or environmental history, rather than as agricultural historians within the profession. This phenomenon is due, in part, to the urban nature of American society and training of most historians.[25]

Indeed, the teaching of agricultural history in the United States remains incredibly undervalued, particularly at land-grant institutions. Yet many historians teach agricultural history without admitting or realizing it, probably because they see the field as pejoratively narrow for their self-definition and professional advancement and too far beyond the mainstream concerns of scholars working in American history on "Big History" projects to willfully accept such self-identification. But this is a problem of training, location, residence, and periodic change of emphasis in their teaching and research fields, not because the field lacks scholarly legitimacy. However the parts are defined, agricultural history itself remains an important subfield in American historical inquiry and for teaching at land-grant institutions.[26]

James H. Shideler, who served as editor of *Agricultural History* from 1965 to 1984, recognized the problem of field identification. Remarkably, Shideler did not consider agricultural history a field of study, and he apparently never taught such a course at the University of California-Davis. For Shideler agricultural history meant the study of production agriculture and nothing more. He wrote: "Agricultural history, broadly defined, is diffuse, discursive, and incoherent; it has no discipline, no unique methodology. It is not even a sub discipline." Shideler affirmed the opinion of Everett E. Edwards, who earlier contended that the Agricultural History Society intended its study to be interdisciplinary and "to promote the field as a contribution to the better understanding of history in general rather than to set it apart as a separate discipline."[27]

Shideler, however, was not the first historian to lament the amorphousness of American agricultural history as a field. In 1948, Rodney Loehr went so far as to say that "The history of agriculture merges insensibly into the totality of human experience." Moreover, in 1973, Clarence Danhof, as president of the Agricultural History Society, worried that the goals of the organization as stated in the constitution were "so inclusive as to provide virtually no restraints upon the use of the very resources available and little guidance to the selection of research objectives." He argued for a tighter, more restrictive definition of agricultural history. "Would not our small guild be able to make a greater contribution if we could agree on a set of boundaries less inclusive in character and more sharply defining the end products we seek for our efforts?" he asked. Fortunately scholars ignored this call for restricting the field by imposing artificial parameters that limited subjects that could be legitimately considered agricultural history. In fact, scholars expanded rather than limited their interests in the field by broadening it to include rural social history in its many manifestations. Today the increasing emphasis of agricultural history as part of the field of environmental history merely continues the tradition of periodic change of interests and emphasis. The teaching and scholarship in the field will be the richer for it.[28]

Certainly any definition of American agricultural history as a field for teaching and research will be as diverse as the individuals asked to provide one. Yet because many scholars teach and work in the field of agricultural story but do not consider themselves agricultural historians, it is best for them to remember the words of Alfred Lord Tennyson who wrote in "Ulysses" that "that which we are, we are."[29]

NOTES

1. Act of July 2, 1862, ch. 130, 12 *U.S. Statutes at Large* 503, 7 U.S.C. 301 et seq ; Wayne D. Rasmussen, ed., "The First Morrill Act, 1862," in *Agriculture in the United States: A Documentary History* (New York: Random House, 1975), 2:616–18; "Celebrating 150 Years of Public Higher Education: The Morrill Act at 150," *Association of Public and Land-Grant Universities*, http://www.aplu.org (accessed November 28, 2012); Lawrence Biemiller, "As Land-Grant Law Turns 150, Students Crowd into Agriculture Colleges," *Chronicle of Higher Education*, June 22, 2012, 10; Vassiliki Betty Smocovitis, University of Florida, to the author, March 3, 2012.

2. Monroe Billington, "Teaching Agricultural History at Land-Grant Institutions," *OAH Newsletter* 14 (August 1986): 12–13.

3. Ibid., 13.

4. For a list of the land-grant institutions, see Coy F. Cross II, *Justin Smith Morrill: Father of the Land-Grant Colleges* (East Lansing: Michigan State University Press, 1999), 90–92; Act of August 30, 1890, ch. 841, 26 *U.S. Statues at Large* 503, 7 U.S.C. 301 et seq; Wayne D. Rasmussen, "Second Morrill Act for Agricultural Colleges, 1890," in *Agriculture in the United States*, 2:1258–60; "Equity in Educational Land-Grant Status Act of 1994," http://ifas.ufl.edu/land_grant_history/native.html (accessed September 26, 2012). The departments of history at the following 1862 land-grant institutions responded to my inquiry: Auburn University; Clemson University; Colorado State University; Cornell University; Iowa State University; Kansas State University; Michigan State University; Mississippi State University; Montana State University; New Mexico State University; Ohio State University; Oklahoma State University; Oregon State University; Penn State University; Rutgers University; South Dakota State University; University of Alaska; University of Arkansas; University of Delaware; University of Florida; University of Idaho; University of Illinois; University of Kentucky; University of Maine; University of Maryland; University of Massachusetts; University of Minnesota; University of Nebraska; University of Nevada-Reno; University of New Hampshire; University of Rhode Island; University of Tennessee; University of Vermont; University of Wyoming; Utah State University; Virginia Tech University; Washington State University; and West Virginia University. The following departments of history at the 1890 land-grant institutions responded to my inquiry: Alcorn State University; Delaware State University; Florida A&M University; Fort Valley State University; Prairie View A&M; Tuskegee Institute; University of the District of Columbia; and West Virginia State University.

5. Billy Peyton, West Virginia State University, to the author, June 13, 2012; David Jackson, Florida A&M University, to the author, June 14, 2012; Richard Spence, University of Idaho, to the author, March 6, 2012; John Hurt, University of Delaware, to the author, March 6, 2012; Fred R. Hartesveldt, Fort Valley State University, to the author, June 14, 2012; Richard Judd, University of Missouri, to the author, June 5, 2012; Thomas E. Burman, University of Tennessee, to the author, June 5, 2012; Jan Golinski, University of New Hampshire, to the author, June 6, 2012; Paul Clemens,

Rutgers University, to the author, June 14, 2012; Will Guzman, Florida A&M University, to the author, August 14, 2012; James Massachaele, Rutgers University, to the author, June 7, 2012.

6. Gary B. Cohen, University of Minnesota, to the author, June 6, 2012; Marla R. Miller, University of Massachusetts, to the author, June 5, 2012; Gerald McFarland, University of Massachusetts, to the author, June 5, 2012; Michael Carl Brose, University of Wyoming, to the author, June 5, 2012; Jan Galinski, University of New Hampshire, to the author, June 6, 2012.

7. G. P. Colman to the author, September 17, 2012.

8. Barry Straus, Cornell University, to the author, June 5, 2012; Cornell University website, http://vivo.cornell.edu/display/individaual 5314 (accessed August 27, 2012).

9. Allan Bogue to the author, September 30, 2012. The Department of History at Wisconsin did not respond to my query. John Cox, North Dakota State University, to the author, August 27, 2012; David Danbom to the author, September 11, 2012; James Hanson, Colorado State University, to the author, August 31 and September 10, 2012; Bill Rowley, University of Nevada, Reno, to the author, August 27, 2012, Raymond C. Sun, Washington State University, to the author, June 13, 2012; David Cherry, Montana State University, to the author, June 4, 2014.

10. David Hamilton, University of Kentucky, to the author, June 6, 2012; Gary B. Cohen, University of Minnesota, to the author, June 6, 2012; Walter Hawthorne, Michigan State University, to the author, June 5 and 6, 2012.

11. Robert R. Rea, *History at Auburn: The First One Hundred Years of the Auburn University History Department* (Auburn, AL: Auburn University, 1991), p. 48; Charles Israel, Auburn University, to the author, June 6, 2012.

12. Mark Barrow, University of Vermont, to the author, June 5, 2012.

13. Joëlle Rollo-Koster, University of Rhode Island, to the author, June 4 and 5, 2012.

14. Rollo-Koster to the author, June 5, 2012; Hawthorne to the author, June 5, 2012; Sally McMurry, Penn State University, to the author, August 27, 2012.

15. April Brooks, South Dakota State University, to the author, June 4, 2012; Will Thomas, University of Nebraska, to the author, June 20, 2012; James C. Giesen, Mississippi State University, to the author, June 4, 2012; Jeannie Whayne, University of Arkansas, to the author, August 27, 2012; Louise Breen, Kansas State University, to the author, June 6, 2012; Bonnie Lynn-Sherow, Kansas State University, to the author, August 27, 2012.

16. Personal recollections of the author from serving on graduate committees in the Department of Rural Sociology, 1978–86; http://registrar.osu.edu/courses/index.asp (accessed November 28, 2012); Debra Reid, Eastern Illinois University, to the author, November 11, 2012; Russell Zguta, University of Missouri, to the author, June 4, 2012.

17. Biemiller, "As Land-Grant Law Turns 150," pp. 10–11, 22.

18. Richard Judd, University of Maine, to the author, June 5, 2012; Norman Jones, Utah State University, to the author, June 4, 2012.

19. Mark Tauger, West Virginia University, to the author, August 27, 2012.

20. Robert Townsend, "History Salaries Lag behind Inflation and the Rest of Academia," *Perspectives in History* 50 (May 2012): 12.

21. Hereafter I draw on my article "Reflections on American Agricultural History," *Agricultural History Review* 52, pt. 1 (2004): 1–19; Wayne D. Rasmussen, "The Growth of Agricultural History," in *Support of Clio: Essays in Memory of Herbert A. Keller*, ed. William B. Hasseltine and Donald R. McNeil (Madison: State Historical Society of Wisconsin, 1958), 162; and Louis B. Schmidt, "The Economic History of American Agriculture as a Field of Study," *Mississippi Valley Historical Review* 3 (June 1916): 40.

22. Schmidt, "The Economic History of American Agriculture," 40–41, 43, 48.

23. Arthur G. Peterson, "The Agricultural History Society's First Quarter Century," *Agricultural History* 19 (October 1945): 193–95; Wayne D. Rasmussen, "Forty Years of Agricultural History," *Agricultural History* 33 (October 1959): 177; Harold D. Woodman, "The State of Agricultural History," in *The State of American History*, ed. Herbert J. Bass (Chicago: Quadrangle Books, 1970), 220–24.

24. Woodman, "The State of Agricultural History," 220. For an example, see John L. Shover, *First Majority—Last Minority: The Transforming of Rural Life in America* (DeKalb: Northern Illinois University Press, 1976).

25. Hurt, "Reflections on American Agricultural History," 17

26. Ibid., 18.

27. James H. Shideler, "Agricultural History Studies: A Retrospective View," in *Outstanding in His Field: Perspectives on American Agriculture in Honor of Wayne D. Rasmussen*, ed. Frederick V. Carstensen, Morton Rothstein, and Joseph A. Swanson (Ames: Iowa State University Press, 1993), 3–4. The University of California-Davis did not respond to my inquiry.

28. Rodney C. Loehr, Agriculture and History," *Journal of Farm Economics* 30 (August 1948): 537; Clarence H. Danhof, "Wither Agricultural History," *Agricultural History* 47 (January 1973): 2.

29. Hurt, "Reflections on American Agricultural History," 19; Alfred Tennyson, "Ulysses," in *Complete Poetical Works of Alfred Tennyson* (Boston: J. R. Osgood, 1872), 81.

Conclusion

Managing the present and future has become the mainstay of the contemporary land-grant university. Management is not just a teaching stratagem. It cuts through every aspect of the land-grant experience. Research is undertaken to manage change, to resolve some perceived insufficiency or inequity. It is also the heart of what has become known as engagement, the very special responsibility of land-grants to serve private and public stakeholders as well as governmental units. Management in these cases relies on a vision of relative scarcity; things need to be managed to do more with less or no more. It is an effort to expand benefits without a corresponding input of additional resources. Management here assumes that waste or inefficiency has been part and parcel of virtually all activities and that tangible benefits can be wrung out by eliminating those two bugaboos.

Such a vision is surely not humanistic. It decides all matters in the name of efficiency. The most efficient solution is the most elegant solution and the most effective solution. It holds no truck with any other form of adjudication. It is the very essence of science, the application of a precise set of discrete principles to all problems, no matter their character.

Science has long been at the center of the land-grant university but management has become its touchstone only relatively recently. Other metrics have predated it. A sense of limits or scarcity did not figure prominently in them. Seemingly limitless possibilities often served as the earlier delineator. Employing the rigid template of science—but not management—to the problems of farmers enabled land-grants initially to carve out a place for themselves in late nineteenth-century America. Its purveyors demonstrated first to farmers and then others that science held the power to improve their yields, their farmsteads, and even their families. Science became the mechanism, basis, and means that the national government employed to establish a national land-grant system around the turn of the century and science served as the cudgel that enabled the states to regain a strong measure of autonomy in the much less distant past. Land-grant science and technology helped America lead the Allies to victory in World War II, made possible the rapid rebuilding of Europe and Japan, and helped make over the world in the war's aftermath. Land-grant science and technology were pillars of what would become known as the military-industrial complex and were instrumental in winning the Cold War. Those same universities fostered a mid-twentieth-century agricultural revolution in America and abroad and fueled rapid and pervasive industrialization in Third World countries. Land-grants welcomed the elites of almost every country to study in the United States and trained more men and women in the sciences and engineering than any other entity. In effect, land-grants established the scientific and technological infrastructure for the entire world. The mechanical contrivances upon which twenty-first-century humanity relies are primarily products of land-grants, run and maintained by land-grant-trained operatives and their students.

In all of these and other endeavors, land-grants avidly participated in the making and reshaping of the modern world. From at least 1930, however, the activities of the land-grants have taken on a characteristically American hue. They are the embodiment of the American presumption that any situation or condition can be fixed or at least mitigated. There are no problems too difficult or too big to handle. Everything can be made better or more palatable, and since it is possible, it is unconscionable not to act. The key to that perspective is that action in the present can and will lead to a modified, improved future. This fundamental tenet of twentieth- and twenty-first-century Americanism persisted through World War II, Vietnam, and the Cold War and continues to influence American foreign policy as the nation's repeated dalliance in the Middle East attests. It characterizes our politics and the passion with which we cling to our beliefs, faith, and bigotries. It is who Americans have become.

It is a profoundly optimistic sentiment. It often results in an equally naïve assessment. Since change seems possible, then change is desirable, essential. Action taken in the present can yield a future without the problem that demanded action. In short, things can be improved simply by taking direct action.

Almost as critical, the mechanisms to take this action seem readily available. Land-grants and contrivances created or discovered by land-grant personnel or graduates constitute a storehouse of expertise, talent, and productions. Even government depends on the land-grant trough for land-grant-derived science and technology, some of which appears likely to come to bear on almost any problem. Land-grants themselves embrace the challenge to form the future and move aggressively to remedy virtually every announced annoyance, condition, or situation that can conceivably fall under their purview.

Such an approach works best in the abstract. It focuses almost exclusively on materialist concerns. It relegates problems and resolutions to tangible matters and applies one type of standard—science and technology—to every issue, without regard to its essentialist character.

This reductionist framework is problematic, but it disguises an even more glaring flaw. It reduces American society to a monolith. Just as it negates all forms of evaluation except science, it also presupposes either that the situations, conditions, and irritations occur without reference to any external factors or that all segments of American society understand these variances similarly.

It is the latter assumption that proves most troublesome. It maintains that action to resolve something will not have repercussions, that those repercussions are easily ameliorable or that the repercussions are unimportant. None is remotely true. America has championed the idea of equality, that each person's or group's concerns has merit. Change often impacts peoples and groups differently and differentially. One person's resolution may well be another person's disempowerment or effective disenfranchisement. Public action in this case is almost Newtonian. Attempts to apply resolutions to one set of problems quite often lead to an equal and opposite reaction; they will cause some other problem and create a new aggrieved party.

As the predominant nongovernmental agents for manipulating or helping to manipulate American society, land-grant universities regularly find themselves in the middle of this quintessentially American morass. Their engagement in the slog is foreordained. To not engage is to fail; it is to surrender the future to chaos or chance. Land-grants are destined to participate in an almost endless array of activities, many of which will certainly be provocative, even divisive. Controversy threatens to erupt whenever these schools act. Questions of motive and ownership surface as pained or wronged parties see themselves as minimalized or menaced and vehemently object to disruptions of the status quo. It is the dualism—this two-faced Janus—that has attended land-grant programs, methods, and initiatives for much of the past century. It makes these crucial institutions endlessly fascinating and so tightly woven within the American social cloth. They have become staples of the American tapestry, as iconic in their way as mom and apple pie. In a fundamental sense, land-grant universities are quintessentially American productions doing characteristically American bidding.

Bibliography

Altschuler, Glenn. *The GI Bill: A New Deal for Veterans.* London: Oxford University Press, 2009.

Amenta, Edwin. *When Movements Matter: The Townsend Plan and the Rise of Social Security.* Princeton: Princeton University Press, 2006.

Anderson, Oscar Edward. *The Health of a Nation: Harvey W. Wiley and the Fight for Pure Food.* Chicago: University of Chicago Press, 1958.

Bacevich, Andrew J. *The New American Militarism: How Americans Are Seduced by War.* New York: Oxford University Press, 2005.

Bailey, L. H. *The Country-Life Movement in the United States.* New York: Macmillan, 1911.

Baker, Gladys L., Jane M. Porter, Wayne D. Rasmussen, and Vivian Wiser. *Century of Service: The First 100 Years of the United States Department of Agriculture.* Washington, DC: US Department of Agriculture, 1963.

Barnes, Roswell P. *Militarizing Our Youth: The Significance of the Reserve Officers' Training Corps.* New York: Committee on Militarism in Education, 1927.

Bates, Tom. *RADS: The 1970 Bombing of the Army Math Research Center at the University of Wisconsin and Its Aftermath.* New York: Harper Collins, 1992.

Beecher, Catherine Esther. *The American Woman's Home: Principles of Domestic Science as Applied to the Duties and Pleasures of Home: A Textbook for the Use of Young Ladies in Schools, Seminaries, and Colleges.* New York: J. B. Ford, 1870.

Beeman, Randal S., and James A. Prichard. *A Green and Permanent Land: Ecology and Agriculture in the Twentieth Century.* Lawrence: University Press of Kansas, 2001.

Bensel, Richard Franklin. *Yankee Leviathan: The Origins of Central State Authority in America, 1859–1877.* New York: Cambridge University Press, 1990.

Berger, Molly. *Hotel Dreams: Luxury, Technology, and Urban Ambition in America, 1829–1929.* Baltimore: Johns Hopkins University Press, 2011.

Berghahn, Volker R. *America and the Intellectual Cold Wars in Europe: Shepard Stone between Philanthropy, Academy, and Diplomacy.* Princeton: Princeton University Press, 2001.

Berry, Wendell. *The Art of the Commonplace: The Agrarian Essays of Wendell Berry.* Edited and with an introduction by Norman Wirzba. Emeryville, CA: Shoemaker and Hoard, 2002.

Beveridge, Elizabeth. *Choosing and Using Home Equipment.* Ames: Iowa State University Press, 1968.

Bishop, Morris. *A History of Cornell.* Ithaca, NY: Cornell University Press, 1963.

Bonnen, James T., John F. Geweke, Andrew A. White, and Jeffrey J. White, eds. *Sowing Seeds of Change: Informing Public Policy in the Economic Research Service of USDA.* Washington, DC: National Academy Press, 1999.

Browne, R. S., "Only Six Million Acres: The Decline of Black Owned Land in the Rural South," New York: Black Economic Research Center, 1973.

Buchele, Wesley F., and Graeme R. Quick. *The Grain Harvesters.* St. Joseph, MI: American Society of Agricultural Engineers, 1978.

Butler, Susan. *East to the Dawn: The Life of Amelia Earhart.* Cambridge, MA: DaCapo Press, 2009.

Caples, V. *A People and a Spirit Serving the Nations of the World.* Normal: Alabama A&M University, 1990.

Carson, Rachel. *Silent Spring.* Boston: Houghton Mifflin Company, 1962.

Curti, Merle, and Vernon Carstensen. *The University of Wisconsin.* 2 vols. Madison: University of Wisconsin Press, 1948.

Clarke, Edward H. *Sex in Education, or, A Fair Chance for Girls.* Boston: James R. Osgood and Co., 1873.

Clarke, Robert. *Ellen Richards: The Woman Who Founded Ecology.* Chicago: Follett Publishing, 1973.

Clemens, Elisabeth S. *The People's Lobby: Organizational Innovation and the Rise of Interest Group Politics in the United States, 1890–1925.* Chicago: University of Chicago Press, 1997.

Condition of Education 2012, The. Washington, DC: US Department of Education, National Center for Education Statistics, 2012.

Coppin, Clayton A. *The Politics of Purity: Harvey Washington Wiley and the Origins of Federal Food Policy.* Ann Arbor: University of Michigan Press, 1999.

Cotton, Barbara, ed. *The 1890 Land-Grant Colleges: A Centennial Review.* Washington, DC: Agricultural History Society, 1992.

Coumbe, Arthur T., and Lee S. Harford. *U.S. Army Cadet Command: The Ten Year History.* Fort Monroe, VA: Office of the Command Historian, US Army Cadet Command, 1996.

Coulter, E. Merton. *College Life in the Old South.* Cited in William B. Parker, *The Life and Services of Justin S. Morrill.* Boston: Houghton Mifflin, 1924.

Cravens, Hamilton. *Before Head Start: The Iowa Station and America's Children.* Chapel Hill: University of North Carolina Press, 1993.

Cross II, Coy F. *Justin Smith Morrill: Father of the Land-Grant Colleges*. East Lansing: Michigan State University Press, 1999.

Cruess, W. V. *Commercial Fruit and Vegetable Products: A Textbook for Student, Investigator and Manufacturer*. 2nd ed. New York: McGraw-Hill, 1938.

Curry, Lynn. *Modern Mothers in the Heartland: Gender, Health and Progressives in Illinois, 1900–1930*. Columbus: Ohio State University Press, 1999.

Danbom, David B. *The Resisted Revolution: Urban America and the Industrialization of Agriculture, 1900–1930*. Ames: Iowa State University Press, 1979.

Daniel, Pete. *Dispossession: Discrimination against African American Farmers in the Age of Civil Rights*. Chapel Hill: University of North Carolina Press, 2013.

Davison, Eloise. "A Course in Home Economics: A Report of a Successful Course Offered to Sophomore Women at Iowa State College." Master's thesis, Iowa State College, 1924.

Day, H. Summerfield. *The Iowa State University Campus and Its Buildings, 1859–1979*. Ames: Iowa State University Press, 1980.

Della Porta, Donatella, and Mario Diani. *Social Movements: An Introduction*. 2nd ed. Malden, MA: Blackwell, 2006.

Developing and Extending Sustainable Agriculture: A New Social Contract. New York: Haworth Food & Agricultural Products Press, 2006.

Diamond, Nancy, and Hugh Davis Graham. *The Rise of American Research Universities: Elites and Challenges in the Postwar Era*. Baltimore: Johns Hopkins University Press, 1997.

Donahue, Brian. *The Great Meadow: Farmers and the Land in Colonial Concord*. New Haven: Yale University Press, 2004.

———. *Reclaiming the Commons: Community Farms and Forests in a New England Town*. New Haven: Yale University Press, 1999.

Dorfman, Joseph. *The Economic Mind in American Civilization*. Vols. 4 and 5, 1918–1933. New York: Viking, 1959.

Economic Research Service. *Progress of Rural and Urban Students Entering Iowa State University, Fall, 1955*. Washington, DC: US Department of Agriculture, Agricultural Economic Report No. 12, 1962.

Eddy Jr., Edward D. *Colleges for Our Land and Time: The Land Grant Idea in American Education*. New York: Harper and Brothers, 1956.

Edmondson, Brad. *Hospitality Leadership: The Cornell Hotel School*. Ithaca, NY: Cornell Society of Hotelmen, 1996.

Elias, Megan J. *Stir It Up: Home Economics in American Culture*. Philadelphia: University of Pennsylvania Press, 2008.

Eppright, Ercel S., and Elizabeth Storm Ferguson. *A Century of Home Economics at Iowa State University: A Proud Past, a Lively Present, a Future Promise*. Ames: Iowa State University Press, 1971.

Ernst, John. *Forging a Fateful Alliance: Michigan State University and the Vietnam War*. East Lansing: Michigan State University Press, 1998.

Ezekiel, Mordecai. *Jobs for All through Industrial Expansion*. New York: Knopf, 1939.

Farber, Daniel. *Lincoln's Constitution*. Chicago: University of Chicago Press, 2003.

Faust, Drew G. *This Republic of Suffering: Death and the American Civil War*. New York: Knopf, 2008.

Fisher, John C. and Carol Fisher. *Food in the American Military: A History*. Jefferson, NC: McFarland, 2011. Kindle edition.

Scigliano, Robert and Guy H. Fox. *Technical Assistance in Vietnam: The Michigan State Experience*. New York: Praeger, 1965.

Freyfogle, Eric T. *Agrarianism and the Good Society: Land, Culture, Conflict, and Hope*. Lexington: University of Kentucky Press, 2007.

———, ed. *The New Agrarianism: Land, Culture, and the Community of Life*. Washington, DC: Island Press, 2001.

Friedberg, Aaron. *In the Shadow of the Garrison State: America's Anti-Statism and Its Cold War Strategy*. Princeton: Princeton University Press, 2000.

Fritschner, Linda. "The Rise and Fall of Home Economics: A Study with Implications for Women, Education, and Change." PhD diss., University of California-Davis, 1973.

Galambos, Louis, and Joseph A. Pratt. *The Rise of the Corporate Commonwealth: U.S. Business and Public Policy in the Twentieth Century*. New York: Basic Books, 1988.

Galpin, Charles J. *My Drift into Rural Sociology: Memoir of Charles Josiah Gilpin*. Rural Sociological Monographs. Baton Rouge: Louisiana State University Press, 1938.

———. *Rural Life*. New York: The Century Company, 1918.

Gates, Paul W. *Agriculture and the Civil War*. New York: Knopf, 1965.

Gillette, John M. *Constructive Rural Sociology*. New York: Sturgis and Walton, 1917.

Gilman, Nils. *Mandarins of the Future: Modernization Theory in Cold War America*. Baltimore: Johns Hopkins University Press, 2003.

Gliessman, Stephen. *Agroecology: Ecological Processes in Sustainable Agriculture*. Boca Raton, FL: CRC Press, 1997.

Goldman, Eric. *Rendezvous with Destiny: A History of Modern American Reform*. New York: Knopf, 1952.

Goldstein, Carolyn. *Creating Consumers: Home Economics in Twentieth-Century America*. Chapel Hill: University of North Carolina Press, 2012.

Goldstein, Carolyn, and Paul Betters. *The Bureau of Home Economics: Its History, Activities and Organization*. Washington, DC: Brookings Institution, 1930.

Goodwin, Lorine Swainston. *The Pure Food, Drink, and Drug Crusaders, 1879–1914*. Jefferson, NC: McFarland, 1999.

Gordon, Lynn D. *Gender and Higher Education in the Progressive Era*. New Haven: Yale University Press, 1990.

Grandt Jr., A. F., W.A. Gustafson, and L. T. Cargnino. *One Small Step: The History of Aerospace Engineering at Purdue University.* West Lafayette, IN: Purdue University Press, 2010.

Greenberg, Milton. *The G.I. Bill: The Law That Changed America.* New York: Lickle Publishing, 1997.

Hall, G. Stanley. *Adolescence: Its Psychology, Anthropology, Sociology, Sex, Crime, Religion, and Education*, 2 vols. New York: D. Appleton, 1904.

Hanson, Victor Davis. *Fields without Dreams: Defending the Agrarian Ideal.* New York: The Free Press, 1996.

———. *The Land Was Everything: Letters from an American Farmer.* New York: The Free Press, 2000.

Hartmann, Susan. *The Home Front and Beyond: American Women in the 1940s.* Boston: Twayne, 1983.

Hassanein, Neva. *Changing the Way America Farms: Knowledge and Community in the Sustainable Agriculture Movement.* Lincoln: University of Nebraska Press, 1999.

Hays, Samuel P. *Conservation and the Gospel of Efficiency: The Progressive Conservation Movement, 1890–1920.* Cambridge, MA: Harvard University Press, 1959.

Heineman, Kenneth J. *Campus Wars: The Peace Movement at American State Universities in the Vietnam Era.* New York: New York University Press, 1993.

Herring, George C. *America's Longest War: The United States and Vietnam, 1950–1975.* 3rd ed. New York: John Wiley and Sons, 1996.

Hoeflin, Ruth. *History of a College: From Woman's Course to Home Economics to Human Ecology.* Manhattan, KS: Ag Press, 1988.

Hofstadter, Richard. *The Age of Reform: From Bryan to FDR.* New York: Vintage, 1955.

Holt, Marilyn Irvin. *Linoleum, Better Babies, and the Modern Farm Woman, 1890–1930.* Albuquerque: University of New Mexico Press, 1995.

Holthaus, Gary. *From the Farm to the Table: What All Americans Need to Know about Agriculture.* Lexington: University Press of Kentucky, 2009.

Horowitz, Helen L. *Alma Mater: Design and Experience in the Women's Colleges from Their Nineteenth-Century Beginnings to the 1930s.* New York: Knopf, 1984.

Horowitz, Irving L. *The Rise and Fall of Project Camelot: Studies in the Relationship between Social Science and Practical Politics.* Cambridge, MA: MIT Press, 1974.

Howe, Daniel Walker. *The Political Culture of the American Whigs.* Chicago: University of Chicago Press, 1979.

———. *What Hath God Wrought: The Transformation of America, 1815–1848.* New York: Oxford University Press, 2007.

Humes, H. Edward. *Over Here: How the G.I. Bill Transformed the American Dream.* New York: Harcourt, 2006.

Hunt, Caroline. *The Life of Ellen H. Richards.* Boston: Whitcomb & Barrows, 1912.

Hurt, R. Douglas. *American Agriculture: A Brief History*. 1st ed. Ames: Iowa State University Press, 1994.

———. *The Dust Bowl: An Agricultural and Social History*. Chicago: Nelson-Hall, 1981.

Jackson, Wes. *New Roots for Agriculture*. Foreword by Wendell Berry. 1980. Lincoln: University of Nebraska Press, 1985.

Jager, Ronald. *The Fate of Family Farming: Variations on an American Idea*. Hanover, NH: University Press of New England, 2004.

Jax, Judy Annette. "A Comparative Analysis of the Meaning of Home Economics: The 1899–1908 Lake Placid Conferences and 'Home Economics: A Definition.'" PhD diss., University of Minnesota, 1981.

Jeffrey, Julie Roy. *Frontier Women: "Civilizing" the West? 1840–1880*. New York: Hill and Wang, 1998.

Jordan, John M. *Machine-Age Ideology: Social Engineering and American Liberalism, 1911–1939*. Chapel Hill: University of North Carolina Press, 1994.

Kaledin, Eugenia. *Mothers and More: Women in the 1950s*. Boston: Twayne, 1985.

Kelley, Brooks Mather. *Yale: A History*. New Haven: Yale University Press, 1974.

Kerr, Clark. *The Great Transformation in Higher Education, 1960–1980*. Albany: State University of New York Press, 1991.

Kerr, Norwood Allen. *The Legacy: A Centennial History of the State Agricultural Experiment Stations, 1887-1987*. Columbia: Missouri Agricultural Experiment Station, University of Missouri, 1987.

Killian, James R. *Sputnik, Scientists, and Eisenhower: A Memoir of the First Special Assistant to the President for Science and Technology*. Cambridge, MA: MIT Press, 1977.

King, David C., and Zachary Karabell. *The Generation of Trust: How the U.S. Military Has Regained the Public's Confidence since Vietnam*. Washington, DC: American Enterprise Institute Press, 2003.

Kirkendall, Richard S. *Social Scientists and Farm Politics in the Age of Roosevelt*. Columbia: University of Missouri Press, 1966.

Kirschenmann, Frederick L. *Cultivating an Ecological Conscience: Essays from a Farmer Philosopher*. Ed. Constance L. Falk. Lexington: University Press of Kentucky, 2010.

Kronenberg, Philip S. *New Civil-Military Relations: The Agonies of Adjustment to Post-Vietnam Realities*. New Brunswick, NJ: Transaction Books, 1974.

Kurlansky, Mark. *Salt: A World History*. New York: Penguin, 2003.

Ladd-Taylor, Molly. *Raising a Baby the Government Way: Mothers' Letters to the Children's Bureau, 1915–1932*. New Brunswick, NJ: Rutgers University Press, 1986.

Lancaster, Jane. *Making Time: Lillian Moller Gilbreth—A Life beyond "Cheaper by the Dozen."* Boston: Northeastern University Press, 2006.

Larsen, Olaf F., and Julie N. Zimmerman. *Sociology in Government: The Galpin-Taylor*

Years in the U.S. Department of Agriculture, 1919–1953. University Park: Pennsylvania State University Press, 2003.

Latham, Michael E. *The Right Kind of Revolution: Modernization, Development, and U.S. Foreign Policy from the Cold War to the Present.* Ithaca, NY: Cornell University Press, 2011.

Leavitt, Sarah. *From Catherine Beecher to Martha Stewart: A Cultural History of Domestic Advice.* Chapel Hill: University of North Carolina Press, 2002.

Leopold, Aldo. *A Sand County Almanac, and Sketches from Here and There.* First published 1949. New York: Oxford University Press, 1987.

Leslie, Stuart W. *The Cold War and American Science: The Military-Industrial-Academic Complex at MIT and Stanford.* New York: Columbia University Press, 1993.

Lindenmeyer, Kriste. *A Right to Childhood: The U.S. Children's Bureau and Child Welfare, 1912–1946.* Urbana: University of Illinois Press, 1997.

Lockeretz, William, ed. *Organic Farming: An International History.* Cambridge, MA: CAB International, 2007.

Logsdon, Gene. *At Nature's Pace: Farming and the American Dream.* New York: Pantheon Books, 1994.

———. *You Can Go Home Again: Adventures of a Contrary Life.* Bloomington: Indiana University Press, 1998.

Lowitt, Richard, ed. *Journal of a Tamed Bureaucrat: Nils A. Olsen and the BAE, 1925–1935.* Ames: Iowa State University Press, 1980.

Madden, Faith. *Household Equipment Experiments.* Ames: Iowa State College Press, 1952.

Marco, Gino J., Robert M. Hollingsworth, and William Durham, eds. *Silent Spring Revisited.* Washington, DC: American Chemical Society, 1987.

Marcus, Alan I. *Agricultural Science and the Quest for Legitimacy: Farmers, Agricultural Colleges, and Experiment Stations.* Ames: Iowa State University Press, 1985.

———, ed. *Engineering in a Land-Grant Context: The Past, Present, and Future of an Idea.* West Lafayette, IN: Purdue University Press, 2005.

Marcus, Alan I, and Howard P. Segal. *American Technology: A Brief History.* Part 3. San Diego: Harcourt, Brace, and Jovanovich, 1989.

Matthews, Glenna. *Just a Housewife: The Rise and Fall of Domesticity in America.* New York: Oxford University Press, 1987.

McAdam, Doug, Sidney Tarrow, and Charles Tilly. *Dynamics of Contention.* Cambridge: Cambridge University Press, 2001.

McClelland, David C. *The Achieving Society.* New York: The Free Press, 1961.

McDougall, Walter A. *Promised Land, Crusader State: The American Encounter with the World since 1776.* Boston: Mariner Books, 1997.

McKenzie, Roderick D. *The Metropolitan Community.* 1932. New York: Russell and Russell, 1967.

McMath Jr., Robert C. *American Populism: A Social History*. New York: Hill and Wang, 1993.

McWilliams, James E. *Just Food: Where Locavores Get It Wrong and How We Can Truly Eat Responsibly*. Boston: Little, Brown, 2009.

Nash, Willard Lee. *A Study of the Stated Aims and Purposes of the Departments of Military Science and Tactics, and Physical Education in the Land Grant Colleges of the United States*. New York: Teachers College, Columbia University, 1934.

Nelkin, Dorothy. *The University and Military Research: Moral Politics at M.I.T.* Ithaca, NY: Cornell University Press, 1972.

Neufeld, Michael J. *Von Braun: Dreamer of Space/Engineer of War*. New York: Vintage, 2007.

Neuhaus, Jessamyn. *Manly Meals and Mom's Home Cooking: Cookbooks and Gender in Modern America*. Baltimore: Johns Hopkins University Press, 2003.

Neyland, Leedell W. *Historically Black Land-Grant Institutions and the Development of Agriculture and Economics*. Tallahassee: Florida A&M University Foundation, 1990.

Niebuhr, Reinhold. *The Irony of American History*. New York: Charles Scribner's Sons, 1952.

Norberg, John. *Wings of Their Dreams: Purdue in Flight*. Lafayette, IN: Purdue University Press, 2003.

Nye Jr., Joseph S. *Bound to Lead: The Changing Nature of American Power*. New York: Basic Books, 1990.

———. *The Paradox of American Power: Why the World's Only Superpower Can't Go It Alone*. New York: Oxford University Press, 2002.

———. *Soft Power: The Means to Success in World Politics*. New York: Public Affairs, 2005.

Okun, Mitchell. *Fair Play in the Marketplace: The First Battle for Pure Food and Drugs*. DeKalb: Northern Illinois University Press, 1986.

Oldenziel, Ruth. *Making Technology Masculine: Men, Women, and Modern Machines in America, 1870–1945*. Amsterdam: Amsterdam University Press, 1999.

Olson, Keith W. *The G.I. Bill, the Veterans, and the Colleges*. Lexington: University of Kentucky Press, 1974.

Parr, Damian M. "Student Farmer-to-Student Farmer." PhD diss., University of California-Davis, 2009.

Pelfrey, Patricia A. *A Brief History of the University of California*. 2nd ed. Berkeley: University of California Press, 2004.

Pollan, Michael. *In Defense of Food: An Eater's Manifesto*. New York: Penguin, 2008.

———. *The Omnivore's Dilemma: A Natural History of Four Meals*. New York: Penguin, 2006.

Pollard, James E. *Military Training in the Land-Grant Colleges and Universities, with Special Reference to the R.O.T.C. Program*. Washington, DC: Association of State Universities and Land-Grant Colleges, 1962.

Pye, Lucien W. *Aspects of Political Development*. Boston: Little, Brown, 1966.

Radke-Moss, Andrea G. *Bright Epoch: Women and Coeducation in the American West*. Lincoln: University of Nebraska Press, 2008.

Rasmussen, Wayne D. *Taking the University to the People: Seventy-five Years of Cooperative Extension*. Ames: Iowa State University Press, 1989.

Rea, Robert R. *History at Auburn: The First One Hundred Years of the Auburn University History Department*. Auburn, AL: Auburn University, 1991.

Reid, Debra A., and Evan P. Bennett. *Beyond Forty Acres and a Mule: African American Landowning Families since Reconstruction*. Gainesville: University Press of Florida, 2012.

Richardson, Peter. *A Bomb in Every Issue: How the Short, Unruly Life of Ramparts Magazine Changed America*. New York: The New Press, 2009.

Riney-Kehrberg, Pamela. *Rooted in Dust: Surviving Drought and Depression in Southwestern Kansas*. Lawrence: University Press of Kansas, 1994.

Rose, Flora, and Esther Stocks. *A Growing College: Home Economics at Cornell University*. Ithaca, NY: Cornell University Press, 1969.

Rosen, Ruth. *The World Split Open: How the Modern Women's Movement Changed America*. New York: Penguin, 2000.

Rosenberg, Rosalind. *Beyond Separate Spheres: Intellectual Roots of Modern Feminism*. New Haven: Yale University Press, 1982.

Ross, Dorothy. *G. Stanley Hall: The Psychologist as Prophet*. Chicago: University of Chicago Press, 1972.

Ross, Earle D. *Democracy's College: The Land Grant Movement in the Formative Stage*. New York: Arno Press and the *New York Times*, 1969.

Rossiter, Margaret W. *The Emergence of Agricultural Science: Justus Liebig and the Americans, 1840–1880*. New Haven: Yale University Press, 1975.

———. *Women Scientists in America: Before Affirmative Action, 1940–1972*. Baltimore: Johns Hopkins University Press, 1995.

———. *Women Scientists in America: Struggles and Strategies to 1940*. Baltimore: Johns Hopkins University Press, 1982.

Rostow, Walter W. *The Stages of Economic Growth: A Non-Communist Manifesto*. Cambridge: Cambridge University Press, 1960.

Rudolph, John L. *Scientists in the Classroom: The Cold War Reconstruction of American Science Education*. New York: Palgrave, 2002.

Sanderson, Dwight. *Research Memorandum on Rural Life in the Depression, Bulletin 34*. New York: Social Science Research Council, 1937.

———. *Rural Sociology and Rural Social Organization*. New York: John Wiley and Sons, 1942.

———. "A Survey of Sickness in Rural Areas in Cortland County, New York." *Cornell University Agricultural Experiment Station, Memoir 112*. Ithaca, NY: Published by the University, March 1927.

Sayre, Laura, and Sean Clark. *Fields of Learning: The Student Farm Movement in North America*. Lexington: University Press of Kentucky, 2011.

Scheuring, Ann Foley. *Abundant Harvest: The History of the University of California, Davis*. Davis: UC-Davis History Project, 2001.

Schilletter, J. C. *The First 100 Years of Residential Housing at Iowa State University*. Ames: Iowa State University Press, 1970.

Seim, David L. *Rockefeller Philanthropy and Modern Social Science*. London: Pickering and Chatto, 2013.

Shephard, Sue. *Pickled, Potted, and Canned: How the Art and Science of Food Preserving Changed the World*. New York: Simon and Schuster, 2000.

Shover, John L. *First Majority—Last Minority: The Transforming of Rural Life in America*. DeKalb: Northern Illinois University Press, 1976.

Schrader, Dorothy H. *History of Ames Municipal Government, Sewers*. Ames, IA: Iowa State University Press, 1965.

Skowronek, Stephen. *Building a New American State: The Expansion of National Administrative Capacities, 1877–1920*. New York: Cambridge University Press, 1982.

Southerners, Twelve. *I'll Take My Stand: The South and the Agrarian Tradition*. Baton Rouge: Louisiana State University Press, 1977.

Starr, Kevin. *California: A History*. 1st ed. A Modern Library Chronicles Book 23. New York: Modern Library, 2005.

Stoll, Steven. *Larding the Lean Earth: Soil and Society in Nineteenth-Century America*. New York: Hill and Wang, 2002.

Suri, Jeremy. *Henry Kissinger and the American Century*. Cambridge, MA: Harvard University Press, 2007.

Tarrow, Sidney. *Power in Movement: Social Movements and Contentious Politics*. 2nd ed. Cambridge: Cambridge University Press, 1998.

Taylor, Henry C. *An Introduction to the Study of Agricultural Economics*. First published 1909. New York: Macmillan, 1911.

Taylor, Henry C., and Anne Dewees Taylor. *The Story of Agricultural Economics in the United States, 1840–1932*. Ames: Iowa State College Press, 1952.

Teaford, Jon C. *The Rise of the States: Evolution of American State Government*. Baltimore: Johns Hopkins University Press, 2002.

Thelin, John R. *A History of American Higher Education*. Baltimore: Johns Hopkins University Press, 2011.

Thompson, Nicholas. *The Hawk and the Dove: Paul Nitze, George Kennan, and the History of the Cold War*. New York: Henry Holt, 2009.

Thompson, Paul B. *The Agrarian Vision: Sustainability and Environmental Ethics*. Lexington: University Press of Kentucky, 2010.

Tomes, Nancy. *The Gospel of Germs: Men, Women, and the Microbe in American Life*. Cambridge, MA: Harvard University Press, 1998.

Topping, Robert. *A Century and Beyond: The History of Purdue University.* Lafayette, IN: Purdue University Press, 1988.

Trescott, Martha Moore. *New Images, New Paths: A History of Women in Engineering in the United States, 1850–1980.* Dallas: T&L Enterprises, 1996.

Urban, Wayne F. *Black Scholar: Horace Mann Bond, 1904–1972.* Athens: University of Georgia Press, 1992.

Vincent, C. *Southern University and A&M College: Its Agricultural Development.* Baton Rouge: Southern University and A&M College, 1990.

Wade, Kathryn Lindsay. "The Intent and Fulfillment of the Morrill Act of 1862: A Review of the History of Auburn University and the University of Georgia." Master's thesis, Clemson University, 1965.

Wang, Jessica. *American Science in an Age of Anxiety: Scientists, Anticommunism, and the Cold War.* Chapel Hill: University of North Carolina Press, 1999.

Warner, Keith Douglass. *Agroecology in Action: Extending Alternative Agriculture through Social Networks.* Cambridge, MA: MIT Press, 2007.

Werhan, Carol. "Why Men Enter the Gendered Profession of Family and Consumer Sciences Education: An Exploratory Case Study." PhD diss., University of Akron, 2008.

Wilson, Elmina. *Modern Conveniences for the Farm Home.* USDA Farmers' Bulletin, No. 270. Washington, DC: GPO, 1906.

Winston, Mark L. *Nature Wars: People vs. Pests.* Cambridge, MA: Harvard University Press, 1997.

Worster, Donald. *Dust Bowl: The Southern Plains in the 1930s.* Rev. ed. New York: Oxford University Press, 2004.

Wyatt, Mary. "A Comparison of Preservice Home Economics Education Programs in Predominantly Black and White Southern Institutions of Higher Education." PhD diss., Florida State University, 1980.

Young, James Harvey. *Pure Food: Securing the Federal Food and Drugs Act of 1906.* Princeton: Princeton University Press, 1989.

Contributors

AMY SUE BIX is an associate professor in the History Department at Iowa State University (ISU) and director of ISU's Center for Historical Studies of Technology and Science. Her work includes *Girls Coming to Tech!: A History of American Engineering Education for Women* (MIT Press, 2014), *Inventing Ourselves Out of Jobs?: America's Debate over Technological Unemployment, 1929–1981* (Johns Hopkins University Press, 2000), and articles on a wide range of topics, including the history of breast cancer and AIDS research, the history of eugenics, the history of alternative medicine, the history of home-tool use, steampunk, and post–World War II physics and engineering.

HAMILTON CRAVENS is Emeritus Professor of History at Iowa State University, where he taught for forty-two years. He has held fellowships from the National Endowment for the Humanities, the National Science Foundation, the Hoover Institution and the Humanities Center, and Stanford University, as well as Fulbright professorships in Germany and the Netherlands. He is the author or editor of about a dozen books, most recently *Cold War Social Science* (Palgrave Macmillan, 2014), and is writing *Imagining the Good Society: The Social Sciences in the American Past and Present* (Cambridge, 2016). He is affiliated with the Graduate Program in History of Science, Technology, and Medicine, University of Minnesota-Twin Cities, where he presently lives.

DONALD A. DOWNS is the Alexander Meiklejohn Professor of Political Science and Affiliate Professor of Law and Journalism at the University of Wisconsin-Madison. His scholarship has covered a wide range of issues such as freedom of speech; academic freedom; American politics; political thought; political and legal movements; citizenship; campus politics; domestic violence, psychiatry, and criminal law; and the relationship among the military, the university, and civic education. His most recent book is *Arms and the University: Military Presence and the Civic Education of Non-Military Students* (Cambridge University Press, 2012), coauthored with Ilia Murtazashvili.

ANNE B. EFFLAND received a PhD in agricultural history and rural studies from Iowa State University and has been a research historian and social scientist with the Economic Research Service, US Department of Agriculture, since 1990. Her historical research has ranged widely, including studies of US farm and rural policy; rural labor, women, and minorities; and the institutional history of the US Department of Agriculture. She is a Fellow of the Agricultural History Society and served as its president in 2008–9.

VALERIE GRIM holds a PhD from Iowa State University in history, with a specialization in agricultural history and rural studies. She is a professor in and the chair of the Department of African American and African Diaspora Studies at Indiana University-Bloomington. She researches and publishes in the areas of African American rural history, culture, and life. Her publications have appeared in such journals as *Agricultural History, Oral History Review, Frontiers: A Journal of Women's History, Black Diaspora Review, and Black Women, Gender, and Families.* She has contributed chapters to such edited volumes as *Beyond Forty Acres and a Mule, Women Writing Women,* and *Outside In: African American History in Iowa.* Grim is currently completing a manuscript concerning Black land-grant universities.

DAVID L. HARMON earned his PhD in the history of technology and science from Iowa State University in 2001. Since then he has taught at the State University of New York-Finger Lakes and Mississippi State University. He is currently teaching online courses for Thomas Edison State College of New Jersey. His research interests include American camping culture and recreational vehicle history, the changing role of engineering programs at historic black colleges and universities from vocational programs to advanced engineering programs, and the shifts from vocational agriculture programs to those supporting extension services and broader agricultural interests.

R. DOUGLAS HURT is a professor in and head of the Department of History at Purdue University. He is a past editor of *Agricultural History,* a past president of the Agricultural History Society, a Fellow of the Agricultural History Society, and an Associate Fellow of the Center for Great Plains Studies at the University of Nebraska. *Gwen Kay* is a professor in the History Department and director of the Honors Program at the State University of New York-Oswego. She is the author of *Dying to Be Beautiful: The Fight for Safe Cosmetics* (Ohio State University Press, 2005) and is currently working on a book manuscript titled "Not Just Stichin' and Stirrin': Changing Identities in Home Economics."

ALAN I MARCUS is a professor in and the head of the Department of History at Mississippi State University. Author or editor of some fifteen books and journals, including *Science as Service: Establishing and Reformulating American Land-Grant*

Universities, 1865–1930 (University of Alabama Press, 2015), he is director of the Virtual Archives for Land-Grant History, a collaboration between the Association of Public and Land-Grant Universities and Mississippi State. His *Death by Analogy: The World's First War on Cancer and Creation of the Modern Cancer Research Establishment, 1875–1915* is out for review.

ERINN MCCOMB is an assistant professor at Del Mar College in Corpus Christi. She received her PhD from Mississippi State University in 2012, where her research focused on gender culture, technology, and diplomacy in US history. She is currently revising her dissertation into a book manuscript titled "Why Can't a Woman Fly: American Masculinity and the Astronaut Image, 1957–1972." She is a reviewer for the *Journal of South Texas* and has presented at the Society for the History of Technology (SHOT), the Society for American Foreign Relations (SHAFR), and at the National Aeronautics and Space Administration (NASA).

ROBERT C. MCMATH is a professor of history emeritus at the University of Arkansas, where he also served as dean of the Honors College. McMath previously taught and held various administrative posts at the Georgia Institute of Technology. His publications include *American Populism: A Social History* (MacMillan, 1993) and *Engineering the New South: Georgia Tech, 1885–1985* (University of Georgia Press, 1985; coauthored with Ronald H. Bayor, James E. Brittain, Lawrence Foster, August W. Giebelhaus, and Germaine M. Reed).

STEPHANIE STATZ received her PhD in history from the University of Houston and is working on turning her dissertation titled "Fruit Cocktail: A History of Industrial Food Production, the State and the Environment in Northern California" into a book. She also works as a historical consultant. Her research interests include the history of the American West and the role of the state in agriculture, natural resource use, and food production.

MELISSA WALKER is the George Dean Johnson Jr. Professor of History at Converse College in Spartanburg, South Carolina. She is the author or editor of eight books on rural and southern history, including *All We Knew Was to Farm: Rural Women in the Upcountry South, 1919–1941* (Johns Hopkins University Press, 2000) and *The Battles of Kings Mountain and Cowpens: The American Revolution in the Southern Backcountry* (Routledge, 2012). Raised on a dairy farm in Tennessee, Walker was active in 4-H throughout her childhood and adolescence.

Index